The Best of Times

Also by Brian Tesler

Before I Forget (Mind Advertising Ltd)

The Best of Times

A personal history of British television
1952–1994

Brian Tesler

First published in hardback in Great Britain in 2016 by
Kaleidoscope Publishing
42 Victoriana Way
Handsworth Wood
B20 2SZ
United Kingdom

ISBN-13 978-1-900203-63-0

Cover/jacket and photo plate design by Mind Advertising
Book text layout by Simon Coward

To Audrey Maclean Tesler,
the best of the Best of Times

Acknowledgements

Readers of my Family Memoir, *Before I Forget*, will know that I have drawn on it for some of my early influences. The full account of my time with the British Forces Broadcasting Service can be found there. I am indebted to Peter Black's *The Mirror in the Corner*; to David Docherty's *Running the Show*, his history of the first 21 years of LWT; and to Bernard Sendall, Jeremy Potter and Paul Bonner with Lesley Aston, the serial authors of *Independent Television in Britain*. And my grateful thanks go to the friends and colleagues who have helped in person and online to refresh my memory of the 42 years this memoir encompasses.

They are here in alphabetical order, peers of the realm, knights of the shires and all: Rod Allen, Jack Andrews, Lord (John) Birt, Sir Christopher Bland, Paul Bonner, Alan Boyd, Gillian Braithwaite-Exley, Warren Breach, Bernard Burke, Michael Chapman, Barry Cox, David Cox, John Donovan, Greg Dyke, Nick Elliott, Sir Paul Fox, Colin Freeman, James Gatward, Rosie Gleeson, Lord (Michael) Grade, Norman Green, John Hambley, Carol Haslam, Richard Hooper, Sir Jeremy Isaacs, Ros Long, Ernest Maxin, Marion McDougall, Ron Miller, Steve Minchin, Bob Norris, John O'Loan, Joy Owen, Robin Paxton, Andrew Pixley, Bill Rawcliffe, Michael Redington, Nick Roberts, Jill Sampson, Brian Scott, Mike Southgate, Andrea Turner, Bob Warren, Leonard White, Jaz Wiseman.

With special thanks to Simon Coward who checked my facts and compiled the index, and Simon Tesler who checked my p's and q's and organised the photographs.

Photo Acknowledgements

Estate of Derek Adkins	A1: "Round About Paris".
Estate of Sydney W. Baynton	A13: With Alicia Markova
Bishops	A4: With Norden and Muir. A7: With the Forresters. A8: 'I suppose you think that's funny'.
Broadcast	B14: Lord Olivier's 80th birthday.
Estate of John Cura	All Telesnaps
Fremantle Media	B1: *Steamboat Shuffle* and ABC programme heads. B2: *Sammy Davis Jr Meets the British.* B3: *Candid Camera.* B4: *Thank Your Lucky Stars*, and Leonard White and Patrick Macnee. B5: Frank Sinatra *ABC TV News / World of Sport* team. B6: *Tempo.* B7: With the Archbishop and the Moderator / Programme Controllers Group. B8: Thames programme department 1968. B8: Horseshoes / Howard Thomas and the Winters. B9: BAFTA winners 1972 / With Philip Jones / The key to the loo. B14: Bill Ward dinner.
IPC Media	A1: With Neville Coghill. A2: *Why?.* A3: *Guess My Story.* A6–A7: *Ask Pickles.* A15: *New Look* – Bruce and Roy.

ITV Pictures	B10: BAFTA Winners 1975 / Cake / John Freeman.
	B11: Visiting us... / Visiting them... / *Cream in my Coffee*
	Prix Italia.
	B12: With two Lords-a-leaping / LWT Board 1982 /
	With David Frost.
	B13: A toast... / A more private toast... / and LWT News.
	B14: At Buckingham Palace.
	B15: Royal Variety Performance / With Princess Diana.
	B16: Franchise Team 1992.
Estate of Bob Monkhouse	B16: Retirement book – Cartoon.
Odhams	A4: *And So to Bentley* (main picture).
	A6: With Wilfred and Mabel.
Photo-Records	A8: With Barbara Kelly.
PIC Publicity	B10: With Audrey and Bryan Cowgill
The Tatler	A1: Footlights
Thomas Rowlandson	B7: *Kick Up at a Hazard Table.*
Trinity Mirror	A2: *What's My Line?.*
	A5: With the Television Toppers.
	A12: *Saturday Spectacular* (control room) / *The Benny Hill Show.*
	A13: *Sunday Night at the London Palladium.*

All pictures are taken from the author's private collection.

Every reasonable effort has been made to trace the present copyright holders, but Kaleidoscope Publishing will be pleased to correct any errors or omissions in any future edition of this book.

Contents

Photo Section A: Programme Production

CONTENTS | xi

The Best of Times

I am sitting in a small, windowless room in Broadcasting House on a chilly afternoon in January 1952.

I am here for an interview, arranged by an amiable but not very optimistic Assistant Secretary to the Oxford University Appointments Committee: "Not much chance, I'm afraid. Simply everybody wants to get into the BBC. Have you considered the advertising industry?"

I don't know the name of my interviewer. I don't even know what he looks like: he hasn't yet raised his head from his desk, where he is filling in details on a form – the details, presumably, of some other aspiring undergraduate. This appears to be Undergraduate Interview Day. However, he did most politely invite me to sit down when I was ushered in, and now he says "Right, that's done; now, just let me get *your* details, Mr...?

"Tesler, Brian Tesler."

"Age?"

"Twenty-two."

"University?"

"Oxford."

"College?"

"Exeter."

"What are you reading?"

"English Language and Literature."

"Taking your Finals this year?"

"Yes: I was held up by National Service."

"Army? Air Force...?"

"Army: Royal Artillery; but I spent most of my two years with the British Forces Radio Station in Trieste."

"So you'd like to pick up your radio career professionally with the BBC?"

"Well no, actually. I've been writing and producing revues and cabaret in Oxford for most of the past three years and I'd like to do that sort of thing on BBC Television, in light entertainment."

"Ah...No chance of that, I'm afraid. Television takes its light entertainment recruits from the theatrical profession or the light entertainment department here at B.H. Our university recruits usually go to Television Talks: you know, news, current affairs, documentaries. Would you be interested in that sort of thing?"

"Not really..."

"In that case, I'm afraid there's probably not very much we can do for you. Is there anything else you'd like to tell me that might be of interest?"

"Well, I've written quite a few songs that have been recorded and broadcast."

My interviewer stops writing and looks up at me for the first time.

"*Broadcast?*" he says. "*On the BBC?*"

"Yes, on radio and television."

"Really? Broadcast, you say. On the BBC! On radio *and* television! Well, well. Which, er, which programmes? Who performed these songs of yours? Anybody I'd know? Any stars...? We must get you an interview, mustn't we?"

I'd arrived in Oxford along with a small army of other ex-National Servicemen in September 1949, at the beginning of Michaelmas Term. We were two years older than the majority of our fellow undergraduates, most of whom had come straight from school. For the rest of us, National Service had been a sort of Gap Year experience before its time, but we were no more accomplished than our younger contemporaries. Oxford theatre and journalism, my particular fields of interest, were not only packed with present talent but still reverberating with the exploits of talent recently past, not least those of a particular blazing star, one Kenneth Peacock Tynan. I don't know which of us would have been more surprised to know that a dozen years later Ken would be working for me in Independent Television.

My childhood and adolescence were full of such pre-echoes. British stars of stage, screen and radio I had admired before the war – performers like Gracie Fields, Arthur Askey, Jack Buchanan, George Formby – would perform in my television programmes. American stars like Bob Hope, Bing Crosby and Jack Benny, whose movies and radio series had helped lift the nation's morale during World War Two, would star in my shows. I would produce television programmes not only from the music halls my family and I used to frequent before and during the war, like the Hackney Empire and the Shepherds Bush Empire, but also from the most famous variety theatre of all, the London Palladium, the family's special treat for red-letter days. The movies I adored in the cinema in the thirties and forties I would be buying for my television schedules in the sixties and seventies. The presenter of my favourite BBC radio show of the late thirties, *Monday Night at Eight*, would be my first television boss a decade and a half later... In Wordsworth's Ode, *Intimation of Immortality*, "Shades of the prison-house begin to close / Upon the growing boy". In my case, happily, the shades seemed to be those of show-business; and at Oxford they first engulfed and then propelled me into the career I would follow for over 40 years.

It would be a career encompassing the best of times for British television: the whole of its post-war evolution from a single-channel BBC to the beginning of today's explosion of cable and satellite channels. In the course of it I would work as a producer in both the BBC and Independent Television and then as a programme executive in ITV; successively Head of a creative department, Director of Programmes, Managing Director, and finally Chairman and Managing Director. I would become a founder-Director of both Thames Television and Channel 4, the founder of ITV's Teletext enterprise Oracle, and the founder-chairman of ITV's first venture into satellite broadcasting, SuperChannel. I would work for four legendary broadcasting bosses: Ronnie Waldman, Lew Grade, Howard Thomas and John Freeman; and when I became a broadcasting boss myself I would appoint four future legends, Jeremy Isaacs, Michael Grade, John Birt and Greg Dyke, to the positions from which they would flourish. It would be a career full of people and programmes, confrontations and negotiations, alarums and excursions, good times, bad times...

It began, as so many stories do, at a university. At Oxford.

Oxford: Gathering Shades

I was fortunate enough to win a State Scholarship in my Higher Schools Exam of 1946 and applied to take it up at Exeter College, Oxford, principally because I was intrigued by the theatrical interests of its Professor of English, Nevill Coghill. Nevill had founded the University's Experimental Theatre Club and in later years would publish a hugely successful modern English translation of Chaucer's Canterbury Tales. He would also collaborate in a musical version of the Tales in the West End, and produce Elizabeth Taylor and Richard Burton in Marlowe's Dr Faustus at Oxford's Playhouse Theatre.

I had been given a letter of introduction to him by my English Master at Chiswick County School for Boys, Charles Garlick, an old acquaintance of his, and on one dazzling, disorienting day I had lunch with Professor Coghill and a handful of other Exeter College dignitaries, including the Rector, E. A. Barber, who was in charge of admissions. I can't remember what we ate or drank or a single word of what I or anybody else said. I only remember thinking, on the train journey home, that I must have seemed a speechless, gormless, talentless loon to them all. Subsequently, however, Mr Barber was kind enough to say that the college would be prepared to admit me in view of the State Scholarship, once I had completed my National Service. And now, two years later, here I was, fresh from the British Forces Broadcasting Station in Trieste, ready to begin my university career.

Exeter was and remains one of Oxford's oldest and most distinguished colleges. It is also one of the smallest, and in September 1949 it was too small to accommodate me.

The customary practice in Oxford is for undergraduates to live in college for the first of their University years and in lodgings for the remainder. In 1949 all the Exeter College staircases were full, so I was allocated a bed-room and study on the first floor of the college's annexe, which occupied the corner of Broad Street and the Turl – local shorthand for Turl Street. I shared the floor and its bathroom with Fred and Homer, two American post-graduates in their later twenties. We used to say Hi and Hello when we passed each other on the stairs, but that was as near to socialising as we ever got. Fred and Homer were in their final University year and much of the time they were enthusiastically celebrating this fact with their fellow post-graduate Americans. It wasn't easy to concentrate on Old English texts with the party sounds coming from the other end of the landing.

Exeter College's entrance was a few hundred yards further down the Turl. I used to make my way there for breakfast in Hall each morning, I signed in for the mandatory number of Hall dinners, I dropped into the Junior Common Room and the Buttery from time to time, and I appeared regularly in college for my tutorials with Nevill Coghill, but there was no opportunity to socialise with any of my fellow undergraduates and I felt like a visitor rather than a resident. I was *at* Oxford but somehow not *in* it.

As an alternative, I contemplated the fellowship of the ring – the boxing ring, that is. My father was an avid fight fan, and a great treat for me as a young lad was to be taken by him to the Devonshire Sporting Club in the Whitechapel Road, a venue for boxing matches run by the promoter Jack Solomons. One of my dad's friends was Jack Greenstock, a profes-sional lightweight who fought in his teens as Young Greenstock and had gone on to promote fights himself and run a gym where he trained young boxers. When I was sixteen my father arranged for him to give me and my friend Barry Levison weekly boxing lessons in the family garage, and fired by my dad's enthusiasm and Jack's training skills I rather took to the sport. I founded my School's Boxing Club and carried on boxing in the early months of my National Service before I was seconded to the British Forces Broadcasting Service.

As a Gunner – a Private – in the Royal Artillery, stationed in Rhyl in North Wales, I entered the Army's North-West Command Novices Championships and managed to reach the Finals of my weight division which I failed to win, but that's the fight game. In Trieste, the nearest I got to boxing was commentating on the Services boxing matches we covered, but now I took my bright orange training gloves, a farewell gift from Jack Greenstock, to the Alfred Street gym where the members of the University Amateur Boxing Club carried out their training.

I found myself in a boxing environment startlingly different from the ones I had known. These were not young tyros squaring up to each other in a family garage, a school gym or a novices tournament. The muscle and sinew working out all around me belonged to committed athletes, relentlessly skipping ropes and pounding punchbags, speedballs, and each other. For a few days I skipped, hit the punchbag and hammered the speedball; I assessed the dedication, discipline and sheer hard physical work entailed in taking up the sport seriously; and I realised that I was simply not good enough for it. I threw in the towel and hung up my gloves. Young Greenstock would have been disappointed in me.

The same week, I tried my luck at the auditions for the Acting Contest run annually by the ETC — the Experimental Theatre Club — for the new intake of aspiring undergraduate performers and producers. I remember being cast as the Senator in Jean-Paul Sartre's *The Respectful Prostitute* and Tegeus in Christopher Fry's *A Phoenix Too Frequent*, but according to an article retained from *The Isis* magazine I appear to have been in a total of three productions, which came first, second and fourth in the adjudication by Francis McKenzie, Head of the British Drama League's Training Department. Whatever the actual number, and whether I lived in the Turl annexe or in my subsequent digs on the Ifley and Woodstock Roads, I had found my fellowship, and for the next three years my true Oxford home would be the rehearsal rooms, stages, cabaret floors, coffee bars and green rooms of Oxford's little theatre world.

University terms are eight weeks long. The rest of that Michaelmas term was packed with activity, though not much of it academic. As well as the Acting Contest, I auditioned for a revue produced by New College's Dramatic Society, and within three weeks of Sartre and Fry I was performing comedy sketches and point numbers in *The New Revue*. The success of that show led to an invitation to take part in a cabaret at the Randolph Hotel, which in turn produced an invitation to join the Oxford University Dramatic Society's Smoking Concert, the annual opportunity for the acting stalwarts of the OUDS to let their hair down in a ribald, boisterous, men-only entertainment.

That year, the Smoker was in the form of a Christmas Pantomime, *Babes in the Wood*. I played the male Babe, and I was in pretty good company.

The Dame, John Schlesinger, would go on to direct *Billy Liar* and *Darling* and win an Oscar for *Midnight Cowboy*; The Demon King, Nigel Davenport, would become a leading actor in British film, theatre and television; The Fairly Wicked Baron, John Bowen, would become a successful novelist; and other members of the cast included the future international ballet critic Clement Crisp and the future presenter of the BBC's *Call My Bluff* and *Brain of Britain*, Robert Robinson. Michael Codron, who wrote and produced *Babes in the Wood*, went on to become one of the West End's most successful independent theatre producers, receiving a Lifetime Achievement Award at the Olivier Awards of 2010 and a knighthood for his services to the theatre in the New Year's Honours for 2014. He's a little heavier today, and his hair is white, but he is otherwise unchanged: as suave and elegant now as he was then, though perhaps no longer a full-time impresario: in 2013 he announced that his production of Simon Gray's *Quartermaine's Terms* would be his last. Not quite, however. Two years later he was still bringing productions to the West End's Theatre Royal, including Bradley Cooper in *The Elephant Man*, from Broadway, and Simon Russell Beale in *Mr Foote's Other Leg*, from London's Hampstead Theatre. In a radio interview, he announced that *Mr Foote's Other Leg* would definitely, absolutely, be his last production. We shall see.

I don't know what became of Michael's rival impresario John Mayer, who was responsible for the New College revue, but he certainly didn't lack ambition or enterprise. For the Easter vacation, John put some new material and performers together with the best of the script and cast of his New College revue, called the show *Spring Fever* and took it to the Torch Club Theatre in Knightsbridge, thereby anticipating the Cambridge Footlights revue debut in London by four years. If there had been an Edinburgh Fringe in 1950, we might have gone there instead; but the London fringe of little club theatres dotted in and around the capital was fine with us, and Knightsbridge had the sort of cachet which suited our show. Were we the first revue team from any University to play London? I've no idea whether we were blazing any kind of trail, but we were certainly well received. P. L. Mannock in the *Daily Herald*: "The performers include personalities sufficiently able and charming to excuse any of the hallmarks of amateurs. They have the fresh confidence and audacity of youth. As for their material, I hereby declare that the wit and blazing topicality of ideas in most of the 25 items adds up to that of all the current British musical shows in the West End put together."

We gave a matinee performance on the Friday of our week in the Big Time, in case any West End professional might want to pop in and see us. At least one of them did. Henry Kendall was a leading actor and revue artiste, the star along with Hermione Gingold and Hermione Baddeley of hit revues like *Rise Above It*, *Sweet and Low* and its successors *Sweeter and Lower* and *Sweetest and Lowest*. He was now enjoying great success in Philip King's play *On Monday Next* at the Comedy Theatre. The day after our matinee, a note was delivered to the stage door which said: "Dear Mr Tesler, I was very impressed by your performance in "Spring Fever" yesterday afternoon. If you are thinking of taking up acting professionally when you leave the University, I might be able to help you, so perhaps you might like to call at the Stage Door of this theatre any evening except Saturday and have a chat? Will you please convey my thanks to Mr Mayer and the rest of the company for a most enjoyable show? Yours sincerely, Henry Kendall."

Flattered and curious – and deeply envied by the rest of the *Spring Fever* cast – I duly presented myself at the stage door of the Comedy Theatre the following week and was directed to the star dressing room for my little chat. Kendall was in his middle 50s, tall, portly, disarming. He was full of praise for our show, had some nice things to say about my performance and asked whether I did in fact want to pursue a career in the theatre when I left Oxford. I told him I hadn't really given it any thought, and he said "Well, dear boy, why don't you slip into the auditorium, see the show and come back afterwards? We'll go to the Buckstone for a little supper and talk about it."

The play was great fun and Kendall's performance a master-class in timing and delivery. When I got back to his dressing room he was taking off his make-up and another young man of about my own age was sitting quietly in the corner. We weren't introduced to each other so I've no idea who or what he was – Kendall's dresser? A nephew? A friend? – but he accompanied us to the Buckstone, a noisy, bustling little show-business club and joined us in a bacon and egg supper. And when Kendall said "Look, we can't hear each other speak here; why don't we go back to my flat? I've got some recordings of a couple of new Broadway shows you're bound to like", he came with us in the taxi and up the stairs to Kendall's flat in Victoria.

The three of us sat and drank a little wine and listened to the original cast recordings of two splendid and now celebrated musicals which had opened on Broadway the previous autumn, *Kiss Me Kate* and *Gentlemen*

Prefer Blondes. Still no word from the anonymous young man. Was he a sort of companion to Kendall? Was he perhaps more than just a friend? He certainly seemed to know his way about the flat, making himself useful by pouring the wine and making some coffee. After a while I went off to use the lavatory – "It's through the bedroom, dear boy: you can't miss it" – and when I returned the young man had gone, his disappearance as mysterious as his presence, to neither of which Kendall referred; whoever or whatever he had been, it appeared that he had become redundant.

We had another glass of wine and Henry finally said "Now, about this acting career of yours. I have a suggestion that could start you off on a pretty sound professional basis if you're interested. I'm taking the company to Australia this autumn. Why don't you come with us as Assistant Stage Manager? You could act as general stand-in while you're learning the business from the inside, and in a few months you could take over one of the smaller parts and gradually work your way up perhaps to second lead. What do you think?"

What I *thought* was: I'm not stage-struck enough to throw away an Oxford degree in order to become Assistant Stage Manager and work my way up to second lead in a touring company on the other side of the world. What I said, however, was: "That's very generous of you, Henry, and it would be a great opportunity – but it's too soon. I've only just come up to Oxford and I'd really like a degree under my belt before I decide what I want to do in the future. So thanks a lot, but honestly I couldn't consider it."

Henry said I should give it a little more thought. He talked about the rapturous reception enjoyed by English theatrical companies in Australia and regaled me with some very funny stories of his experiences as a touring actor, until I looked at my watch, saw it was half past one and said I really must be getting home. "You'll never find a taxi at this time of night, dear boy. Why don't you stay here? I can offer you a comfortable bed and a decent breakfast, and we can go and see Redgrave's Hamlet – there's a matinee tomorrow. Why don't you ring home and tell them you're staying here for the night?"

I knew about the bed: I'd seen it on my way through to Henry's bathroom. It might well have been comfortable but it wasn't what you would call particularly *large*, and I had a vision of my mother's reaction to being woken up at 1.30 in the morning and told that I would be spending the night with an actor I had met for the first time just a few hours earlier. So I said

"Thanks again, Henry, but I ought at least to try. If I can't get a taxi, I'll come straight back." I walked down the stairs and out of the front door to flag down a taxi. It wasn't difficult. This was Victoria; I had a choice of three.

Looking back with the hindsight of 65 years, did I genuinely not understand the sub-text of that evening? Was I really that naïve? Or was I, consciously or unconsciously, being the most appalling little tease? I actually phoned Henry the next morning to say I'd managed to get a taxi, thanked him for his hospitality and asked what time we should meet for the Hamlet matinee. Henry, decent, generous man that he was, didn't tell me to take a running jump; he named a time and we spent the afternoon watching Michael Redgrave's stunning performance, to which we paid tribute in his dressing room after the show.

If Henry felt any displeasure at my turning down his offer he never showed it. He invited me to a party the following week, and I found myself talking to the two legendary Hermiones, Gingold and Baddeley, and being chatted up by some of his male show business friends, including Robert Helpmann and Eric Portman. At neither that party nor any of the others to which I was invited before he took his troupe to Australia did Henry make another move on me, presumably because he realised what my reaction would be. Nor did his friends, presumably because they thought I belonged to Henry.

Back in Oxford a day or two before the start of the Hilary Term, I was enjoying a long hot bath when Michael Codron burst into the bathroom, dragged over the bathroom stool, sat down and folded his arms, and said "Right. Tell me all about it!"

"Tell you all about what?" "You and Henry Kendall! The show! The invitation to see him! Going into the profession! Oxford is buzzing with it!" I told Michael everything that had happened and at the end of my recital he said "So *did* you spend the night with him?" I said "No!" Michael said "And *wouldn't* you? Not even for the sake of your *career*?" I said "No!" again. Even with the hindsight of 65 years, I'm still not certain whether my reply made Michael think more of me or less.

Have Songs, Will Travel

The music for *Babes in the Wood* was composed by Leopold Antelme, with additional music by Stanley Myers. The two of them also wrote the music for *The New Revue* and *Spring Fever* and accompanied all three shows on the piano so we got to know each other very well. We were joined from time to time by another brilliant pianist, Julian Dale, who was playing at the University Jazz Club one Saturday night when I asked if I could sing a chorus or two with the band. My contribution to "I Wish I Could Shimmy Like My Sister Kate" seemed not to frighten the dancers, who were intent on their own versions of Sister Kate's shimmying, and Julian and the boys said I could perform at the Club any time I chose to drop in. So I finally got to sing "Sweet Lorraine" and my other favourite standards in public – or as Cherwell magazine put it, "Brian Tesler shouted down a microphone and, when it died on him, the band."

I don't know whether Leopold or Julian pursued a career in music when they left Oxford, but Stanley certainly did. He became a prolific movie composer, winning international acclaim with his score for Michael Cimino's The Deer Hunter, and writing the music for over 60 films before he died, far too young, in his early 60s. Together with Leopold and Julian, Stanley composed the music for *Make It A Date*, a revue I produced for the ETC the following Michaelmas; and he and I began to write songs together and perform them in cabaret. Julian collaborated on some of the numbers and accompanied fellow fresher Colin George and me when we assailed our cabaret audiences with the music hall cross-talk act – "I say! I say! I say!" – that I had performed with an equally show-biz-struck friend half-a-dozen years earlier at our youth club in Shepherds Bush. I have to say that the act went down better in Oxford than Shepherds Bush, but what did they know of music hall who only dreaming spires knew?

The five of us, Colin, Stanley, Julian, Leopold and me in various combinations, were considerably in demand and, hams that we were, never turned down an invitation to perform at a College dance, a Society dinner or the drop of any other hat. Many years later, at one of David Frost's marvellously eclectic garden parties, I was introduced to George Carman, the eminent Queen's Counsel then at the height of his fame. I said how glad I was to meet him and that I was a great admirer of his work. "Thank you, Mr Tesler", he said, "But you should know that I am a great admirer of *yours*."

"You must be confusing me with somebody else" I said: "I haven't produced a television programme for nearly 40 years. I can't believe you'd remember them from all that time ago."

"No, I don't watch television and I'm not confusing you with anybody else. I'm remembering you from much further ago than 40 years. I'm speaking of your song and dance entertainments at Oxford. I used to watch your cabarets for the Law Society and your other musical shows with great pleasure. They were a most welcome restorative after a hard day's work poring over law books. You know, you quite cheered me up."

In London, during the Long Vacation of 1950, Stanley and I decided to try our luck in Denmark Street, off the Charing Cross Road – the Tin Pan Alley of the day – where most of the popular music publishers had their offices. The first door we knocked on introduced us to the big, burly proprietor of Carolyn Music and Belinda Music, Charles Forsyth, whom we recognised as the American straight man of the successful British music-hall act Forsyth, Seaman and Farrell. Music publishing was a side-line for him and it was a slow afternoon so he was prepared to indulge a couple of amateur song-writers from Oxford for a while. "Okay, guys: let's hear what you've got." Stanley sat down at the upright and we performed half-a-dozen of our numbers for him and his partner, Bert Barnes. Mr Forsyth – "Call me Charlie, guys" – bought five of them for five pounds apiece, as an advance against royalties. We'd made 25 quid in 15 minutes, and in 1950 25 quid was not to be sneezed at: its equivalent in today's scale of average earnings is over £2,000. Was song-writing really that easy?

No, it wasn't. Brim full of confidence, we went next door to Noel Gay Music, the publishing offices of one of the most celebrated names in popular music. We were ushered into the office of a bald, bespectacled gentleman who appeared to be in his late 30s. He wasn't old enough to be Noel Gay himself but he obviously knew his business: he turned down everything we played for him.

After a succession of courteously patient rejections, he finally said "No, gentlemen, what we're looking for is a good, catchy six-eight. Do you have any good, catchy six-eights?" I looked at Stanley, who said "No, we haven't at the moment – but we could bring you one tomorrow." I was very glad to hear it, since I hadn't the faintest idea what a six-eight was. Back outside in Denmark Street, Stanley explained. "It's a time signal, like three-four: three-four is a waltz tempo, six-eight is a sort of rumpty tumpty tempo. You'll recognise it as soon as you hear it: no problem." So we took a taxi back to his uncle's flat in Kensington where Stanley was living during the vacation, requisitioned the baby grand and went to work on our six-eight. Next morning we presented ourselves at the Noel Gay offices and sold them the result, a little piece of nonsense called "Don't Feed An Elephant Rubber Buns", which comedian Terry-Thomas sang on a BBC Television show a few weeks later.

The bald, bespectacled gentleman who wasn't Noel Gay was in fact Noel Gay's son, Richard Armitage, Armitage being the family's true surname. Ten years later, when I was a television executive and Richard had built Noel Gay Music into an extremely successful talent agency, I got to know and like him enormously. In 1950, however, he was nowhere near his late 30s. He was a mere 21 and a college freshman like Stanley and me. He'd come down from Cambridge for the Long Vacation and was learning his father's business minding the music department. Ten years later, in 1960, he didn't look a day older, and in fact never did: Richard simply grew into his appearance and stayed that way until he died at the age of 58 – like Stanley himself far too young.

Charlie Forsyth called us one day and asked if we'd like to try plugging some of our stuff to Noble and King, an American cabaret act due shortly to open at the Savoy Hotel. Wouldn't we just! We high-tailed it to the Savoy to meet Harry Noble and Frances King, a sophisticated New York cabaret duo looking for some British material for their first London appearance. Stanley sat down at yet another baby grand – this was the sort of luxurious hotel suite you used to see in black and white Fred Astaire and Ginger Rogers movies – and we rattled off some of our by now quite extensive repertoire. Frances King's husband was the song-writer Sam Coslow, whose contribution to popular music included classic standards like "Cocktails For Two" and "My Old Flame", so we were particularly flattered that she and Harry liked our songs well enough to pick two of them for their act. They also recorded them for Columbia Records, so perhaps somewhere there still exists an old, worn-out 78 rpm shellac recording of Noble and King singing "Let's Ride Round the Park Again" and "Cold Hands, Warm Heart". Please let me know if you ever come across it. I still have the last royalty statement I received for "Cold Hands, Warm Heart". It was in fact the last royalty statement I received for any of our songs, and it came from Southern Music in July 1968, passing on the copyright earnings from a broadcast on Swedish radio. It was for three shillings and three pence, just over 16p in today's currency. This is a living?

Sixteen years earlier our songs were doing rather well on radio broadcasts. Ted Heath and his Orchestra recorded "The Girl Next Door" for Decca Records, with Dickie Valentine and Lita Roza singing the vocal, and Terry-Thomas performed another of our numbers, "I Wanna Talk About Tootsie", on television. Stanley and I were also kept busy during our vacations as performers. Song-plugging for Carolyn and Belinda Music led to our being invited to perform at show-biz parties – I remember with particular pleasure the shindigs thrown by John Metcalfe, a big wheel in advertising, and Arthur Ferrier, the eminent newspaper cartoonist and caricaturist of West End shows and show people. We did a gig at the little supper-club then occupying the top floor of the Royal Court Theatre, which was run by a young Clement Freud, who not only supervised the kitchen and acted as his own maitre d' but also introduced the cabaret, exercising with great success the lugubrious wit that continued to delight his audiences until his death almost six decades later. Stanley and I were paid in suppers.

We were also booked into a show at The Nuffield Centre by Patrick Burton, a theatrical agent who heard us at a party and asked us to fill in for one of his professional acts who couldn't make the date. I still have the letter he wrote after the show: "My dear Brian and Stanley, Just a note to thank you for your help at the Nuffield Centre on Friday night, and I hope you enjoyed the experience. Since then I have received various reports from people who saw the show – some of them conflicting – but everyone I have spoken to thought that your three numbers were delightful. I think you two could have quite a future in cabaret. You have an excellent style, and it is only a question of finding a policy suitable for cabaret audiences and the rest would be up to you. If you ever decide to do this when you leave Oxford, and I can be of any assistance, please let me know at once. Thanks once again for your help. Kind regards, Patrick." The printed strap-line at the bottom of his letter read ANY OFFER MADE IN THIS LETTER DOES NOT CONSTITUTE A CONTRACT OF ANY KIND. We took the hint.

Back at Oxford, at the beginning of Trinity Term 1950 I joined the reporting team on *The Isis*, still the longest-running independent student magazine in England – my pride at seeing my name listed for the first time as a journalist in that exalted journal only slightly dimmed by its being spelt Brian *Tester*. Most of my reporting assignments that term were to cover the flying visits from British film and theatre luminaries invited to speak at meetings of the OUDS or ETC. These distinguished artistes were usually paid expenses, accommodated at The Randolph Hotel and given a slap-up dinner at White's, the most exclusive restaurant in Oxford. I was there to report the event on the evening Peter Ustinov talked to the ETC, and the Committee members were kind enough to invite me to join them at supper with the star afterwards.

Britain's post-war austerity in 1950 extended to public eating-places. Oxford's City Council still operated one of the British Restaurants set up by the Government during the war in church halls and similar premises to provide cheap, wholesome food for people to consume without using up their precious ration book coupons. Ration books were still very much in use in 1950: rationing didn't end fully in post-war Britain until 1954, and the B.R. was packed every day. My own fairly regular eating-place was the ABC tea-room in the High, where I used to polish off my plate of egg and chips before an evening of study at the Bodleian. Enterprising little restaurants were just beginning to spring up over the city however, and undergraduates would seek them out for lunch. But walking into the warmly panelled luxury of White's for the first time – the wineglasses sparkling, the tablecloths gleaming, the black-jacketed waiters bowing and scraping – was like walking into an Emperor's palace.

I was born in the East End of London and brought up in Walthamstow, and the family moved to Chiswick when I was thirteen. We didn't have restaurants like this in Walthamstow or Chiswick; and we certainly didn't dine like this at home. I was used to a knife and fork by the side of my plate and a fork and spoon at the top of it. Here, I was confronted by a seemingly endless array of knives, forks, spoons and other implements on either side of my plate, with not the faintest idea which to use for what purpose. Sitting opposite me, Michael Codron saw my predicament and, accomplished young *bon viveur* that he was as well as impresario, he leaned across and murmured "Start at the outside and work your way in." Why couldn't I have thought of that?

During that term and the next *The Isis* gave me the occasional theatre production to review, and at the beginning of the following year I was appointed the magazine's Theatre Editor. It was a role I filled for three consecutive terms, a record for *The Isis* at that time I was told, and an absolute delight for me. Oxford was and still is blessed with two professional theatres. The New Theatre, a large auditorium with a magnificent art deco interior, was the first port of call for major touring productions and the final stop for shows on their way to Shaftesbury Avenue. The Playhouse Theatre – the Oxford Playhouse to give it its formal name – was the more intimate home of a first-class repertory company. Add to these the productions by the OUDS, the ETC and the various college dramatic societies, and my year in the theatre editor's complimentary seat in the stalls exposed me to everything from intimate revue to Chekhov, from variety-bills to Gilbert and Sullivan, from Playhouse productions of Shaw and Priestley to Univ's presentation of *The Insect Play* and Worcester's of *As You Like It*, from Noël Coward's first straight drama for ten years, *Relative Values*, to Irving Berlin's latest stage musical, *Call Me Madam*.

The range of responses to my notices was almost as wide. E. Martin Browne, the much respected producer of all T. S. Eliot's plays, wrote "Dear Mr Tesler, I was sent, by one of the cast, a copy of *Isis* with your notice of *The Cocktail Party*. I read it with great pleasure, and particular gratitude for the appreciation of its theatrical values as well as for the quality of your writing. Thank you! The sender demands her copy back. Can you very kindly send me one to keep?" The same week, from the PR representative of British film starlet Jean Kent, who was about to open in a touring production at the New, I had a tempting request "to do something personal on Miss Kent."

I was still involved directly as well as indirectly with straight theatre. In the spring of 1950, I produced Thornton Wilder's *Pullman Car Hiawatha* for a season of experimental plays organised by the Experimental Theatre Club, and in the same year played Lodovico in Alan Cooke's OUDS production of *Othello* at the Playhouse. After Oxford, Alan would go on to become one of Sydney Newman's outstanding drama directors for ABC Television's *Armchair Theatre* (*look out: another pre-echo coming up*) and I would become his boss as the company's Director of Programmes, but for *Othello* he was very much my boss. Early in the following year, Tony Richardson cast me as Delio in his production of Webster's *The Duchess of Malfi*, also for the OUDS and also at the Playhouse. Tony's post-Oxford career would of course be spectacular. Within five years he would revolutionise British theatre with his production of John Osborne's *Look Back in Anger* at the Royal Court Theatre for The English Stage Company, which he co-founded with George Devine, and he would go on to make such classic movies as *Tom Jones*, which won him Academy Awards for Best Director and Best Film, *The Loneliness of the Long Distance Runner*, and *The Charge of the Light Brigade*. No pre-echo this time: our paths never crossed after Oxford.

But we did go to France together. Along with the rest of *The Duchess*'s cast.

Engulfed

The OUDS was invited to take Tony Richardson's production to France that spring. I don't remember under whose auspices the tour was arranged or which organisation co-ordinated it, but it did give me some experience of the delights of touring that Henry Kendall had described the previous year.

We played university theatres and provincial entertainment venues, and were mostly put up in hostels and college dormitories. In Paris, however, the company was booked into a number of small hotels and *pensions*. Colin George was playing Antonio, the Duchess of Malfi's lover, and Delio was his confidant, and Colin and I tracked down our particular little backstreet hotel, checked in, dumped our bags and went off to the Cité Universitaire to have a look at the stage and its facilities. When we returned and asked for our keys we were told that our rooms were not yet ready. "There must be some mistake: we were in our rooms this morning – we left our luggage there when we checked in and they were perfectly ready then." "Ah, m'sieur, your luggage is quite safe, and we will move it back into your rooms when they are available, which" – the concierge looked at his watch – "will be very shortly." And Colin and I suddenly realised why the staircases were bustling with housemaids trotting in and out of rooms, taking armfuls of freshly ironed bed-linen up the stairs and bringing freshly crumpled armfuls down them. We had been booked into a house of *assignations amoureuses* and we were clearly interrupting the traffic.

For our one-night stand in Poitiers, where we played La Grand Salle des Pas-Perdus du Palais de Justice, we were welcomed into the homes of local farmers and discovered that in this part of France at any rate the hearty local breakfast was accompanied *de rigueur* by lashings of good strong local wine. That afternoon's matinee performance was a little more light-headed than usual, and it wasn't helped by what preceded curtain-up. Our hosts, Le Syndicat d'Initiative de Poitiers, keen to emphasise the symbolic significance of this cultural event, had arranged the playing of the national anthems of our two countries on gramophone records as we took up our opening positions on the stage. The short burst of "La Marseillaise" went perfectly smoothly, but the military band rendition of "God Save the Queen" failed to finish after the customary first 16 bars. The gramophone operator had been supplied with an extended ceremonial recording of our anthem – we could see it on the turntable in the wings: a ten-inch HMV plum and gold label – and he simply didn't know where or how to stop it; all he could do was wait for the record to run its course. So for two and a half minutes, as chorus followed chorus after chorus after chorus, while the local dignitaries and fellow members of our distinguished audience stood to attention on one side of the curtain, the shamefully disloyal members of the British and Commonwealth cast on the other side of the curtain, tears rolling down our cheeks, slowly collapsed onto the stage, writhing with helpless, aching, agonisingly suppressed laughter.

I had forgotten until I re-read the French newspaper cuttings that, in Tours, L'Institut de Touraine threw a big party for us after our performance, with entertainment by L'ensemble Lucky Mario, the young dancers of the Conservatoire de Mme Pesche and – how could I have forgotten it? – ourselves."*Enfin, Brian Tesler, Colin George et le guitariste Chuck Tilly, revelerent des aptitudes d'artistes de cabaret que la 'Duchesse d'Amalfi' ne nous avait pas soupconner.*" Even in the middle of a tour of Webster's darkest tragedy, Colin and I couldn't resist the opportunity to trot out our cabaret act, with Chuck, the company's Canadian Assistant Stage Manager, gamely depping on his guitar for Stanley Myers's baby grand.

The Duchess of Malfi was my last straight play. My penchant was clearly for musical theatre. I was having too much fun in revue and cabaret to go straight. Back at Oxford even my fiascos were greeted as coups. Overweening ass that I was, I thought I would open the second half of my ETC Revue *Make It A Date* with the sort of extravaganza I had always loved in West End shows and Hollywood musicals. Stanley Myers, Julian Dale and I wrote the words and music for a romantic production number called "Caribbean

Spell", set on an exotic island in the West Indies. The stage was dressed
with palm trees and sand dunes to look like a tropical beach at dusk, lit by
the rays of the setting sun. Dressed as a beachcomber, I stood stage right
to sing the passionate lyric while Colin George and Liz MacEwan danced
an ardent pas de deux against a background of swaying silhouettes supplied by the rest of the cast. The full romantic works. And the audience
roared with laughter. Half-way through the first eight bars, I realised with
horror that they thought "Caribbean Spell" was a send-up, a *parody* of the
romantic production numbers of stage and screen and not a pastiche. The
more passionately I sang, the more ardently Colin and Liz danced, the more
seductively the silhouettes swayed, the more the audience roared.

Incredibly, and quite unjustifiably, the number was a hit. So was the
rest of the show: the Oxford Mail's reviewer thought *Make It A Date* "well
deserved the rapturous applause with which it was greeted by a full house. It
was one of the brightest, merriest and most melodious shows of its kind that
I have seen for a very long time." So I got away with it. I modestly accepted
praise for the ingenuity of the send-up and learnt a great lesson about not
taking audiences for granted. But I still find myself hot with embarrassment
at the memory of it all.

Fortunately, I was able to manage the next pastiche rather better. Browsing in the Charing Cross Road bookshops during the Christmas vacation
I found a sheet music collection of songs of the twenties. I couldn't and
still can't read music, but most of the numbers were familiar to me: great
standards from the Jazz Age, when ragtime was king and Irving Berlin, the
Gershwins, Cole Porter and Rodgers and Hart were beginning to fill the
pages of The Great American Song Book. I'd already sung half of them at
the O.U. Jazz Club, and the others looked delightful.

Back at Oxford, Stanley, Julian and I worked our way through the numbers
we didn't know, and put together a running-order of familiar and unfamiliar
material that might make an attractive cabaret for an evening of *The Roaring Twenties*. The ETC Committee liked the idea, and the following month
Mimi Kenny transformed the Agricola Restaurant's big upstairs room on
George Street into a Speakeasy, a smoky cellar dive – just like the movies. A
platform accommodated The Original Jellybabe Kings, the name we gave the
great little band from the University Jazz Club; the centre of the floor was
cleared for the dancing and cabaret; the surrounding tables and chairs were
lit by candles stuck in the tops of old liqueur bottles; coloured spotlights

swept over the dancers and the Jellybabe Kings; and "Prohibition liquor" was served by the Agricola's wine-waiter dressed in period, complete with bow-tie, rolled-up sleeves and apron.

We'd advertised "Period Or Evening Dress Welcomed. Minor Outrages In Period Condoned" and the idea of a *Roaring Twenties* evening appeared to have caught the eye of the *Daily Express* as well as the ETC members and guests. The *Express* sent their columnist Eve Perrick to have a look at it; and, as she said in her column two days later, "Undergraduates in bow ties, striped blazers, Oxford bags (one enterprising male even managed a racoon coat); undergraduettes in those terrible fringe-and-spangle furbelows, long earrings, longer necklaces and near-blinding hairdo's surged in. Mr Robinson's Jellybabe Kings made the appropriate noises – bouncy, brassy and deafening. The dancers jigged and kicked. Everyone shouted and stomped..." It was quite a night.

That Charing Cross collection of sheet music provided superb material not only for our established revue artistes from *Spring Fever*, *The New Revue* and *Make It A Date* but also for newcomers like Shirley Catlin – Baroness Williams of Crosby as she now is – who sang "Falling In Love Again" in a husky contralto, and for others whose normal role was producing rather than performing, like Michael Codron, who rose from behind Julian Dale's upright piano with a giant sombrero on his head to deliver the deathless "When Yuba Plays The Rumba On The Tuba". And Colin George and I, with Stanley Myers at the piano, were able to add two new old numbers to our cabaret repertoire: Irving Berlin's "Play A Simple Melody", which had been around since 1914, and "Hard Hearted Hannah (The Vamp of Savannah)", written in 1924 and not revived until the 1955 movie Pete Kelley's Blues: we got to it first.

The Oxford Clarion said "This was Oxford at its best; it is in this sort of revue – half cabaret, half parody – that her most obvious talents appear." And forgive me if I also quote from the review in *The Isis*: "Excellent though the individual numbers were, the most striking feature of the floor-show was its smooth presentation. The slick showmanship of Brian Tesler's production was of a standard rarely found in an amateur entertainment. The effect of this was to leave his crowded audience in the right mood to enjoy the final session from the Jazz Club Band. As they stamped their feet and surged round the instrumentalists, the evening drew to a close; an evening which provided some of the brightest entertainment likely to be seen in Oxford for some time." Well, *something* had to have rubbed off from all those hours spent at the theatre, the movies and the music-hall.

But it was time for me to turn to a very different kind of study. The Rector of Exeter College had asked me to see him. Mr Barber said he was aware of all that I had been doing and delighted to see a member of the college playing a prominent part in University activities, but Schools – the final degree exams – were approaching and he was concerned that I might be devoting insufficient time to my preparation for them. He would not want me to endanger my chances of a respectable degree. Did I not think it was time for me to cut back on these other interests and concentrate on my academic work? He was right, of course. I knew that my tutors, Nevill Coghill for English Literature and Lord David Cecil for English Language, felt that my work was adequate but no more and thought that I was capable of better. And I loved the literature and the language and the opportunity to immerse myself in them; I just hadn't taken that opportunity zealously enough. This was October 1951; the degree exams were in the middle of the following May, so I determined to resist all distractions and dedicate myself to study.

There were, however, a few prior commitments to fulfil. I had to complete that Michaelmas term as Theatre Editor of *The Isis*. Michael Codron had asked me to arrange the musical routines for *Cinderella*, the 1951 Christmas Pantomime for the OUDS. Not a smoking concert this time: *Cinderella* was to be a major production at the Playhouse, written and directed by Michael, with a score by Stanley Myers. And there was another commitment. As President of the ETC – I succeeded Michael early in 1951 – I had been invited to take a company to Cambridge as guests of honour at the University's annual Theatre Ball, where we would join members of the Footlights and other dramatic clubs in providing the cabaret. This was an undertaking I couldn't resist.

In *The Tatler* of 12 March 1952, under the caption "CABARET WAS HIGH-LIGHT OF UNIVERSITY THEATRE BALL", there's a typical *Tatler* photograph of the top table enjoying a jolly conversation at dinner. It's a pretty crowded table. Among the group are Stanley Myers and our lead female performer Liz MacEwan, together with Cambridge Footlights committee members Peter Jeffrey, Peter Firth and their chairman Andrew Davidson. I am also in the group, though you'll have to take the caption-writer's word for it: all you can see of me is the back of my head.

Leaving Oxford

There was an additional distraction. As well as the work for my degree I had to think about work post-Oxford. When I left the BFBS station in Trieste I had more or less assumed that radio was where my future would lie. I even attempted to reactivate the old University Radio Club in my first college year by producing for the ETC a radio adaptation I had made of Elmer Rice's play *The Adding Machine.* That turned out to be a somewhat surreal event, with the cast performing to a microphone in one room and the audience sitting and listening in the room next door. During the louder passages, when they could hear us through the wall as well as through the radio's loudspeaker, it must have sounded like stereo-broadcasting decades before its time. Not surprisingly, the Radio Club remained un-reactivated.

Now, two years later, I wasn't at all sure about radio as a career. My parents had acquired a state-of-the-art television set and I'd begun to watch this newfangled thing during vacations. It's difficult to remember just how different our TV technology was in the early fifties from today's world of king-sized screens flat and slim enough to hang on the wall. In the early fifties it was the television *set* – the console – that was king-sized: it had to be, to accommodate the huge cathode-ray tube fitted perpendicularly inside it: no flat-screen LCD magic in those days. The early fifties television screen looked up at the ceiling from the top of the tube; it was a mere nine or twelve inches wide, and you watched it via its reflection in the angled mirror suspended from the lid of the console. That seems a bizarre and convoluted procedure today, but for us it was the latest, most ingenious technology, and the experience – these moving pictures, this world of entertainment and information in your own front room – was magical. I wanted to be part of it, which is how I ended up in the small windowless interview room in Broadcasting House where this story began...

My anonymous interviewer at B.H. was as good as his word. A month later I was interviewed by Ronnie Waldman, BBC Television's Head of Light Entertainment, at the Corporation's Lime Grove studios in Shepherds Bush. Ronnie was in his middle 30s, stocky, dark-haired, good-looking; a graduate of Oxford's Pembroke College with a background in radio that went back a dozen years. He'd joined the BBC's Radio Variety department as a producer and presenter in 1938, which was when I began listening to his *Monday Night at Eight* programme. Ronnie had served with the Royal Air Force Volunteer Reserve during the war and, once demobbed, had returned to BBC Radio as Assistant Head of Variety. When the BBC's Television Service started up again he was transferred to Lime Grove as a senior producer and appointed Head of Light Entertainment in 1950. Ronnie was immediately and immensely engaging and gave me a sympathetic hearing – after all, as he pointed out, he'd spent his years at Oxford doing exactly what I had been doing and during the war had also worked for the British Forces Broadcasting Service.

"Look," he said, "I like the sound of what you've done at Oxford, and you've certainly picked up a good deal of knowledge about musical enter-tainment and variety and so on, but I run a professional department; my producers are all experienced professionals from radio or the theatre, and inevitably you have no professional experience at all. I could tell you to go out and get some – join a repertory company, do some summer season work, try for an Assistant Stage Manager job somewhere" – like Australia? Where are you, Henry Kendall, now that I need you? – "However...I'm prepared to take a chance. I'll recommend you for an interview with the Appointments Board for the Training Course. If you pass that, you'll be offered a six-month contract. For the first six weeks they'll teach you the basics of the business. You'll then join the Light Entertainment Department here at Lime Grove as a trainee assistant to one of my senior producers. How much you manage to learn about making light entertainment programmes during the rest of the six months will be up to you, and you'll have a couple of 15-minute programmes of your own to produce as your trainee exercises. But at the end of your contract you'll be thrown out to join the rest of the ex-trainees, to be hauled back if and when something comes up for which we think you might be suitable. How does that sound to you?" Like the Hallelujah Chorus, Mr Waldman, if you really want to know.

My interview with the BBC's Appointments Board took place at the end of April. I sat in front of a long table in a conference room at the Redbourne Hotel in Great Portland Street. Ronnie Waldman's was the only face I recognised among the six or seven dark-suited men on the other side of the table. They asked the expected questions about my education and interests, my National Service experience with the British Forces Broadcasting Service and my reasons for wanting to join the BBC, and then handed me over to Ronnie to find out what I knew about light entertainment. After a pretty intensive grilling Ronnie slid a piece of paper across the table. It contained a list of variety performers – singers, dancers, comedians, speciality acts – and Ronnie said "I want you to put this list into a variety bill for Saturday night. Tell us where you would place each of them in your running order, and why."

I recognised the artistes and I'd spent enough evenings at the music hall to know how they might most effectively be placed in sequence, so I constructed a running order as requested and gave my reasons one by one. But Ronnie had thrown in a little catch. I had an artiste left over: there was one comedian too many on his list. "So what would you do with this performer?" he said. "Where on the bill would you place him?" In desperation I replied "Oh, he'd be the show's compere." Another pre-echo. That left-over comedian on Ronnie's list was Tommy Trinder. Three and a half years later, Tommy would indeed be the compere of a variety show: ITV's hugely successful *Sunday Night at The London Palladium.* And two years later still, I would drop him from the show when I took over as its producer; but that's another story. At the 1952 Board my answer satisfied Ronnie and impressed the others; and a few days later I received a letter to say that I had been granted a place on the Television Training Course for the coming September.

Had I left myself enough time to put up a decent show in the Degree Finals? During the previous two-and-a-half years I'd managed to keep my head above the academic water. I hadn't failed Mods, the exams at the end of an undergraduate's first year, designed to monitor progress; I had attended all the necessary lectures; I had never failed to deliver my weekly essay to Nevill Coghill – and I was by no means the only undergraduate who had to stay up most of the previous night in order to do so. It wasn't the case, therefore, that I had to cram three years of study into my last six months, but I certainly had a lot of catching up to do. With my Language tutor David Cecil I'd found Old English and Middle English the most amenable of subjects so I was pretty confident about the History of Language papers. I loved the big beasts, Chaucer and Shakespeare, and felt I could communicate that love with the help of a short-term memory honed on learning parts for plays and sketches; I would be getting quotations instead of lines off by heart and I knew enough by now about playing to an audience to ensure that the quotations would be apt and unhackneyed. But the splendours of English literature are infinite and, though the syllabus I had to cover was not, it was too great for me to cover in the time I had left. Some of the authors in the remaining papers would have to be skated over.

I decided that the best I could do if I were confronted with any of them would be to know enough about these authors to provide an eye-catching opening paragraph or two for my answers – and then stop, as if I had run out of time. The strategy would play havoc with my plans for the summer vacation because I would have to mug up on the truncated answers in case I was asked to complete them at the Viva Voce, the live examination which would follow at the end of June, but it seemed the only way to go. And that's the way I went. Alexander Pope and his contemporaries were given short shrift in Paper B9, English Literature from 1400 to 1800 – but they got some great opening paragraphs.

With the exams over I was able to concentrate on my last Oxford show. The ETC had been asked to put on an entertainment to close the rather grand occasion of a Garden Party sponsored by the Oxford International Committee. The handbill read

OXFORD INTERNATIONAL COMMITTEE
GARDEN PARTY
In New College Gardens and Cloisters
On Saturday June 16th
Entertainment by
BRIAN TESLER AND MEMBERS OF E.T.C
FRENCH CLUB MADRIGALS
O.U.SCOTTISH SOCIETY
O.U. REEL CLUB
LES CHANSONS DE LAUSANNE
Those present will include:
The Very Reverend THE VICE-CHANCELLOR

His Excellency THE ITALIAN AMBASSADOR
His Excellency THE AUSTRIAN MINISTER
His Excellency THE SWISS MINISTER
THE GERMAN CONSUL-GENERAL.

Also present, unbilled, would be a Mr Graeme Muir of BBC Television's Light Entertainment Department and his wife. Ronnie Waldman had asked me to keep in touch after the Appointments Board, and when I told him about the International Committee affair he said he would send one of his producers to have a look at what I did in such a setting and before such an audience and report back to him; so it would have to be pretty special.

We'd been given the closing hour and our show would go on at 5 pm, when the college gardens and cloisters would still be bathed in sunlight. I dug deep into childhood memories of the sunbathed pier-end shows I had loved so much with my family in Southend and Margate, and the ETC's own handbill announced

The O.U. Experimental Theatre Club
will present
THE SUNBEAM FOLLIES
An Informal Concert-Party
not at all to be taken seriously
UNDER THE DIRECTION OF BRIAN TESLER
STANLEY MYERS AND JULIAN DALE AT TWO PIANOS

We had just about enough time to write two new numbers to open and close the show but otherwise we adapted the best of our revue and cabaret material of the past three years – concert-party being the perfect setting at last for the George-Tesler music-hall act – and put together the best of our revue and cabaret performers, with one scintillating addition. Eighteen-year old, red-headed Maggie Smith was a student at Oxford High School, not an undergraduate, but she had just made her stage debut as Viola in *Twelfth Night* for the OUDS and was the girl friend of a most fortunate member of our group, Michael Murray. She thought it would be fun to try her hand at revue, and that flaming hair and talent helped to light up what became a very successful show. Anyway, that's what Graeme Muir and his actress wife Marjorie Mars reported back to Ronnie Waldman. We had plied them with enough pre-show champagne to ensure a receptive mood in both of them, just in case.

After *The Sunbeam Follies*, at the end of term, Colin George forsook music-hall and started up his own touring Shakespeare company, beginning a career which has encompassed theatre, film and television, two residences with the Royal Shakespeare Company in Stratford and London, the setting-up of Sheffield's Crucible Theatre, and long periods as Artistic Director of theatres both at home at Leicester's Haymarket Theatre and Sheffield's Playhouse and abroad in Australia and Hong Kong. Maggie Smith joined Frank Shelley's repertory company at the Oxford Playhouse and four years later was on Broadway starring in Leonard Sillman's *New Faces Revue*; it's nice to think that the song and dance part of her remarkable career started with *The Sunbeam Follies*.

As for me, at the end of term I left a dozen red roses at the Playhouse stage door for her – well, who *wouldn't* be sweet on Maggie? – and drove away from Oxford to four weeks of intense preparation for the Viva. It was a time-consuming but not unduly onerous task because I liked the authors I had treated so cursorily in my exam papers: I just hadn't known enough about them to produce full-length answers. My most provocative stand-alone opening paragraphs had been on Alexander Pope and his contemporaries, so I concentrated on cramming as much Pope as possible, ready to complete my essay if the examiners pressed me, as they surely would. Any remaining revision time I would spend mugging up enough about the other authors to bluff my way through if called upon to do so. For four weeks I was a red-eyed resident of the Chiswick Public Library's Reference Section from opening time to closing.

I duly presented myself the following month alongside my fellow English School examinees at the Examination Schools building on the High Street, still mentally rehearsing what I would say to complete those abbreviated Honours answers, and waited to be called into the inquisition. When my turn finally came, I entered a large, sparsely furnished room and was directed to a hard-backed chair placed in front of a long table. On the other side of the table sat half-a-dozen or so dark-suited, black-gowned, mortar-boarded dons. It was like a re-run of the interview with the BBC's Television Training Scheme Board but with gowns and mortar-boards and without a single familiar face. As it happened, I couldn't have recognised a familiar face even if there had been one because the dons were in silhouette. Their backs were to the sun, which poured in through the windows behind them and shone relentlessly into the eyes of the now dry-mouthed, apprehensive victim before them. Silence. Where would they start? What was it I had said about Pope's *Dunciad*? Had I mugged up enough about Dryden's plays? The silhouettes slowly removed their mortar-boards, paused, and put them back on again. The central silhouette said "Thank you, Mr Tesler. You may go."

I stumbled into the waiting room dazed and bemused. "How was it?" someone asked: "You weren't very long." I told him what had happened. "That's a First" he said. "More like an execution" I said. "No, that's what they do when you've been awarded a First. They don't say anything, they just doff their mortar-boards. You've got a First, you lucky bugger!" I didn't believe it. What about those unanswered questions, those unfinished exam papers? I joined my parents on holiday in Bournemouth still not believing it, until a congratulatory phone-call came in the middle of lunch one day from a friend who'd seen the results posted on the Schools notice-board.

Nevill Coghill sent me a card detailing the marks on each of the papers, with the comment "All the way!" They were all alphas, alpha-betas or alpha-minuses except for B9, and even that had managed a beta-plus. In the wonderfully warm letter Nevill sent with the card, I learned at last what his reaction to our original meeting seven years earlier had been: "I knew from the first sight I had of you that you were able, but I thought you might be an idle rogue, possibly even a Smart Alec!" So, at least he hadn't thought me a loon.

The Rector sent his congratulations: "Considering all the other claims on your time here (which, as you will remember, caused me some apprehension!) it reflects the greatest credit on you." Merton College's Robert Levens, another English don heavily involved in undergraduate theatre, also sent me a note: "My dear Brian, The sight of your name among the Firsts was a great delight, all the more because it was – I'm sure you won't mind my saying – a great surprise... We never suspected that you would have *time* to get a First!... And what a class list for the acting world" – two of our straight actresses had also got Firsts – "So much for those who say it is a ruinous waste of time."

Amen to that. Oxford gave me a degree. Oxford's acting world gave me a career. The shades of show business that had begun to close in on my childhood and adolescence had finally engulfed me. Now they were to propel me into the world of television.

Back to School

Number 27 Marylebone Road is occupied today by the Methodist Missionary Society. In September 1952 it was the home of the BBC's Television Training Course and grandly designated Luxborough House, the entrance being round the side in Luxborough Street. Luxborough House must previously have been some kind of teaching establishment, perhaps a sixth-form college. It had a Lecture Room – Room 317 – equipped with a dozen or so bench and desk units designed to accommodate two students per unit, and an impressive blackboard stretching across the wall behind the instructor's desk and chair; there was a Common Room for the students, a Canteen in the basement and offices for the administrative staff.

The executive in charge of Television Training was Royston Morley, an authentic television veteran even in 1952. He had been a producer with the BBC's pre-war television service from its inauguration in 1936 until its close-down in 1939 for the duration of hostilities, and in those three pioneering years he had produced plays by authors ranging from Edgar Wallace to Oscar Wilde as well as topical interview programmes like *Picture Page*. Morley's office boasted the only television set on the premises and, television sets still being comparatively rare – none of the students staying in hotels or boarding-houses had access to them – we were free to use it after school and at weekends for our required viewing.

Room 317 would be home base for the next three weeks for a dozen trainees, half-a-dozen guest students from Swedish, German and Australian television networks and a drama producer from the theatre, John Fernald, who had been invited to try his hand at the new medium. Now, at 9.45 a.m.

on the morning of 22 September 1952, we were milling about, disoriented, unfamiliar with each other and with our surroundings, just like any other first day at school. I sat down at one of the double-desks and took my papers out of my briefcase. A broad-shouldered, thick-set man in his late 20s, tough-looking but light on his feet – a sort of cross between Gene Kelly and the light-heavyweight boxer Gus Lesnevich – made his way toward my desk and loomed over me. He spoke. "Are you a Jewish boy?" I swallowed nervously and replied. "Yeeess..." "Can I sit with you?" he said.

This, it transpired, was Ernest Maxin, who had somehow in the madding crowd sensed a kindred ethnic as well as creative spirit: we were the only Jewish as well as the only Light Entertainment trainees on the Course. Ernest was not a University graduate: he had come from the theatre, where he had been a producer and choreographer; but we got on well at once and would find ourselves working productively together in the future. Later still in the future, Ernest would devise and produce the great television routines – "Singing In The Rain"; preparing breakfast to the music of "The Stripper"; the acrobatic newsreaders vaulting their way through "There Is Nothing Like A Dame" – which would help to keep the Morecambe and Wise shows forever fresh in the memory of the television audience.

Ernest was not the only member of the class of '52 who would make his mark. Over on the other side of the room was Peter Graham Scott, who would become a leading film and television producer. Next to him was Patricia Foy, who would go on to be an Emmy-winning producer of music and ballet programmes, the only one to succeed in persuading Margot Fonteyn to tell the story of her life and career in a television series. At the next desk was Michael Peacock, who would produce *Panorama* at the age of 25 and go on to be the first Controller of the new BBC television channel, BBC 2, which he would launch in 1964 before becoming Controller of BBC 1 and subsequently the founder-Managing Director of London Weekend Television. And there in the back row was David Attenborough, who would enjoy the most remarkable career of all: beginning as a producer, then moving to administration as Controller of BBC 2 before being appointed the BBC's first Director of Programmes for both television channels and then, in 1972, rejecting the position of Director General in order to return to programme-making, where he would become the producer and presenter of an internationally acclaimed succession of television series about the natural world. All in all, not a bad year for talent, 1952.

The Training Course was comprehensive, meticulously planned, and absolutely jam-packed. Nothing like it existed in the world of communications then, and nothing like it exists today: the BBC Film and Television Production Course is now available to purchase as a 13-part series, the price of the parts ranging from £25 to £160. We students had no idea how fortunate we were. We were taught the constitutional and legal status of the BBC. We heard lectures from the heads of Engineering and Administration. We were given specific programmes to watch in the evenings and weekends so that we could discuss them with their writers and producers next day. We explored the BBC's Research Department at Kingswood Warren. We spent days in the television studios at Alexandra Palace and Lime Grove, where we watched programmes at every stage of rehearsal and production. We toured the Film, Newsreel, Design, Wardrobe & Make-up, Programme Planning, Presentation, Outside Broadcasts, Engineering and Technical Departments and discussed with their heads the respective roles they played in the BBC's output. We learned about the work of the Booking Department, the Audience Research Department, the *Radio Times* and the rest of the BBC Publications Department. At Marylebone Road and in viewing theatres at both studios we attended lectures by the heads of the creative departments: Drama, Light Entertainment, Children's Television, Religious Broadcasting, and Talks, which in the fifties subsumed Documentaries and Current Affairs. We also heard from some celebrated guest speakers: the novelist C. P. Snow, who discussed *The Writer and Television*, the West End impresario Henry Sherek, whose subject was *Television and the Theatre*, and the celebrated documentary-maker John Grierson, who talked about *The Documentary Film in Relation to Television*.

The guest speakers were familiar to us by their reputation; so too was at least one of the creative heads, since most people knew Ronnie Waldman from *Monday Night at Eight* on radio or *Puzzle Corner* on television. But not until we were actually working in the medium itself would we realise what legendary broadcasting figures our other lecturers were: Cecil McGivern, the Controller of BBC Television Programmes; Cecil Madden, the Assistant Controller; Grace Wyndham Goldie, the Talks Producer; Mary Adams, the Head of Television Talks; Freda Lingstrom, the Head of Children's Programmes; S.J. de Lotbiniere, the Head of Television Outside Broadcasts; D. R. Campbell and D. C. Birkinshaw the Production Engineeers... I doubt if many of these or their fellow pioneers are remembered by anybody other than the broadcasters of my generation but there were giants in television broadcasting then, and these were amongst them.

At the end of the Course, four days were set aside for our trainee exercises at Alexandra Palace. We were divided up into six groups by Royston and his team and supplied with rehearsal rooms and any advice we needed about technical support. John Fernald was the nominated producer of my group and I the assistant producer, sitting at his side in the gallery and previewing his shots before he called them up. This was not the easiest of procedures because Alexandra Palace was still operating with pre-war facilities and equipment. You couldn't simply call up the picture you wanted from among the screens in front of you; each shot had to be selected in advance on one of two preview screens and switched to the second screen before it could be transmitted. Needless to say, we decided against trying our hand at a quick-cutting sequence.

John chose a one-act play for our production exercise and it appeared to go quite well, as did all the other exercises, though I have absolutely no recollection of the title or content of any of them. All I remember is the general euphoria of our last day, with a final discussion of the course and a boisterous farewell tea party. John Fernald never got the chance to make use of the knowledge he had acquired: not long afterwards he was appointed Principal of RADA, the Royal Academy of Dramatic Art. Our guest students from Sweden and Australia were evidently impressed by their experience and reported glowingly back home – and Royston Morley found himself spending most of the next ten years setting up and running Television Training Schools for both the Swedish and Australian Broadcasting Corporations. Our fellow trainees departed for their respective departments: Talks, Documentaries, Music, Design and Wardrobe. And Ernest Maxin and I headed off to Light Entertainment at Lime Grove. Now for the real thing.

The Real Thing

We had no way of knowing it, but we were arriving at a remarkable time in the history of British television. The BBC's post-war service was only six years old in 1952. The Government had encouraged its resumption partly to raise the nation's morale and partly to stimulate a market for manufacturers like EMI, Pye and Marconi, whose TV sets and other electronic equipment could then be exported to other emerging markets to earn much-needed overseas revenue. But if the BBC's pre-war studios and equipment hadn't already existed at Alexandra Palace, post-war austerity Britain could not have afforded a television service at all.

As it was, the combined radio and television licence of £2 introduced in 1946 when the service re-started was barely enough to keep the service ticking over. In 1952, television had only recently ceased being just one department among others within the BBC's Home Broadcasts Division, and it was still very much radio's infant offspring. Its only news broadcast was a late-night radio bulletin, read by an announcer over a still picture of Big Ben. Its drama output was supervised along with that of radio drama at Broadcasting House, by the BBC's Head of Drama, John Gielgud's brother Val. Its programmes were relegated to a handful of pages at the back of the *Radio Times*; and the programmes themselves were broadcast for only a few hours each day, from 3 pm to 4 pm in the afternoon, 5.30 pm to 6.30 pm in the early evening and 7.30 pm to 10.30 pm at night. It would not become self-supporting until 1954, when the combined licence fee was increased from £2 to £3.

But if television was an infant, it was an infant Hercules. By the end of 1952, when Ernest and I and the other Training Course graduates were making our way to Lime Grove, there were already a million and a half combined licences, and another 150,000 homes were thought to be watching without a licence: the first TV detector van was commissioned in 1952 to track them down. Television had begun to catch the public's imagination and the newspapers' attention, and incidents that occurred in its most popular programme, the Sunday night panel game *What's My Line?* – panellist Barbara Kelly losing an ear-ring or co-panellist Gilbert Harding losing his temper – would be featured on the front pages next day. As Peter Black observed, in his indispensable study of British television *The Mirror in the Corner*, newspaper placards used to announce changes in the *What's My Line?* panel as if they were Cabinet re-shuffles.

Most of the basic formats and techniques with which television programming re-started had been more or less invented by Alexandra Palace's pre-war service. Broadcasting only three hours a day in the three years before war closed it down, freewheeling young programme makers like Royston Morley had transmitted hundreds of plays, features, interview programmes, music, dance and variety shows, relays from West End theatres and scores of other Outside Broadcasts, including the very first Outside Broadcast itself, the Coronation of King George VI in 1937. And those pre-war producers of the world's first regular television service had had no star to guide them: they were making it up as they went along.

This sort of cheerful have-a-go enthusiasm had re-established itself in the post-war service, but in 1950 the job of running it as controller of programmes was handed to Cecil McGivern, a radio producer with a background in cinema and theatre and a passionate belief in the new medium. By the time the Class of '52 made its way to Lime Grove, McGivern and his lieutenants had tempered the dashing amateurism with a hard professional edge; and that's what Ernest Maxin and I found in its Light Entertainment Department when we knocked on Ronnie Waldman's door on 20 October 1952.

Ronnie had put together a team of professionals with years of production experience in radio, theatre, cabaret, revue and television itself. Some of his most senior producers had actually preceded him into the department. Michael Mills had joined in January 1947, when a producer was still known simply as 'producer, television' and was expected to turn his hand to every kind of production, just as the pre-war producers at Alexandra Palace had done. Mills was the first to be designated 'producer, light entertainment' and was now responsible for some of the department's most ambitious programming, including 90-minute extravaganzas dedicated to the musical theatre called *The Passing Show*. Richard Afton and Henry Caldwell, *grands seigneurs* of the department, who appeared to be allowed to combine their work with various show-business ventures outside television, were responsible for cabaret-style entertainments like *Café Continental* and *Rooftop Rendezvous*.

Bill Ward's experience was practically a history of television in itself. As an engineer he had worked at everything from sound-boom operator to vision mixer at Alexandra Palace. Just before the war, he had moved to production and become a studio manager, and he had rejoined the television service in that capacity in 1946. The story went that the Appointments Board turned him down when he applied for a producer's job but Cecil McGivern had insisted on what the rest of the Board considered an ill-advised appointment and agreed to take full responsibility for it. If the story was true, McGivern's gamble had paid off handsomely: Ward was the doyen of the department, the most successful and highly regarded of them all, responsible for comedy series featuring stars like Arthur Askey and Terry-Thomas as well as the spectacular *This is Show Business*, a regular salute to the entertainment profession.

Ernest fitted into this environment without much difficulty because he shared the production background and experience of these and other producers like Bill Lyon-Shaw, Bryan Sears, Dicky Leeman, T. Leslie Jackson and Graeme Muir. But what was a 22-year old English graduate doing in a professional light entertainment department? Why wasn't he in Talks with the rest of the graduates? A wisecrack swiftly became a rumour: I was Ronnie Waldman's illegitimate son. After all, we were both of medium height, dark of skin and Jewish: what else could explain it? The department's old pros gave me a pretty tough time. If they didn't totally ignore me, like Richard Afton and Henry Caldwell, they treated me with a mixture of suspicion and disdain, like Bill Ward and Michael Mills. I would have to work hard to win their acceptance, let alone their respect.

Ernest and I were designated Assistant Light Entertainment Producers and attached to Bryan Sears and Graeme Muir respectively. At least Graeme knew something of my production potential and might take me seriously – that is, if he could remember anything at all from the champagne haze of *The Sunbeam Follies*. We were allocated a desk in the corner of our respective mentor's office and followed our leaders through the preparation, rehearsal and production of their shows, learning as much as we could about the practicalities of programme-making before we took our own solo flights at Alexandra Palace at the turn of the year.

There were no Alexandra Palace productions by Graeme or Bryan for us to study during the next few months but we knew its studios pretty well as a result of the Training Course. High on Muswell Hill in North London, the Palace had been an exhibition centre before the BBC rented the premises in 1936 and constructed its first television studios and control rooms there. The control rooms themselves were built in the Palace's Minstrel Gallery so they were referred to as galleries. The studios had changed very little, but apart from their archaic camera preview systems and the fact that their control rooms were up steep metal staircases to the galleries overlooking them, Alexandra Palace's studios A and B were not all that different from the studios at Lime Grove.

Lime Grove itself runs between Goldhawk Road and the Uxbridge Road in Shepherds Bush. It's a perfectly ordinary residential street today; and so it was in 1952 – except for a vast, five-storey television studio complex which seemed to have materialised in the middle of its west side like some great Tardis from another planet. Four decades earlier Lime Grove had been an unused cul de sac, part of a railway company's industrial site. The French film company Gaumont bought the plot in 1915 and built a silent movie studio on it. Over the years, talkies succeeded silents, Gaumont became Gaumont-British, the industrial site was swallowed up by the houses, pubs, restaurants and shops of Shepherds Bush, and Lime Grove itself became a perfectly ordinary residential street. The studio got there first: the residential street – and the rest of Shepherds Bush – had simply grown up round it.

As a film studio, Lime Grove had been the home of many notable British film-makers. Michael Balcon was director of production there for six years. Michael Powell, David Lean and Carol Reed began their careers there; so did Alfred Hitchcock, all of whose early British movies, including *The Lady Vanishes* and *The 39 Steps*, were made at Lime Grove. The films that boosted our spirits during the war and helped us escape the shabby austerity that followed it – wartime adventures like *We Dive At Dawn* and costume melodramas like *The Wicked Lady* and *Fanny By Gaslight* – were produced at Lime Grove. The Rank Organisation took over the studio in 1942 as part of its enormous film empire, but by the end of the forties the British film industry was hit by one of its periodic financial crises and Rank was forced to put everything but Pinewood Studios up for sale. The BBC acquired Lime Grove on the last day of its auction, in October 1949.

The studios were intended to be a temporary measure while the Corporation's custom-designed Television Centre was being built nearby at White City, and they were converted in great haste: the first production from Lime Grove was transmitted only seven months after the Corporation moved in. Being temporary, no attempt was made to transform the building overall or even to renovate it. It was a rabbit-warren of corridors, staircases, fire escapes and offices, with mysterious locked rooms and cupboards dotted throughout the building.

The converted movie sound-stages, re-designated Studios D, E, G and H were piled on top of each other and the unconverted ones were used to store scenery and equipment – including the vast, square stage 4, re-designated Studio F, which would have made a marvellous light entertainment studio if the need for a giant scene-dock to service all the studios had not taken precedence. The lettering was meant to follow on from the Alexandra Palace studio designations A and B, and if you really want to know what happened to the Studio C missing from the alphabetical list, the engineers had decided that the 'C' might be confused with the 'C' of CCR, the Central Control Room, so they left it out. It must have seemed a sensible idea at the time.

Lime Grove was a warren in which to get lost, and staff as well as visitors frequently did. You needed a map to find your way to the Canteen, and studio audiences often found themselves being shepherded up fire escapes to get to their shows. The sound-proofing on the walls of Studio G, which *was* the light entertainment studio, looked like old sacks held temporarily in place with chicken wire. It was this sort of unfinished, improvisatory, Alice in Wonderland character of the place that endeared it to everyone who worked there: it made us feel that we were all still pioneers.

Remarkably, that's the condition in which this temporary measure remained for the next 42 years, long after the Television Centre at White City was up and running. Television's exponential need for studios and technical facilities meant that Lime Grove would remain in use until its very last programme was transmitted on 13 June 1991. Throughout all those years, the Gaumont-British logo remained untouched on the Studios' façade: no one ever got round to removing it. And in 1995, when the studios were finally demolished and the rubble ended up as hardcore for widening the

M25, the name lived on. The parade of flats and houses that occupies the space today is called Gaumont Terrace and to its right is Gainsborough Court. It's pleasing to know that someone in the local planning office had a sense of show business history.

There's another pleasant little tug of nostalgia for any Lime Grove old-timer walking down the road today. Public swimming baths built for Hammersmith Council used to occupy a large site on the other side of the road opposite the Studios, and from time to time they would be covered over to provide the venue for televised wrestling matches on Saturday afternoons. The baths were converted long ago into a block of apartments. But at the top of this rather smart block's façade the original name of the site still remains, worn and weather-beaten, carved into the stone: HAMMERSMITH PUBLIC BATHS AND WASH HOUSES.

The studios at Lime Grove were bigger than those of Alexandra Palace and the control-rooms were at the top of normal staircases instead of the peril-ous metal spirals that led to the Palace's Minstrel Gallery, but their floors featured the same maze of cables snaking from cameras and microphones, the same microphones hung from sound-booms on wheeled platforms, their cameras mounted on the same pedestals pushed by cameramen or dollies pushed by trackers. It's true that the pictures in the camera view-finders were no longer upside-down and reversed left-to-right as they were at Alexandra Palace, but the cameramen had to push their pedestals perilously near their subject's face to get a close-up – though they didn't attempt that move in-vision because it wasn't easy to keep in focus while they pushed.

If you walk into a television studio today you will find that the control-room is still called the gallery whether it's up a flight of stairs, down on the ground floor or buried in the basement, but radio microphones and hand-held cameras have swept away the cable-clutter, and zoom-lenses will keep you in perfect focus all the way to your close-up. No doubt there are different technical challenges today, but production teams regard them just as we did in the fifties; they are facts of life: you just get on with them.

Television evening transmissions in 1952 were still restricted to three and a half hours and in order to fit programmes of differing lengths into this tight time-band the planners were often left with odd chunks of airtime to fill. The smallest of these chunks were filled with hypnotic little filmed Interludes – a potter's wheel, a sandy shore, a farmer and his horse plough-ing a field – which no one who watched television in those early days will ever forget. The larger gaps, those of 15 or 20 minutes in length, would be taken up by pocket programmes, usually musical and usually provided by Light Entertainment under the generic title of *Starlight*. These were ideal vehicles for a trainee's solo flight and Ernest was presented with one of them, together with a designated artiste, Petula Clark. Later an illustrious international performer, Pet had been a singing star from childhood and in the fifties she was already a television favourite. As a result, her fifteen-minute fillers were granted their own title; Ernest was by no means the first or last Light Entertainment trainee to cut his teeth on the sunnily forbearing Petula and her *Pet's Parlour*.

Since Pet was already taken, Ronnie Waldman proposed another fine performer for my first solo venture. Pat Kirkwood was a leading lady of musical comedy and revue, a star of British movies and a famously glamorous principal boy in the lavish West End pantomimes of the day – Ken Tynan described her legs as "the eighth wonder of the world". Ronnie introduced me to her in her flat. We talked about the sort of one-woman show she might do, found we had similar ideas about her material and the way it might be presented and struck an accord that would last throughout my time at the BBC. It certainly gave me an auspicious start. Mark Johns, in the *Daily Sketch* of 3 January 1953:

"PAT WAS THE STARLIGHT OF THE SHOW

"Sometimes it is the little shows, the TV programmettes that score. This happened last night. After an absorbing 'special inquiry' into the smoke menace, lasting 45 minutes, we had another 40 minutes or so of high jinks with the Magic Circle.

Then, for a scant quarter of an hour – and why was it so brutally whisked off the air at the end? – came a really delightful 'Starlight' programme, featuring Pat Kirkwood. It had a snappy, intriguing opening, then the attractive Pat sang us several bright songs well out of the usual rut. She danced, too, and her linking dialogue was unusually sensible. Eric Robinson's accompanying music was just right, and we ought to have been told the name of the producer who gave us this diminutive TV gem."

I'm afraid it was my fault that the programme was so brutally whisked off the air before the viewers could be told the name of the producer: I had misjudged its timing and the programme over-ran. I made sure that my next two *Starlight* slots, with Joyce Grenfell and Pearl Carr and Teddy Johnson respectively, came out on time, complete with their producer's credit.

My next assignment was very different. The panel-game had caught on as a form of television entertainment, thanks to the huge success of *What's My Line?* Fellow trainee David Attenborough, over in Talks Department, was cutting his teeth on a television version of the popular parlour-game *Animal, Vegetable, Mineral*. And as well as *What's My Line?*, Light Entertainment was responsible for a second weekly game, also based on an American format, a slightly more cerebral crossword-puzzle exercise called *Down You Go*. It was hosted successfully in the States by a professor from the University of Chicago, Dr Bergen Evans, so it had seemed perfectly reasonable to cast an Oxford don as the host of the British version. Unfortunately, while Dr Evans was an experienced and consummately professional American television host, young Marcus Dick, a Fellow of Balliol and a noted philosopher, was not. The programme was awkward and slow and appeared from our audience research to be sustained almost exclusively by the sex-appeal for female viewers of Marcus Dick's dashing good looks. The show was dying, and Ronnie asked me to take it over for its final weeks. That was fine with me: I thought I could see where the programme might be improved.

It wasn't an act of genius. Marcus Dick's contract was about to expire so I replaced him with Roy Rich, an agreeable and experienced broadcaster who took to the role of chairing a TV panel-game with ease, and I added to the panel the courteous charm and good humour of another radio personality, the admirable Kenneth Horne. The show almost instantly became the fast, funny, intelligent game it was designed to be; and although I was swamped for a few weeks with postcards from indignant housewives and female university students rather unnervingly proclaiming WE WANT DICK!, *Down You Go* stayed in the schedule and Ronnie handed me another panel-game as my next assignment.

I should have ducked.

Why?

((Why?" was a format devised by Gordon Crier, an ex-radio colleague
of Ronnie's who had moved into advertising. It was intended to fill
the Sunday night slot occupied by *What's My Line?* when that show
took its summer break, but it was a very different kind of game. Instead of
featuring ordinary members of the public taking on a group of professional
panellists, as in *What's My Line?*, it set two groups of panellists against
each other as Parents and Children. In each round, a member of one panel
took on the role of the Parent, a member of the other took on the role of the
Child, and they proceeded to engage in the age-old battle of wits and will
power in which children ask "Why?" to every pronouncement from their
long-suffering parents. The host would set the subject for each tussle and
the studio audience would decide who had achieved the upper hand. I cast
sports presenter Peter West as the host, and the panellists were performers
well versed in witty improvisation: actors Richard Attenborough, Brenda
Bruce, Judy Campbell, Hugh Griffith and Patricia Burke and comedians and
comedy-writers Bob Monkhouse and Denis Goodwin.

Unfortunately, the programme was burdened with two major disadvantages, neither of which I had foreseen. First, it wasn't *What's My Line?*; it
wasn't even remotely *like What's My Line?*; and the audience didn't want
an entirely different kind of panel-game in the hallowed *What's My Line?*
slot. And second, like every other television programme in those days, *Why?*
was *live*: we were asking our panellists to scintillate live, non-stop, for half
an hour on the same theme – not, as we would be doing today, recording them for at least an hour and cutting out the not so scintillating bits

before transmission. It was too much to expect of either the panellists or the audience, and the BBC switchboard on its opening night was swamped with calls from indignant viewers. We made the front pages all right next day. They were blazoned with variations on a single theme: "'Why?' was broadcast by the BBC last night: *Why?*"

After a sleepless night, the next morning I was summoned to two administrative offices one after the other. Cecil McGivern, the Controller of Programmes, was the first to send for me, and I went into his office in the greatest trepidation: he was known to be merciless to anybody who fell below the high standards he had set for the service, and he had the morning newspapers open on his desk. "I watched your programme last night" he said. "How old are you?" "Twenty-four, sir." "Good" he said. "You'll learn. Your programme won't survive, but you made a decent fist of it. Ignore the critics: they don't know anything."

Ronnie Waldman was equally non-recriminatory. He thought the fiasco would be a salutary experience for me – "Flops happen; this one would have happened whoever produced it." He blamed himself for letting the programme invite such direct comparison with the BBC's most popular show by taking over its time-slot: it might have fared better on a different day and at a different time; but the format was flawed anyway. "See what you can do to sharpen it up, but it won't sustain more than a short run. You're going to have to find a game show that *can* follow *What's My Line?* We'll run a season of pilots and let the audience tell us if they like any of them. It'll be a hunt for the next big panel-game success. Invite the viewers to send in their ideas. See if Radio is doing anything that might be suitable. Think up something yourself. And get Press Department to publicise the project, advertise it in the *Radio Times* and *The Listener*. You've got six months to work on it, so you'd better have a new contract. I'll get Administration to call you."

Astonishingly, my debacle seemed to have done me no harm at all. I hadn't had to be thrown out into the pool of ex-trainees at the end of my six-month training contract, and I wasn't being thrown out now. What was more, my flop seemed to be considered a sort of rite of passage by the old pros in the department. I was commiserated with, clapped on the back – "We've all been through it, old boy" – *accepted*. Was that all it took? Messrs Afton and Caldwell nodded to me in the corridor. Michael Mills, who was preparing a celebration of the life of the showman C. B. Cochran in studio G at Lime Grove, invited me to produce a 15-minute programme from Alexandra Palace to introduce it, interviewing a dozen of the surviving Cochran Young Ladies, the West End's equivalent in the twenties and thirties to Broadway's Zeigfield Girls. Ah, but what about Bill Ward? What was his reaction? I wouldn't have long to find out.

Those gaps between the television schedule's set pieces were allocated by the legendary Joanna Spicer and her programme planning department, in consultation with the various department heads. Producers used to scan the advance schedule as soon as it was available to see whether their initials had been set against any of these slots, and on 2 June 1953, my initials were attached to a 20-minute spot to follow the coverage of the Coronation of Queen Elizabeth II. My programme would need to be particularly eye-catching if it was to stand a chance of inheriting any part of the huge audience that this Outside Broadcast would attract, and the brilliant D. R. Campbell, our Training Course lecturer on television engineering, had devised an innovative piece of visual trickery called Inlay and Overlay which might be just right for it. D. R. and I worked closely together on this project. Even so, it would be another fifty years, in a visit to Alexandra Palace's Studio A, lovingly restored by the Alexandra Palace Television Society, before I discovered that the D of D. R. – which was how everybody always referred to him – stood for Desmond.

Scouring the internet for a layman's description of the technique, I found this account in the 1956 records of the Australian Broadcasting Commission. Arthur Wyndham, a Sydney TV announcer, had gone back home after a course at the BBC Television School, which had included an attachment to Lime Grove. He wrote the following in his enthusiastic report. "When an artist's reflection in a mirror suddenly changes before your eyes to the face of another, when tiny figures dance on a piano keyboard and then disappear, when actors appear at the window of a building you know was bombed out during the war, then you can be certain that Mr Campbell or one of his followers is at the back of it. Briefly, the object of Inlay...is to superimpose all or part of one picture into part of another picture but without the obvious disadvantages of transparency apparent with normal superimposition....Overlay is laying a secondary picture *over the top of* instead of *into* a primary picture. Whereas an inlaid subject is restricted to movement within the confines of the masked area and will be obliterated when moving beyond it, an overlaid picture may move freely across the whole of the primary picture."

In other words, Arthur Wyndham's tiny dancers would be shot on one camera and overlaid onto a piano keyboard which was shot on another; and the actors who appeared in the empty windows of that bombed-out house would be shot on one camera and inlaid *into* the windows of a photograph of the house which was shot on another. Mr Wyndham went on to say something that I quote for two particular reasons. The first of them is simple vanity, and I hope you will excuse it. The second is that, unknown to Mr Wyndham, he was reporting what turned out to be the most significant day of my time with the Corporation.

This is what he said. "The most ambitious use of Inlay I saw while training with the BBC was by Brian Tesler, one of the Corporation's youngest and most imaginative producers. A compere stepped through a simulated movie screen and stood beside it to introduce in turn excerpts from old musical films and live studio routines which appeared to be projected continuously on to it. If anyone has the time to listen I will be glad to explain how, but space does not permit me to do so now." Nor does it permit me, but I will return to the programme and the significance of that day in due course.

To be honest, Mr Wyndham was too easily impressed: those movie-screen effects were among the most basic applications of Inlay and Overlay. I needed my little post-Coronation show to be rather more enterprising. It was called *The Girl Next Door*. The song Stanley Myers, Julian Dale and I had written at Oxford provided the scenario for a romantic story about two young lovers, played and sung by Dickie Valentine and Lita Roza, the two featured singers with the Ted Heath Orchestra who had recorded the number for Decca Records. The magic of Inlay and Overlay made it possible for me to place the lovers within and among a variety of hand-drawn cartoon settings as their romance progressed.

It was quite a complicated piece of work; and to my consternation Bill Ward suddenly appeared just as we went on air, to stand beady-eyed at the back of the control room. Was this his way of indicating that the *Why?* debacle had reconciled him to my presence in the department, as it had with his colleagues? If that was the case, he seemed to be regretting it again almost at once: throughout the show, at almost every trick effect, I could hear a wincing intake of breath from him. What was I doing wrong? It all seemed to be going smoothly enough: the effects were working, the music was appealing, Dickie and Lita were at their best; so how was I cocking it up? As we went off the air, I finally turned and said "I'm sorry you didn't like the show, Bill. What was the problem? Where did I go wrong?" "You didn't go wrong, old love. I thought it was fine, and I liked the effects. It's just that I'm in agony with this flaming toothache. I've really got to see a dentist tomorrow."

Before I was due to embark on the great panel-game hunt, Ronnie had another assignment for me. Frank Muir and Denis Norden, the writers of the hit radio show *Take It From Here*, were also responsible for the off-beat *Breakfast with Braden* and *Bedtime with Braden* radio shows, which they wrote for Bernard Braden and Barbara Kelly, the husband and wife team from Canadian radio who had brought a little Transatlantic bezazz to British show business when they arrived here in the late '40s.

Ronnie introduced me to the four of them and suggested that if we all got along we might make a one-off show which could serve as the pilot for a future series. A previous foray into television by the Bradens had not succeeded and this would be the first attempt at writing a situation comedy series for the small screen for Frank and Denis, but we did in fact all get along. The four of them knew they would be putting their fate in the hands of a 24-year old producer whose only credits so far were half-a-dozen little musical shows and two panel games, one of which had been a resounding flop, but they trusted Ronnie's judgement and agreed to take the risk.

We called the show *Barbara with Braden* and translated the Bradens' radio show to the screen more or less in its entirety, retaining its cast, its air of spontaneity and its studio setting. We augmented the regulars with Dick Bentley, one of the stars of *Take It From Here*, to enable us to open out the show with sketches that could be set outside the studio; and we used Barbara, when she wasn't in one of the sketches, as a wry commentator on the proceedings, set into the corner of the screen by courtesy of Inlay. As *The Birmingham Mail* commented next day "It is not as deceptively easy as it looks. The trick of mounting the beautiful Miss Kelly in the corner of the screen was not always immaculately managed". But the rest of the review was pretty good: "Who would have thought it possible? Who other than Mr Braden would even have risked translating a highly successful programme, deriving all its force from verbal wit, into the as yet uncertain medium for humour of television? Who else, having ventured, could have achieved such a triumph of simplicity?" Other reviews were just as enthusiastic: "*Barbara with Braden* was like bomb with bullet", and "The brilliant Bradens, the success of the week with their new TV show *Barbara with Braden*". The

Daily Sketch was a little more tolerant of my own technical cock-ups: "Into the witless vacuum of current TV variety there came last night an artless fugitive from sound radio to give us a spanking good lesson in putting fun on to the screen. *Barbara with Braden*, a visual version of the Bradens' radio show, is the sort of programme that drives TV technicians frantic. It was really too fast to avoid occasional imperfections, but small blemishes were drowned in a refreshing wave of spicy, telling fun."

Barbara with Braden did indeed spawn a future series but, for various reasons, not for another two years, although I would work with Frank and Denis again before then, and with Bernie and Barbara too. Meanwhile, I could embark on the panel-game hunt feeling that I could handle television comedy well enough to hope that Ronnie Waldman might at some time let me do more of it.

The Game's the Thing

It wasn't difficult to analyse the reasons for the popularity of *What's My Line?* American television had over years of test and trial forged a guaranteed template for panel-game success: an affable host, an entertaining mix of panellists, a simple but interesting challenge for its theme, and ordinary members of the public as its challengers, winning their own five minutes of celebrity in what was in effect an early form of what would become known as reality television. But the ingredient that could turn a successful panel-game into an unmissable one was unpredictability. *What's My Line?* possessed this ingredient in spades in one of its panellists. David Nixon was amusing, Barbara Kelly engaging, Lady Isobel Barnett coolly intuitive, but you never knew what Gilbert Harding was going to say or do. Crusty and irascible in manner but capable of great charm, Gilbert enjoyed his popular success but despised what he felt was its essential triviality; and this dichotomy gave an edge of danger and the unexpected to his performance. Would he be gruff or gentle with a contestant? Would he explode with irritation or subside into glowering silence? Would Eamonn Andrews, the programme's host, be able to cajole him into conformity? The newspaper columnists as well as the mass audience tuned in every Sunday to see what would happen, and the BBC Press Office had a formula at the ready to cover the more exceptional incident: "Mr Harding was overcome by the heat from the studio lights".

Inspired by *What's My Line?*, the public had been sending in game-show ideas by the hundreds even before we invited them to do so, and the first task for my newly-appointed secretary Iris Jones and myself was to tackle the back-log. Most of the proposals were variations on *What's My Line?* itself, the two most frequent being *What's My Hobby?* and *What's My Hometown?* Another great pile was for television versions of familiar parlour games like Dominoes, Battleships and even Postman's Knock. Others were pretty bizarre inventions, like *Mind the Baby*, in which the contestants had to compete in bathing and dressing a real-life infant, *Disagreeing with Gilbert*, in which contestants quite literally had to try to win an argument with Gilbert Harding, and something called *Fun on The Billiard Table*. Don't ask.

One of these unsolicited ideas did seem promising, however. A viewer from Billericay working for the Southwark Borough Council suggested a game in which the panel was challenged by contestants who had been involved in a recent news story: the panel had to work out what the story was. If the prospective panellists couldn't provide the element of surprise or unpredictability, the news story ought to do it and, with any luck, it might also provide some interesting characters among the contestants with stories to tell. I took the idea to Ronnie and suggested that we shouldn't wait to include it in the season of panel-game pilots – "Let's do the show right here!" so to speak. He agreed, and the first series of *Guess My Story* was on the air within a month. The admirable Peter West was host (I had to make up for lumbering him with *Why?*); the regular panellists were screenwriter Michael Pertwee and actresses Helen Cherry and Pat Kirkwood, my good-luck charm from my first production. They were joined by a guest panellist each week; and the celebrity guest was a Fleet Street editor or reporter, to be quizzed on his or her most memorable scoop. I hired Larry Forrester, a young Scottish journalist and scriptwriter, to scour the newspapers for me and track down suitable contestants. We soon discovered that this was too time-consuming a chore for one person so we brought in his wife Pauline to join him, and the pair swiftly became the best and most sought-after researchers in television.

Guess My Story was the sort of show that simply couldn't exist today. 24-hour rolling television news covers most of the people involved in any worthwhile story and renders them all immediately identifiable, but in the early fifties television news was still non-visual, so that all the panel had to go on was what they had read in the newspapers or seen several days later in a cinema newsreel. This visual anonymity greatly added to the appeal of the programme for viewers at home, who were curious to see what people in the news actually looked like. It occurred to me that they would also be curious to see what some of the elements in the news stories themselves looked like. It might seem old hat today, but it caused a tremendous stir when the last story in one edition of the programme was about that same day's London to Brighton Race and concluded with the veteran car from the Genevieve movie clanking and banging its way round the studio with the panellists, the contestants and Susie, the movie's giant St Bernard, on board.

The Forresters and I tried to find a light-hearted story with equal visual appeal to end each edition of the programme – a sort of precursor of News at Ten's "...and finally"; and we usually managed it. The actor James Robertson Justice was the guest panellist when the team was challenged by someone who turned out to be the keeper of a team of performing monkeys which had escaped from its circus that week. When the panel finally guessed his story we let some of the monkeys onto the set. To the delight of the studio audience and the shocked surprise of Peter West and the panel, whom we hadn't forewarned, they performed as if they'd been scripted and rehearsed, wandering round the studio, stealing Peter West's notes, walking up and down the panellists' desk, one of them putting its arms round James Robertson Justice and stroking his beard as we faded the programme out. Health and Safety would have forbidden that sort of fun today; in 1953 it made the front page.

Another guest panellist, the best-selling novelist Gerald Kersh, was himself the story on another occasion. Pauline and Larry burst into the control room half an hour before airtime to tell me that he had apparently drunk himself pie-eyed in his dressing-room and could hardly stand, let alone perform. There was no time to get hold of a substitute so we poured black coffee down Kersh's throat and walked him up and down the corridor like a scene from a Hollywood B movie, and he was more or less recovered by the time we got him into the studio.

Unfortunately, the hot studio lights did for Gerald; and after the first round of questioning it was clear that he was incapable of carrying on. We had warned Peter and the panel about this possibility just as we went on the air and they took over magnificently, gently abbreviating Gerald's turn to ask questions – Helen tapping him on the head with her pencil, Pat saying "Now, Gerald, you've had your go" to his puzzled protests – and generally jollying him along so that he didn't have the opportunity to say or do anything appalling – that is, until the end of the programme. With the audience applauding over our theme music, I cued in the closing credits with great relief – and the studio sound abruptly cut out. I turned to the sound supervisor and asked "What happened?" He said "Well, Gerald leaned forward into his microphone and I thought it best to cut the studio output in case he said something awful." I dashed into the studio to find the audience still laughing and the panel still stunned at what Gerald had in fact said. Still very slurred, he had leaned into his microphone to announce "I want you to know that I would have got every question right tonight if I hadn't had a sudden attack of the worms."

Guess My Story rapidly became popular, and not only with the mass audience. London's *Evening Standard* featured a distinguished writer as a guest critic each week and *Guess My Story* seemed to appeal to them all: Alan Melville: "This is TV light entertainment at its very best"; Jill Craigie: "*Guess My Story*, the best of the television games with its speed, humour and glamour, is one of the reasons why people stay away from movies"; Wolf Mankowitz: "The beauty of Helen Cherry and the earnest charm with which she pursues her clues, the quizzical seriousness of Michael Pertwee and the warm vivacity of the unparalleled Pat Kirkwood are more than enough. Add to them the most amusing minor stories of a week's newsprint; the interest of meeting the fascinating ordinary people who make that news; the brilliant Fleet Street talents like Chapman Pincher of the *Daily Express* who write that news; the spice of a guest like James Robertson Justice; and the equable fairness of Peter West, the game's chairman. Surely you have the answer to the common question, what's happened to *What's My Line?* It is, dear questioners, that *Guess My Story* has taken over."

Guess My Story did in fact take over from *What's My Line?* in its precious Sunday night slot the following year, when the Line took its summer break – no protests from viewers this time – and the format was also bought by the Canadian Broadcasting Corporation so I hope our viewer from Billericay did well out of it. The hunt for a successor to the *Line* had patently succeeded before it had even begun, and it was clear that the public's appetite for this kind of entertainment was keen and growing.

Ronnie had suggested radio as a source for panel-game possibilities and the BBC's Light Programme was enjoying some success with another American format from Goodson and Todman, the panel-game kings of American Television who had devised *What's My Line?* So why not see if they would agree to transfer it to television where, after all, it had begun its life in the States? We did; they would; and *The Name's The Same* joined our little stable of successful panel-games. And all this before we had seen the results of our nation-wide search for new panel-game ideas, which were already beginning to flood in from our game-struck viewers.

The Name's The Same had as simple a format as *What's My Line?* Instead of guessing the contestant's job the panel had to guess the contestant's name, which could also be the name of anything from a household appliance to another person, real, historical or from the pages of fiction. We adhered firmly to the Goodson and Todman template. Bernie Braden was our affable chairman, though we knew we could only have him for a couple of months because of prior commitments, and the panel was an agreeable mix of witty and articulate people. I borrowed Frank Muir and Denis Norden from the radio show, and added Brenda Bruce, another casualty of *Why?* to whom I felt I should make amends. They were joined by one Viscountess Boyle – Katie Boyle – a young fashion model who had made her first television appearance only a few weeks previously on a Richard Afton programme called *Quite Contrary.*

In my continuing trawl for likely panellists I had interviewed this part-Italian, part-Russian, part-English member of the aristocracy, discovered she had an attractive personality as well as good looks, and thought she would fit in very well with the other more seasoned performers. The critics agreed. Emery Pierce of the *Daily Herald*: "Radio's parlour game *The Name's The Same* had its TV try-out last night – and was the hit of the year. It is the only TV show that can beat *What's My Line?*" – how fickle these critics are! I thought *Guess My Story* had already been appointed the *What's My Line?* beater – "The panel was pure delight – Frank Muir (moustached, lazy and cynical); Viscountess Boyle (a famous model bubbling with life and laughter); Denis Norden (perpetually puzzled but guessing everything); and Brenda Bruce (sweet and husky-voiced). The idea was for the panel to guess the famous names of ordinary folk who challenged them – like Dick Whittington, Mark Antony, Kenneth Horne, Mrs Grundy, and even A. Radish. It was glorious fun. The chairman, Bernard Braden, started out by referring to Lady Boyle. He faltered a little then called her Catherine. By the end of the show, with Frank Muir rubbing noses with her, he said "Well, you can call her Kiss Me Kate!" "Kate it is, you may call me Dream Boat," said Muir, to a burbling, beautiful Viscountess. So there it is – Kate and "Dream Boat" are the overnight stars with Denis and Brenda in a show that was a breath of fresh air." Frank's Dream Boat stardom was not something he thanked me for, though it was mercifully brief. Years afterward, he remembered catching Denis's eye in the middle of chasing down the identity of some contestant or other on the programme, and thinking "Dear God, was it for this that my parents spent all that money to get me into private school?"

The Name's The Same lacked a central controversial figure like Gilbert Harding, but the good humour and vivacity of the panel as a whole made up for it, and when Bernie Braden had to leave the show I was lucky enough to be able to replace him with the ideal successor. I'd heard a young actor called Peter Martyn compere *People Are Funny*, a Radio Luxembourg programme, and had been very impressed by him. He made an immediate impact on our show, as Clifford Davis noted in the *Daily Mirror*: "Peter Martyn – London actor borrowed from commercial radio – came to TV last night as its latest parlour game chairman. And very good he was, too. With fair, wavy hair, good looks and a diffident smile, Mr Martyn, 28, ran *The Name's The Same* with such assurance that it's a wonder to me TV has managed to do without him for so long." The audience took to Peter at once. His wit, charm and authority made him an immediate and overwhelming success, but having done without him for so long, TV all too soon had to do without him entirely: tragically he died of leukaemia only a year after his debut.

Parlour Game Parade

Peter was the programme's host on the one occasion in my time at the BBC that I earned a severe carpeting from Ronnie Waldman. Like most of these shows, *The Name's The Same* featured a celebrity spot. One of the contestants would bear the name of a particularly well-known individual, who would then make an entrance after the panel's attempt to guess his or her name; there would be a few light-hearted exchanges between them and the panel, and celebrity and namesake would move off to applause while the game continued.

A viewer had written in to say his name was George Robey and he would dearly love to challenge the team and meet his namesake, the great master of early 20th century music hall, now ennobled and retired. Why not? I thought, and tracked down Sir George to see if he would be interested in appearing on the programme. I spoke to Lady Robey, who said her husband had been ill but was now much better; she'd have a word with his doctor and call me back. Why didn't that sound a warning bell? Sir George's doctor thought that an appearance in front of an audience once again would be the best thing in the world for his patient, so I handed Lady Robey over to my secretary to make all the necessary arrangements. Where on earth was that warning bell? Why didn't I have the sense to talk to the doctor myself, or ask to talk to Sir George, or even suggest a train journey to their home to discuss the appearance?

The day of the live transmission began ominously: the Robeys' train would be delayed, and they would be unable to get to the studio until just before we went on the air. Sublimely and idiotically cocky, I thought fine, we'll wing it: Peter will handle the proceedings perfectly well in the studio and

I'll ad lib the camera shots without any difficulty. No problem. That damned warning bell finally tolled just five minutes before the celebrity spot was due. The studio manager advised us over his intercom that Sir George and Lady Robey had arrived; he was in a wheelchair and she would be pushing him on, "but be warned: Sir George has Alzheimer's".

It was a hideous experience. Befuddled by the heat and bright lights of the studio, Sir George wasn't at all encouraged by the audience's rapturous reception when he was wheeled on by Lady Robey: he was visibly terrified by it. Wheeled into position at Peter Martyn's side, all he could manage when Peter welcomed him was an indistinguishable mumble. Lady Robey was cheerfully ready to speak for him. Perhaps she really did think this was doing her husband some good, but I could see from the preview screens that poor Sir George's vacant eyes were watering and his trembling mouth was beginning to drool. I couldn't possibly take a close-up or even a medium shot of him. I could only show the unhappy scene in long-shot and pray that Peter would end it as quickly as he could, which he did with skill and grace.

There was, thankfully, no reference to this appalling scene in the next morning's newspapers, but Ronnie was incandescent with anger when I was called to his office. "How could you humiliate a great man like George Robey in that way? Didn't you *know* he'd had a stroke? Didn't you do any research on him? Didn't you try to find out what he'd been ill *with*? Didn't you even try to talk to him yourself? How could you be so ludicrously slapdash? You've disgraced yourself and deeply disappointed me. Don't ever let it happen again." It didn't happen again; and I deserved every word of that tongue-lashing. I just hoped that the episode would finally exorcise the cockiness that Nevill Coghill had spotted and which clearly existed in me.

My search for new panel-game ideas had produced thousands of responses and I had sorted out eight possible runners, which we planned to transmit one a week for two months in the summer of 1954. A chastened and now more circumspect Tesler, aware of the danger of squabbles over owner-ship, discussed the question of rights with the BBC's Legal Department and asked the *Radio Times* to print an explanatory introduction to the season. No one could own the rights in an idea, we pointed out, but the BBC would recognise the rights in any programme *layout* submitted in writing which we proceeded to broadcast.

If a programme layout suggested by only one viewer was accepted, that viewer would receive the sole credit. If a programme layout was sent in by many viewers with different variations on the same theme, we would choose the version we considered the best, which would not necessarily be the first to be received. And if a roughly similar idea was submitted by many different people but none of them in a satisfactory layout, we would devise our own programme layout for it if we thought the idea a potentially popular one. Amazingly enough, we had no copyright quibbles whatsoever.

A large number of viewers submitted ideas for a game-show involving music, but none of them seemed to work, so I devised one myself. It was called *Music, Music, Music* after the popular juke-box song of the time and featured two teams, led by Petula Clark and Julie Andrews respectively, with panellists including Gerard Hoffnung and B. C. Hilliam, who was half of the witty musical duo of Flotsam & Jetsam. David Jacobs was the chairman and the panellists had to identify and perform music of which various recorded scraps were played in vision by an attractive BBC grams operator named Joyce Wooller. There was no truth whatsoever to the rumour that I had devised the show simply because I fancied all three of the young ladies involved – that's my story, anyway – but you would have thought that this combination of beauty and wit would be warmly greeted by our viewing audience; alas, *Music, Music, Music* ended up at the bottom of the viewers' list. I don't think David ever forgave me but it didn't disrupt his long and remarkably successful career. Joyce ended up as a Director on the Board of Granada Television. I don't know what became of Julie and Pet. I hope *Music, Music, Music* didn't damage their careers too much.

Of the remaining seven in what the *Radio Times* called the Parade of Parlour Games, four others found their way swiftly to the bottom of the viewers' list and need detain us no longer than they detained the audience, but the three winners would provide several seasons of attractive television alongside *Guess My Story, The Name's The Same* and *Down You Go. What's My Line?* would never be short of a stablemate or a summer replacement again.

The Tall Story Club, a simple and fairly common idea submitted in its most effective form by an actor called George Margo, featured a handful of much-travelled competitors sitting in a comfortable gentleman's club telling tall stories which they claimed to be true. The storytellers, some of whom were women – this was an *enlightened* gentleman's club – quizzed each other to discover whether the stories were fact or fiction and club trophies were awarded to the storytellers who managed to hoodwink their fellows as to which they turned out to be. It was an idea that depended on the appeal and skill of the storyteller and we managed to find enough colourful exponents to attract large audiences to its series of short runs, most notably the beguiling Irish actress Barbara Mullen and Commander Douglas Duff, a fiery old seadog who was the nearest we ever got to discovering a television panellist as unpredictable and compelling as Gilbert Harding or *Animal, Vegetable, Mineral*'s Sir Mortimer Wheeler.

One of the Family, the best version of a particularly popular idea, in which the contestants were related to celebrities in every walk of life, came from a viewer in Hove; and *Find the Link*, in which the panel had to guess the connection shared by two, three or even four contestants, was submitted by a viewer from Watford. I produced both of them, along with the six others in the season, while remaining responsible for the department's regular panel-game output of *What's My Line?*, *The Name's The Same*, *Guess My Story* and *Down You Go*. Not all the regular games were broadcast concurrently – the series often alternated with each other – but I see from a *TV Mirror* press cutting that in August 1954 I produced 13 editions of this, that or the other of them in four and a half weeks.

It seems extraordinary today that a statistic like that should have been considered important enough to feature in a magazine article, but television was still so new in the early fifties and the public's interest in it so avid that television producers as well as television celebrities found themselves written about in newspapers and TV magazines. Panel-games and panel-game people were particularly high-profile. Although Ronnie gave me other shows to do while I was still in charge of panel-games – one of which became an award-winning success – in the TV columns I was referred to as "TV's panel game chief" or "King of the Panel Games" or even, by Clifford Davis of the *Daily Mirror* who should have known better, "Quiz Kid with the Crazy Touch". By the end of 1954 I was longing to be known as "*former* parlour-game King", a description finally achieved in March 1955 in *She* magazine.

Don't get me wrong. I enjoyed my time with panel games. They saved me from the ex-trainee pool, and they provided me with interesting employment while I watched what the other producers were doing and worked my way from amateur to professional status. I enjoyed the never-ending search for panellists and contestants. Today, I would have had several teams of researchers to do the legwork, but in those early fifties my team comprised only Iris Jones and myself, aided on *Guess My Story* and *One of the Family* by the formidable Forresters. Looking for panellists, I interviewed writers, journalists, broadcasters, actors and actresses, people recommended to me, people I met at dinner parties. Some I had to coach a little, some were naturals from the start.

The relationship between panel-game producers and panellists was a professional one but you were often friends as well as colleagues, and sometimes even nannies: I wasn't the only panel-game producer who had to fish Gilbert Harding out of the pub next to the Television Theatre in Shepherds Bush just before airtime. I dated one of my panellists for a while, and she actually went on to marry the producer who succeeded me on that particular game-show. But as far as I was concerned there was never any question of collaboration with the panellists, of giving them the answers before the show in order to enhance their performance, though I was asked to do so once: "But honey, we do it like that all the time in the States: don't you *want* me to put on a good show?"

I enjoyed looking for contestants too, though that wasn't so intensive an activity. Mostly they found themselves, writing in to tell us their unusual jobs or names or connections with the famous; though during the *Guess My Story* runs I used to go through the newspapers every day with Pauline and Larry looking for the telegenic human element in a news story. While lining up contestants for *The Name's The Same*, I remember wondering about the sense of humour of parents who could saddle their offspring with names like Topsy Turvey, River Jordan, Valentine Card, Christmas Carroll or Malvern Hills. I loved the rosy-cheeked, outrageously outspoken 82-year old Granny Knot, the sort of character panel-game producers pray for in their contestants. From *Guess My Story* I particularly remember challengers like the 6ft 6in American airman who waded into the floods near his base in Britain to save people – waded, because he couldn't swim; or the two bowls finalists in a sporting news story, aged respectively 98, the champion, and 91, the challenger – who respectfully referred to the champion as "the old gentleman". And, from *Find the Link*, the Mrs A and Mr B whose unlikely link was they were both lion tamers; or another Mrs A and Mrs B whose rare connection was that they were both mothers of quads – how I longed to bring both sets of quads on to the set at the end of the programme as a surprise for everyone, including the mothers. Or challenger Mr C, Gilbert Harding himself, at his most benign in one edition alongside another Mrs A and Mr B, all three of them having in their earlier days been Yorkshire police constables.

But I had had enough. Thirty-eight years later, Michael Winner, sitting opposite me at a British Film Institute dinner, called across our large round table "Mr Tesler! Mr Tesler! Have you forgiven me yet?" I told him I was sure I would be prepared to do so, but what on earth for? "Well," Mr Winner told our table, "In 1954, when I was an undergraduate at Cambridge, I managed to get some holiday work during the Christmas Vacation as a call boy at Lime Grove, and one of the shows I worked on was *Find the Link*." The call boy's duty on panel-games was to ensure that the contestants were standing by for their entrance and cue them on to the set at the appropriate moment. On this particular occasion, apparently, the programme host was talking to James Mason, the guest celebrity, at the foot of the stairs down which all the programme's appearances were made, and temporary call boy Michael Winner was behind the entrance at the top of the stairs, standing by with the next two contestants.

The programme host at that time was Peter Martyn, who had come over from *The Name's The Same* to give the new show a kick-start when it began. The next two contestants, Michael Winner went on to explain, were Eric Williams, the ex-prisoner of war who had written The Wooden Horse about his tunnelling escape from Colditz, accompanied by one of his fellow-tunnellers. They were roped together and equipped with tunnelling picks and shovels as they had been in their original tunnel, ready to make their entrance. And Michael Winner cued them on too soon.

Eric Williams and his fellow-tunneller came clattering down the stairs and pitched into James Mason and Peter Martyn in the middle of their conversation. "Uproar and consternation all round" said Michael Winner, the situation being rescued by Peter Martyn, who took the tunnellers over to the contestants' desk, returned to finish his chat with Mr Mason and seamlessly continued with the show. As Michael Winner told it, when I came on to the studio floor to thank everybody after the show, I pierced the young Mr Winner with an icy look of anger and contempt. "So have you forgiven me yet?" he asked. I'm afraid I had to say that for the life of me I couldn't recall the incident at all. "Sorry, Michael: so many panel games, so many contestants, so many call boys..."

Fresh Fields

P anel games remained my principal preoccupation for much of 1954 and 1955, but Ronnie gave me the opportunity to flex any unused creative muscles I might have had on a number of very different projects. Some of them were for the occasional 15 or 20-minute filler slots in the schedule against which I would find my initials, and I remember booking artistes like Larry Adler, Petula Clark and the glamorous zither-playing Australian Shirley Abicair for these. Others were for the elongated luxury of 45 or 60 minutes, and I remember the pleasure I derived – and, I hope, gave – from producing shows like *We Got Rhythm*, with an all-black cast of singers, dancers and cabaret artistes, including the legendary Hutch, Leslie Hutchinson; *Music and Magic*, which combined illusionists like David Nixon and performers like Frankie Vaughan with the technical trickery made possible by D. R. Campbell and his colleagues; and a welcome-home production with Ted Heath and his Orchestra after their first record-breaking tour of America.

I was also able finally to make amends to Bob Monkhouse and Denis Goodwin for their entanglement in the *Why?* debacle by producing *Fast and Loose*, their first half-hour comedy series as performers as well as writers. I've forgotten everything about the show except its vivid embodiment of the oldest of show-business adages. In the dress-run of a sketch, comedian Charlie Drake forgot to duck when Bob fired a pistol through the door of the wardrobe in which his character was hiding. The shot was a blank, but the door was the thinnest of balsa wood and the full force of the cartridge wad hit Charlie in the side of his face. When he recovered consciousness, blood pouring from his ear and his face pitted with bits of wood and wadding, Charlie flatly refused to be taken to hospital and insisted on doing the transmission three hours later. He was deaf in one ear and a little dazed but, as he said, The Show Must Go On.

It had occurred to me that the unknown performers who understudied the stars of West End revues and musicals ought to be good enough to carry a show on their own, so I sat in on the understudy rehearsals of some of London's most successful musical productions and picked the best of these unknowns to star in a part-revue, part-documentary called *Stand-In*. Stanley Myers joined me to write the special material for it, including the opening and closing production numbers, Ernest Maxin devised the choreography, and the story of these stars for a night was narrated by Peter Martyn. Fortunately, none of the stars they understudied was off for that evening's performance. The show helped to boost the careers of Shirley Eaton and Andrée Melly and enabled Peter Glaze to progress from understudying Flanagan and Allen and the rest of the Crazy Gang at the Victoria Palace to becoming a star in his own right in children's television. It also taught me to curb my production ambitions until I was a little more versed in the technology: at one stage, in rehearsing a tricky little sequence, I found myself with all four of my cameras in the centre of the studio, pointing at each other.

Ronnie was also keen to feature some of the big popular orchestras of the day like Mantovani, Ray Martin and Frank Chacksfield and seeing what kind of a television fist his producers made of what was essentially radio material. I drew Frank Chacksfield and his superb orchestra, which like the others was of symphonic size, and to break up the orchestral sequences I used guest artistes and exotic settings – scrupulously avoiding Caribbean islands in the setting sun of course. I also used Inlay and Overlay, and discovered how easy it was to trip up with this technique on a live show with no chance of a re-take or re-position.

Vanessa Lee was the beautiful blonde soprano who had played the lead opposite Ivor Novello in his romantic operettas *Perchance to Dream* and *King's Rhapsody*. I featured her in one Frank Chacksfield show and used Overlay to give her a variety of filmed settings in which to wander while she sang: it was easier than filling the studio with elaborate and expensive scenery. In one number, Vanessa was pictured in a jungle setting with a magnificent waterfall cascading down behind her. It happens that Overlay, as

Arthur Wyndham didn't have time to tell his Australian bosses, required the person or object you wished to overlay to be shot against a black background because black would not register on the picture over which it was laid: it would in effect be transparent. And there's the rub: anything *else* that was black in the picture you were overlaying would also be transparent. Vanessa's blonde colouring was ideal for the effect, and she looked gorgeous singing something from *Rose Marie* against the waterfall, but she was slightly off her lighting mark, and when she opened that beautiful mouth for the big notes at the end of the number it was unlit. That made it appear black, and therefore transparent, so the waterfall was seen by our viewers to be cascading down the back of her throat.

The biggest non-panel game projects, however, were very different affairs, and didn't require tricky embellishments. Frank Muir and Denis Norden had enjoyed their initial attempt at writing for television with *Barbara with Braden*, and rather than wait for the Bradens to be available for a follow-up, they suggested a series built round Dick Bentley, the Australian comic actor who was enjoying great success in their radio show *Take It From Here*. Ronnie was delighted with the prospect and, with their agreement, handed the series to Ernest Maxin and myself as a team, on the grounds that it would benefit from two people sharing the creative and logistical responsibility: a typically wise decision on his part since neither of his two tyros was ready to handle such a major project by himself.

Ernest and I had worked well together on *Stand-In* and had similar tastes in both music and comedy, so we had no difficulty in working with Muir and Norden or setting up the show. We cast Peter Sellers, Bill Fraser and a clever young revue artiste named Charlotte Mitchell as supporting artistes to Dick Bentley, but since we clearly couldn't direct the cameras together on transmission days, we alternated in the control room show by show, and also in producing it show by show. Quite unwittingly, therefore, *And So To Bentley* set a precedent. Traditionally, the light entertainment producer did everything. He or she set up the show, put together its script, cast and music, planned its design, costumes and technical requirements with the relevant departments, rehearsed the show and finally, on transmission day, directed it from the studio control room. For purely practical reasons Ernest and I separated the functions of producer and director, but it would be years before those separate functions became a norm, in most major series and not just in light entertainment.

For me, And So To Bentley was notable for three particular reasons. It introduced me to the genius of Peter Sellers, who was booked as a supporting artist but proceeded to steal the series in the character parts Frank and Denis wrote for him. It confirmed my belief, and I'm happy to say, Ronnie's confidence, in my ability to handle television comedy. And it demonstrated for me the value of a live audience to a comedy show.

The big sketch in each edition of *And So To Bentley* was a satire of a particular genre of entertainment. For the second show the victim was Ruritanian musical romance, with Dick Bentley as a rather ageing Student Prince and Charlotte Mitchell as his commoner sweetheart. Charlotte's children's nanny had been invited to watch the transmission in the Lime Grove viewing room as a special treat, but when we met her after the show she was in tears: "Oh, Miss Charlotte, it was lovely but it was so sad – he was a Prince and you couldn't marry him because you didn't come from a royal family, and I *cried!*"

Charlotte's nanny was a romantic little soul but she wasn't stupid; she simply didn't realise that the sketch was meant to be funny: it was too subtly close to its stereotype, which was what we all fondly believed *made* it funny. So we cut back on the scenery for the next show in order to squeeze in a studio audience, and though that audience was small it laughed in all the right places and our viewing audience's appreciation figures grew substantially from then on.

Television viewers in the early fifties knew all about comedy in variety bills and sketch shows but they were comparatively unused to situation comedy and totally unaccustomed to satire, and for the rest of my time as a producer I never failed to find that a live studio audience added atmosphere and warmth to a live show. Pre-recorded canned laughter was anathema – not because it was fake but because it *sounded* fake, it discomfited the home audience and it didn't help the performers, whose timing it tended to throw; but the real thing in those early days of television comedy reassured and prompted both viewers and cast. Fifty years or so later, of course, the viewing audience is very much more experienced and sophisticated, and doesn't need studio laughter to help it recognise that programmes like *The Office* or *Extras* or *Peep Show* are *funny*.

The follow-up series to *Barbara with Braden* finally happened, but without Barbara, who was appearing in a West End play. *Bath Night with Braden* was broadcast on Friday night, the traditional night in those far-off days for a bath and hair-wash – "Friday night is Amami night", the shampoo advertisements used to proclaim. It was a visual version of the radio shows Frank and Denis were writing for Bernie, complete with his radio cast of Benny Lee, Pearl Carr, announcer Ronald Fletcher and Nat Temple and his orchestra. Until the advent of ITV, BBC TV's comedy shows with the very rarest of exceptions were transmitted on a fortnightly basis, presumably because it was thought scripts couldn't be written and learnt or scenery designed and constructed on a weekly turn-round. Bernie wanted *Bath Night* broadcast weekly like his radio shows, but this wasn't radio, where the team could read their lines from a typed script; would they be able to learn a new script by heart each week?

"We'll use a teleprompter to help us, like they do in the States and Canada. You know, the script rolls through on little screens below the cameras so if they forget their lines they can just take a look at the nearest camera. Some guy has licensed the process over here." That guy was one John Whitney, an astute young businessman who had seen how valuable this visual aid could be for television broadcasters. Thirty years later John would become the Director-General of the Independent Broadcasting Authority. He should have held on to the teleprompter licence.

Bath Night was a free-and-easy show, fond of making fun of the television process itself. On one transmission, Bernie called the studio manager into his shot and said he'd always been puzzled by the ear-muffs worn by him and the cameramen. "They're not ear-muffs, they're headphones, so that we can hear what the producer is saying while we're on the air." "You mean the producer is on the other end of the cable?" "Yes, Bernie." "So if I pull that cable, sooner or later he's going to..." And of course Bernie couldn't resist pulling, and I was yanked through the studio wall at the other end of the cable in an explosion of brickwork and masonry dust. Well, that was the illusion Props and Scenery helped us to achieve; and when the laughter of our live audience died down, I was able to deliver the time-honoured tag-line "I suppose you think that's funny!"

I have a photograph of that scene, taken on the studio floor, and the striking thing about it is that though I am not wearing a jacket and my sleeves are rolled up – I *have* been working in the control room, after all – I am still wearing a tie. How formal! What quaintly old-fashioned pioneers we were! I know the sixties had not yet hit us and the fifties were pretty constrained and decorous, but this was *show business* and we were in the thick of it. Male producers and directors were still wearing formal suits and ties to work, just as they did at Alexandra Palace before the war. I can still remember Bill Lyon-Shaw's silver grey houndstooth check – he must have had more than one of them because I don't recall ever seeing him in anything else; and for my first few months as a trainee I even emulated Graeme Muir's elegant turn-out and took to wearing shirts with stiff separate collars, fiddling daily with front and back collar-studs. We television producers were *suits*, just like our managers and administrators. Today's street-wise, street-clad producers and directors wouldn't recognise us as being in the same profession.

Enter Caliban

The pressure for a new television channel had been growing from the beginning of the decade. Like so much else in the early fifties, newsprint was still rationed and advertisers and retailers believed that an additional television channel could provide an ideal new outlet for their advertisements. Television manufacturers and the electronics industries wanted an additional channel to help boost the development and sale of their equipment; and Conservative politicians, convinced that the BBC was biased against the Tory party, wanted to break its monopoly of the television screen.

But there was fierce opposition to a new channel and to the proposed method of its funding through advertising, expressed in the most rancorous terms during no fewer than six full-scale Parliamentary debates. Quintin Hogg in the Commons called "commercial television" a dangerous and unworkable animal, a Caliban emerging from his slimy cavern. Lord Reith, in the Lords, famously compared the introduction of sponsored television to this country to the introduction of smallpox, bubonic plague and the Black Death. But on 30 July 1954 the Television Bill was enacted, establishing the Independent Television Authority, and the Authority promptly set to work creating a new competitive channel to the BBC, with advertising as its source of funding.

In the BBC itself, or at least in the production departments, we were remarkably complacent about the competition's chance of success. We believed that Commercial Television – it would be years before the Corporation could bring itself to refer to its rival as *Independent* Television

– would be brash and vulgar. Viewers would hate it; they certainly wouldn't tolerate having their programmes interrupted every few minutes by those ghastly American-style advertising jingles. There wouldn't be enough viewers anyway: the service was only going to be broadcast in London to begin with; it wouldn't extend to the Midlands for another six months and wouldn't cover the whole of the North for more than a year, by which time it would be bankrupt. We didn't know how prescient we very nearly were.

Most of us blithely returned to the studio floor and concentrated on our next production. Some of us, perhaps, mused about the prospects of employment – probably more *gainful* employment – that a competitive channel might provide. No such musing for me. I had gone from one sheltered environment to another, from school to National Service, from university to the BBC; for someone like me, the idea of working in the cut-throat commercial world outside was repugnant. And there were plenty of attractive production prospects to look forward to at Lime Grove.

Wilfred Pickles was a hugely popular BBC radio performer of the day, the host of a touring radio quiz called *Have a Go!*, with Mr and Mrs Joe Public as its contestants. It was a simple, homely little show but Wilfred's warm Yorkshire accent and genius for putting ordinary folk at their ease made it enormously successful, with audiences regularly exceeding 20 million. *Have a Go!* was broadcast from town halls, church halls and local institutes all around the country. The contestants were asked simple general knowledge questions for modest money prizes and encouraged to talk about their lives.

These were innocent days, in which merely answering Wilfred's question about your age – "'Ow old are yer, luv?" – with a proud "I'm sixty-five!" would receive thunderous applause from the audience and an immediate "Give 'er the money, Barney!" from Wilfred, Barney being Barney Colehan the producer. The money would be handed over to Barney by "Mabel at the table" – Mabel was Wilfred's wife – to the accompaniment of a rousing eight bars of the programme's signature tune, "Have a Go, Joe! Come and Have a Go!" played on the upright piano by one Violet Carson, who would go on to become one of Independent Television's very first stars as Ena Sharples of Coronation Street. Small world, show-biz.

In the spring of 1954, while what Wilfred would have called all that argy bargy about Commercial Television was going on in Parliament, Ronnie Waldman asked me if I'd like to do a simple little series with him and Mabel, a request show, perhaps – "Let's call it *Ask Pickles*" – in which viewers could write in and ask for a piece of film or music or some such – a quiet, laid-back little show with which Wilfred and Mabel could ease their way gently into the new medium. And that's how it started, in a small studio in Lime Grove with a small orchestra and no studio audience. I brought in the Forresters to help me wade through the requests that the BBC press department hoped to drum up with their publicity – "Do you want to feed a lion or pat a giraffe on the tiny top of his head?"… "Do you want to meet a film star?"… "Do you want to ride pillion on a motor bike?"… "It doesn't matter how old you are, you can still make your own special dream come true if you get in touch with Wilfred Pickles".

As it turned out, nobody wanted to pat a giraffe, but one housewife did want to cuddle a lion: when it made its entrance on the studio floor she rushed to meet it with open arms and the lion turned in horror and ran back into its cage. We were inundated with homely little requests which, with the North Country warmth and sincerity that came so naturally to Wilfred and Mabel, proceeded to charm a modest but appreciative viewing audience every other Friday evening. Someone wanted to see the newsreel sequence of the Oxford crew sinking in the 1952 Boat Race. Mrs Nell Hughes wanted to waltz with the television Dance King Victor Sylvester. Viewers wanted to know what the potter in the famous Potter's Wheel Interlude was making, and the potter, George Aubertin, was able to explain that he wasn't making anything, just doodling away for ten minutes because that's what the Film Unit had asked him to do. One viewer wanted to shake hands with the Queen but "if you can't manage that, my alternative is the Littlewood Songsters singing O Mein Papa".

And then, one Friday early in our run, Studio D was unavailable and no other Lime Grove studio was free, so we were scheduled into the BBC Television Theatre for our show. We decided to take advantage of the vast increase in scale that this new venue offered – the Television Theatre used to be the Shepherds Bush Empire – so we asked the BBC's Audience Ticket Unit to fill the theatre, told Eric Robinson he could book his full BBC Television Orchestra for the gig and scoured our post bag for requests that would work well on a stage in front of a large audience. We still fulfilled the often touching little requests that had characterised the show in Studio D at Lime Grove, but such a large venue also allowed for some more extravagant set-pieces.

When ex-Tiller Girl Mona Mason asked to hear one of the numbers she had danced to 30 years ago, she saw her fellow-Tiller Girl troupe come high-kicking on stage in their old routine – and got up and joined them. When Harry Bishop, a survivor of the 1918 Battle of the Khyber Pass, asked to hear the Band of his old regiment, the Royal Sussex, play "Sussex by the Sea" on the anniversary of the Battle, we invited him on stage for the performance and reunited him with half a dozen fellow survivors whom he hadn't seen for decades – and they all stood proudly to attention when their Regimental Band marched on playing the Regimental march. The wife who wanted Eric Robinson to cheer her up with her husband's favourite song because he himself would be on duty with the British Army in Germany on their first anniversary, saw her husband walk on stage to give her a kiss, courtesy of a persuasive Pauline and Larry Forrester and a compassionate BAOR Colonel. The elderly gentleman who wanted a ride in a helicopter was taken by Wilfred around the corner to a floodlit White City sports ground where the helicopter and a BBC Outside Broadcast Unit were waiting for him, while Mabel carried on with the show in the Theatre, and we could see that particular dream come through on a large Eidophor screen and enjoy our guest's ecstatic reaction when Wilfred returned with him to the theatre in due course.

The show was a huge success. The BBC's switchboard was jammed with appreciative calls – and still more requests – and the rest of that initial run was hastily rescheduled to remain in the Television Theatre. The series enjoyed the highest Audience Appreciation figures of any BBC production bar the Coronation and won the *Daily Mail* National Television Award for The Most Entertaining Programme of the Year. Its mixture of request and reunion initiated a genre of its own, followed across the years by programmes like *Jim'll Fix It*, *Ask Aspel*, and *The Big Time*. Forty years later, when I was Chairman and Managing Director of London Weekend Television and Alan Boyd was preparing his Cilla Black series *Surprise! Surprise!*, he debriefed me of everything I could remember about what we did in *Ask Pickles* and how we did it. In the event, *Surprise! Surprise!* was a sort of tribute show. Wilfred and Mabel and Pauline and Larry, all, alas, now gone, would have been tickled pink.

The *Daily Mail* National Television Awards – there were no BAFTAS in the early '50s – were televised in February of 1955. In the following eight months, 350 men and women from departments across the whole of BBC Television left to join the two London ITV companies, Associated-Rediffusion and Associated Television, known familiarly as Rediffusion and ATV. A little belatedly, the Corporation began to issue new contracts to some of its key personnel and to tie down its most important sports contracts and other outside broadcast events, some of them for as much as seven years. Paul Fox remembers the queue of producers summoned to wait in line outside the Head of Establishment's office to discuss their new contracts. Michael Peacock, my ex-trainee colleague in Talks department, was offered a new five-year contract starting at a salary nearly twice his previous one. In Light Entertainment, I was more than happy to sign a two-year contract, taking me to the end of 1956, for a very much more modest increase. But Bill Ward left us, to set up the production department at Associated Television, taking with him Bill Lyon-Shaw and Dicky Leeman and a sizeable number of senior engineers and technicians.

Some of these BBC personnel left for more money: as a monopoly, the BBC hadn't needed to pay big salaries, so it didn't. Some of the technicians left for career enhancement, with cameramen promoted to producers, and designers, engineers, wardrobe assistants and makeup artists given the opportunity to become heads of their own departments. Some left for the fun of doing something new and the prospect of doing it with artistes and performers that the BBC couldn't afford to hire. The television service had only just become self-supporting the previous year and it didn't have the money to lavish on big name entertainers. How very different from today!

Caliban finally emerged from his cavern, blinking in the spotlight, on Thursday, 22 September 1955; and, to the surprise and dismay of his detractors, turned out to be not such a slimy beast after all. ITV's programmes were by no means brash and vulgar: they were just as good as the BBC's – after all, most of them were made by ex-BBC people – but they seemed glossier, zippier, somehow *friendlier*. The commercials, jingles and all, were lively and funny, and not an irritating interruption. The news was delivered not by anonymous voices over a succession of still pictures but by *newscasters*, personalities who were not only engaging in themselves, like Robin Day and Christopher Chataway, but also clearly engaged in what they were delivering.

In their first four days, Rediffusion and ATV began the weekly transmission of quiz and giveaway shows in which Mr and Mrs Joe Public could now win significant sums of cash – in Hughie Green's *Double Your Money* as much as £1,000. They could also win valuable prizes – in Michael Miles's *Take Your Pick* prizes as valuable as motorbikes, refrigerators, kitchen units, even round trips to Australia. In the game shows I had been producing at the

BBC the prize for winners would at best have been a certificate to indicate that they had beaten the panel.

Viewers found themselves introduced to fast-moving American comedy shows and drama series – Lucille Ball's *I Love Lucy* began its British run on ITV that opening weekend. They had their very first experience of variety on a *Sunday* night – unthinkable at the BBC – with *Val Parnell's Sunday Night at the London Palladium* presenting international stars they had previously only seen in the movies or heard on radio or records. The opening Sunday night bill was topped by Gracie Fields and American recording star Guy Mitchell. And British stars who had previously featured only in occasional guest slots for the BBC were now appearing in their own weekly series: on ITV's opening Saturday night, Harry Secombe starred in the first of six weekly shows written for him by Eric Sykes.

The two London companies were instantly popular with their audience. But that audience was dauntingly small: on September's opening night, no more than 188,000 homes had a TV set capable of receiving ITV. Throughout its first few months on the air, the anti-ITV press headlines claimed that the new channel was struggling to get on its feet, that it was not pulling in sufficient advertising revenue, that its programmes were failing to persuade people to buy the new TV sets. It looked as if the prophecies of financial doom for the new channel would be realised. Those of us left behind at Lime Grove were beginning to feel a little sorry for our ex-colleagues, though we still envied them their new programme-making opportunities and the artistes they were fortunate enough to be working with.

However, not every artiste appearing in his or her own ITV series was enjoying the experience. Billy Cotton and his Band were one of British variety's biggest draws and BBC Radio's star entertainment attraction with their Sunday lunchtime *Billy Cotton Band Show*. They followed Harry Secombe into ITV's Saturday night schedule with a six-week series of their own, and Billy wasn't happy about it. He was uncomfortable with the show's format, which used up far too much of the music-hall material he and the band had built up over the years, and a weekly television series was too big a disruption of the band's regular tour of the halls, which paid the wages of his sixteen musicians year in, year out whether they worked or not. His music publisher son, Bill Cotton Jr, encouraged him to see Ronnie Waldman, whom he knew well from Ronnie's radio days, to explore the possibilities of a combined BBC radio and television deal which might find a way of protecting his touring schedule, and to discuss the kind of programme format that might suit the band without using up the material which its music-hall audiences paid good money to see.

And that was where I was to come in. Billy and Ronnie agreed financial terms and hit on the simple idea of producing the television series on a fortnightly basis so that the band could tour on alternate weeks when the show was not on the air. And Ronnie, with his genius for unlikely casting, persuaded Billy to take a chance on a university graduate with no music-hall experience as his producer. Billy reluctantly agreed to consider a pilot show to see how we got on.

As a music-hall devotee and avid radio listener, I knew the act well. Billy, with his bluff Cockney humour, led a band which was full of both first-class musicians and natural comedians and I could see how both the music and the comedy could be translated to the screen. I went up to Manchester to watch the band's stage act at the Opera House and over a late-night supper with Billy told him some of my ideas for the television show. My years in the stalls of the Hackney, Chiswick and Shepherds Bush Empires stood me in good stead once again. To Billy's surprise, as he told me months later, he found that for all my university background we were speaking the same language; and when we parted, he patted me on the back and said "Sleep well, son. Don't worry. I'm much too good for you to bugger up."

He was right. In *Wakey! Wakey!*, which is what we called *The Billy Cotton Band Show*, we managed to add the gloss and glamour of television to the band's boisterous music-hall fun. Scriptwriter Jimmy Grafton and I deployed the band's comedy skills in new comedy numbers without ransacking its precious stage material; I used every available technical device to add visual appeal to its musical numbers; we introduced guest artistes in comedy routines with Billy; and I persuaded him to perform dance numbers with a line of dancers. The juxtaposition of a dozen beautiful, glamorously dressed girl dancers with this bluff, portly, 60-year old man – who, like many large men, was capable of the lightest and most delicate movement – was irresistible.

The pilot show became a series; and the series ran for twelve years. I saw it through its first year, and in the process became acquainted with the music halls, railway stations and station-hotel dining rooms of quite a few of the nation's cities. On those alternate touring weeks I would take the morning train to York or Leeds or Cardiff or wherever the band was playing, and have lunch with Billy to tell him my suggestions for the next *Wakey! Wakey!* In the afternoon we would join the band in the theatre, walk through some of the material I had brought with me, try out any new ideas Billy and the boys had been working on, and have a cup of tea before I caught the next train back to London. On the journey home, I would map out the running-order for the show, incorporating the material we had worked on that afternoon, and arrive in my office next morning with a rough script. A practical and not at all disagreeable procedure, but for years I was left with the impression that York and Leeds and Cardiff and all the other cities I visited consisted exclusively of a railway station, a railway-hotel dining room and a music hall. And they all looked exactly the same; a case of constant déjà vu.

Wakey! Wakey! wasn't my only preoccupation in 1956. I was still filling the occasional one-off slots against which the schedulers placed my initials. *Ask Pickles* remained my responsibility until the Cotton show became a series, and then Wilfred and Mabel found themselves in the congenial hands of Ernest Maxin. I also produced Petula Clark in what, after an initial quarter-hour run, became her first half-hour television series, complete with guest stars and a large studio orchestra, both of us thereby finally graduating from the era of *Pet's Parlour* and 15-minute *Starlight* trainee exercises. And Pat Kirkwood came back into my professional life in a 90-minute play about the Edwardian music-hall performer Vesta Tilley, written by Pat's then husband, Hubert Gregg.

Work in ITV? Never!

Vesta Tilley had been a star in Britain and the United States for over thirty years, the most famous and highly paid male impersonator of her day and the originator of such classic music-hall songs as "Burlington Bertie", "Jolly Good Luck to the Girl who Loves a Soldier" and "After the Ball". A little working-class girl from Worcester, she made her first appearance on stage at the age of three. She proved so effective as a singer of patriotic songs during the First World War that she was known as Britain's Greatest Recruiting Sergeant; and she ended up as Lady de Frece, the wife of a prominent Conservative MP. We pulled out all the stops to depict her remarkable career. *The Great Little Tilley* was a huge two-studio operation occupying both D and E on the fourth floor of Lime Grove, the dramatic sequences staged in Studio D and the musical sequences in Studio E, which was filled with a reproduction of an Edwardian music-hall, hurriedly dressed and re-dressed between sequences to resemble the different venues in which Tilley had performed.

The cameras for both studios were linked to the control-room in D, so I was comfortably stationary in my producer's chair while Pat dashed between the two studios, frantically changing costumes, wigs and props on the way: ah! the joys of live television! She had been a sensation four years earlier in a dramatisation of the life of another great Edwardian music-hall star, Marie Lloyd, produced by Michael Mills at Alexandra Palace. She was a sensation again in *The Great Little Tilley* and repeated her triumph the following year in the movie version, re-titled *After the Ball*, which was directed by Compton Bennett with Laurence Harvey as her co-star. And she was still sensational the last time I saw her, forty years later, in a Noël Coward/Cole Porter revue at the Chichester Festival Theatre.

Ronnie Waldman had been busily recruiting new young producers to replace those who had left to join ITV, among them Francis Essex from revue, Bill Cotton Jr from music publishing, Duncan Wood from BBC radio in Bristol, Josephine Douglas from the stage, and Jack Good from Oxford, a fellow graduate who trumped my Presidency of the ETC with his Presidency of the OUDS. They were assigned to various members of the Department for training, as I had been to Graeme Muir, and I drew Bill Cotton and Jack Good as my pupils. Neither needed much instruction. Bill was a television natural – more importantly, he was a *BBC* natural: over the years he would move ever upwards in the Corporation, from light entertainment producer to Head of the Department to Controller of BBC 1 to Director of Programmes to Managing Director of BBC Television itself. When, many years later, I failed to prise him away from the Corporation to join me at LWT as my Director of Programmes, I used to refer to him at industry gatherings as an immovable barnacle on the soul of the BBC. He in turn would say "Brian taught me everything I know about television; unfortunately, he didn't teach me everything *he* knew." No one could top Bill's punch-lines. We became lifelong friends, until he died more than 50 years later.

Jack, on the other hand, didn't want to know *anything* about television comedy shows, panel games or variety spectaculars. He had undergone an almost religious conversion in 1956 – he actually said he "saw the light" – when he came across the Bill Haley movie *Rock Around The Clock* and decided from that moment on to devote his career exclusively to the new phenomenon of rock and roll music. The rest of the Department thought rock and roll couldn't possibly last; it was a fad, a musical dead end. But in 1957 the BBC needed a Saturday night show to fill the blank screen between 6 pm and 7 pm, which television had been required to observe with the resumption of broadcasting after the war as a "toddler's truce" to enable parents to bundle their youngsters off to bed. Ronnie Waldman handed the slot to Jack Good and Josephine Douglas with the brief to aim their show at a young audience.

Six-Five Special, television's very first pop music show for teenagers, began in February 1957 and Jack crammed as much rock music into it as he could get away with. It wasn't enough to satisfy him, so he took his rock and roll ambitions to ABC Television, the newest of the big five ITV companies. With the enormously gifted Rita Gillespie as his director, he began a run of strikingly original rock and roll shows – *Oh Boy!*, *Boy Meets Girls*, *Wham!* – which broke new ground in production techniques, kick-started the careers of previously unknown performers like Cliff Richard, Adam Faith, Marty Wilde, Billy Fury and Jess Conrad, and brought an entirely new teenage audience to television. Jack and Rita repeated their success in America with a similar show, Shindig, for the ABC network. Jack went on to write and produce rock music stage shows, including *Catch My Soul!*, a rock opera adaptation of Shakespeare's *Othello*, which played both Broadway and the West End comfortably ahead of *Joseph and the Amazing Technicolor Dreamcoat* and *Jesus Christ Superstar*, the rock operas of Andrew Lloyd Webber and Tim Rice. Some dead end.

What, meanwhile, of Caliban?

It's difficult to remember what a close-run thing it was for ITV in that first year. There were delays in rolling out the transmitter coverage from London to the rest of the United Kingdom; viewers were slow to spend the money to convert their old television sets or buy new ones able to receive the ITV signal; and without audiences advertisers were reluctant to divert their budgets to the new medium. Granada Television, the weekday ITV contractor for the North of England nearly went belly up and had to be rescued by Rediffusion, who agreed to supply it with 85 percent of the network schedule for the next four years in exchange for 85 percent of Granada's advertising revenue.

In his autobiography, Howard Thomas, the Managing Director of ABC Television, the weekend programme contractor for the North and Midlands in ITV's first crazy quilt of a network, remembered how he and Denis Forman, Granada's Managing Director, used to travel up on the train together from London to their respective studios in Manchester, anxiously counting the ITV aerials as they approached the North. It was only when the aerials became too profuse to be counted that they realised the tide had turned. And, at the BBC, we watched it turn. In the new-fangled ratings books over which we all began to pore each week, we saw the ITV line in the daily audience graphs gradually pull further and further up and away from the BBC's. It girded us on, of course. The cut-throat commercial world was still anathema. We had to admit that their programmes were pretty good, but we could take them on: not a problem: we were the BBC.

I was rehearsing Frank Chacksfield and his Orchestra in Studio G, preparing my own little contribution to taking on ITV, when I was summoned to see the Establishment Officer, Leslie Page, to discuss a new contract. Eamonn Andrews, the presenter of *What's My Line?*, was a star guest in Frank's show. His double-sided recording of a narrative song, "Shifting Whispering Sands", had risen to number eighteen in the Top Twenty and I was busily turning it into a visual narrative for Eamonn and the Orchestra with the aid of Inlay, Overlay and the hand-operated animated graphics of the great Alfred Wurmser. It was the technical trickery of this particular programme about which Arthur Wyndham enthused to his bosses at the Australian Broadcasting Commission. And it was this particular production day which would prove to be the most significant of my time at the BBC.

"Ah, Tesler", said Mr Page, "Your contract's up for renewal shortly. You've been doing well and we're happy to keep you on. We'd like to offer you another contract for two years. Would that be satisfactory?" "Yes, very, thank you", I said. "Excellent. We'll send you the contract and if you'll just sign it and send it back that will be fine. Do you have any questions or comments?" "Well", I said, "I'm earning £1,700 a year at the moment; could it go up to £1,800 for the next two years?" "Oh no", said Mr Page, "Working for the BBC is reward enough."

I returned to the studio considerably disheartened, and my disappointment was apparent not only to Eamonn and Frank but also to their joint manager, Teddy Sommerfield, who had happened to pop in to see how rehearsals were going. Teddy was a well-established literary and artistes agent, good-humoured and good-natured, and as soon as I walked in he said "You're looking glum. What's up?" I told him my story. "You can do better than that", he said. "Would you be prepared to work for ITV?" "Dammit!" I said, "Yes!" "Let me make a few calls" said Teddy. When he came back he said he'd been on the phone to Lew Grade, who would like me to join ATV. "He offered £3,500 a year for three years. I told him I didn't think that was enough, so he threw in two weeks in New York for the first two years to study American television, all expenses paid. What would you like me to do?" "Bite his hand off" I said.

It wasn't ATV's money that spurred me – I was more attracted to those weeks of studying American television in New York. What hurt was the feeling that the BBC didn't think I was worth another £100 a year to keep me. If I had been a little more street-wise I would have haggled for that extra £100. If I had had any sense, I would have gone to Ronnie Waldman and asked if he would support me in my request for this modest rise. And if Teddy Sommerfield had not been in the studio on that fateful day there would have been no question of an offer from Lew Grade. I was too naïve, too unused to commercial reality to realise that a little negotiation might not only have been in order but was actually expected by Leslie Page. Two weeks later, the Assistant Establishment Officer, Kinchin Smith, wrote to offer me £2,000 a year for three years. But it was too late. I had committed to ATV.

What was I letting myself in for?

A six-page, hand-written letter from Ronnie Waldman made me no easier in mind. "You know that ATV believes in money and not much else. You must know that commercial television is in grave danger, within a very short time, of being run entirely by the advertisers. You must know, therefore, that any creative thoughts you have about Television (and you have plenty) must be subservient in ATV to considerations other than those of the real future of TV programmes.... Your type of creative mind will not react happily when, after you've done a show, you're told to 'rough it up' (a phrase used very recently by one of your future bosses)....What do you believe in, and what do you want as far as TV is concerned? If you know the answers to those questions then you're safe anywhere (even in ATV, though I doubt whether anyone there will share your beliefs). If you don't, then I feel I should do everything, even at this fantastically late hour, to prevent you from going...."

Ronnie himself left the Department the following year – but not the BBC, though I cannot believe he wasn't offered a position as Managing Director or Programme Controller in at least one of the 15 ITV companies. Like Bill Cotton decades later, he was too much of a BBC man to be tempted away from the Corporation; and the Corporation appointed him Business Manager, BBC Television Programmes. Cynics in the industry wondered why they hadn't appointed him Cecil McGivern's successor as BBC Television's Controller of Programmes. Was it because the Corporation still considered Light Entertainment too lowbrow a background for the Service's senior executive? That background certainly didn't impede Bill Cotton's future rise through the Service's hierarchy. Or was it because Ronnie was Jewish? Jews are supposed to be good at business, aren't they, so why not make him Business Manager instead?

I was never conscious of any kind of anti-Semitism, institutional or otherwise, in my years at the BBC, although Ernest Maxin tells me that *he* was. During the Six Day Israel-Arab war some moron had amused himself by scrawling on Ernest's office door the injunction "Go back to where you came from". Where he came from was Upton Park as it happened, which was where he was born. I must confess, however, to being startled to find in going through my BBC Personal File, courtesy of the Freedom of Information Act, that the Assistant Secretary of Oxford's University Appointments Committee, in writing about me to the BBC's Appointments Officer in 1951, had found it appropriate to begin his letter with "Brian Tesler is a Jew". Would he have felt obliged to begin other letters about prospective candidates with a statement of their religious denomination? Certainly, being Jewish at the BBC never impaired Paul Fox's career: he went from Head of Current Affairs to Controller of BBC 1 to Director of Programmes and finally to Managing Director of BBC Network Television without any difficulty, in spite of taking eleven years out between the third and fourth of those appointments to run ITV's Yorkshire Television as its Managing Director.

No, I think Ronnie's move to the business side of television programming was a deliberate choice on his part and entirely consonant with the questions he put to me in his letter. He believed in the BBC and its programmes and he wanted those programmes to be seen and admired throughout the world. In 1960, two years after he became Business Manager of Television Programmes, the organisation was restructured to become BBC TV Enterprises, with Ronnie as its General Manager. Thirty-five years later still, long after he died in 1963, the organisation he had built with the skill, ingenuity and charm that characterised his years in Light Entertainment had grown so large that it was restructured again to become BBC Worldwide Ltd, the commercial subsidiary of the BBC. In 2014-15 BBC Worldwide reported sales of £1 billion and returned £136.6 million to the Corporation.

I knew what my own answers to Ronnie's two questions were. I believed in pleasing a great many people, including myself, with the best entertainment programmes I was capable of producing. I wanted to be proud of my work, to feel at times that I had perhaps achieved something more than ephemeral. Would I be able to achieve any of this in the rough, tough commercial world of Independent Television?

Working for Val and Lew

I t wasn't an auspicious beginning.

Associated Television was very much a show business company. In its original incarnation as the Associated Broadcasting Company it was an amalgamation of two consortia, the Associated Broadcasting Development Company and the Incorporated Television Programme Company, and its combined shareholders included Howard and Wyndham Theatres, the H. M. Tennant production company, the Stoll Moss and General Theatre Corporation and the Lew and Leslie Grade variety agency, which had merged with the actors' agency London Artists. Between them they owned some of the most important theatres in the West End and the provinces, produced a significant proportion of the plays, musicals, operas, ballets and variety shows that filled those theatres, and represented many of the actors and artistes who performed in them.

Their original application for an ITV franchise was in fact turned down because the Independent Television Authority felt their consortium would control a near-monopoly of the available entertainment in Great Britain and suggested they became programme suppliers to the successful franchise holders instead. It was only when the Kemsley-Winnick Group, which had been awarded the franchise for weekends in London and weekdays in the Midlands, hit financial difficulties that the Authority reconsidered and proposed a fifty-fifty partnership between both consortia.

The new partners called their company Associated Broadcasting, its television subsidiary ABC and its production subsidiary ITPC. The TV company went on the air as ABC Television but three weeks later was obliged to change its name when Associated British Cinemas became the new weekend franchise-holder for the North and Midlands and successfully sued for the right to use the inititials for its own television company. So the company providing television programmes for weekends in London and weekdays in the Midlands finally became Associated Television, or ATV.

The merger had been relatively painless and its show-business element was in no way diluted. ATV's Managing Director was the legendary showman Val Parnell, who continued to run the London Palladium and the rest of the Stoll Moss theatres, and its Deputy Managing Director was Lew Grade, who continued with his brother Leslie to run the Lew and Leslie Grade artistes' agency. ATV's biggest and most successful light entertainment shows were *Val Parnell's Saturday Spectacular* and *Val Parnell's Sunday Night at the London Palladium*, and both shows were booked by the Grades. What could be more propitious for yours truly? Which international show-biz top-liners would they present me with for my first ATV show? What glittering cascade of stars? I went to my first meeting with them in that first week of January 1957 heady with anticipation.

Val and Lew shared an office in Adastral House on Kingsway, sitting diagonally across from each other behind identical desks: the tall, imposing impresario and the short, endearing variety agent, the oddest of Odd Couples but the most formidable in show business. They welcomed me warmly and we exchanged a few general pleasantries before Val wished me good luck and went off to a Palladium rehearsal. Lew invited me to take a seat, flourished his king-sized cigar and exulted "You're doing your first show on the 19th, a *Saturday Spectacular*, and have we got a show for you!" He slid a typed list of names across his desk, and my heady anticipation instantly evaporated.

It didn't remotely resemble the sort of list Ronnie Waldman had presented me with at my BBC interview five years earlier. It was a simple run of the mill variety bill: a list of singers, speciality acts, a ventriloquist, a comedian, one of the dizzy blonde panellists from ATV's panel game *Yakity Yak*; not a top-liner among them, not a star. Lew could see my disappointment. "My boy, it's the pantomime season. Everybody's working. Nobody else is available. But you can dress it up with your production ideas, get some dancers, a big orchestra – you'll make a great show of it!" I said "Thank you, Mr Grade" – "Call me Lew!" – "Thank you, Lew, but could I just... think about it? If it's OK with you I'd really like to do something more than a straightforward variety bill for my first show: could I think about it, and come back to you?" "Of course, my boy, but come back quick: you're on in two and a half weeks."

Whatever production values I might have been able to dress Lew's list with, a run-of-the-mill variety bill would have been no fun to produce, and no way to make a mark in independent television with my first show. I had to find some focal point, someone not working in pantomime around whom I could build a *show*; and by the time I'd left the lift on the ground floor I knew exactly who.

During my last few months at the BBC I had booked Dick Henderson, a much-loved survivor of the music hall in its prime, as a guest on *The Billy Cotton Band Show*. Dick was an amiable comedian who shared Billy's rotund profile and lightness of foot, and it occurred to me that it might be fun to add their respective sons to the mix. At that time, Bill Cotton Jr was a thriving young music publisher and Dickie Henderson Jr was a successful variety performer in his own right. The young men were slim and dashing; their fathers were most definitely not: visually, the quartet would be irresistible. So Jimmy Grafton dreamt up some cross-talk for the four of them, Leslie Roberts choreographed a nifty soft-shoe dance routine, and one memorable Wednesday evening at 8 pm, live of course, they sang, danced and wisecracked their way through three choruses of "Tiptoe Through The Tulips", to the delight of our theatre audience and, judging from the phone calls received by the BBC switchboard, our viewers. Young Bill was as nervous as a kitten throughout: I like to think that the experience helped to induce in him the empathy which would in the future endear him to every artiste he ever worked with as a producer and programme executive. His young co-performer was a revelation.

Dickie Henderson Jr was then in his middle 30s, a good looking singer, dancer and comedian, with a breezy American style that relied on observational humour rather than jokes; and he had a repertoire of knockabout physical routines that had made him equally popular in America, where he was a regular guest on *The Ed Sullivan Show*. He and I had found ourselves on the same entertainment wavelength at once, and I had booked him on the Petula Clark series, my last production for the BBC, where he sang and danced and chatted with Pet with great skill and charm.

I called Dickie from the nearest telephone booth and asked how he'd feel about doing *The Dickie Henderson Show* as one of *Val Parnell's Saturday Spectaculars*. "Val wouldn't like it," he said. "For Pete's sake, why?" "Well, last year, he persuaded me to star in a show called *Young at Heart* though I told him that with that cast, those writers and that production team, it wouldn't work. And it didn't. And Val sort of blamed me for it." "Well let's get together with Jimmy Grafton anyway and see what we can come up with. It's worth a try."

Over a boozy lunch somewhere in the Aldwych, the three of us mapped out a format that looked a great deal more interesting than a succession of middle-range variety acts and I phoned Lew Grade with the good news. Lew said "Val wouldn't like it" and explained the *Young at Heart* problem. So I called my last hope, Bill Ward, who as ATV's Head of Production was now my immediate boss. Bill called back and said because it was my first programme for ATV he'd persuaded Val to let me use Dickie – "but he says on no account can it be called *The Dickie Henderson Show*."

It was a minor restriction and we thought we'd risk a minor infraction. The standard opening format for ATV's big Saturday night show was a succession of captions: ATV PRESENTS...VAL PARNELL'S SATURDAY SPEC-TACULAR...THE (*STAR'S NAME*) SHOW. For our own opening sequence I moved the camera along a line of glamorous show girls in leotards and fish-net stockings, posed against a black velvet background glittering with stars and sequins, each gorgeous girl holding a sparkling, elaborately designed caption card – ATV PRESENTS...VAL PARNELL'S... SATURDAY SPECTACU-LAR... – until the camera came to a scruffy piece of cardboard suspended from a lamp-post on which was scrawled "the dickie henderson show?" and we panned down to find Dickie himself leaning against the lamp-post with a few wry, self-deprecating remarks before he went into the opening production number.

We threw pretty well everything we could into that show – including the kitchen-sink, which fitted quite naturally into a domestic sketch with Arthur Askey's daughter Anthea playing Dickie's wife. We featured songs, dances, production numbers, a little inlay/overlay trickery, sketches with great "feeds" like Charles Hawtrey, who would go on to become a star in his own right in the *Carry On* films, and Freddie Mills, the ex-British and World Light Heavyweight boxing champion. We incorporated one of Dickie's knockabout physical routines: the inept Frank Sinatra impersonator making a hash of "One For My Baby" at the speakeasy bar, singeing his eyebrows lighting his cigarette, spilling his drink checking the time, entangling his legs in the bar stool, ending up helplessly entwined with the stool on the floor but still resolutely singing "... and One More For The Road". And we turned the difficulty of getting a guest artiste to a production advantage.

Shani Wallis, a delightful young singer and dancer who would a decade later star as Nancy in the film version of *Oliver*, was featuring in a West End Revue. We persuaded the producers – not too difficult: it was a Stoll Moss theatre – to switch her First House appearance to the revue's first half, rushed her by taxi to the television theatre in Wood Green for our show and rushed her back again in time to appear in the second half of the revue's Second House. Tight, but workable. To get Shani onto our own stage as dramatically as possible, we built a long, curved slide from the back of the Circle all the way down the side of the Wood Green auditorium, so that while Dickie was explaining why he wasn't certain she would arrive in time, Shani could make a last-minute appearance bursting into the back of the Circle – "I'm here, Dickie! I'm here!" – and, game little trouper that she was, jumping onto the slide to helter-skelter all the way down to her co-star. Another Health & Safety No-No today. The audience didn't know just how nail-bitingly last-minute Shani's arrival really was: the evening traffic to Wood Green was diverted by a road accident and she reached our theatre only just in time for her cue.

The show worked wonderfully well, and Val Parnell was generous enough to send a congratulatory telegram thanking us for giving *Saturday Spectacular* a new look and saying YOU CAN DO AS MANY MORE DICKIE HENDERSON SHOWS AS YOU LIKE. So we did, until Val's rival impresario, Jack Hylton, engaged by Associated-Rediffusion to mastermind its own light entertainment output, made Dickie an offer he couldn't refuse the following summer: a weekly domestic situation comedy series adapted from the Sid Caesar-Imogene Coca scripts which Hylton had bought from American television's *Your Show of Shows*. Anthea Askey continued to play Dickie's wife until she married and retired from show business two years later, at which point June Laverick took over the role in a series which eventually ran for 135 episodes. And I was never offered another run-of-the mill variety bill again.

The Buccaneering Years

The late fifties were freewheeling, buccaneering years for Associated Television, when cash flow had ceased to be a problem, no programme ambition seemed unattainable, and programme budgets were effectively limitless. It was a period of particularly exhilarating freedom for all of us in ATV's light entertainment department. The designers and technicians and engineers we worked with had come from the BBC, with all the Corporation's experience and expertise behind them. The casting directors we worked with – Alec Fyne and Myrna Malinsky – had the power and know-how of the Grade agency behind them. And we had no budgets to circumscribe us. For me, it was like finding myself in the British Forces Broadcasting Station in Trieste again exactly ten years later, free to devise, to originate, to experiment, as long as it worked.

I had stopped collecting newspaper reviews by then, being too busy to cut them out and paste them in, but I see from Mark Lewisohn's *Guide to TV Comedy* that, in 1957, as well as the Dickie Henderson shows, I produced *Saturday Spectaculars* with some of the top British comedy stars of the time – Max Bygraves, Frankie Howerd, Norman Wisdom, Benny Hill – as well as American luminaries like Rosemary Clooney, Ray Bolger and Johnnie Ray, flown over from the States for *Sunday Night at the London Palladium* and a Moss Empire tour. To my delight, I also produced *Saturday Spectaculars* with some of my pre-war entertainment idols like Jack Buchanan and George Formby, whose show business careers had both been given new life – Buchanan by co-starring with Fred Astaire in MGM's *The Band Wagon* and Formby by packing out his West End theatre with a musical version of *Brewster's Millions*. And in not one of these shows was I presented with a budget.

The nearest I ever got to a budget in fact was in a telephone conversation with Leslie Grade. In the wonderfully synergistic world of Associated Television, the Grade agency was in effect the casting office for ATV's light entertainment programmes, which were packaged by ATV's production company ITC and bought by the television company for transmission in the U.K. That certainly seemed to be the case when Leslie phoned me during the preparation of one of the Dickie Henderson shows. "How's it going, Brian?" he said, in his quiet, purring voice. "Fine, thank you, Leslie." "Have you booked everybody for the show yet?" "Not quite. Bob Hope's in town and we think we can get him to do a spot with Dickie." "Well, be careful: you're nearly over budget." "Tell me what the budget is, Leslie, and I'll be careful to stay inside it." "Never mind what the budget is, you're nearly over it." "Would you like me to drop Bob Hope?" Pause. "No. Keep Bob Hope. Drop the violins."

Early in that first year with ATV, I had begun to notice the young Production Assistant who worked along the corridor for fellow light entertainment producer Albert Locke. Her name was Audrey Maclean; she was blonde and bright and extremely attractive; and increasingly I would find myself wandering into Albert's office to ask his advice about something or other, casually, in passing, having a word or two with this beguiling young woman. Sometimes I was lucky enough to find Albert absent, so I could chat to Audrey without having to drum up some idiotic excuse; and that summer I was luckier still: my own Production Assistant had to change her holiday dates just before the Johnnie Ray *Spectacular* I was scheduled to produce; Albert didn't have a show of his own to work on, and Audrey was assigned to my show instead.

As possible bookings for the Johnnie Ray production, the Grade agency had asked me to have a look at some of the international speciality acts who were playing that season's Summer Shows in Great Yarmouth; so before rehearsals began Audrey and I took a trip to the coast to check them out. We saw the shows, booked one of the acts, stayed overnight in a hotel – in separate rooms of course – and drove back to London after a long, sunny, chatty walk along the promenade. The attraction appeared to be mutual; the Yarmouth expedition had been an ideal opportunity to get to know each other; and in the Johnnie Ray rehearsals the following week we found we worked well together as a team. By the time the show was over we were, as they say, an item; and at the beginning of the autumn schedule ATV agreed to make Audrey my P.A. on a permanent basis. Audrey bade her fond farewells to Albert Locke, and she and I embarked on a partnership that lasted fifty-one wonderful years until she died in October 2008, three weeks before what would have been our Golden Wedding Anniversary.

It was a particularly busy autumn. Val Parnell asked me to take over the new season of *Sunday Night at the London Palladium*, more of which anon, but I was still being scheduled for Val's *Saturday Spectaculars* – I produced shows with Dickie Henderson, Norman Wisdom and Benny Hill that autumn – and, in addition, Bill Ward asked if I'd like to take on a 90-minute slot for a Christmas special, "Fill it any way you like – but let me know what you're thinking of doing."

In an emergency, send for Dickie Henderson and Jimmy Grafton. I turned to my trusty buddies once again, and we devised a story-line show called *A Santa for Christmas*, the plot for which couldn't have been simpler. Dickie's agent phones on Christmas Eve to say that the artiste he'd booked to perform as Father Christmas the following day at a big charity children's party has fallen ill and Dickie has got to help out by deputising for him. Only problem: aforesaid performer's Father Christmas costume is miles too big: Dickie has 24 hours to get hold of a new one. And we followed his attempts to track down a costume that would fit him: at his friends' houses, at other people's Christmas Eve parties, at the costumiers, rehearsal rooms, film sets, theatres, anywhere you might hope to find a Santa Claus suit on Christmas Eve and, of course, anywhere we could find a legitimate reason for introducing musical numbers, comedy routines and performers playing themselves. We even looked for a Santa suit in Jack Solomons's gym – it seemed perfectly logical at the time – where Freddie Mills was able to use his contacts to gather together half a dozen other past and present British boxing champions for us, and where I was able to tell Jack, now a television host with his own boxing archive show, how much my father and I had enjoyed those Sundays at the Devonshire Sporting Club twenty years previously.

A Santa for Christmas was an extremely complicated show. Apart from anything else, the studio schedules couldn't accommodate a 90-minute production and we had to borrow the studios and audiences of a couple of other shows to record some of our sequences after they themselves had wrapped: an added delight for those audiences but an additional headache for my Production Assistant, who had enough of a problem organising the rest of the show as well as the *Palladium* Sundays and the *Saturday Spectaculars*. I thought I'd make it up to her with a screen credit which, against all custom and regulation my special pleading finally managed to achieve, so that Audrey Maclean was the first – and for some time the only – P.A. ever to receive on-screen recognition.

All the hard work in that first year at ATV was worthwhile. I still have the handwritten note received after the transmission of *A Santa for Christmas*: "Dear Brian, My very sincere 'Congrats' on the Santa Show. It was truly a wonderful effort and for my money the best thing of its kind I have ever seen on T.V. <u>ANYWHERE</u>. Thanks. Val Parnell." And at the Television Ball and Dinner at the Dorchester given by The Guild of Television Producers and Directors – the predecessor of The British Academy of Film and Television Arts – I was the first recipient of their award for Production-Light Entertainment, which in 1957 joined Production-Drama and Production-Factual as a category eligible for the one-eyed bronze Mitzi Cunliffe mask which became internationally recognised as the BAFTA Award. Rudolph Cartier was the winner for Production-Drama and Donald Baverstock and the Production Team of *Tonight* for Production-Factual. Robin Day won the Award for TV Personality of the Year, Michael Hordern for Actor-Drama and Tony Hancock for Artist-Light Entertainment. It was a great honour to be in their company.

All my studio shows that year and throughout my years at ATV, with one exception, were produced at the Wood Green Empire in North London. The exception was three Sally Ann Howes Shows in 1959 under Val Parnell's *Saturday Spectacular* banner at the Hackney Empire, one of the music halls in which I had spent so many happy hours before the war. Twenty years later, the theatre was instantly familiar the minute I walked through its foyer, although the seats my parents and I used to occupy were now covered by the studio floor which extended from the stage through the entire stalls area. ATV's Stoll-Moss company owned the Empire circuit and it had been quicker and easier to convert some of their theatres – New Cross Empire was another – than build new television studios from scratch. Wood Green, Hackney and New Cross, together with the Shepherds Bush Empire, which the BBC had converted to its own Television Theatre a few years earlier, were all custom-built as music halls for the great Victorian theatre impresarios Sir Edward Moss and Sir Oswald Stoll, whose rival companies merged in 1898.

Like the London Palladium, the London Coliseum, the Victoria Palace and 200 other Stoll-Moss theatres throughout London and the United Kingdom, they were designed by the remarkable architect Frank Matcham, whose skill and style could make an auditorium of any size feel warm and intimate. That was certainly the case with Wood Green, even after its conversion. Like the Hackney Empire, Wood Green's stage was extended out over the stalls to provide a studio floor as large as any of the BBC's. The audience was confined to the Circle, which enabled them to see over the cameras and microphone booms; and the control room and orchestra room were both tucked in under the Circle within easy reach of the studio floor and each other: here was one production gallery to and from which you didn't have to run up and down flights of stairs.

I still treasure the memory of my first Wood Green band call, walking into the band room to be greeted by ATV's then Musical Director, Geraldo. Gerry was one of our best known band leaders and had led his own orchestra in the smartest West End night clubs and on radio and television for decades. Now he was about to rehearse the music for our first Dickie Henderson *Spectacular*, suave, elegantly dressed as always, welcoming smile on his face, baton in hand, and black brilliantined hair combed back over his head — which was crowned with a *hairnet*. Practical and efficient as ever, Gerry was not going to allow the constant taking off and putting on of his headphones to muss up that magnificent mane.

There was just time, before the new season of the *Palladium* show to make my first trip to New York to study American television, courtesy of Teddy Sommerfield's ingenious contract negotiation. It was a magical fortnight. The majestic old Plaza Hotel on Central Park was both my base and, for quite a lot of the time, my viewing room, since much of network television — particularly comedy shows like Jack Benny's and Lucille Ball's — had already made the move to film and the Hollywood studios. But I was able to sit in on the production of most of the live shows still emanating from New York, including *The Ed Sullivan Show* from CBS's Studio 50 on West 57th Street; Perry Como's *Kraft Music Hall* and Jack Paar's late night chat show from the NBC studios in Rockefeller Centre; and the early morning *Today Show* with Dave Garroway and his chimpanzee side-kick J. Fred Muggs, from the glass-fronted studio in RCA's Exhibition Hall a block down from the Centre.

I envied the production skills I saw, particularly the camerawork. I was appalled by the biliously fluctuating quality of the NTSC colour TV transmissions just being introduced (the National Television System Committee's initials popularly standing for Never Twice the Same Colour). I admired Jack

Paar's charm and the number of A List celebrities prepared to turn up for a little late night conversation; and I made a particular note of the amiably casual Garroway show with its audience of passers-by and out-of-towners on the other side of the studio's glass wall.

Five years later, at ABC TV, I introduced British television's own late night chat show with Eamonn Andrews – "*Live from London!*" – the forerunner of every subsequent home-grown chat show from Michael Parkinson to Graham Norton. And at Thames Television, six years later still, Eamonn Andrews and Bill Grundy (without the assistance of a chimpanzee) presented London's own daily news and entertainment *Today* show from a specially constructed glass-fronted studio on the corner of Kingsway and the Aldwych. Not for long, unfortunately: the Metropolitan Police closed us down because our outdoor audience of tourists and passers-by declined to pass by and caused a major obstruction. The London panorama visible through a glass-walled studio was too interesting to pass up, however: it was adopted by the local news programmes at London Weekend and for many years remained the backdrop for the London newscasts of ITV.

Happily, the 1957 season on Broadway was the setting for one of the periodic flowerings of the great American musical; and, through Teddy Sommerfield's contacts with U.S. music publishers, I was fortunate enough on this trip to see the original Broadway productions of now classic shows like *West Side Story*, *My Fair Lady*, and *Bells Are Ringing*. I also managed to catch some of the musicals that never made it to Shaftesbury Avenue, like Harold Arlen's *Jamaica*, with Lena Horne, and *Happy Hunting*, with Ethel Merman, whose now legendary status was marked at this and apparently every other performance by a standing ovation when she walked on, as well as at the final curtain.

I flew back to London very much aware of my good fortune; and even more aware of it the next day. Before I left New York I had treated myself to the traditional American shave, haircut and shoe-shine in the hotel barber shop. Next morning, the notorious Albert Anastasia, boss and chief executioner of the crime syndicate Murder Inc., chose to do the same – in the same barber shop and, as I like to tell it, in the same barber's chair. Two contract killers burst in and shot him dead. I was dark and Italianate-looking and about the same size and shape as Anastasia...what if the killers had got their dates wrong?

New Looks

Sunday Night at the London Palladium was still one of ATV's most successful shows; but after two 39-week long seasons it was beginning to look tired. Its centre section, *Beat the Clock*, a game show featuring contestants from the theatre audience who were challenged to perform various knockabout physical tasks against the clock for quite valuable prizes, was still popular, and the variety bill that constituted the rest of the show was by no means run-of-the mill − its artistes were still the best and biggest available. But its format had become routine, its novelty and glamour were fading, and its compere, Tommy Trinder, another of my pre-war show-business idols, whose cheeky cockney patter had been one of the show's principal strengths at its outset, now alas seemed old hat.

So, when Val Parnell asked me to take over the show at the beginning of the autumn season, I said I would want to make some changes. "Like what?" "Well, for a start, I'd like to bring in the Tiller Girls to give the show some spectacle − nothing like a line of glamorous high-kicking girl dancers to open a show." "Agreed. What else?" "I'd... I know he's been great for the show in his time, but I think he's wrong for it now, so... I'd like to drop Tommy." Pause. "Agreed."

What I didn't know until much later was that Val and Tommy had had a falling-out and Val himself was contemplating dropping Tommy, so I had just pushed at a wide-open door. "And who do you want to replace him?" "Well, no one, to start with. I'd like to try out various comperes, a month at a time, let them bring their own style to the show; and I'd like to integrate them into the show a bit more − you know, let them do little routines with some of the artistes if they agree and if there's time to rehearse. And we can see how they work, how the audience and the critics react, and pick the best of them to take over as permanent compere next year." Longer pause. "And who do you have in mind to kick off for the first four weeks?" "Dickie Henderson." "Now why did I think you'd say that? OK with me. Good luck."

The audience and the critics reacted exactly as we had hoped. The Tiller Girls were a sensation – even today, those who still remember the original Sunday night show think it featured the Tillers from its very beginning and not two years later. Dickie was at his best; and we were fortunate enough to have both Harry Secombe and Shani Wallis in the opening show, both of them available during the previous week to rehearse a neatly integrated song and dance routine which stopped the show and got the season off to the best possible start. Each of the succeeding guest comperes – Bob Monkhouse, Hughie Green, Alfred Marks and – an off-beat choice suggested by the Grade agency who represented him, Robert Morley – brought something fresh to the show.

Morley, the large, portly West End straight actor, was a particular and most unexpected success, taking the line that he didn't know who any of the people he was introducing were, or what they did, or indeed what on earth he was doing in the show in the first place. The audience, both at home and in the theatre, found him hilarious and we had to bring him back for a second month later in the run. Dickie and Bob, the most popular of the other guest comperes, also made repeat appearances; but the idea of trying out guest comperes until we found a permanent successor to Tommy Trinder was too successful for its own good: all these seasoned performers had shows and careers of their own which they weren't prepared to put aside for a long-term commitment to the Palladium. The search continued. So did the Tesler-Maclean work-load.

The Palladium season ended at the end of June 1958. Bill Ward asked us to cover some of its summer replacement weeks at the Prince of Wales Theatre before we returned to the Palladium again in the autumn. New venue, new impresario, new opening titles – *Bernard Delfont Presents... Sunday Night at The Prince of Wales* – same star-studded variety bill, but no *Beat the Clock*. So, apart from our own summer break, 1958 saw Audrey and me working every Sunday at the Palladium or the Prince Of Wales and most months at Wood Green Empire for one *Saturday Spectacular* or another, first with Dickie Henderson, who made his last show with us in March before going off to Jack Hylton, and then with the hugely popular comedian Dave King, whom ATV had lured away from the BBC.

ATV certainly got its money's worth out of the two of us. It worked because this particular producer and his P.A. were more than happy to be together most of the time, working late at the office on camera scripts, sorting out caption requirements, props and wardrobe lists over dinner, looking for acts over a drink at a nightclub – the two of us together with Dickie Henderson were thrown out of Edmundo Ros's one night by Edmundo himself for sitting through his lavish cabaret with only a glass of wine and a cup of coffee each.

My second New York trip managed to squeeze itself in before the Palladium season began. I watched more TV shows, both in and out of my hotel room, and saw more Broadway musicals, among them *The Music Man* with Robert Preston and Frank Loesser's *Most Happy Fella*; but I also had another preoccupation. Teddy Sommerfield had negotiated a commission from the pop-music journal *Disc* for me to write a weekly column about the American music scene under the title of Broadway Melody. As a result, I had to pay a little closer attention to Peter Potter's West Coast disc jockey show, Alan Freed's *The Big Beat* and the daily *Rate the Records*. None of them, I thought, markedly superior to the BBC's *Six-Five Special*. I drove down to Philadelphia to see Dick Clark's *American Bandstand* in action, spent two stomping rhythm and blues evenings at Harlem's fabulous Apollo Theatre, and interviewed Elvis Presley's music publisher Freddy Bienstock and some of the other denizens of Broadway's famous Brill Building, a sort of vertical Tin Pan Alley crammed with the offices of music publishers and song pluggers.

I also indulged myself – and I hope intrigued my readers – with seeing and hearing live performances by some of the jazz musicians whose genius I had known through the years only on gramophone records: Errol Garner, in a recording session at Leidercrantz Hall; Count Basie and his orchestra at Birdland; a couple of sets of Bobby Hackett's little Dixieland Band at the Henry Hudson Hotel; and several nights at the 30ft long bar of the Metropole Café, listening to the music of great jazzmen of the past like Henry Red Allen, Buster Bailey and Cozy Cole, strung out in single file on a narrow platform behind the bar where the bottles usually go.

I was also fortunate enough, at a party in Freddy Bienstock's penthouse apartment, to meet another celebrated black jazz musician of the past,

Willie 'The Lion' Smith, who was entertaining Freddy's guests at the piano, signature derby hat tipped on his head and giant cigar in the corner of his mouth. Sitting beside him on the piano stool during a bourbon break, I discovered that The Lion was a great Anglophile and wanted to know all about my East End background, after which he proceeded to perform Fats Waller's "Squeeze Me" in my honour in authentic Yiddish. That was one of the more bizarre Broadway Melodies I was able to report to the gentle readers of *Disc* before I took my long Comet flight back to the UK.

The search for a new permanent compere for *Sunday Night at the London Palladium* ended that year, somewhat to my cost. I wanted to do another kind of show, something different from the Palladium, a studio show at Wood Green featuring new talent. Not a talent show with a succession of acts, but a revue with a regular team of attractive young all-round entertainers who could sing and dance and perform sketches specially written for the show. There was no shortage of suggestions for such performers, from friends in the business as well as the talent agencies who got wind of the project. I remember auditioning a young Des O'Connor and a double act one half of which was an even younger Roy Hudd – this was, after all, well over 50 years ago; the *Daily Mirror*'s Clifford Davis drove me down to Oxford to see a 24-year old newcomer called Roy Castle in Dickie Valentine's show at the New Theatre – good to be back there without an Isis deadline to meet; and Dickie Henderson suggested I caught the act of a gangly young comic called Bruce Forsyth, who was wowing the audience at the Chiswick Empire.

I finally booked what I thought would make a well balanced team: Roy and Bruce, the double act of Joe Baker and Jack Douglas, revue artistes Ronnie Stevens, Stephanie Voss and Gillian Moran, and Joyce Blair, a bubbly young star of the West End musical *Grab Me A Gondola*. I added Joyce's brother Lionel as choreographer and the Vernons Girls, a choir of attractive girl singers who could dance well enough to help out in the production numbers. The Girls had already appeared on BBC radio and television and Jack Good's rock and roll shows for ABC TV, and I could never understand how they got past the broadcasting authorities because they were, by definition, a walking, talking, singing promotion for Vernons football pools, for whom they all worked; but who was I to raise an eyebrow?

According to Mark Lewisohn's *Guide*, "*New Look* was undoubtedly an outstanding success – even before it went on the air." That's because when I showed the pilot programme to Val and Lew, Val immediately added Roy

Castle to that November's *Royal Variety Performance* and wanted Bruce Forsyth to take over as the permanent compere of *Sunday Night at the London Palladium*. I suggested we try Bruce out with a six-minute spot the following Sunday to see how he took to the Palladium stage. As was apparent to everybody who saw that spot, Bruce didn't just take to the Palladium stage: he took it over. The audience loved his bossy, fussy personality and the following January he began a run as the Palladium show's presenter that lasted four years and led to a career that has endured more than five decades and still counting.

We lost Bruce from *New Look* after three editions, but the team was strong enough to continue its popular and critical success. The show also kick-started Roy Castle's brilliant but too short career. Lionel Blair moved over to take Bruce's place as Roy's tap-dancing partner in a series of stunning routines and began his career as an all-round performer, not just a dance director: when I began writing this memoir he was preparing a tour of his one-man song, dance and chat show after playing Sir Peter Teazle in Sheridan's *School for Scandal* at the Edinburgh Festival. And a young paint salesman called Jeremy Lloyd, recruited by Jimmy Grafton for the *New Look* writing team, was persuaded by me to use his lanky physique and silly-ass style in some of our comedy sketches. He went on to co-write *Are You Being Served?* and *'Allo 'Allo!* for BBC Television and appear in British and American TV series and movies ranging from *The Avengers* to *Laugh In*, from *Goodbye Mr Chips* to *Those Magnificent Men in Their Flying Machines*. He also married Joanna Lumley. *New Look* had nothing to do with that.

Leaving ATV

After seeing Bruce comfortably settled in at the Palladium I handed the show over to my successor Albert Locke. It had been a joy to work on, not just for the pleasure of meeting and working however briefly with artistes ranging from Markova to Mario Lanza, from a very young Woody Allen to a much older but still vibrant Gracie Fields, but also because that Sunday experience was an extraordinary mix of the glamorous, the practical and the downright homely.

The Palladium was a working theatre, with its own weekday variety shows, summer revues and Christmas pantomimes, so the scenery and props of the current show had to be cleared overnight after its Saturday evening performance for our own scenery to be brought in and hung. On Sunday morning our Outside Broadcast van would park by the Palladium's Stage Door in Ramillies Place, the camera crew would bring in the unit's cameras, and the morning would come alive with the noise and bustle of setting the scenery, testing the sound and organising the lighting, while the orchestra and musical director ran through the music for the night's show with the artistes: the singers with their immaculately maintained scores, the jugglers and acrobats with their music cues on dog-eared bits of manuscript. People dropped in on the Band Call: Val Parnell and his twinkling middle-aged secretary Miss Wood – "Woody" – with her customary bag of sweets for the control room crew; a 13-year old Michael Grade with his father Leslie; agents, music publishers, song-pluggers.

Val Parnell's barber, Jack Lee, from his hairdressing establishment at the Piccadilly Hotel, would set up his barber's chair in one of the dressing-rooms, available for other customers after Mr Parnell had had his weekly trim. I jumped at the opportunity since there was no time to have a haircut during the week, and Jack became my own hairdresser too until he retired. A snack lunch in the Palladium's Tudor Bar with Val Parnell and Woody – Audrey was usually too busy with cue scripts and organisational detail for anything other than a sandwich. Then, in the afternoon, a walk-through for cameras and lighting of the scene changes, the stunts for *Beat the Clock*, the Tiller Girls' routine, the occasional sketch and any other complicated bit of business.

The Outside Broadcast Unit was restricted to four cameras, two of which were static, side by side on a platform at the back of the stalls so that long shots, mid shots and close ups could be on the same eye line. A mobile camera on a pedestal dolly was positioned in the prompt corner of the stage and could only vary its shots by coming out of the wings to roam behind or beside the performers, which was distracting for the theatre audience and perilous for the director because of the risk of its getting into the shots of the other two. The fourth camera was mounted on a tracking dolly which was usually positioned in one of the aisles. Their coverage was necessarily limited, which was what had helped make the show appear tired by the end of its second year. On a big light entertainment show today a director could have at his disposal as many as ten cameras. In 1957 you were limited to four, so I worked out some variations with the designer and camera crew to make our coverage look more enterprising for the viewers, more interesting for us and less distracting for the theatre audience.

We built up quite a repertoire. A section of black gauze was designed into the scenery or cloth at the back of the stage, through which our pedestal camera could give us wonderfully atmospheric shots of the audience and auditorium from behind the artistes, particularly effective when the Tiller line was high-kicking its way to and from the footlights. There might have been only four cameras, but the O.B. van carried a spare pedestal dolly, so during the commercial breaks the camera crew would take the camera off the tracking dolly and rush it to wherever we had placed the spare, and suddenly we had brand new shots of the stage, from the Royal Box, the back of the Dress Circle or way up in the gods. We placed an eight-foot high mirror at an angle in the wings on one side of the stage and shot its reflections from the wings on the prompt side, so that we had in effect a camera covering the performers from both sides – as long as we remembered to reverse the right to left mirror image in our stage camera: at a function a few weeks after we featured the Johnny Dankworth Band, Johnny's trombonist, Jackie Armstrong, told me his friends had ribbed him mercilessly about his appearing to play his trombone left-handed on the show.

As for the glamorous part of the *Sunday Palladium* experience, it really was an extraordinary thrill when the theatre's house lights went up and the audience started filing into Frank Matcham's beautifully designed auditorium, buzzing with excitement and anticipation. All the last-minute changes and checks had been made, you'd wished good luck to the artistes, the crew and the stage staff, you'd exchanged your sweater for a shirt and jacket and tie, and five minutes or so before the show went on the air, you took a deep breath and walked out into the spotlight, onto the Palladium stage, for the audience warm-up.

Nowadays at a light entertainment show, it's usually the job of a professional entertainer to get the audience into a good mood and explain some of the technicalities of what it's about to see. In those days, the producer usually did the warm-up himself, and there was no finer forum in which to do it than the London Palladium. When you walked out onto that stage to enthusiastic applause – the audience didn't know who on earth you were, but you were obviously *someone*; when you introduced yourself, the orchestra, the Musical Director and the Stage Manager to even warmer applause; when you got your laughs from two and a half thousand appreciative theatregoers with time-honoured warm-up lines like "Remember, the camera will be on *you* from time to time, so if you're sitting next to someone you *shouldn't* be sitting next to...." or "There's two minutes to go, so if you *want* to...", you understood why performers considered the Palladium the best variety theatre in the world in which to work. And then you dashed out of the theatre, climbed into the O.B. van's control room, grabbed a handful of Woody's sweets, and cued the orchestra for the show's opening theme. For a ham like me, still missing the kick of performing to a cabaret or revue audience, it was pure magic.

New Look ended in June of 1959; so did my professional partnership with Audrey. I had asked her to marry me and after our holiday break she handed in her notice and turned her P.A skills to finding and organising a home for us. I lost the best Production Assistant in the business and gained the best wife. In the six months before she left, we worked not only on *New Look* but also on at least one *Saturday Spectacular* a month – Mark Lewisohn's *Guide* records three in February alone, with Dave King, Arthur Askey and

Harry Secombe. Looking for a flat must have seemed like a rest cure by comparison; and though the P.A.s who replaced her were first-rate the pressures were beginning to tell on me, too. The Dave King, Arthur Askey and Harry Secombe shows continued to the end of the year. And Lew asked if I'd like to come up with an idea to feature the West End's latest showbiz venture, Bernard Delfont's Talk of the Town. How could I refuse?

Audrey and I were married in October at Caxton Hall, in a ceremony that might have come straight out of a comedy sketch: the Registrar had a twisty, whiny voice like Pa Kettle in the Ma and Pa Kettle movies, and the two of us and most of our witnesses choked with suppressed laughter throughout the proceedings. Our honeymoon was in Paris, and by the time we had had our long, chatty, autumn walks in the Bois de Boulogne we had agreed that I would reduce my work-load pressure and go freelance when my contract was up at the end of the year. That way, I could pick the shows I wanted to produce, and if I chose to work as hard as I was doing at ATV I would at least be paid commensurately: we had a home to find and furnish and hopefully a family to start. I had also decided on a format for the *Talk of the Town* show and composed the music for its opening titles – as always, in my head: I never could read or write music, alas, and Kenny Powell, the rehearsal pianist on all my ATV shows, would have to follow my Oxford collaborators in writing the music down for me.

Bernard Delfont and restaurateur Charles Forte had acquired the lease of another of Frank Matcham's marvels, the London Hippodrome, a vast auditorium in the heart of the West End, and converted it into a theatre restaurant – the biggest in the world, their publicity claimed, with 40 cooks and 100 waiters catering for more than 200 diners. The Talk of the Town was certainly impressive. The diners sat at glamorously lit tables round an expansive dance floor. Two orchestras played alternating dance sets on a band rostrum which would split down the middle every half hour for the two halves to glide to each side of the stage and, with each half-orchestra still playing the change-over melody, slowly descend, while another rostrum slid gently forward from the back of the stage with the other orchestra seamlessly continuing the change-over melody in its own characteristic rhythm. Almost worth the price of entry just to witness this operation – but that wasn't all. For the floorshows, Sydney Simone and his house orchestra played a suitably dramatic overture as the dance floor itself descended 20 feet and came up again to form a stage, four feet higher than before, dressed with gorgeous showgirls while more equally gorgeous showgirls descended from the ceiling on an exotically decorated bridge to join them. The two spectacular floorshows were devised by Robert Nesbitt, the leading theatrical producer of the day: you always got your money's worth with Mr Nesbitt.

Our outside broadcast cameras would cover part of one of the floorshows in the first half of our programme and a big name cabaret act or two in the second; and, while the diners danced to the music of Sydney Simone and the Hermanos Deniz Cuban Rhythm Band during the rest of the hour, we would interview celebrity guests at their tables enjoying their night out. Well, that was the idea; and it seemed a good one at the time; but the logistics were murderously difficult. Night clubs are noisy, bustling places; our cameras and microphones were cabled and cumbersome and difficult to manoeuvre through the happy crowd of diners, dancers, waiters and guests. Live TV shows are irresistible to gremlins, and ours abounded with them. My unthinking cockiness just about got away with it, but I had perilously over-reached myself. I should have waited another twenty years for the arrival of cable-free microphones and hand-held cameras.

There seemed one bright personal aspect to this near-debacle. The two Talk of the Town bandleaders liked the show's title tune so much that they used it for their change-over music every half-hour, and not just on our show night. It cheered me, just a little, to hear that tune morph from fox trot to rumba and back again every time the orchestras switched places. Every night! Not just during the TV show, but *every night*! The Performing Rights royalties would be huge! When they failed to make an appearance on my royalty statements I asked my music publishers, Southern Music, how come? They referred me to ATV's Copyright Department, whose Head cheerfully announced that since I had written the music on ATV time the royalties belonged to ATV. I didn't have the heart to argue.

I told Teddy Sommerfield that I planned to go freelance when my ATV contract came to an end. "Good idea", he said, "but don't do anything in a hurry. You're tired. Take a couple of months off. I'll talk to a few people, see what kind of freelance work might be out there for you, and come back with some suggestions." "That's fine", I said, "but what are we going to live on? No work, no salary; and I have no savings to speak of." "Yes you do" said Teddy. "The manager of the Vernons Girls was so pleased with the exposure you gave them that he wanted to give you a really expensive gift as a mark of appreciation. I told him that wasn't necessary but if he really wanted to show his appreciation he might like to put a little something in a deposit account for you every time you used the Girls. You did twelve shows with them and he put £50 into a deposit account in your name each time, so that account now holds £600. Plus interest. That's a bit more than two months of your current salary. That should be enough to tide you over while I find you some freelance work." Does it count as Payola if you haven't the faintest idea you're receiving it?

When I told Val and Lew and Bill Ward that I intended to go freelance at the end of my contract they said they hoped I would continue to do some work with ATV in my new capacity. I said I very much hoped so too and Teddy Sommerfield would be talking to them about it. I went back to *Talk of the Town* and my remaining *Saturday Spectaculars*, Dave King in November and Arthur Askey in December. The final edition of *Talk of the Town* was on New Year's Eve. We finished the show at 10.30pm. I had an hour and a half of free time before my contract expired. Happy New Year!

Entering ABC

B efore I could make my farewells at ATV, Teddy Sommerfield had lined up two six-month freelance contracts for me, one with ATV, one with the BBC. All that was needed to clinch the deals was for me to agree dates and projects with Bill Ward and, at the BBC, Eric Maschwitz, now its Head of Light Entertainment. I asked Teddy if that could wait until Audrey and I returned from a week's break in Yorkshire with her family. Teddy said "Fine, but before you go, do me a favour and go and see Howard Thomas at ABC. He keeps phoning, says he wants to talk to you about something – probably some freelance project or other – but he won't tell me what it is and he keeps calling, every day. Do me a favour and get him off my back."

In 1955, the Independent Television Authority had divided the United Kingdom into a network of fourteen regions in which four major programme companies of approximately equal strength were committed to supply the bulk of the network programme schedule to ten smaller regional companies, which filled the remainder of their airtime with programmes of local interest. The smaller companies, whose names proudly proclaimed their regional identities, were Southern, Television Wales and the West, Westward, Ulster, Tyne Tees, Grampian, Border, Scottish and Anglia. The roll call would be completed in 1962, when Channel Television and West & North Wales – Teledu Cymru – would go on air.

The four major companies were based in London, the Midlands, and the North; and, since a single London company would have been dispro-portionately large and powerful, the network had been constructed roughly to balance their strength in terms of potential audience and advertising revenue. Associated-Rediffusion was awarded the contract for London weekdays; ATV for weekends in London and weekdays in the Midlands; Granada Television for weekdays in the North; and ABC for weekends in both the North and the Midlands. Crazy the quilt might have seemed, but it worked and it would hold together for the next thirteen years.

ABC TV was the smallest of the majors and the last to be granted a franchise – by default, as it happened. When the Authority was still in its planning stage, Howard Thomas had urged his company, the Associated British Picture Corporation, to apply for a franchise; and the ITA had actually offered them a provisional contract for seven days in the Midlands. But, wary of a medium which they considered a threat to their business as cinema proprietors and film producers, the ABPC Board had turned the offer down. The programme company formed by impresario Maurice Winnick and Press baron Lord Kemsley had been awarded the franchise for weekends in the North and Midlands, but it broke up in disarray only seven months before its opening night in Birmingham, and the ITA let it be known that an application from ABPC to take over the franchise would be welcomed. They also promised the company part of the £750,000 set aside by the Government if Independent Television should fail, so ABPC's bet would be helpfully hedged.

This time Howard Thomas had C. J. Latta on his side, and C. J. had muscle. Warner Brothers, the Hollywood film company, owned a substantial piece of ABPC and had appointed C. J., an Anglophile American, as its representative on the Board and Managing Director. Together, he and Howard Thomas persuaded the rest of the Board to change their mind about television – more or less on the basis that if we think we can't beat it, let's join it – and ABPC signed its franchise contract the night before ITV's London opening.

They had five months to get on the air in Birmingham, eight to opening in Manchester. There were a few advantages to entering the race at such a late stage. The equipment was immediately available: they simply bought it from Kemsley-Winnick at a discount. ATV also needed a studio in the Midlands to service their weekday franchise and they were happy to form a joint company with ABC – Alpha Television – to operate it, converting the Astoria cinema in the Birmingham suburb of Aston into a TV studio. As a result, ABC were spared the costs of lengthy preparation which their fellow majors had had to bear. But the pool of available production talent had been more or less scooped by the time they started recruiting and they had found it difficult to prise their way into a weekend network programme schedule which had been commandeered by ATV's home-grown television film series like *The Adventures of Robin Hood* and its big light entertainment guns.

ABC had managed it with one show: Sunday Night's *Armchair Theatre*. The legendary drama producer Dennis Vance had originated this – I should perhaps say 'legendary drama producer and impresario' since, in my tattered copy of the *TV Times* for 26 January 1958, under the *Armchair Theatre* header the programme billing has "Dennis Vance presents" above both the names of the stars and the title of the play. Later in 1958 Denis had been promoted to another position within the ABC Corporation and had suggested Canadian producer Sydney Newman as his successor. Telerecordings of Sydney's productions for the Canadian Broadcasting Corporation had been shown by the BBC to great acclaim and he had been invited over to Britain to discuss his forthcoming productions with its drama department.

While he was here Dennis persuaded him to come and talk to Howard Thomas, and Howard offered him the job of running ABC's Drama Department and producing *Armchair Theatre*. Sydney had trained in North American television's Golden Age of live drama and he brought with him to ABC its fast-moving, flexible camera-work and emphasis on new writing and new writers dealing with contemporary subjects. The subsequent influence of Sydney's *Armchair Theatre* on the style and content of British television drama was prodigious.

However, apart from Jack Good's ground-breaking rock shows *Oh Boy!*, *Boy Meets Girls* and *Wham!* – shows which would disappear with Jack's departure to the States – ABC's remaining contributions to the network seemed more or less restricted to outside broadcast coverage of sport and religious services and a weekly television youth club programme of music and chat called *The Sunday Break*. The period between 6.15 pm and 7.00 pm on Sunday evening was one of the few periods still closed to broadcasting, the legislators believing in this particular case that television would affect church service attendances. However, Howard Thomas had persuaded the ITA that *The Sunday Break* could legitimately fill what became generally known as the Closed Period because the chat would include serious discussion of religion and morals between the young club members and religious leaders of all denominations. Howard was clearly not short of either ideas or the powers of persuasion, but what kind of freelance work could he offer me?

A musical drama or two to fill an *Armchair Theatre* slot? A more ambitious light entertainment input to *The Sunday Break*?

I met him in ABC's offices in Hanover Square. Brisk, burly, broad-shouldered, with thick-lensed horn-rimmed spectacles; not a showman like Val Parnell or an agent like Lew Grade, but a media man, with a background in journalism, advertising, radio and cinema newsreels. Now he was running a television programme company seemingly single-handed: ABC appeared not to possess a Controller of Production like Bill Ward at ATV or John McMillan at Associated-Rediffusion. So what freelance work was he about to offer me?

Nothing.

Nothing at all.

"How old are you?" he asked. "Thirty." "That's getting on for a light entertainment producer, isn't it? I like your work; I think it's excellent; but you don't want to do that for the rest of your life. Isn't it time you settled down and started to tell others what to do? I want you to join ABC as our Supervisor of Features and Light Entertainment. I've got Sydney Newman supervising Drama and David Southwood up in Manchester in charge of our Outside Broadcasts. You'd be in charge of everything else. Free hand. Answerable only to me. What do you say?"

What could I say? "Um. Er. Well, that's very flattering, and I admit I've thought about moving on to being a programme executive some time in the future, but not yet. I've been a producer for only seven years and I enjoy it, and there are lots of things I want to do and artistes I want to work with. So, thank you very much, but No Thanks."

Howard Thomas went into his persuasive mode. I told him it was impractical anyway: I had some major freelance contracts lined up. "No, they aren't signed yet but I couldn't let ATV and the BBC down; look, I'm going up to Yorkshire for a break tomorrow and I don't want – all right, I'll think about it while I'm up there, but I really don't... yes, I'll call you when I get back." "Excellent. Let me have your telephone number in case I need to get in touch."

And get in touch he did, 48 hours after Audrey and I had arrived at her parents' house in Sleights. "I've talked to my Board and they're delighted that you're interested in joining us." "But I'm not interested, as I told you. Not yet, anyway." "Tell you what, why don't you just come down and meet them, have lunch with us, take a look at our brand new studio in Teddington – you'll love it, state of the art, not a converted theatre – what can you lose?"

So I did. I drove back down to our little basement flat in Knightsbridge; I was chauffeured to Teddington to look at what had been a film studio owned by Warner Brothers; and I joined the Associated Picture Corporation Board at their Golden Square headquarters for lunch after their monthly Board Meeting. I was welcomed by the tall, diffident Chairman Sir Philip Warter, the Deputy Chairman Robert Clark, the large and ebullient Managing Director C. J. Latta and the rest of the Corporation's Directors who ran the ABPC studios at Elstree, the Associated British Newsreel division and the ABC cinemas throughout the U.K. I smoked a big Havana cigar along with them all as we talked TV and movie business after lunch, and yes, of course, it was flattering and alluring and I began to think "Well, why not?"

Why Not?

I was perfectly aware why not. I'd been a television producer for only seven years and it was the only profession I knew. I would miss the sheer fun of it; the thrilling danger of a live production; the exhilaration of seeing something come off – an elaborate production number, a piece of technical trickery, a complicated comedy sketch – something I'd assiduously planned and rehearsed – live, on air. I would even miss the gripe of apprehension that used to hit my stomach like a knife before every show.

I would miss the skilled and talented professionals I'd been fortunate enough to work with: the writers, artistes, dancers, choreographers, musicians, Musical Directors. I'd miss the buzz of the rehearsal room and the camaraderie of the control room. I'd miss the expertise and ingenuity of the designers, the lighting directors, the sound and camera crews and everybody else on the studio floor, though heaven knows I'd tested their patience and loyalty enough times. I still felt guilty about the effort the camera crew had to devote to lining up the multi-level overlay sequence for a *Dickie Henderson Show* in which the dancers' silhouettes, curled into the shape of notes on a page of sheet music, sprang into life and danced up and down around and along the staves of the Benny Goodman arrangement of "Bach Goes To Town". I still winced at the hard labour required of the caption operators for "Stop, Look and Listen", the production number in a *Harry Secombe Show* in which Lionel Blair was overlaid onto scores of carefully calibrated caption cards to create the illusion of his dancing with the cartoon figure of a giant white rabbit, the caption operators changing the cards on their caption easels in time with the music while I cut between them. No computer-generated trickery in those days!

And I still felt hot with shame at the memory of the totally deserved reprimand I had received from the senior cameraman on a *Saturday Spectacular* when, in order for Audrey and me to attend the wedding of Ronnie Stevens, one of our *New Look* stars, I was cocky enough to think I could get away with cancelling the Friday camera rehearsal for the show and cram all the rehearsals into Saturday. We did get away with it, just about; but after the show the crew's senior cameraman, Johnny Glenister, strode into the control room to say "I want you to know that this has been the most unprofessional behaviour I have ever experienced. You had no right to cancel Friday's rehearsals. You knew the risk you were running on an under-rehearsed live show. It could have been disastrous. You should be ashamed of yourself." And I was.

Many years later at some industry function, when I found myself face to face with Johnny, by then *John* Glenister, a highly regarded drama director in his own right and father of two fine professional actors, Robert and Philip Glenister, I told him how effective his rebuke had been, how right he was to have bawled me out and how guilty I'd felt all those years over that particular *Saturday Spectacular*. John said "Sorry, old love. Which rebuke? What *Saturday Spectacular*?" He had absolutely no recollection of it. But it was a salutary lesson for me, so thanks anyway, Johnny: I like to think it finally put to rest the cockiness that Nevill Coghill at Oxford and Ronnie Waldman at the BBC had spotted in me.

There were more persuasive calls from Howard Thomas. I began to think that taking on the responsibility of running an entire features and light entertainment output more or less from scratch would be a tempting, even an exciting challenge. And perhaps I wouldn't have to miss production after all. Bill Ward at ATV managed to run his company's total programme output and still combine it with TV productions of the Moscow State Circus. Why couldn't I combine it with the occasional big show? I had long discussions about the offer with Audrey and Teddy Sommerfield. And I accepted it.

While Teddy negotiated a contract with Howard Thomas I wrote to Eric Maschwitz at the BBC and Val Parnell, Lew Grade and Bill Ward at ATV to explain why I wouldn't be taking up their freelance work. I had amicable replies from Eric Maschwitz – "You must do what suits you best and with some trepidation I wish you the best of luck in the new job" – and from

Kenneth Adam, who had succeeded Cecil McGivern as BBC Television's Controller of Programmes – "I was sorry to hear the news, glad to have your letter, and hope that one day we may work together." Val and Lew wrote to wish me luck. Bill didn't reply and wouldn't take my calls. I learned from a mutual friend that he considered my move from ATV to ABC an act of personal betrayal, carefully planned from the start, and it was years before he would speak to me again.

My parents, naturally enough, were delighted with the move, my father especially, because it helped him in his running game of one-upmanship with Jack Lyons, whose carpet business occupied the factory floor above his in Great Sutton Street. By now, television was front-page news in all the newspapers: not just every little off-beat incident in the live programmes that went out each night but also gossip about the comings and goings between the two rival channels of performers and writers and even produc- ers. When I left the BBC to join ATV at the end of 1956 there were press stories about my departure and the salary for which I was allegedly leaving: the *Daily Telegraph* quoted £10,000 a year, which was about three times the actual figure. My father had been particularly pleased with himself on that occasion when he came home for dinner. Apparently, everybody he'd seen that day had congratulated him on his son's success, including Jack Lyons. "But you didn't tell him the salary in the *Telegraph* was right, did you Dad?" "No, of course not" he said. "...but I didn't tell him it was wrong either."

Now, three years later, reporting on the move from ATV to ABC as an executive, the newspapers were quoting my new salary as £5,000, which happened this time to be correct. How was my father going to handle this apparent drop? "Well, what did Jack Lyons say, Dad?" "He said 'So tell me, Dave: your son's new job: it's a promotion, no?' I told him 'Yes, of course.' And he said 'But Dave, if it's a promotion, and he was getting £10,000 a year for the old job, how come he's only getting £5,000 a year for the new one?" "So what did you say, Dad?" "I said 'Ah, that's *as well!*'"

Like Lime Grove, Teddington began as a silent film studio. Not on a disused industrial site, however, but on the riverside lawn of a wealthy stockbroker's Surrey country house next to Teddington Lock, the longest Lock on the River Thames. Exercising his dogs one morning in the early teens of the 19th century its owner, Henry Chinnery, saw a group of local film makers trying to shoot a dramatic scene by the river in the rain and invited them into his greenhouse to complete it. He caught the film-making bug;

the film makers stayed; and several silent films were shot in the Chinnery greenhouse until 1916, when he converted it into a purpose-built film stage. Sound stages were added in 1931 and from then on it expanded horizontally, rather than vertically like Lime Grove, until Mr Chinnery's site became as tightly packed as the engine under the bonnet of a high-powered automobile.

Warner Brothers bought the studio in 1934 to help fill the quota of British films required by legislation to make up British cinema programmes, without which American movies could not be exhibited; and though Teddington's quota quickies were no more distinguished than any of the others being turned out by the industry, it did help to provide an invaluable training ground for British actors and technicians: Rex Harrison and Margaret Lockwood made their earliest movie appearances at Teddington, Errol Flynn's first film as a leading man, *Murder at Monte Carlo*, was shot there in 1934, the great music hall hero Max Miller made no fewer than eight film comedies there, and it chugged along cheerfully making patriotic movies and programme-fillers during the war until it was destroyed by a flying bomb in 1944.

The studio was rebuilt in 1948 and reopened by the great Danny Kaye with much ceremony and celebration; but in the early fifties, with the British film industry once again in crisis, it fell into sad disuse, reduced at one time to a storage site for the Hawker Aircraft company which operated a factory on the other side of the river. Like Lime Grove, however, television came to its rescue. With its weekend programme franchise for the North and Midlands, ABC had not planned to operate a London studio. It rented the Hackney Empire from ATV for Jack Good's rock and roll extravaganzas and the converted ABC Capitol cinema in the Didsbury suburb of Manchester could comfortably accommodate its other big network success, *Armchair Theatre*.

However, *Armchair Theatre*'s productions had to be transmitted live and, since many of the artistes were appearing in West End theatres, their casts were obliged to rehearse in London during the week, travel up to Manchester on the overnight sleeper after their Saturday night performances, perform their television plays on Sunday night and travel back on the overnight sleeper again: a tiring and time-consuming process, though a good time was had by all apparently – and, I'm afraid, somewhat notoriously. When I went to Manchester for my first look at the Didsbury studio, the Midland Hotel porter who brought my suitcase and me up in the lift to my room, said

"ABC Television, are you sir?" "Yes, I am." "You'll be wanting a woman then?" he said. Needless to say, I politely declined and he left the room.

In order to sustain this weekly *Armchair Theatre* commitment, ABC needed a full-time London-based studio. It wasn't possible to move into the parent company's film studios at Elstree because union members operating under the rigid, time-honoured film agreements would not welcome their brothers working under the far more relaxed television agreement alongside them, but Warner Brothers had been only too happy to let their ABC colleagues take over Teddington, which they did in 1958.

And here I was in February 1960, walking into what was now, in a brilliant conversion, an absolutely top of the art television studio, with features which would in due course be copied by broadcasters around the world. The conversion was designed and executed, under the studio's General Manager Bernard Greenhead, by a gifted team of engineers and technicians recruited from EMI, Marconi and High Definition Films, and by the time they had finished Teddington was a stunning piece of work. I was shown round the complex again a few years ago and, having kept itself firmly in the forefront of technical development for half a century, it was still stunning, with no fewer than eight studios packed into it instead of the original three. Now, alas, it is scheduled to be demolished and replaced by a luxury riverside development of houses and apartments. I hope, like Lime Grove, its past will be remembered in the names of its drives and terraces.

Howard Steele, George Taylor and Stuart Sansom and some of the other engineers who carried out the studio's conversion had stayed on to run its engineering and technical operations, and I met them on my introductory tour. I also met Sydney Newman, the stocky, swarthy, charismatic Canadian with a Viva Zapata moustache, who had transformed British television drama with his *Armchair Theatre* productions. Sydney took me aside and said "Tell you what you gotta do, kid. Get yourself a show: one big weekly light entertainment show, *your* show, *your* production: the rest of the stuff will fall in behind it and the company will make a name for itself; and so will you."

ABC's Sunday Spectacular? Brian Tesler's Saturday Night at the Blackpool Empire? I didn't think so. Light entertainment isn't that easy. Television drama starts with a text. Light entertainment starts with a blank sheet of paper. A television play needs writers, directors, actors and designers. A light entertainment show needs writers, directors, actors, designers, comedians, dancers, singers, musicians, choreographers, conductors, *stars* – and an idea that can bring all those elements together on that blank sheet of paper; and that's a lot for one person to handle personally week in, week out.

Besides, Howard Thomas had brought me to Teddington not to produce light entertainment alone but to supervise the production of all ABC's light entertainment and features programmes. There wasn't an ABC features and light entertainment department in February 1960, and there weren't many ABC features or light entertainment programmes either. I had to find some shows to supervise – and quickly. The department would have to grow out of the programmes, not the other way round. But where to begin? Well, ABC was ITV's weekend programme contractor for the North and Midlands. What sort of presence did we have in our regions?

Getting It Together

I t hadn't been easy for ABC to establish a regional presence. For a start, it served the North and the Midlands, two very different regions, concurrently. The only other Independent Television company with a dual franchise was ATV, which operated consecutively, on weekdays in the Midlands and weekends in London. Weekdays in the North were served by Granada, so both ATV and Granada enjoyed the luxury of five days a week in which to establish and build their regional presence. ABC, with offices, headquarters and now a studio complex in London, seemed to turn up on Saturday morning in each region like the big-city owner of a second home visiting his property for a weekend break. In 1960 the *TV Times* was still getting it wrong: the weekend programme pages in its Midlands edition displayed ABC's station ident all right but stated that the programmes were brought to the viewers by ATV.

ABC had sought to dispel this wildly erroneous impression by deploying its Outside Broadcast Division, the largest in ITV, throughout both regions, covering sport and other local events on Saturday afternoon and religious services on Sunday morning. It also produced two regular outside broadcast series: *The Other Man's Farm*, an enquiring look at farms throughout the North and Midlands for much of the year, and *Holiday Town Parade*, a summer tour of the seaside resorts on our east and west coasts, which included a TV Bathing Beauty Queen contest and a contest to find Great Britain's TV Adonis, though the rest of Great Britain appeared to have little to do with it.

We needed to add some local news and current affairs to the mix, so I set up a team in each of the Didsbury and Aston studios to produce a weekly programme of local interest, transmitted simultaneously to their respective regions on Saturday night. It wasn't difficult to think of a title. *ABC of the North* and *ABC of the Midlands* were welcomed by our viewers and managed to give a sizeable number of bright young journalists their first taste of television, including Michael Parkinson as an on-screen reporter, and Anthony Howard as a programme editor. Anthony went on to become editor of the *New Statesman* and *The Listener*, a prolific broadcaster and the most highly regarded political commentator of his day until his death in 2010. Parky – Sir Michael –is happily still with us, a hale and hearty knight of the realm with his broadcasting career very much alive.

We also needed more regionally oriented entertainment to add to *Holiday Town Parade*'s brief annual run. ITV's Saturday afternoon sports coverage and the Sunday morning *Church Service* roster were shared with our fellow weekend broadcaster, ATV, so ABC's Outside Broadcast Division wasn't overly stretched. Perhaps I could beg a unit or two to deploy around our regions? I needed programmes fast, and I was prepared to beg, borrow or steal to acquire them – well, beg and borrow anyway: I only stole once, and that was unwittingly, as I will relate in due course.

I rang David Southwood, the Head of ABC's Outside Broadcast Division, in full begging mode. David had been an outside broadcast producer and presenter for BBC radio before he joined ABC. I remembered as a teenager listening to him on a programme called *A Seat in the Circle*, in which he used to watch a movie from the circle of a cinema each week and, with the movie's soundtrack playing in the background, describe in a hushed voice what was taking place on the screen. For half an hour each week. A procedure as bizarre as making a ventriloquist's dummy the star of a radio situation comedy. But that worked for Peter Brough and Archie Andrews in Educating Archie, and *A Seat in the Circle* must have worked for David Southwood if I could still remember it after at least fifteen years.

"Mr Southwood isn't available" said his secretary, and she referred me to the Department's Organiser, Lawrie Higgins. As I would discover, Mr Southwood was seldom available: in my eight years with ABC I can remember no more than half a dozen conversations with him, all of them brief, all of them distant. I used to think this remoteness was only with me until, in my research for this memoir, I discovered that it was with everybody. This, from one of his old colleagues: "David was aloof. Never mixed with the crew, even when he was directing. Always immaculately dressed: white shirt, collar and tie, blue blazer. He was the Commanding Officer and everyone else was Other Ranks." That distinction seemed to extend to Sydney Newman and me: in the company's literature Sydney was referred to as Drama Supervisor and I as Light Entertainment and Features Supervisor; David was a *Chief*: "Chief of Outside Broadcasts". Well that was OK with me: I didn't want David's companionship; I just wanted his OB units. And with the help of Lawrie Higgins I got them.

The great British tradition of theatrical farce was lusty and alive in the sixties, just as it is today. Actor-manager Brian Rix – now Baron Rix – took over London's Whitehall Theatre in 1950 and dedicated it to farce, as the Aldwych Theatre had done in the twenties and thirties. The Aldwych Farces written by Ben Travers had been a huge success and ran for eight years. Rix's Whitehall Farces, both classic and newly commissioned, proved even more successful: they would run for an extraordinary 19 years; and BBC Television had signed up Rix and his company in 1952 to provide a number of excerpts and full-length performances of their productions each year, so live relays of farce from the theatre clearly worked on TV.

Farce was also a staple of the repertory theatre, that other great British theatrical tradition, and our regions were served by some of the finest repertory theatres in the United Kingdom. So I borrowed the BBC's initiative, applied it to our own repertory theatres, and asked my old BBC colleague Michael Mills, now freelance, to produce a series of Sunday afternoon adaptations of some of the best theatrical farces from some of our best regional theatres under the umbrella title of *Comedy Matinee*. We would ask our repertory theatres which farces they were planning to present, on which dates, and marshal their productions into a weekly transmission schedule, suggesting wherever necessary that this or that production might move back or forward a week or so to even out the continuity. By the time we reached transmission on the Sunday each cast would have performed to a paying audience for an entire week, resolving any production problems, polishing the laughs, perfecting the stage business. All we would have to do was rehearse our adaptations, which in the experienced hands of comedy writers Dick Vosburgh and Brad Ashton would principally be abridgements for time, and televise them live in front of another enthusiastic local audience.

So ABC's OB units criss-crossed our regions on Sundays from one celebrated theatrical venue to another: the Belgrade in Coventry, the Palace in Nottingham, the Coliseum in Oldham, the Theatre Royal in York, the Opera

House in Harrogate, the Playhouse Theatres in Derby and Salisbury, the Civic Theatres in Rotherham and Chesterfield, and our audiences both in the theatre and at home were regaled with the well-rehearsed work of old and new masters of farce from Ben Travers and Ronald Gow to Philip King and William Douglas Home: *A Cuckoo in the Nest*, *See How They Run*, *Ma's Bit 'o' Brass*, *Queen Elizabeth Slept Here*, *Master of Arts*, *The Happiest Days of Your Life*... Watch out for them all at your local rep: they're still being played today.

The success of this venture prompted one of Howard Thomas's bright double-edged ideas, admirable in itself and invaluable for the company's image – with HT's ideas you always got two for the price of one. "These Repertory Theatres of ours: they need to foster new talent, don't they? Talent that sooner or later television will benefit from as well as the theatre? That talent will need somewhere to learn its trade. Promising young theatre directors have to make a living while they are learning. Why don't we set up a scheme in which we find promising young trainee directors for our Repertory Theatres and pay their living expenses while they're on attachment? It would help the theatres, help the directors, and help us. Yes? Over to you, Tesler."

So we set up ABC's Regional Trainee Director Scheme, in which the Artistic Directors of four Repertory Theatres from the North and Midlands joined us each year to select four promising young directors to train with their respective companies on a two-year attachment, during which time ABC would grant the successful candidates a bursary of £5,000 free of tax for their living expenses. I chaired the early panels of Artistic Directors and in a happy reunion had the pleasure of inviting Nevill Coghill, my old Oxford tutor, to add his wisdom and theatrical nous to our deliberations. We didn't do badly: the Scheme still thrives after more than fifty years (the residential bursaries are now £27,500), and as a way of repaying television's debt to the theatre for its supply of creative talent it has had a remarkable impact. Some of the most illustrious names in British theatre are among the Scheme's graduates. They include Sir Trevor Nunn, Ken Loach, Ronald Hayman, Michael Ockrent, Rupert Goold, Adrian Noble and many Artistic Directors now running theatre companies of their own. Now funded by the Arts Council, the Scheme was reconfigured in 2012 and re-named the Regional Theatre Young Director Scheme. I'm proud to have been one of its original Patrons.

We embarked on some more borrowing for ABC's other venture in regional entertainment, another challenge for Lawrie Higgins's Outside Broadcast schedules. The North and Midlands were the heart of British manufacturing in the sixties, booming with factories of every kind. What better way of reinforcing our regional presence than featuring those factories and their workers on our screens? But exactly how?

Joe Henderson had been Petula Clark's accompanist when we worked on her shows at Lime Grove. Now he was Joe "Mr Piano" Henderson, a star in his own right with two hit record albums, *Sing it with Joe* and *Sing it Again with Joe. Sing Something Simple* was a popular BBC radio series featuring non-stop medleys of familiar songs performed by Cliff Adams and the Cliff Adams Singers. And *Worker's Playtime* was a BBC radio variety show created in 1941 to support the war effort, broadcast weekly from factory canteens "somewhere in Britain". It had proved so successful in raising the morale of industrial workers that it continued to be broadcast after the war while Britain and the British economy were being rebuilt; it would in fact not end its run until 1964.

I borrowed elements from all three to devise *Sing Along with Joe*, in which Joe Henderson and a rhythm section accompanied a group of singers each week in one of our regions' most photogenic factories, performing non-stop sequences of standards and current pop-tunes. They would be singing their medleys in and around the factory floors, workshops, production lines, conveyor belts and anywhere else that would make for exciting television pictures in the hands of a bright young ABC director named Ben Churchill. As well as a Talent Contest, we threw in another Beauty Contest: an annual search for Miss Industry. Today's Health and Safety officers and Political Correctness monitors would have been competing with each other to close us down, but we didn't receive a single complaint on either count in all the years in which the programme ran. On the contrary: our Didsbury staff were overwhelmed by the sackfuls of mail we received each week praising the show and voting for the contest winners. If only we'd thought of today's voting by phone and charging for it.

Our *Sing Along* factories provided a fascinating snapshot of the variety of British manufacturing in the North and Midlands in the sixties: Fox's Biscuits in Batley, Fox's Steel Works in Sheffield, Basset's Liquorice All Sorts in Pontefract, Wynsmore Garments in The Fyled, JCB Tractors and WYPACS' car parts in the Midlands, Robert Hurst Raincoats in Harrogate,

Hammonds United and John Smith's Breweries in Tadcaster... Alas, only a few of them exist today, but they were flourishing then. Conscious of the promotional value of an on-screen appearance and the goodwill it would create among their staff members, the owners opened up the factories for us on the Sunday and offered our artistes and crews the most lavish hospitality, and the workers flocked in to act as audiences for our contests. I sincerely hope that the crews had dedicated drivers for the journeys back to their base after each show. From what I heard, they needed them.

Getting on the Network

I f ABC's task in registering a regional presence was difficult, registering a network presence was positively Herculean. I'd met George Noordhof at Lime Grove, where he worked in Mary Adams's Talks Department as BBC Television's first producer of science programmes. George was now freelance, and he rang me with an interesting idea for a series on the scientific principles behind the feats of show business, from the skills of the circus ring to the illusions of stage and cinema. It was called *You'd Never Believe It!* and it seemed a television natural to me. By its second series the *TV Times*' Northern and Midlands editions were labelling it "easily the most popular science programme ever on British TV". But viewers in London never saw it. Getting ABC's programmes on to London's television screens at the weekend wasn't as easy as fire eating, lion taming or producing Pepper's Ghost on the stage.

You didn't exist as a major television company if your programmes were not seen in London and consequently reviewed by the national television critics. However, London's screens were controlled at the weekend by ATV and filled with ATV programmes. Granada's financial deal with Associated–Rediffusion meant that their programmes had no difficulty in reaching London's screens during the week but there was no such arrangement for ABC at the weekend. Howard Thomas told me about the Monday morning meetings he used to have with Val Parnell and Lew Grade to agree the weekend schedules. He would sit between the two of them in their vast office, now transplanted to ATV House in Great Cumberland Place, just as I had done on my first day in ITV three years before, and haggle: haggle over programmes with Val and haggle over programme prices with Lew.

The prices were important. ABC's audience in the North and Midlands at the weekend was twice the size of ATV's in London, so in theory ABC should have paid two-thirds of the cost of ATV's network programmes while ATV paid only a third of ABC's. But London was ATV's showcase. It was proud of its programmes and the press coverage and publicity they attracted. It simply didn't want to schedule ABC programmes in place of its own and, when it did, Lew enjoyed haggling over prices. Jack Good's rock music programmes had made it, but they had been remunerative tenants for ATV's Hackney Empire studio and were now no more. *Holiday Town Parade* and the odd panel game scraped in; *The Sunday Break* was allowed to share the Closed Period airtime with ATV's *About Religion* series. The two companies alternated off-peak afternoon drama serials for children. Val and Lew respected *Armchair Theatre* – though they quibbled over costs when its casts were small or its sets economical – but they argued that ABC had no light entertainment credentials and no respectable light entertainment producers and directors. So why didn't Howard simply contract out the rest of his programmes to ATV? There's a revealing little sentence in Howard Thomas's autobiography: "To survive in the jungle of the network I had to build production power into ABC." He wanted ABC to be one of the big beasts of the network jungle and that required production power all round, not just in drama.

I was one of Howard's double-edged swords. My job was not just to make programmes to entertain and inform our viewers in the North and Midlands at the weekend. It was also to prise ATV's hands from the weekend's network schedule, which they had monopolised from the beginning of ITV five years before. After all, I had been responsible for some of ATV's biggest light entertainment successes, so Val and Lew could hardly refuse to network ABC's light entertainment programmes now that I was responsible for them, could they? Well, yes they could; they would; and they did. But none of these considerations occurred to me at the time. I was too busy drumming up programme ideas, looking for producers, writers, directors, *stars.*

In 1960, Sammy Davis Jr was one of the few American stars yet to perform in Britain; we knew him only from his records and his reputation. Sammy's British agent was Harry Foster, who also represented Dickie Henderson Jr, and through Dickie Harry and I had become good friends. The Foster agency was one of the most respected in the business and Harry himself was urbane, shrewd – and not a little mischievous. I'd heard that Sammy Davis Jr was coming to Britain in June to play the Pigalle, a glamorous new theatre-restaurant in Piccadilly, and assumed that Val and Lew had already snapped him up for the Moss Empire circuit, the London Palladium stage and ATV's *Sunday Night at the London Palladium*, which was the almost automatic routine for international variety stars visiting Britain. "Not so," said Harry. "Well, in that case," I said, with blithe presumption – after all, he could only say No – "how about letting me have him for ABC, for a one-hour special?" With a little twinkle in his eye, Harry said "Well, Val and Lew won't like it... but I don't see why not. Who would produce?" I didn't have a light entertainment department and I didn't have a light entertainment producer, so this was my chance to do a Bill Ward and produce it myself. I said "Me." Harry said "OK."

I didn't know what I was letting myself in for.

Sammy would be working to a tight schedule, coming into London at the end of May, opening at the Pigalle at the beginning of June, flying back to his show in Las Vegas at the end of the month. The first chance to meet him would be at his hotel the morning after his opening night. He'd be available for rehearsals the following week and would do our show live on the Sunday. What kind of show? Not just his nightclub act, I thought, though we could devote part of the hour to it, dress the studio as a nightclub and invite a celebrity audience to sit at the tables. A big entrance, of course: down a great white staircase perhaps? Something entirely different for the middle section: I'd decided to call the show *Sammy Davis Jr Meets the British*, so why not let him meet some of the British in some eye-catching location away from the studio? Another treat for a Didsbury Outside Broadcast crew.

Sammy's opening night at the Pigalle was a triumph and the reviews next day were a universal rave, a happy augury for my first meeting with our star. I took my old *New Look* colleague Lionel Blair with me to Sammy's hotel. I wanted Lionel to choreograph the show, and had brought him back from Los Angeles where he was holidaying with Roger Moore and Dorothy Squires to do so. But then Harry Foster told me that Sammy's entourage would include his own choreographer, so as a consolation prize I had retained Lionel as Associate Producer. Good move.

"So *you're* Lionel Blair," said Sammy when I introduced them; "Jack Cassidy and Shirley Jones told me I've just got to meet you: they said you're *adorable!*" The fact that Lionel was a fellow dancer clinched the relationship; they got on at once. When we discussed the possibility of an outside broadcast location for the middle section of the show, Sammy didn't like the sound of Madame Tussauds or any of the other locations I proposed but jumped at Lionel's suggestion of the Battersea Fun Fair, which happened to be closed for renovation at the time.

"We could have you driving a bunch of kids to the Fair for a fun day out," Lionel said, "but it's closed. The kids are heartbroken, you find a way to get into the fairground and you cheer the kids up with – you know, that number from *Anchors Aweigh* where Gene Kelly danced with the cartoon mouse –"

"You mean 'The Worry Song' – yeah, and we can use the fairground stuff, the roundabouts and sideshows, the slides and swings, maybe the rollercoasters –"

"Yes, you're a sort of Pied Piper, singing and dancing all over the fairground with them – you could do some of your impressions, you know, make them laugh, get them to sing and dance with you..."

They were getting on like a house on fire. I warmed my hands at the blaze, realised that a standby fireman would be redundant, and went back to the office. Lionel rang me that afternoon to say that after their Battersea love-in Sammy had asked him to go shopping with him – "introduce him to some high-tone British stores so that he could get some typically British stuff – bowler hats, umbrellas, spats, that sort of thing – and he wants me to do a number with him based on that, with me as a snooty British shop assistant. You know, he asks for a derby hat and I tell him in this country, sir, we call it a bowler, and so on, and we get into a sort of challenge dance routine... I told him well it's Brian's show, I'd have to ask *you*. What do you think?" I thought Yes, and jumped at the idea as quickly as Sammy had jumped at the Fun Fair.

I persuaded the authorities to let us rent the Fairground, wheedled an OB Unit from Lawrie Higgins, booked a mixed bunch of talented kids from a couple of Stage Schools, and a week later we all gathered at Battersea to work out a routine for the Fun Fair sequence and a schedule for rehearsals. Sammy and Lionel would rehearse their own number at Cecil Sharp House each morning – a pepped-up arrangement of Rodgers and Hammerstein's "Shall We Dance?" – then they'd work on the "Worry Song" sequence at the Fun Fair with the kids each afternoon. My Associate Producer was now both the show's choreographer and its guest artiste, with Sammy's choreographer teaching Lionel some of Sammy's signature steps but otherwise supplying nothing more than a benign and approving presence throughout the proceedings.

The rehearsals went well when they actually went, but Sammy had set himself a punishing routine. Meeting the British every day, playing the Pigalle every evening, partying after the show every night: it was bound to have an effect. One member of the OB crew had this to say on that subject: "I'm not sure how many days were allocated for Battersea but because of the antics of the star we were there much longer than scheduled. He turned up when he felt like it, sometimes late, sometimes leaving early, and one day not turning up at all. This gave the crew a lot of spare time." Well, I suppose it's an ill wind...

Unfortunately, the ill wind didn't blow much good when we got to the studio. Sammy's first reaction to the magnificent white staircase Timothy O'Brien had designed for his entrance was "I ain't going up there, baby", so we scrapped it and set up a pair of stage curtains on the studio floor as the backing for his opening sequence, the best we could find at short notice on a Sunday. Howard Steele had acquired a lavalier microphone from the States, a rare and expensive piece of equipment in those days, which would hang round Sammy's neck and give him the freedom to move wherever he wanted without worrying about boom microphones and their shadows. Unfortunately, it took a while for our sound engineers to establish its wavelength and our rehearsals were interrupted by so many sound howl-backs that Sammy finally tore the mike from his neck and hurled it from one end of the studio to the other. Back to the microphone boom, and another time-consuming lighting set-up. It was a tetchy and disagreeable day all round, but I certainly didn't expect what happened at the end of it, when I was in the control room giving last-minute notes to the camera crew and the rest of the production team.

Our make-up assistant ran in and said "I've just been to Sammy's dressing-room to make him up. He says he's not going to do the show. And he's not joking!" I rushed off to Sammy's dressing-room and said "What's going on, Sam?" "I'm not doing the show, that's what's going on. It's been a lousy day. I don't like the set, I don't like the equipment, I don't like anything about this goddam studio. You're all a bunch of amateurs and I'm not going to put my career on the line for you. I'm not doing the show. Period. *That's* what's going on!"

I heard myself saying "Yes, Sammy, it *has* been a lousy day: for us as well as for you. I know things haven't gone well but we've sorted them out and you're a pro. Look, the studio's buzzing with excitement; there's a huge audience at home waiting to see you for the first time on British television. Think of them. Think of all your friends and celebrities sitting at the nightclub tables out there in the studio waiting for you to knock 'em dead. Think of *Lionel!* This is a big moment for him, and that number you do together is great. You can't let all those people down...Do the show, Sammy. *Do the show!*" It was like a scene from yet another B movie, a schmaltzy back-stage musical B movie: I could hear the strings welling up in the background.

And of course Sammy did do the show: that's the way those back-stage B movies always end, isn't it? His staggering talent burnt up the screen and the show was a great success. He and Lionel were invited to reprise the "Shall We Dance?" routine in the following year's Royal Variety Show, and the two of them became lifelong friends until Sammy's death in 1990. Me? I never really made it up with Sammy. The experience of working with him was enough to persuade me to hang up my producer mittens alongside Jack Greenstock's boxing gloves. I told myself I had more than enough to do with looking for programme ideas and building a department capable of realising them; so I tipped my hat to Bill Ward's multi-tasking talent and walked away from the control room. I would produce only one more show in the remainder of my television career. And I would be sure to have a director on it to deal directly with its stars.

Stealing the Show

L ooking for programme ideas and building up a department to realise them, I diligently pursued my beg, borrow or steal policy. I begged – or rather *commissioned* – Norman Hudis, the writer of the first half dozen *Carry On* films, to write a comedy series which might attract as many as possible of the *Carry On* repertory company of artistes, and put him together with my old friend and ex-BBC colleague Ernest Maxin who, like Michael Mills, was now a freelance producer. They came up with the idea of an oddball collection of very different people pooling their financial resources to purchase a house together, with their individual stories sometimes separate, sometimes intertwining.

It was called *Our House* and it attracted Hattie Jacques, Charles Hawtrey, Joan Sims and Norman Rossington from the *Carry On* films among many other first-class comic actors, including Hylda Baker, Deryck Guyler, and Bernard Bresslaw who went on to become a future *Carry On* star. Played live in front of a studio audience, it was probably the first 60-minute situation comedy in British television and it was almost certainly the last, but it was successful enough to run for thirty-nine episodes and inspire another series for Charles Hawtrey and Hylda Baker in 1963, *Best of Friends*.

In 1960, jazz of the New Orleans and Chicago variety – traditional jazz – was all the rage, and our studios were conveniently situated on the bank of a river – the Thames rather than the Mississippi, but you can't have everything. I borrowed the jiving teenagers of the BBC's *Six-Five Special*, put them aboard a mocked-up New Orleans riverboat we called Cottontail, which we moored where Mr Chinnery's lawns had once swept down to the river, and let the kids jive the afternoon away to the music of the best of the British trad bands, from Acker Bilk to Alex Walsh, from Kenny Ball to Humphrey Lyttelton.

I borrowed the great trumpeter Kenny Baker from Ted Heath's orchestra as the show's musical director, and borrowed the show's title, *Steamboat Shuffle*, from Hoagy Carmichael's 1924 toe-tapper "Riverboat Shuffle" – I still don't know why I didn't go all the way and call the show *Riverboat* Shuffle: it would have provided us with the perfect signature tune. I didn't need to borrow an OB unit from Didsbury this time, however. Mr Chinnery's lawns had long been tarmacked over to provide a car park for the studios, so to shoot the show we simply wheeled the cameras and microphone-booms out of Studio 2. Robert Fuest's design for the boat was literally a work of art: he was so taken by its setting among the lush riverside trees that his original design was not the customary black and white sketch but a handsome watercolour which still graces a bedroom wall in my house in Chiswick. Bob Fuest went on to become a successful movie director. The riverboat itself gave Howard Thomas another of his double-edged ideas.

The Corporation's Board meetings were sometimes held in Teddington but not often, because the lunching facilities in our modest little executive dining room were no match for those in Golden Square. Walking back to Howard's office across the car park after a Board lunch one Thursday, ABPC's amply framed Managing Director, C. J. Latta, was grumbling about how cramped the dining room was. Howard explained that there wasn't enough room on the site to build a larger one and then, spotting the *Steamboat Shuffle* set said "But look at this. What about a boat? We could buy a motor launch of some kind and convert it into a dining room not only for the Board but also to entertain special guests: you know, advertising executives, newspaper editors, politicians, the Television Authority and so on. The Board could use it any time they wanted to show off the studio to some important contact. What do you think? Would they agree to the cost?"

C. J. looked, was hooked, persuaded the Board to agree; and Howard acquired a facility none of his fellow TV Managing Directors could match. One of Dunkirk's little motor vessels, plying its trade as a ferry on the south coast, was found for us by an agent, renamed M.V. Iris after ABC's production subsidiary Iris Productions, and firmly moored beyond the car park, alongside the studios. In the years to come its charms would facilitate many negotiations, help to close many deals, witness the signing of many contracts.

The one case of my *stealing* a programme idea – inadvertently, m'lud, so help me – was the result of culpable ignorance on my part and the dark impenetrability of the mind of one Jonathan Routh. Jonathan was a practical joker in the great tradition of the British hoaxers of the 18th and 19th centuries, though the latter were usually leisured amateurs and Jonathan was an experienced professional who advertised his skills in *The Times*: "Practical joker with wide experience of the British public's sad gullibility organises, leads and guarantees success of large-scale hoaxes."

I came across him early in 1960, not from the newspaper but from a vinyl LP in a local record store. The record was *Candid Mike*, a collection of sound clips from a Radio Luxembourg series in which the engaging prankster set up a number of ingenious practical jokes involving ordinary members of the public unaware that they were being recorded for a radio programme by a concealed microphone. It was very funny, and I thought it would be even funnier on television with a concealed camera. I tracked Jonathan down, found him equally engaging in the flesh, with a craggy, beetle-browed face just made for the TV screen, and asked if he'd like to do a television version of his radio show. "We'll call it *We've Got You Covered*" I said. "Fine with me" said Jonathan.

Ronnie Taylor, the brilliant writer and producer of Al Read's radio show from BBC North, had rung to tell me he had gone freelance, and *We've Got You Covered* seemed an ideal vehicle for him to handle. Jonathan agreed, and four weeks later the show went into our Didsbury studio with the Irish actor Joe Lynch as its host, Jonathan as its prime prankster and a team of practical joke-devisers headed by Andy Atkins and the ubiquitous John Whitney. It was a success from the start and the show quickly began to receive coverage in the national newspapers even though ATV had declined to network it in London. It was the press coverage that actually did for it. The Company Secretary burst into my office one afternoon to say that an American production company was accusing us of stealing their programme: *Candid Camera*, a big hit on America's CBS Network. Its producer, presenter and production company boss was Allen Funt, and his lawyers required us to cease production forthwith and make available to them the programmes we had already transmitted so that they could advise Mr Funt of the legal action he should take.

I rang Jonathan Routh and said "Jonathan, we have a problem. *Candid Mike* wasn't your idea, was it?" "No, it was an old American radio show from the forties: I just leased the rights." "But did you know that there was a television version, *Candid Camera*?" "Yes, of course, that was an old format, too." "For Pete's sake, Jonathan, why didn't you tell me?" "Oh, I thought you knew." Oh, but I didn't, Jonathan. I *should* have known, but I didn't. How could I have been so unquestioning, so uninformed? How could I have been unaware of the existence of a hit show called *Candid Camera* during my New York trips of 1957 and 1958? And – dammit – how could I not have realised that *Candid Camera* was a far better title for a TV version of *Candid Mike* than *We've Got You Covered*?

Far too belatedly I did the research, and did at least find a little mitigating evidence on my behalf. Allen Funt's *Candid Microphone* had indeed been a U.S. radio show in the forties, but it had ended its run in 1948. *Candid Camera* had succeeded it in 1948 on both network and syndicated television, but it had been off U.S. TV screens for years until it was revived as an insert in Jack Paar's late night show and again in 1959 as an insert in Gary Moore's late night show, after my second U.S. trip. And it didn't return to the CBS network as a show in its own right until 1960, at just about the time we ourselves went on the air with *We've Got You Covered*.

Extraordinary coincidence; and that timing saved the day for us: we couldn't have stolen *Candid Camera*'s CBS format, though we certainly nicked Allen Funt's essential idea in devising our own television version of *Candid Mike*. Happily, Allen didn't dislike what we had done with that idea, and since we were both new to the air with our respective shows and each needed a regular flow of ideas for our stunts, we struck a deal. He would excuse our inadvertent theft. We would retitle our show *Candid Camera* and pay a licence fee for the format. We would send each other tapes of our show each week and be free to borrow any of the stunts our respective teams of hoaxers devised, at no cost. And we would be spared our day in court.

During the legal hiatus, Joe Lynch had committed himself to a stage play so we offered the role of programme host to Bob Monkhouse, who added his own lively mind to the construction of its practical jokes. We had a hit show on our hands from the moment Jonathan famously coasted his car minus an engine into a garage and asked the bemused attendants to check its oil and water. The British version of *Candid Camera* ran for eight years. Many of its stunts are still remembered. Some have been re-worked in the shows that became its legacy, from *Game for a Laugh* and *Beadle's About* to Dom Joly's *Trigger Happy TV* and *The Pranker*. But I can't help thinking, as I look back on the whole episode, that keeping quiet about both the provenance of *Candid Mike* and the existence of *Candid Camera* when we first dreamed up our show was Jonathan's biggest and most successful practical joke of the entire series. And the joke was on me.

The little embryo Light Entertainment and Features department ended 1960 with its Supervisor's very last production. A Christmas show, I thought. A Christmas show too big, too star-studded, for ATV to turn down. Something on the lines of *A Santa for Christmas* perhaps: a quest, which could accommodate in its episodic progress all the stars we could get hold of before they were swallowed up by Christmas pantos. I called in Jimmy Grafton, ever-reliable friend and scriptwriting colleague of my production days at ATV and the BBC, put him together with Sid Colin, another leading scriptwriter, invited Michael Mills to join our team as the show's director, and the four of us brainstormed a version of *Alice Through the Looking Glass* which fitted the bill perfectly.

Alice Through the Looking Box was networked on Christmas Day 1960. Alice herself was played by the delightful Jeannie Carson, star of the West End musical *Love From Judy*. In our story she was a baby-sitter for the real-life married couple of Jackie Rae, host of the TV game show *Name That Tune*, and film and stage actress Janette Scott. Alice falls asleep while watching TV and dreams that she has lost her charge. Spike Milligan appears as the White Rabbit and invites her into Tellyland to look for it (*Alice in Tellyland* lost the toss with *Alice Through the Looking Box* for our title), and off they go, searching for the baby.

Their search led them in to scenes mirroring Lewis Carroll's but each with a TV twist. His characters were played by comedians, actors and personalities famous on the TV screen then and still remembered now, including Harry Secombe, Bob Monkhouse, Ronnie Corbett, Mike and Bernie Winters, Ron Moody, Dora Bryan, Donald Pleasence, Fanny Cradock, Bernard Braden and Barbara Kelly. And also with the somewhat bizarre assistance of the principal characters from some of television's popular crime and detection series, including – here's a trip down Memory Lane for the archivists – Raymond Francis as Inspector Lockhart from *No Hiding Place*, Donald Gray as Mark Saber, Ian Hendry as Dr Geoffrey Brent of *Police Surgeon*, John Bentley as Inspector Paul Derek from *Elephant Patrol*, even Conrad Phillips as William Tell. I can't remember how the Swiss crossbow expert got himself involved in it but, after all, this *was* a dream.

We made the cover of the Christmas edition of *TV Times* and won ITV's biggest audience on Christmas Day. And on New Year's Day, the Features element of our department produced *Crystal Ball 1961* for the network, an hour-long review of what the future might bring in politics, international affairs, sport and the arts, with George Ffitch, Brian Glanville, Katharine Whitehorn and Kenneth Robinson. Not a bad first year for ABC TV's new department.

Hardball

A part from Drama and Outside Broadcasts, Light Entertainment and Features were responsible for everything else the company transmitted, including its advertising magazines. Remember advertising magazines? In order to preclude American television's system of programme sponsorship, the Independent Television Authority Act had laid down that "there should be no connection between the actual programme and advertising, except in shopping guides." What the Act was unable to preclude was the inevitability that these shopping guides would themselves become programmes, a commercial curiosity unique to British television. Advertising magazines, familiarly known as admags, sprang up throughout ITV, little 15 minute programmes in which popular personalities in various settings recommended and chatted about goods and their prices. It was an attractive opportunity for small advertisers who couldn't afford a 30-second commercial in an advertising break, and an effortless way of maximising ITV's advertising revenue.

Some of the admags became major attractions in their own right. Associated-Rediffusion's *Jim's Inn* featured actor Jimmy Hanley and his wife Maggie as the owners of a village pub whose customers could be found each week on one evening or another discussing their latest household or gardening acquisitions and how much they had cost. Its audience ratings rivalled those of BBC Radio's *Mrs Dale's Diary* and *The Archers*, and there were cries of protest, particularly from the BBC and those newspaper proprietors who were not ITV shareholders themselves, that the Act intended to protect the distinction between programmes and advertising had actually led to the blurring of that distinction.

ABC's own admag output was certainly not onerous to supervise. It was handled very efficiently by the two-man team of Lloyd Shirley and Mike Hodges, Mike as script-writer and Lloyd as organiser/producer/director. Both would go on to bigger things in film and television, but this was 1961 and I had only lesser things to offer, particularly to Lloyd. But this amenable young red-bearded Canadian seemed perfectly happy to produce or direct or organise any programme I threw at him, and I'm afraid I threw him some tricky ones.

In an attempt to open *up* Saturday night viewing for our audiences I had embarked on yet another spree for Lawrie Higgins's Outside Broadcast units. For example, *Big Night Out*, a visit once or twice a month to some major entertainment event, sometimes authentic, sometimes manufactured: an all-star pop concert from the Empire Pool in Wembley; *The Best of the Big Top* from Blackpool's circus arena; a celebration of the best of the summer shows from The Arcadia, Skegness; a tour of London's night club cabarets reuniting Dickie Henderson and Freddie Mills as our guides; that sort of thing. I landed Lloyd with a couple of lulus.

Wolf Mankowitz and Monty Norman had turned Beverly Cross's play about Dr Crippen and his wife into what they called a Music Hall musical – *Belle: The Ballad of Dr Crippen*, a sort of latter day *Threepenny Opera*. They agreed to let us cover it before it opened in the West End. Rather than simply televise an excerpt we thought we would compress its action into an hour's show. Backbreaking work for Lloyd and everybody involved, but at least it worked on the screen, though the show didn't work on the stage: *Belle* folded after 44 performances.

Alas, that order was emphatically reversed by *Big Night Out*'s exclusive, first-time visit to The Green Room Rag, also produced and directed by Lloyd. *The Green Room Rag* in the sixties was one of two annual one-night performances in aid of the Combined Theatrical Charities Appeal, in which artistes from the West End theatre and international guests from stage and screen let their hair down in sketches and musical numbers not normally associated with them. We couldn't afford the better known of the two, *The Night of a Hundred Stars*. Its cast in the one show at the London Palladium I was fortunate enough to see included Laurence Olivier, Judy Garland, Noël Coward and Danny Kaye. Instead, we aimed for the other one, The Green Room Rag.

If I had had the good sense to see an edition of it before we put our cameras into the Victoria Palace I would have realised why it wasn't difficult to secure an exclusive, first-time visit. *The Green Room Rag*, alas, was a Smokers' Concert writ large, and the air was blue with more than smoke. Stanley Holloway and the other artistes who entertained their raucously appreciative audience that night let their hair down so far they were in danger of tripping over it. Poor Lloyd recorded a three hour performance of which only 40 minutes were remotely useable. Two days later he had to fly up to Manchester to record a couple of acts which could be edited into whatever was salvageable from the *Green Room*: a last-minute booking for Frankie Howerd and American singing star Vaughn Monroe, both fortunately appearing at the Palace Theatre that week.

There simply were not enough attractive major events out there for us to cover. Our *Big Nights* would clearly be better off "In" than "Out": a television studio offered much greater control and infinitely more production possibilities. But for whom? Ernest Maxin was busy with *Our House*, Michael Mills with *Comedy Matinee*, Ronnie Taylor with *Candid Camera*. I needed another top-rank light entertainment producer. Chance and geophysics provided one for me.

Whenever Audrey and I were on holiday at her parents' home in Yorkshire, I tried to take a look at ABC's weekend output to us folk in the North. Unfortunately, the signal from the Emley Moor transmitter was unable to pierce the hills surrounding the little village of Sleights where her parents lived. When we switched on the Maclean TV set all we could receive was the signal from the Burnhope transmitter: Tyne Tees Television, the programme company for the North East. With that signal, however, came the bright, imaginative, remarkably consistent work of a producer named Philip Jones, on screen every day, sometimes twice a day. I asked Teddy Sommerfield to track Philip down and persuade him to join me at Teddington. Within weeks he was producing his first situation comedy for us, *Happily Ever After* with Dora Bryan and Pete Murray; within months he was producing one of the most influential popular music shows of the decade, *Thank Your Lucky Stars*.

Meanwhile, Lew Grade was playing network hardball with Howard Thomas. Howard's new production power at ABC was beginning to make itself felt, and Lew wasn't happy about it. He had agreed to take the Ian Hendry drama series *Police Surgeon*, and also *Candid Camera* and *Steamboat Shuffle* and *Our House* and *Comedy Matinee* and *Happily Ever* After and *Alice*

Through the Looking Box. Now Howard wanted him to take *Thank Your Lucky Stars* and this new series from Sydney Newman's Drama Department called *The Avengers.* No! And again No! Howard kept pitching and Lew kept hitting him out of the ball park, until he finally relented. *Thank Your Lucky Stars* was a lost cause, but as for *The Avengers...* The series had already gone to air in the North and Midlands but if Howard was prepared to schedule *The Avengers* every other week and alternate it with ATV's new action series *Deadline Midnight*, he might agree to take it − but in return Howard had to follow suit with *Armchair Theatre*: schedule it every other week, alternating with an ATV series of one-off plays under the title of *Drama 61.*

Howard agreed.

It was a bitter blow for Sydney, though quite how bitter was yet to be revealed. He had lost half his *Armchair Theatre* output and seen its identity and impetus diluted by the alternating *Drama 61.* In addition, the cockeyed fortnightly scheduling of *The Avengers* threatened to deprive his brand new series of the opportunity to build its audience week by week. The fact that *The Avengers*' audience *did* build, in spite of *Deadline Midnight* being sandwiched between each episode, was a tribute to its writers, directors and actors, and its doggedly dedicated producer Leonard White. But Lew's brinkmanship deprived London audiences of nine episodes of that first series. ATV began its run with the show's two opening episodes in order to establish the characters played by Patrick Macnee and Ian Hendry. It then skipped the next nine shows before catching up with ABC's weekly transmission at episode 12, from which point *The Avengers* was transmitted by both companies fortnightly. As a result, episodes 3 to 11 were never seen in London.

ABC's feature programmes were not immune from this network hardball. I was a great admirer of the BBC's *Monitor*, Huw Wheldon's inspired television series devoted to the arts, and I wanted to start an ITV series to rival it, to extend its coverage, to out-*Monitor* it. It was a vainglorious ambition, but a television company's reach should exceed its grasp, should it not? To realise that ambition, I needed an editor of wide interests and fierce enthusiasms, and Audrey and I found him at the London Palladium one Saturday night. Sitting in the row in front of us, watching the American singer Johnnie Ray crying his heart out at the top of the bill, was Kenneth Tynan, *The Observer*'s much admired theatre critic. Tynan's impact on the Oxford arts world had been still resonating when I arrived there ten years previously; his incisive reviews were now galvanising London's theatre world. Yet here he was responding to Johnnie Ray's strange, manipulative talent as rapturously as the rest of the audience. It seemed to me that this might be the sort of eclectic maverick I needed for our arts programme. I wrote to him the following day and we arranged to meet.

Ken was intrigued by the idea, enthusiastic about its prospects, and reassured by the knowledge that he would be supported by two of ABC's most experienced professionals, Lloyd Shirley as executive producer and Reginald Collin as producer. The three of them got together, found they were on the same wavelength, and came up with a title for the show which I was more than happy to accept: *Tempo*. They also rented a suite at the Piccadilly Hotel in central London for their production office because, they argued, Teddington was too far away for the sort of busy creative people they hoped to attract. It was certainly convenient and impressive. And also handy for a haircut whenever I dropped in to see the team: Jack Lee, Val Parnell's old Sunday Morning at the London Palladium hairdresser, had his barbershop on the hotel's ground floor.

Losing Sydney

*T*empo opened with a tremendous scoop. In the summer of 1962 the newly appointed Board of the National Theatre announced that Sir Laurence Olivier was to be its first Director. In a glorious summer of firsts, Sir Laurence, who had previously been appointed the first Artistic Director of the brand new Chichester Festival Theatre, was preparing to launch the Theatre's first season. The core of the National's company would be formed from the company at Chichester, and *Tempo*'s first edition had Olivier talking about his plans for both. It also had Vicky, the great political cartoonist, interviewed on the art of the political cartoon, and the *Beyond the Fringe* team – Alan Bennett, Peter Cook, Jonathan Miller and Dudley Moore – adding their observations on the arts in general, the first of several regular appearances on the programme.

The Earl of Harewood was *Tempo*'s first presenter, and Ken and his team had a magnificent roll call of future guests to perform, to be interviewed or to make films for us, from Orson Welles to Peter Sellers, Yehudi Menuhin to Sophie Tucker, Kingsley Amis to John Osborne, Truman Capote to Elia Kazan. But ATV declined to network it weekly. Like *Armchair Theatre* and *The Avengers*, *Tempo* would have to be screened fortnightly, alternating on Sunday afternoons with ATV's new Bernard Braden series, *The Time, the Place – and the Camera*. Both of them were fine programmes, but why could they not both be screened weekly?

I wasn't party to the negotiations between Howard and Lew, but I must confess that I wondered why the ITA didn't step in and have a quiet word about the lunacy of this alternate scheduling. We could have done with a little forbearance on the part of the BBC too. Piqued at the attempt to encroach on *Monitor*'s territory by this upstart little commercial company from the sticks, the BBC scheduled the American western film series *Overland Trail* against *Tempo*'s debut, Sunday afternoon not the usual home for westerns on the BBC.

Ken ran *Tempo* brilliantly, exactly as I had hoped. My only problem with him was his tendency to include among the lively arts the art of sexual arousal. We never did get to transmit his edition on Indian erotic temple art, or Norman Mailer solemnly reading to camera a four-letter-littered description of sexual intercourse from his latest novel, like some mad Olympia Press version of *Jackanory*. But we did do a programme about Maurice Girodias, the proprietor of the Olympia Press, and covered an extremely louche Happening in Paris. These were not the only occasions on which Ken and I sat with the ITA's Deputy Director General, Bernard Sendall, patiently previewing a programme's material and weighing the artistic value of each explicit shot or phrase against its potential to offend or sexually inflame, both of which seemed to be Ken's obsessive intent. It was some years later that he was able to achieve both goals in his notorious nude revue *Oh! Calcutta!* Looking back, it seems to me that some of those proposed items in *Tempo* were a kind of tentative dry run.

Ken moved on in 1963 to become the literary manager of the National Theatre, though he would return from time to time as *Tempo*'s literary adviser or consultant. The programme continued to build on the foundations he had laid, with editors like Peter Luke and presenters like Clive Goodwin, and it remained ITV's only regular programme on the arts until the weekend franchise changed ownership in 1968. Its creative baton ultimately found itself in the safe hands of Melvyn Bragg and *The South Bank Show*.

Tempo, *Thank Your Lucky Stars*, *Armchair Theatre* and *The Avengers* were not the only ABC programmes to be treated cavalierly by ATV, but elsewhere on the network something new and strange was beginning to happen. *Sing Along with Joe* was getting bigger audiences on Sunday afternoon in the North and Midlands than the *London Palladium* show on Sunday night. *Comedy Bandbox*, introducing a new generation of comedy talent to television like Les Dawson, Mike Yarwood and Jimmy Tarbuck, was getting bigger audiences on Saturday evening than *Val Parnell's Saturday Spectacular*. The regional companies, impressed by our ratings, were taking more of our programmes and fewer of ATV's. London's other ITV company, Associated-Rediffusion, wanted to buy *Thank Your Lucky Stars* for its weekday audiences. World-famous American entertainers like Peggy Lee, Bing Crosby and Frank Sinatra were following Sammy Davis Jr in making their first British TV specials for ABC not ATV: *Frank Sinatra at the Festival Hall*, and Peggy Lee and Bing Crosby, together with two celebrated masters of The Great American Song-book, Sammy Cahn and Jimmy Van Heusen, videotaped at Teddington. Both shows were produced by Philip Jones, and both were taken by ATV. ABC was beginning to be recognised as an all-round programme company. In October, 1962, Howard Thomas told me that the Board was pleased with my progress and had accepted his recommendation that I be appointed the company's Programme Controller. A few weeks later, the BBC announced that Sydney Newman was leaving ABC to join BBC Television as its Head of Drama.

This was one hell of a bombshell. Sydney had been crucial to the company's success and it was devastating to think that my promotion might have had anything to do with his leaving. That was the instant impression. I'm afraid it was an impression Howard did nothing to dispel; indeed, fifteen years later in his autobiography he was still encouraging it. "It was obvious," he wrote, "that my choice would be either our head of Drama or the head of Features and Light Entertainment. There are always agonising moments like this for an executive who has schooled two top men to be capable of succeeding him. It was the first of several such occasions when I knew that whichever man I chose I would lose the services of the other." That was simply not true in this case, though it would be years before I discovered what actually happened. The BBC had offered the post to Sydney a year earlier, in September 1961 but the ABC Board had insisted on Sydney working out his contract, which did not expire until the end of 1962.

In his 1969 autobiography, the great reforming Director-General of the BBC Hugh Carleton Greene said that when he was appointed in 1960 he was determined to "open the windows and dissipate the ivory tower stuffiness which still clung to some parts of the BBC." In his view the BBC's Drama Department was one of those parts, and he was determined to revitalise it with the energy and social realism that Sydney had injected into British television drama with new writers like Alun Owen, Clive Exton, Bill Naughton and Harold Pinter. The opportunity to revitalise it with Sydney himself, new writers and all, fell into his lap when ABC lost half its *Armchair Theatre* output and experienced the humiliation of the remainder being reduced to alternate fortnightly transmission with *The Avengers*.

Hugh Greene saw that this blow would have shaken Sydney's morale if not his pride, and the Corporation's Director of Television, Kenneth Adam, was charged to tempt him with the rich, untrammelled pastures of BBC Drama. Sydney's own memoir, unpublished at his death but coming to light in 2011, makes it clear that Kenneth Adam succeeded. It seems that I hadn't been the cause of Sydney's departure after all. And whatever agonising moments my appointment might or might not have caused Howard, he now had someone else to pitch the company's programmes to Lew Grade. That same someone else also had to find a successor to Sydney as Drama Supervisor.

My first call for Sydney's successor was Leonard White, Sydney's right hand producer. Quietly capable, softly-spoken Leonard was the only other producer in ABC's drama department. Sydney produced *Armchair Theatre*; Leonard, who had just completed the second season of *The Avengers*, seemed to produce everything else. He had begun his career as an actor and in fact had appeared for Dennis Vance in *Armchair Theatre*'s very first season. He had gone on to direct in the theatre as well as act, in Canada as well as in Britain, and it was in Canada that he first met Sydney, then CBC's Head of Drama, when he joined the Canadian Broadcasting Corporation's first training course for TV producer/directors.

Family business had brought Leonard back home and his CBC training had won him freelance work as a TV director for Television Wales and West, Southern Television and Tyne Tees Television. Sydney discovered that he was back in Britain and offered him a job: not as a director – he said he had plenty of those – but as a producer. Leonard joined ABC in February 1960, a few days after me, to take over *Inside Story*, a new drama series which had Ted Willis as its story editor but no producer; and he had been working flat out ever since. By the time he knocked on my door, he had produced the last nine episodes of *Inside Story*, Ian Hendry's *Police Surgeon* series, 40 episodes of *The Avengers*, 1960's summer season of *Armchair Mystery Theatre* and 1962's summer season of science fiction plays *Out of This World*: a total of 76 one-hour plays and nine half-hours in less than three years. I thought he could do with a change of pace.

It seemed to me that it was time to separate the functions of Drama Supervisor and *Armchair Theatre* producer. I wanted to relieve the head of the department of day-to-day production responsibilities, to give him the time and freedom to build on the success of *The Avengers* with more prime time series. So I offered Leonard a choice: *The Avengers*, head of the department or producer of *Armchair Theatre*. He chose *Armchair Theatre*. Good call for both of us. In his first full season, *Armchair Theatre* provided 13 of Television Audience Measurement's Top Twenty Plays of the Year, including the top three. Before he retired Leonard would personally produce a total of 165 *Armchair Theatre* teleplays, most of them specially commissioned new writing. That's more productions and more specially commissioned new plays than Sydney.

I still had to find a new Drama Supervisor. Before I could start looking for a suitable outside contender there was another knock on my door. This was George F. Kerr, one of the department's story editors. George had been associated with *Armchair Theatre* from its beginnings under Dennis Vance, indeed he had adapted its very first production, "The Outsider", from a stage play by Dorothy Brandon. Under Sydney, story editors like Irene Shubik, John Bryce, Terence Feely and Robert Banks Stewart didn't adapt or edit scripts; they looked for stories. They were the department's essential core, finding new writers, encouraging them, persuading producers and directors to commission them. George was one of the most experienced exponents of this art and he thought that he was ready to apply it to running the department. And since new ideas from new writers for new series were exactly what I hoped the department would produce, I agreed. "Why not, George? Take the job, see how you make out. Sydney's a hard act to follow but I'll do anything I can to help you, and I wish you every success."

So, as Programme Controller, I had a new Drama Supervisor. Lloyd Shirley and Ronnie Taylor were my obvious and natural choices as Features Supervisor and Light Entertainment Supervisor respectively. Lloyd was already happily involved with *Tempo*, *The Sunday Break*, other Closed Period religious programmes and *ABC of The North* and *The Midlands*, their resources now merged to form a weekly omnibus *ABC at Large*. But I'm afraid I had a couple of problems already cooking for Ronnie in the persons of Hughie Green and Al Read.

Trouble At T'Mill

Hughie Green was the hugely successful quiz-master of Rediffusion's *Double Your Money*, a simple quiz in which members of the public were invited to answer general knowledge questions for a possible Jackpot Prize of £1,000, a significant sum in those early sixties. I thought we could add the skills of an amateur detective to Hughie's status as a quiz-master and let him work Britain's music halls each week with his quiz show, helping the local gendarmerie to solve local crimes wherever he travelled; and we had an irresistible title for it: *Green for Danger*.

Hughie thought it was a great idea; I signed him up to do 13 shows and handed the project to Ernest Maxin. Ernest hired some first-rate writers and an excellent supporting cast and they produced two pilot shows, but the idea remained stubbornly dead in the water. I had dreamt up a preposterous premise which even Ernest's expertise as a producer and Ronnie's own scriptwriting ingenuity were unable to breathe into life. We couldn't possibly proceed to a series, but I had a contract with Hughie for thirteen shows; how were we going to get out of those?

Fortunately, I remembered that Hughie had been the presenter of a successful radio talent show, Opportunity Knocks, which had begun its life on the BBC's Light Programme before transferring to Radio Luxembourg in the early fifties. The show had enjoyed a brief and nondescript television outing in 1956 on Associated-Rediffusion before it was abandoned for Hughie's much more successful *Double Your Money* quiz. Perhaps it was capable of a revival? Hughie's agent was the ever accommodating Harry Foster. Could we possibly convert the discontinued *Green for Danger* into thirteen editions of *Opportunity Knocks*? "Why not?" said Harry, stroking his immaculately trimmed moustache. "Provided Hughie agrees." Hughie owned the format so, not surprisingly, Hughie agreed. And seriously folks, as Hughie might have said, that's how Hughie Green's *Opportunity Knocks* came back to British television and began its 14-year residency in ITV's Top Twenty: the result of a calamitous creative cock-up on my part. Its ghost has lived on through many subsequent versions of the talent show format, and still walks today in *Britain's Got Talent*. Sorry, folks; and I mean that sincerely.

Al Read presented Ronnie with a very different problem. This Salford comedian featured a new kind of observational comedy: wry monologues and duologues based on his Lancashire working-class experiences, with Al playing all the characters. Al, who started work in his family sausage-making business and ended up as its managing director, had in his 40s become a popular after-dinner speaker and an occasional performer in Northern working-men's clubs, where he was seen by a BBC North talent-scout in 1950. He was given a spot on the Light Programme's *Variety Fanfare* show for new artistes and thereby met its producer Ronnie Taylor. Ronnie's own sense of comedy was a perfect match for Al's. They found they worked well together, dreamed up a format, and *The Al Read Show* for BBC Radio North, written and produced by Ronnie, was a huge success from 1951 to 1968, with audiences of up to an astonishing 20 million.

Al had taken his radio act into the theatre, where he was equally successful – and not only in the north of England. He topped the bill at the Adelphi Theatre in London for a year and appeared in two Royal Variety Performances. I loved his radio show, and when I saw him on stage at Blackpool's Opera House in the early sixties I thought his comedy could work just as well on television. I asked Ronnie to introduce me and persuaded Al to let us have a go at transferring his unique gift to the TV screen. At which point I became Programme Controller and handed the transfer process over to Ronnie, although my conscience led me to sit in on it.

The process was, let us say, tortuous. Al had previously worked in clubs and theatres with material he knew by heart, or at the microphone in a radio studio with new material which he could read from a script. Now we were asking him to work in an unfamiliar setting and play to the unblinking eye of a television camera with new and unfamiliar material, and that came neither naturally nor easily to him. Rehearsals for the first pilot were disastrous. Al said it was difficult to remember the new material, so we put the script on to teleprompters suspended beneath the camera lenses. But Al's eye line was then aimed at the teleprompter, so he appeared to be looking off camera throughout the show and not at the audience at home.

Al said he had a new idea: let him have an earpiece so that Ronnie could cue him in from the control room whenever he seemed uncertain about what came next in the script. We tried that, and found that Al was now relying on Ronnie's feed from the very beginning of the show. He found it difficult to say even the opening "Good evening" without it, which led to an uncharacteristically stilted performance. Al said the problem was that he was used to seeing the friendly faces of his theatre audiences, but the studio audiences were hidden from him by cameras and microphone booms and technicians. He needed a friendly face to work to. "How are we going to manage that, Al?" "Simple. David Hamilton has a friendly face..." Indeed he did: David "Diddy" Hamilton was one of ABC's popular on-screen presenters, much loved by our television audiences and, apparently, by Al. So we stuck a large photograph of David's friendly face onto each of our four studio cameras for him to address. Television was not a comfortable medium for Al.

We tried hard. To give Al some respite in the show I commissioned the graphics company of Halas & Batchelor to produce an animated cartoon to the voice track of one of Al's monologues. John Halas and his wife Joy Batchelor had made several successful children's cartoon series for ABC, and if *Life and Al Read* had worked, we might have anticipated *The Simpsons* by thirty years or so in creating a cartoon element in a comedy show which grew into a successful comedy show in its own right. But Ronnie managed to get only six half-hours of *Life with Al Read* on the air. Three years later, BBC Television were no more successful in their attempt to capture Al's genius on videotape: they achieved only six half-hours of *Al Read says What a Life!* And in 1972 ATV tried again to crack the problem with *It's All in Life*, but managed to complete only eight episodes. A total of 20 television half-hours in a comedy career that lasted 35 years, none of them showing this superb entertainer at his best. Thank goodness some of those radio shows still exist.

ATV took both series: Hughie and Al were far too popular to turn down. But in any case networking relations seemed to be less fraught between our two companies. Howard Thomas was taking me along with him to those weekly meetings now and it was my job to pitch our programmes to Lew Grade, though when it came to haggling over prices and payment I was relegated to the outer office while Howard and Lew engaged in single combat behind closed doors. I must say I enjoyed those programme sessions with Lew, which, however competitive, were always good natured and considerate of each company's programming problems and ambitions.

Lew agreed to take the second and all subsequent series of *Thank Your Lucky Stars* – and not just because I was able to tell him that John McMillan wanted the show for Rediffusion's weekday London schedule: he could see it was a ratings-winner. He accepted my suggestion that alternating series made much more sense than alternating episodes, so *Tempo* and *The Avengers* reverted to weekly transmission for their subsequent outings. He even accepted the argument that our relative two-to-one share of the audience at the weekend should be reflected in the number of slots occupied respectively by *Armchair Theatre* and ATV's *Drama '62* (and '63 and '64 and so on); and in the following year he also agreed that these slots would be more sensibly filled by whole series rather than by piecemeal alternation.

I don't know to what we owed this unaccustomed amenability. Val Parnell retired towards the end of 1962 so presumably Lew as sole Managing Director had considerably more to occupy him than the question of who should schedule what or when. Perhaps his determination to break into the American network market was diverting some of his attention too. Because British television operated on a different line standard from America – 405 lines rather than 525 – we could only transmit each other's live or videotaped programmes by filming them from the television screen itself, and the fuzzy quality of such telerecordings, or kinescopes as the Americans called them, made for most unattractive viewing. Today, computers can clear up the fuzz, sharpen the pictures and render those old recordings perfectly playable, but in the sixties television programmes were only widely marketable internationally if they were filmed in the first place rather than transferred to film subsequently.

ATV's production and distribution company ITC had been supplying half-hour action-adventure film series to ITV ever since the service's opening night. *The Adventures of Robin Hood* was a star attraction of ITV's first weekend and it had been followed by the adventures of, in turn, *Sir Lancelot*, *The Buccaneers*, *William Tell* and *Sir Francis Drake*, most of which had sold well internationally and in syndication to the States, though not yet to any of the American networks.

Now Lew was expanding into one-hour series with *The Saint*, starring Roger Moore and *Danger Man*, starring Patrick McGoohan. *The Saint* would finally make ATV's primetime network breakthrough with a sale to NBC, the first one-hour British television series to do so, and since Lew was forever flying back and forth to the States making the sales pitches to network bosses in person, it was perhaps understandable if his concentration on ITV's network schedule was a little distracted. Or could Lew's change of heart on these scheduling anomalies possibly have been the result of a little pressure being applied by the ITA at last?

It wouldn't have been at all surprising. The Pilkington Report on the future of British broadcasting, including the practicability of a third and fourth television service, was published in June 1962. It proposed among other recommendations that the Independent Television Authority should take over the planning of all ITV programming, let alone the matter of alternate scheduling. ITV was, alas, roundly tarred and feathered by Sir Harry Pilkington's Committee. In their view, while the BBC was the very pinnacle of public service broadcasting, ITV was Caliban come again, just as those who had resisted its very concept at the outset always said it would be. The Committee considered the companies to be money-grubbing and their programmes vulgar; the Authority was the feeblest of regulators; the system was devoid of social conscience and the whole structure should be scrapped and begun again from scratch. I paraphrase; but not much.

The Committee's proposals for a radical restructure of ITV required the Authority not only to plan all the network's programme schedules but also to commission all its programmes, sell all its advertising time, and exercise the firmest regulatory control over all its activities. As for the BBC, its exemplary national service deserved to be extended and complemented by an additional channel. As the Postmaster General, Reg Bevins, observed at the first meeting of Tory backbenchers to discuss the Report, Pilkington had painted the BBC whiter than white. Indeed it had; and along with the whitewash it gave the BBC the third channel. A fourth channel might ultimately be given to the Independent Television Authority but only after far-reaching structural and operational changes to the system. All Pilkington gave ITV was a severe drubbing. But the Committee's excessive, almost unrelieved criticism defeated its purpose. Independent Television was far and away the more popular service, watched by more than two thirds of the viewing audience. No Tory Government could ignore that fact, nor could any Labour Opposition; and Fleet Street – most of which now had a stake in one or other of the ITV companies – made sure they didn't. According to the *Daily Mirror*, the public had been told to "Go to hell!", and the possible electoral repercussions of such an attitude towards the people's channel were not lost on either Party.

A year of prolonged Parliamentary debate followed, including the consideration of not one but two White Papers. *The Yorkshire Post* observed that "although the Pilkington Report gave birth to both White Papers, neither of them looks like mother". Although the new Television Act, when it received its Royal Assent at the end of July 1963, implemented Pilkington's allocation of the third channel to the BBC, it incorporated none of the Report's proposals for the organic restructuring of Independent Television. Nevertheless, Pilkington's identification of weaknesses in the ITV system resonated throughout both the Act and the action which flowed from it. An 11 percent levy was slapped on the companies' advertising revenue to curb their excessive profits. Advertising magazines were abolished. And the Authority was given complete responsibility for all the programmes transmitted by the system, and all the statutory powers to enforce it. Those powers would not fail to be energised by the strength of will and personality of the Authority's new Chairman, Charles Hill, who took up his post four weeks before the Bill became law.

In the ensuing years significant changes would be made to the ITV system under the new Television Act. In addition to the conversion to UHF, 625 lines and colour, all of which would be introduced with BBC 2 and then extended to both BBC 1 and ITV, the Authority would insist on adequate provision for minority programmes, more competition with the BBC in sport and children's programmes, and more time and resources devoted to ITN, including the introduction of British television's first daily half-hour news programme. It would set up a system of detailed consultation with the companies both individually, on a day to day basis, and jointly, in regular meetings of a new Programme Policy Committee, chaired by Charles Hill. The arrangements for scheduling and payment for programmes between the four major companies and between those four and the eleven regional companies would be rationalised and regulated.

The companies' own Network Planning Committee would be joined by a permanent observer from the ITA staff. Within the Authority itself, a Programme Schedules Committee would be established, also chaired by the indefatigable Mr – soon to be Lord – Hill, as well as a number of small specialist committees in which Members of the Authority would play a more active role in specific areas of policy. Significant changes indeed. Happily however, two of them would make it possible for ATV and ABC to extend the amenability which had resolved the scheduling of drama and the arts to a successful collaboration in two very different areas of programming.

Any kind of additional airtime in ABC's tight little two-day franchise was of value to the company, even if advertising were debarred from it: extra airtime earned extra advertising minutes, which could be deployed elsewhere in the schedule. Howard Thomas's success in opening up the Closed Period on Sunday for *The Sunday Break* and, in the process, earning additional advertising airtime for peak hours later in the evening, encouraged him to propose a similar dispensation for adult education programmes, to be broadcast during another closed period, Sunday morning, closed in this case to programmes other than Church Services. He had a fellow advocate in Norman Collins, the Deputy Chairman of ATV, and in January 1962 the two of them put a proposal to the ITA for an hour of adult education between 10 am and 11 am on Sundays.

Events moved at an unusual pace thereafter. In June 1962 the Pilkington Report recommended the continued inclusion of educational broadcasts in all future television services. A few weeks later the first White Paper agreed that education should have a place in all broadcasting services and announced that additional hours would be authorised for adult education as well as schools. And in October the Postmaster General wrote to the ITA to say that he was ready to consider any application for additional television hours to be used for adult education programmes.

He didn't know what would hit him. A speedy eleven days later Mr Bevins received the ITA's application for the ABC/ATV proposal. "We have been a little taken aback by the speed with which your application followed my letter of 4 October" he replied, but he agreed to accept it as an operational trial. On Sunday, 10 January 1965, ABC and ATV introduced British television's first regular adult education series: three 20-minute programmes under the overall title of *Sunday Session*. No haggling over costs this time: the relative sizes of the two weekend services were duly observed and the programmes were simply swapped, two of the weekly series being produced by ABC and one by ATV.

ABC's initial programmes, inspired like the project itself by Howard Thomas, were *You Don't Say*, on speaking effectively, and *Pen to Paper*, on writing effectively, or as Howard liked to refer to them, *How to Speak*

Proper and *How to Write Proper*. ATV's series sandwiched between the two was *Mesdames, Messieurs*, a guide to conversational French. *Sunday Session* quickly established itself as the central pillar of ITV adult education; and ABC's participation in it gave our Features Department the opportunity to expand its programme-making range to a remarkable degree with series as varied as *The Law is Yours*; *An Anatomy of First Aid*; *Psychology for Everyman*; *The ABC of Do It Yourself*; *The Grammar of Cookery*; *Clear Thinking*, on the exercise of logic; and *Your Environment*, on the workings of town planning and local government. The Features Department range would soon be expanded still further by a second, considerably more onerous, programme responsibility. But that was still to come. First there was the little matter of the new ITV franchises.

Above: "Footlights hosts and guests of honour" at the Cambridge University Theatre Ball of 1952. BT in the foreground, back to camera, with Footlights president the Hon. Andrew Davidson on my right. Future actor Peter Jeffrey is far left; Stanley Myers is sitting back left.

Above: Singing "Round about Paris" in the Torch Theatre's *Spring Fever* 1950 revue. Could this be why Henry Kendall thought I might have a future as an ASM?

Below: The cast of *The Duchess of Malfi* 1951 on tour in France. BT in centre, with Nigel Davenport second from left; future actor Hugh Dickson to the left; Paul Almond, future film and TV director, behind to the right; Tony Richardson partly obscured further to the right; and "le guitariste" Chuck Tilley foreground right. I don't know where Colin George is; perhaps he's taking the picture.

Above: With Nevill Coghill, founder of Oxford's Experimental Theatre Club, discussing my production of *Make it a Date* 1950.

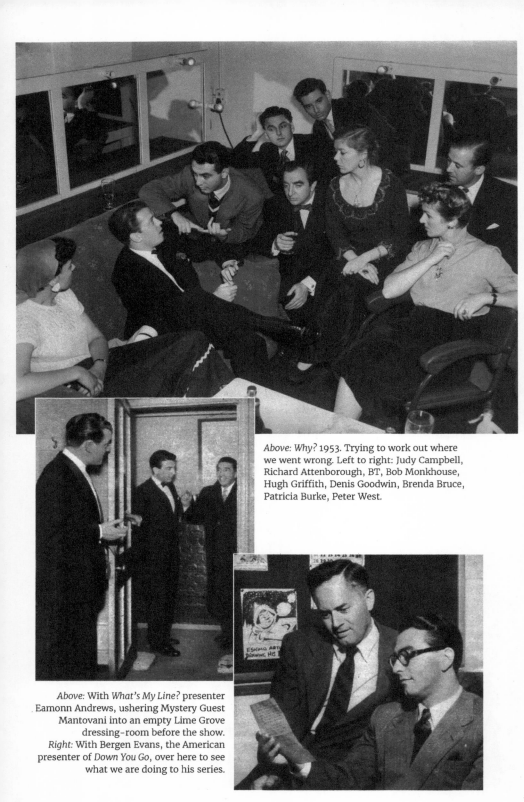

Above: Why? 1953. Trying to work out where we went wrong. Left to right: Judy Campbell, Richard Attenborough, BT, Bob Monkhouse, Hugh Griffith, Denis Goodwin, Brenda Bruce, Patricia Burke, Peter West.

Above: With *What's My Line?* presenter Eamonn Andrews, ushering Mystery Guest Mantovani into an empty Lime Grove dressing-room before the show.
Right: With Bergen Evans, the American presenter of *Down You Go*, over here to see what we are doing to his series.

Studio G, Lime Grove in 1953. *Above:* Panoramic shot from *Illustrated* magazine of the *Guess My Story* studio with cameras, lights, studio manager, studio audience, host Peter West and the panel of Michael Pertwee, Helen Cherry, Pat Kirkwood and guest panellist Wolf Mankowitz, at their respective desks.
Left: Briefing some of the challengers.

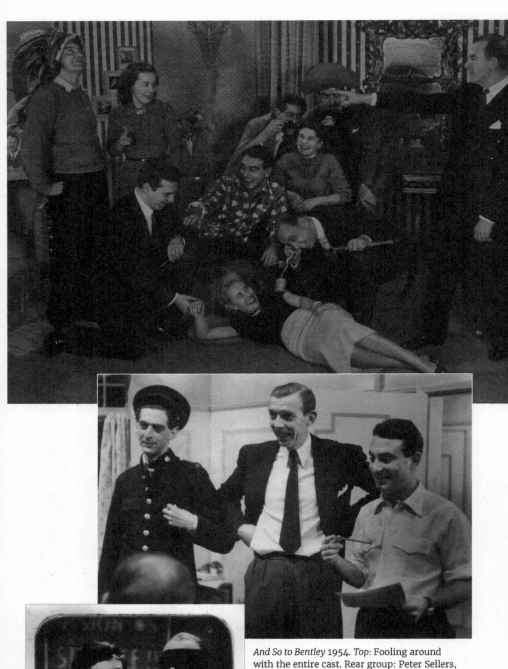

And So to Bentley 1954. *Top:* Fooling around with the entire cast. Rear group: Peter Sellers, Rosemary Miller, Denis Norden, Charlotte Mitchell, Frank Muir, Dick Bentley, and the show's MD Eric Robinson; centre group: Ernest Maxin, BT, guest star Jill Day, Bill Fraser. *Above:* Studio rehearsal with Denis, dressed for his walk-on appearance, and Frank. *Left:* Telesnap of Dick Bentley and Peter Sellers.

Wakey! Wakey! The Billy Cotton Band Show 1956. *Right:* With Billy Cotton on holiday in Alassio in 1956. *Inset:* Telesnap of Billy and Max Bygraves in the show.

Above: Sizing up the Television Toppers, who danced for us in the early editions of the show.

Ask Pickles 1954–55.
Above: To celebrate the success of the first series of the show, Wilfred invited ten people who appeared in it to 'meet the stars' at Lime Grove. BT is wheeling Wilfred and Mabel in on a camera dolly and the guests are happily star-gazing at the TV personalities gathered up from among those working at Lime Grove that day, including Eamonn Andrews, Sylvia Peters, Peter Dimmock, Helen Cherry, Frankie Howerd, Janette Scott, Helene Cordet and Philip Harben.
Left: With Wilfred and Mabel.

Left: Telesnap of BT breaking the news on air to Wilfred and Mabel that the show had won the The Daily Mail National Television Award 1954. *Above:* With Pauline and Larry Forrester and the Award.

Above: Barbara with Braden 1955. With Barbara.
Left: Telesnaps of Pat Kirkwood as Vesta Tilley delivering three of her celebrated songs.
Below: Bath Night with Braden 1957.
"I suppose you think that's funny!"

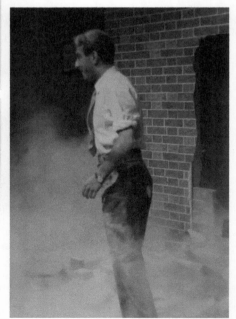

The Dickie Henderson Show 1957–1958. From top to bottom: Shani Wallis's entrance on a slide on the first show; Dickie with Bob Hope: "Keep Bob Hope. Drop the violins"; Dickie with Jack Buchanan; Dickie with Diana Dors.

The Rosemary Clooney Show 1957. George's Aunt Rosie was very pregnant at the time but, great trouper that she was, didn't opt out of any of the strenuous production numbers.

*Dear Brian
Thank you for one
of the most famous
memories I have
of TV any where —
with great
Admiration
Love
Rosemary*

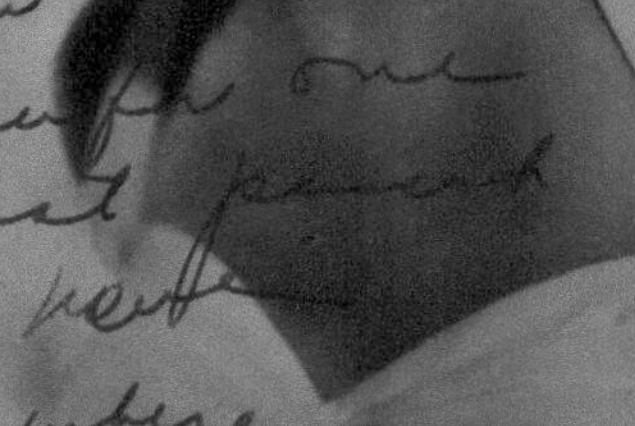

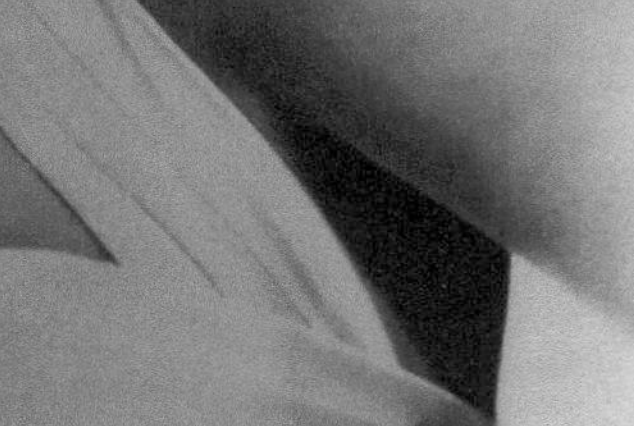

The Johnnie Ray Show 1957. Johnnie also gave me a state
of the art wristwatch with "Johnnie Ray" emblazoned
where the manufacturer's name is normally positioned.
I never wore it, but my father happily did.

A11

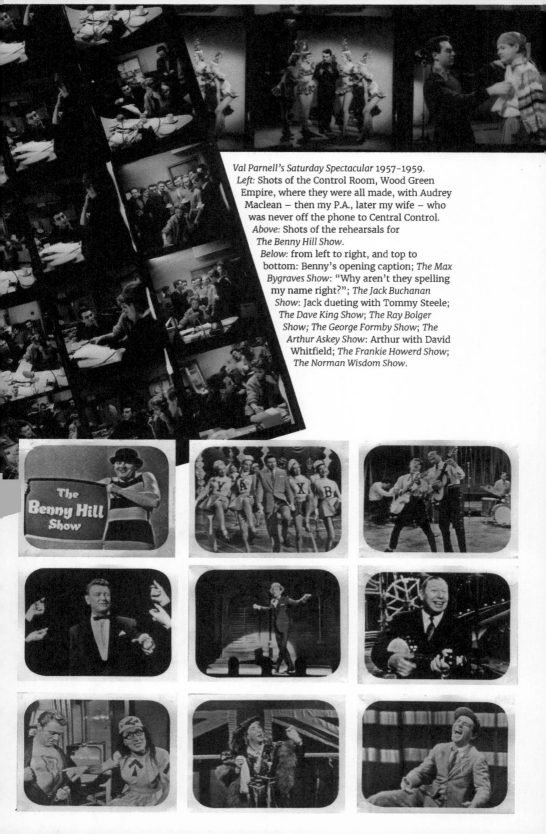

Val Parnell's Saturday Spectacular 1957–1959.
Left: Shots of the Control Room, Wood Green Empire, where they were all made, with Audrey Maclean – then my P.A., later my wife – who was never off the phone to Central Control.
Above: Shots of the rehearsals for *The Benny Hill Show.*
Below: from left to right, and top to bottom: Benny's opening caption; *The Max Bygraves Show*: "Why aren't they spelling my name right?"; *The Jack Buchanan Show*: Jack dueting with Tommy Steele; *The Dave King Show; The Ray Bolger Show; The George Formby Show; The Arthur Askey Show*: Arthur with David Whitfield; *The Frankie Howerd Show; The Norman Wisdom Show.*

Val Parnell's Sunday Night at the London Palladium 1957–58. *Above:* Val Parnell's production right-hand man Charles Henry is squeezed between Audrey and Dickie Henderson (the first of our monthly Palladium comperes) alongside me and Frankie Vaughan. Two of The King Brothers are in the background and choreographer George Carden's back is on the right. *Right:* With Alicia Markova.

More *Sunday Night at the London Palladium*. Telesnaps of some of the Presenters. *Top row L to R:* Dickie Henderson in the first show of his first Palladium stint, with Shani Wallis and Harry Secombe; Bob Monkhouse; Hughie Green, with George Sanders. *Above Right:* Alfred Marks. *Below Right:* Robert Morley, with Line Renaud. *Below:* Bruce Forsyth; followed by front and back views of The Tiller Girls high-kicking their way to the audience.

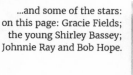

...and some of the stars: on this page: Gracie Fields; the young Shirley Bassey; Johnnie Ray and Bob Hope.

... Don Ameche; Ella Fitzgerald;
Guy Mitchell... Max Bygraves
with Peter Sellers and Eric
Sykes; Larry Parks and Betty
Garrett; Juliette Greco...
Liberace... and Mario Lanza.
Below: New Look 1958–59.
Bruce Forsyth and Roy Castle.

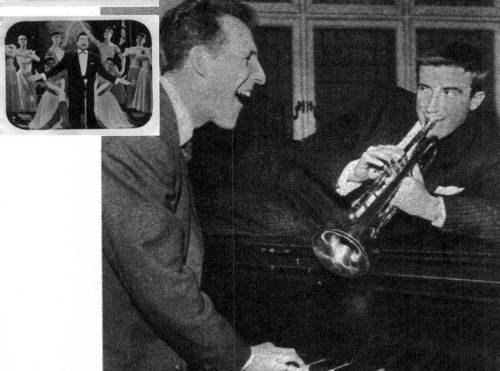

BBC & ATV: The joys of Inlay and Overlay. This technique was developed by BBC engineer D.R. Campbell and his team. With Inlay you inserted a picture shot by one camera into a picture shot by another. With Overlay you superimposed a picture shot by one camera on top of a picture shot by another. It was great fun as well as hard work. Clockwise from top: *The Dickie Henderson Show* ATV 1957; *The Petula Clark Show* BBC 1956; *Music and Magic* BBC 1956; *The Harry Secombe Show* ATV 1957; *The Dickie Henderson Show* ATV 1958; *Secombe and Friends* ATV 1959; *New Look* ATV 1958; *Ted Heath and His Music* BBC 1956.

All Change

ITV's current contracts were due to expire at the end of June 1964. The new Television Act committed the Government to a decision on a possible second ITV channel within three years so the Authority decided to run its new contracts from July 1964 until the end of 1967 and, with the exception of Wales where there were specific problems to overcome, to run them with the current areas and regions unchanged. The advertisement inviting applications for the new contracts appeared on 16 September 1963. By the closing date of 18 November all the existing programme companies had applied, together with eight new contenders, two of them for the ABC franchise. Interviews would begin forthwith and the allocation of contracts would be announced in January 1964.

As the company's Programme Controller I was now regularly attending its monthly Board meetings and the Board was not at all looking forward to its forthcoming interview. My presence was required in order to report on our programmes and I was called in along with the company's Advertising Manager, Bob Norris, who was there to report on our advertising revenue. When revenue failed to meet its targets he and his boss George Cooper, ABC's vastly experienced Director of Sales, would explain that our programme schedule was at fault, that this or that programme was not working and that we needed to play such and such in that slot if we wanted to maximise our audience and our revenue. A baptism of concentrated fire for a tyro executive, but I learned a great deal from these encounters – not least how to fight my corner against acute and articulate opposition.

As a producer I had simply made the best programmes I could. As a programme executive I encouraged my producers and creative heads to do the same. Now, from these monthly challenges from George and Bob, both of whom were to become close and lifelong friends, I learned how those programmes could most effectively be deployed. I learned about the television audience and its demographics, how to build that audience by the ingenious juxtaposition of programmes, how to apply the dark skills of programme scheduling and counter-scheduling. Half a century later, those skills have been rendered redundant by the profusion of television channels and the accessibility of recording systems, iPlayers, and DVD box sets. Today's viewers can choose what they want to watch and when to watch it; they are their own programme planners. But it was an exhilarating exercise while it lasted and it is gratifying to find it acknowledged in the official history of *Independent Television in Britain*. The author of Volume Two, Bernard Sendall, is generous enough in one of his references to Howard Thomas to note that "in Brian Tesler as his programme controller he possessed one of the most skilful programme planners ITV has ever had." Aw, shucks!

With its interview for the new programme contract looming, ABC's Board was becoming increasingly apprehensive. This would be its very first contract application. No application, no interview, had been necessary for the current franchise: the contract had been offered to the parent Corporation by the ITA with a money-back guarantee if it should fail. It wasn't the strength of our rival applicants that concerned us: neither of them seemed a substantial threat. Our apprehension was about the impositions that might be laid on us in the light of the Pilkington Report and the new Television Act. We were conscious of the difficulty we continued to have in establishing an identity in our very different regions. We were aware of the constrictions of a two-day franchise, though we thought we were making a pretty good fist of it. Our programme range was extensive; our network drama and light entertainment programmes were well received; we had been praised for the minority programmes – religion and adult education – we had managed to cram into our tight little schedule. But were we doing enough?

We knew we were vulnerable in our coverage of sport; were we also vulnerable in the number and range of the programmes aimed at our regional viewers? It was a markedly uneasy group of ABC representatives which assembled at the ITA's headquarters in the Brompton Road on the cold November morning of our interview. The team comprised Chairman Sir Philip Warter, Deputy Chairman Robert Clark, Managing Director Howard

Thomas and the Corporation's Secretary Jimmy McDonald, with George Cooper, Bob Norris, Bernard Greenhead and me on hand to answer questions on advertising revenue, engineering or programmes; and our joint apprehension was cruelly inhibiting.

The interview was disastrous.

It wasn't helped by the gloom of the cavernous first floor conference hall in which it took place, with Lord Hill, Sir Robert Fraser and the senior officers of the Authority looking down on us from an elevated dais and the huge windows behind them revealing a melancholy, overcast sky. The self-effacing Sir Philip was thrown by what we slowly realised was the protocol for such interviews: the ITA Chairman would put the Authority's questions to the Company's Chairman and he was expected to pass those questions on to whichever colleague he felt appropriate to answer them. Unfortunately, Sir Philip tried to answer them all himself: all the questions about engineering, advertising and programming, everything, whether it was within his field of expertise or not. And the rest of us were too inhibited by the procedure, too frozen by the formality, to interrupt him by jumping in with an uninvited response.

We were dying.

And then suddenly, faintly, in the distance we heard the sound of a Scottish military band playing "Scotland the Brave", a sound which grew nearer and nearer, as if the band were marching to our rescue, the pipes and fifes and drums coming closer and closer, louder and louder, until their heart-stirring sound was filling the room, seeming to come up through the floorboards, through the windows, through the conference room doors, overwhelming, magnificent. Authority and ABC members sat equally open-mouthed until the music came to a triumphant climax and stopped, and we all burst into laughter, the gloom that had enveloped us totally dispelled. Lord Hill said "Gentlemen, I have absolutely no idea where that came from: I assure you it was not provided by the Authority, but it was a most amusing diversion. Shall we continue?" And continue we did, but this time in a far more relaxed and congenial atmosphere, with Lord Hill putting his questions very much more helpfully – "Perhaps, Sir Philip, you could ask Bernard Greenhead to tell us about your plans for the conversion to UHF and colour?" – and all of us being given the opportunity to answer the appropriate questions directly.

When the interview was over and the ABC contingent left the conference room we mobbed our Scottish members: surely, if the Authority wasn't responsible for the pipe band, it had to be the work of Robert Clark and Jimmy McDonald? How on earth had they contrived that miraculous, life-saving interruption? But Robert and Jimmy were as nonplussed as the rest of us. It wasn't until we were outside the premises and saw the posters on its walls that we realised the sound really had been coming through the windows and up through the conference room floorboards. The building was occupied from the first floor upwards by the Authority. The entire ground floor belonged to a brand new branch of Boots the Chemists and today had been its grand opening, dramatically celebrated by the Band of the Scots Guards marching up the Brompton Road and reaching its thunderous conclusion of "Scotland the Brave" inside the store itself. Serendipity had been with us every step of its way.

When the new contracts were announced in January, the Authority recognised in ABC's case the difficulty of establishing a clear regional identity for a company operating two days a week in two service areas and its only stipulation in renewing our franchise was the appointment to the Board of a director drawn from the life of the areas. In April, ABC's Board invited the distinguished Merseyside doctor, Lord Cohen of Birkenhead, to join it. After a few meetings, Lord Cohen advised the Board that he felt there was little he could contribute to its proceedings, wished it well, and withdrew. The Authority didn't ask for a replacement, and the Board didn't look for one. We seemed to have come out of the franchise round extraordinarily well. All the other incumbents retained their franchises too, but with considerably greater reassurances and changes required of most of them, particularly the other majors. Nothing more was required of us; no criticism was made of our regional programming, and no mention was made of sport. Not yet; but not for long.

A few months later, Robert Fraser called Bill Ward and me together for a little private chat. This was payback time. Having delivered on adult education for ABC and ATV, the Authority now demanded something in return. "Sport, gentlemen. What are we going to do about sport? Or, rather, what are *you* going to do about it? ITV's sports coverage at the weekend is a disgrace. Your companies are responsible for the network's programmes at the weekend and your performance against the BBC's Grandstand is shamefully weak. Something must be done. You're the Programme Controllers. I look to the two of you to do it. Go away, and come back when you have a plan."

Of course he was absolutely right. On Saturday afternoons the people were deserting the people's channel. The one precaution taken by a complacent BBC before ITV went on the air in 1955 was to sign up as many of the important sport contracts as it could, and it had paid off triumphantly. You could see the audience graphs in the weekly TAM ratings books abruptly switch places on Saturday afternoon, the BBC's rocketing up, ITV's plummeting down, completely reversing the two-thirds/one-third supremacy we enjoyed in the rest of the week

The viewers simply wanted sport on Saturday afternoon. ITV had tried to give it to them, but the rights to all the major events belonged to the BBC. We could always find an afternoon's horseracing to cover; we had wrestling and tenpin bowling as potential attractions and we tried to interest the viewers in other Saturday afternoons out under the generic title of *Let's Go!* I blush now to remember some of those outings: lunchtime dance sessions with Joe Loss and his Orchestra from the Hammersmith Palais, for example; Driving Tests at the RASC Parade Ground, Bulford Camp, Salisbury; Ice Skating from the Manchester Ice Palace "with George Kay at the organ"; fashion shows and hairdressing demonstrations like "Crowning Glory" in which "John Cornel, Mayfair Hair stylist, will be demonstrating hair styles and fashions for women from 16 to 60 from a large Croydon Store." Not surprisingly, the great majority of viewers preferred to watch the BBC's coverage of the British Lightweight Championship boxing match, a Rugby Union International between England and Ireland, the Covered Court Tennis Championships from the Queen's Club. Wouldn't you?

Nevertheless, we had to go back to the Authority with a plan – in order to achieve which, Bill was obliged to speak to me again after four years, enabling us at last to resume our friendship, a case of ill wind blowing favourably for a change. We agreed that cooperation was essential but co-production impractical: one of the companies had to take the lead in setting up a production team and running the show and the other would share the costs, the coverage and, via a liaison committee, the planning. ABC had the bigger audience to serve at the weekend and a much larger Outside Broadcast Department with which to serve it, so it was agreed that ABC should take the lead. Over to Lloyd Shirley and ABC's Features Department.

I wanted to borrow the title of the American ABC Network's Saturday afternoon sports programme and call our show *Wide World of Sport*, but we dropped the "Wide" as soon as we realised just how many major national and international events the BBC had under long-term contract: ITV's world of sport would have to be pretty narrow for a while. As Programme Editor, Lloyd suggested John Bromley, the *Daily Mirror*'s sports columnist, and I accepted that engaging, energetic, expertly knowledgeable young man as soon as I met him. He and Lloyd put together a fine production team which included fellow sports writer Ian Marshall and ex-Olympic athlete Adrian Metcalfe, Executive Producer Geoffrey Gilbert and Director David Wickes. What we needed was an authoritative front man to host the show, preferably someone who would appeal to more than an audience of sports buffs. And I knew just the chap.

Eamonn Andrews, the hugely popular presenter of BBC Television's *This is Your Life*, *What's My Line?* and the afternoon children's programme *Crackerjack*, was also a sports enthusiast – indeed, a sports commentator for the BBC on boxing; and I had admired him for years as the genial host of BBC Radio's *Sports Report*. This was the weekly Saturday afternoon show in which Eamonn interviewed major sporting figures, reported on the day's key events, introduced the Sports Results and generally helped to make sport interesting and entertaining even to people who weren't especially enthusiastic about it: people like me. He would be the ideal host for our programme. Could we possibly prise him away from the BBC?

There was no harm in asking, particularly since he and I still shared the same manager, Teddy Sommerfield, who had managed me out of the BBC and into ITV in the first place. Now *there's* serendipity for you. I broached the subject to Teddy, who told me that, fortuitously, Eamonn wasn't too pleased with the BBC at that moment: his contract was due to expire and nobody had said a word to him about a new one, so he might just be persuadable. "Let's meet." Serendipity was working overtime: I couldn't believe that the BBC would take one of their best-loved personalities so much for granted, but who was I to complain? Yes indeed, Teddy. Let's meet. Quickly.

Teddy wanted our meetings to be in absolute secrecy, so I found myself in the middle of another B Movie. No: this time an A Movie, with a Teddy Sommerfield scenario. I would drive up to Portman Square, where Teddy and his wife Dorise had an apartment, park my car, and walk across the Square to a parked black Mercedes with tinted windows. Its uniformed chauffeur would get out and take himself off for a walk, and I would sidle into the back seat with Teddy, like Marlon Brando and Rod Steiger in *On The Waterfront* – I coulda been a contender, Charlie – to talk terms. When we'd finished, I would get out of the Mercedes and walk back to my car, and Teddy's driver would return. Teddy would report to Eamonn that evening and we would resume our talks the next day, following the same scenario. The car and the tinted windows were negotiation-specific: Teddy's office was just round the corner in Oxford Street; he didn't need a car or a chauffeur; he normally walked to his meetings. If I'd owned a fedora hat I would have pulled it down it down over my eyes as I walked back to my car.

Finally, we had a deal. Eamonn would do *World of Sport*, but he had to have a second network show: he couldn't leave *This is Your Life*, *Crackerjack* and *What's My Line?* for Saturday sport alone. Nor could ABC afford his fee for just one show. We needed another vehicle for him, and I already knew what that was going to be. I'd been itching to do a British version of *The Jack Paar Show* from the moment I had seen it in my ATV days in New York. Eamonn was the ideal host for this kind of informal chat among celebrity guests, and if the American experience was any guide, celebrities would queue up to come on such a show for fun, a fee and the chance to plug their latest book, movie, play or TV series. Teddy and Eamonn knew the *Paar Show* and were intrigued by its possibilities as a second vehicle for Eamonn.

I clinched the deal by saying I would try out the format on our North and Midlands transmitters so that we could get it right without the glare of network exposure before we handed it over to Eamonn. And so we did, during the first six months of 1964, in a show called *Gazette*, with a young performer called James Lloyd in the chair and two bright young researchers, Tom Brennand and Roy Bottomley, finding not only celebrities but also some fascinating local characters for its guests. The format worked; and in the autumn Jimmy Lloyd went back to the folk music circuit where we had found him, Tom and Roy came down to Teddington to adapt the format for Eamonn, and *The Eamonn Andrews Show − Live from London!* − went on the air at 11 pm on Sunday, 4 October 1964. It was British television's very first late night chat show, seven years before Michael Parkinson's chat show made its debut on the BBC.

The show was a great popular success, appearing regularly in the Top Twenty TV ratings, with a guest list that ranged from Randolph Churchill to Zsa Zsa Gabor, A. J. P. Taylor to George Raft, Sir John Barbirolli to The Beatles, J. B. Priestley to Tony Hancock. One edition featured both Bing Crosby and Bob Hope, another had Noël Coward, Muhammad Ali, Dudley Moore and Lucille Ball all on the same show. The audience loved Eamonn, though the critics tended to look down their noses at him, finding him ill at ease and uncomfortable.

It's true that this bluff, genial presenter, with years of success at the very top of his profession – he was voted Television Personality of the Year four times – could be thrown by an off-colour remark or an unplanned incident. Woody Allen's jokes about religion gave Eamonn – a Papal Knight and staunch Catholic – cause to swallow and force a laugh; the actor Laurence Harvey visibly embarrassed him with a risqué joke. The live show by its very nature presented other problems; ABC had to settle several libel cases out of court as a result of the off-the-cuff comments by some of our guests. So Howard Steele and his team of engineers devised a delayed transmission recording process which gave producer Malcolm Morris just enough time to cut or bleep the odd incautious remark. The proud announcement "*Live from London!*" had quietly disappeared by the show's third season; "*Almost Live from London!*" didn't have quite the same ring.

Three months later Eamonn embarked on the second leg of his Weekend Double. *World of Sport* made its debut on the afternoon of Saturday, 2 January 1965. More hard work for our engineers. In a remarkably short time, Teddington's facilities had been radically transformed to build a news-gathering and disseminating service as proficient as the BBC's with all its years of radio and television experience in sport. Existing circuits had to be reversed and new ones added, a new micro-wave link installed, a newspaper editorial office created from nowhere, fed with teleprinter circuits, telephone links to all OB points, service lines from Exchange Telegraph, Reuters and the Press Association – and a private wire to the managing director's office at Vernon's Pools in Liverpool. Brommers – inevitably, in the way of the sporting world, John Bromley had become Brommers – and his team put together as strong a package as they could provide without the assistance of the BBC's Contracts Department.

Our opening programme featured International Ski-jumping, Racing from Catterick, Motor Cycle Scrambling and Wrestling. We had Peter Lorenzo of *The Sun* on the day's football, Ian Wooldridge of the *Daily Mail* on the MCC Tour in South Africa, John Rickman on the day's racing, Jimmy Hill on the problems besetting contemporary British soccer, and Freddie Trueman on cricket and anything else he wanted to sound off about. We had a Pools Service bringing our viewers up to date on the Treble Chance and the day's probable dividends; and we had the day's Sports Results in full. All hosted with charm, insight and enthusiasm by Eamonn at his most authoritative, and all organised and produced by ABC, though credited in the *TV Times* as An Independent Television Presentation.

This was the beginning of ITV's fight against the BBC's supremacy in televised sport. It would be a long and bitter battle which would ultimately embroil the Independent Television Authority, the BBC Board of Governors, the Law Courts and the Government itself. ITV's baton would in due course be passed from ABC to its weekend successors in the franchise rounds of the future, with John Bromley still doggedly in there, fighting the good fight for ITV until his retirement. And in the end it would be transformed by the advent of subscription television. But for now it was beginning; and it was beginning well.

Major League

In 1964, the year of our renewed franchise, the Associated British Picture Corporation's annual profit was £5,246,439. ABC Television's contribution was 63.6 percent of that figure: £3,337,185. Howard Thomas was elected at last to the parent company's Board, a fitting and long-deserved reward. And, along with Bernard Greenhead and Bob Norris, I was elected to the Board of the Television Company, ITV's very first Director of Programmes. Six months later, Associated-Rediffusion followed suit and appointed its own Programme Controller, Cyril Bennett, to the Board. Cyril and I, who had been good friends from the beginning of our respective involvement in ITV, drank a toast to each other in the White Elephant restaurant in Curzon Street. We didn't know how much closer our respective careers would bring us ten years into the future.

In the turbulent present, meanwhile, far-reaching changes were having to be made in ABC's Programme Department. At the end of the year, Ronnie Taylor decided to return to freelance work in radio and television. He would continue to be available to us as a producer and writer through his production company, but no longer as our Supervisor of Light Entertainment. The obvious choice as his successor was Philip Jones, whose work for us had been outstanding, from Dora Bryan's situation comedy *Happily Ever After* to *Thank Your Lucky Stars*; from the specials with Peggy Lee and Frank Sinatra to *Big Night Out* studio spectaculars built round stars like Bob Monkhouse, Petula Clark and The Beatles. And also music shows like *Thank Your Lucky Stars*, which that year had been chosen as ITV's entry for The Golden Rose Light Entertainment Festival in Montreux. I was torn between Philip's brilliant contribution as a producer-director and Light Entertainment's need for a brilliant department head. I chose the latter. Another good call, as would be rapidly apparent.

Times were changing in Drama Department too. George Kerr told me he wanted to stand down as its Supervisor and return to writing and story-editing. The Department's creative drive had not lessened with Sydney Newman's departure to the BBC at the end of 1962. With story-editor John Bryce moving up to become its producer, *The Avengers* had continued on its triumphant way until the end of its third series in the spring of 1964, when Honor Blackman went off to play Pussy Galore in the James Bond movie *Goldfinger* and left us with the task of replacing the key Cathy Gale character. But *Armchair Theatre* was still flourishing under Leonard White. Our drama serials for younger viewers continued to alternate successfully with ATV's on weekend afternoons. Several popular new peak-time drama series had been created and taken by ATV and the rest of the network, including *Undermind*, a science-fiction thriller written by Robert Banks Stewart and *Jezebel Ex-UK*, with its stories of the passengers and crew of ocean-liner Jezebel on its journey back from Australia to the UK. *Redcap*, an action series about the work of the Special Investigation Branch of the Royal Military Police, starred John Thaw in his first major television role. *Public Eye*, a crime and detection series which would become one of ITV's most highly regarded programmes, had been commissioned during George's watch, though they would be transmitted during his successor's. And George had had the nous to spot the creative potential of his business manager Michael Chapman and invite him to leave programme administration for production, where he had flourished.

The department seemed still to be in good shape but I didn't try to dissuade George from leaving. I had sensed for some time that he was not entirely comfortable in his executive role. Years later, Roger Marshall, the originator of *Public Eye*, told me how difficult it had been to pitch that programme's concept to George; apparently he didn't think there was any mileage in the story of a shabby private enquiry agent in a run-down seaside town, even if he was to be played by Alfred Burke. I had begun to feel that the department's successes were being driven more by its producers and story-editors than by its head: *Redcap* was very much John Bryce's project and *Public Eye* Richard Bates's. So I wished George every success and agreed to let him go. But who to succeed him?

Before I could even start looking for a likely candidate, Lloyd Shirley knocked on my door. As usual, the grapevine had beaten the official announcement to the news. "I guess you'll be looking for a new head of drama?" "Yes indeed," I said. "I can do that" Lloyd said. "But Lloyd, you're a features and current affairs man; you're happy running the department and you're doing a great job. Why would you want to leave it? And anyway, what do you know about drama?" Lloyd said "Well, I was a drama director in the theatre in Canada, I came to England to take up an offer from The Old Vic Theatre School, I played two seasons for Robert Atkins in Regents Park, I toured the UK in Shakespeare for the Arts Council: my whole professional background is in drama." I said "You never told me that." Lloyd said "You never asked me."

I knew he could run a department. He had tackled every project I handed him with skill and intelligence, from *The Green Room Rag* to *The Ballad of Dr Crippen*, from *The Sunday Break* to adult education, from *Tempo* to Eamonn Andrews's chat show and *World of Sport*. Why not drama? I gave him the job. It turned out to be one of the best appointments I ever made, but it left me with the need to fill yet another senior programme department slot. No knock on the door this time: I knew the man I wanted.

When I was working for Lew and Val, ATV's contribution to Sunday evening's previously closed period was *About Religion*, a lively current affairs series dealing, often most obliquely, with religious matters. Michael Redington was its producer, a bright, cheery individual who, appropriately enough, looked like an ex-priest but was in fact an ex-actor, having started in repertory at the Theatre Royal, Leicester and finished at the West End's New Theatre in Laurence Olivier's Old Vic Theatre Company. Michael had been a first-rate producer, responsible for ATV's religious programmes until he was awarded an Eisenhower Scholarship in 1964 to travel throughout the United States. We had become good friends at ATV and now he was back in Britain. I thought he was capable of holding down a wider brief than just religion so I invited him to run ABC's Features Department, limiting his load a little by moving Eamonn Andrews's Sunday night chat show to Light Entertainment, where it seemed more naturally to belong. Michael accepted.

I now had three first-rate creative heads in the department. We were geared at last for the Major League. And so too was Howard Thomas, who was about to take on Lew Grade in what had previously been exclusive ATV territory.

Two years previously, ABC had commissioned its first television film series. Julian Wintle was an enterprising British film producer, joint head with Leslie Parkyn of the Independent Artists production company. This had several successful films to its credit, including the much admired *Waltz of the Toreadors*, starring Peter Sellers, and Lindsay Anderson's *This Sporting Life*, considered probably the best to come out of the kitchen-sink era of British cinema. In 1963 Independent Artists decided to diversify into television production and Julian Wintle brought an interesting project to ABPC, which passed it on to us at ABC with its blessing. *The Human Jungle* was built round the casebook of a fictitious Harley Street psychiatrist, Dr Roger Corder, to be played by Herbert Lom.

Howard Thomas and I drove down to Beaconsfield Studios to meet Julian and Leslie. We liked them, and we liked the human interest concept of the series and the impressive list of writers and directors they had lined up to work on it, so we commissioned an initial thirteen episodes. The first series of *The Human Jungle* went on the air in the autumn of 1963 and was an instant success, networked in London by ATV. For the second series, in 1964, John McMillan at Rediffusion outbid Lew Grade so we had the unusual experience of seeing an ABC programme transmitted in London during the week instead of at the weekend. When the time came for us to consider a third series for 1965, however, Julian Wintle had a better idea.

After three successful seasons, ABC's hit drama series *The Avengers* had ground to a halt in 1963 with the departure of Honor Blackman. The show's producer and story editor had moved on to other projects and there were no plans for its resuscitation. Rather than commission another series of *The Human Jungle*, said Julian, why not transfer *The Avengers* to film instead? Why not, indeed? *The Avengers* seemed tailor-made for film; and Julian and his team had shown they could produce a television film series of high quality at affordable cost. And, just possibly, this could be the opportunity to compete with ATV in trying to break into the American network television market. So Howard persuaded the ABPC Board to invest the money and it was Goodbye to *The Human Jungle* – Herbert Lom was now free to take up the role of Inspector Clouseau's boss in the *Pink Panther* films – and Hello to the film series of *The Avengers*, destined to crown the success of one of the most popular and influential British television drama series ever made.

The show was still making waves fifty years after the original series began. To celebrate its 50th Anniversary in 2011 the University of Chichester mounted a two-day conference on *The Avengers*, and the BBC's Radio Three arts series *Night Waves* examined the programme's political and cultural significance, with Brian Clemens, the associate producer, story-editor and principal writer of the film series, as its guest of honour. There was a sublime moment in Night Waves, with its panel of social and cultural commentators showering extravagant praise on the programme and the effect it had had on them personally, when the chairman turned to its guest of honour and said "Brian Clemens: look at what you've done to these people. How did you do it?" and Brian completely floored the panel by saying "By accident! And serendipity!"

The convoluted history of *The Avengers* could fill a book by itself, and has indeed filled several, by many different writers. I've touched on it in previous chapters but it's worth encapsulating again here as an example of how television so often works. The programme's originating producer Leonard White, who died at the age of 99 in January 2016, says in one of his volumes of autobiography that no one person can claim to have created *The Avengers*. He was being characteristically modest: Leonard laid the programme's foundations, gave it its title, made some of its key casting decisions and guided it through its first forty episodes. But he was essentially correct: long-running television series don't spring fully formed from the brain of their creator. They evolve. And the way in which *The Avengers* evolved is particularly interesting.

Allow me to take you through it.

In the summer of 1960, writer Julian Bond brought a half-hour series project to Sydney Newman called *Police Surgeon*. It had as its adviser a real-life police surgeon working under the pseudonym of J. J. Bernard and it was an ideal vehicle for up-and-coming actor Ian Hendry. Sydney commissioned a series and, short of producers, asked Julian to produce as well as write it. The lead character's name was Dr Geoffrey Brent.

Writing and producing a weekly series proved too onerous for one person, so after four episodes additional writers were brought in and Leonard White was asked to take over the production in addition to his daytime job of producing *Armchair Mystery Theatre*.

When his initial contract for 13 episodes ended, J. J. Bernard demanded half the writing fee for any further contribution to the series or he would sue. He picked the wrong person to challenge. Sydney simply cancelled *Police Surgeon* and charged Leonard to come up with a new vehicle for Hendry, hour-long this time, and fast: it had to be on the air in two months.

Leonard and story-editor Patrick Brawn put together a format for an undercover crime-busting series with Ian Hendry, still in doctor mode as Dr David Keel, avenging the murder of his fiancee with the aid of a mysterious undercover agent named John Steed, played by one Patrick Macnee. An initial series of 26 episodes was planned, to be transmitted live, weekly. It was too much for any single writer or writing team; they would end up commissioning a total of 19 writers to keep up with the pace of transmission.

Some way into the writing process, Leonard decided to call the series *The Avengers*. Sydney didn't like the title – "Jesus, Leonard! I don't even know what it means!" – but was persuaded to accept it. As we've already seen, a bizarre networking arrangement with ATV resulted in nine episodes of the series not being shown in London and the rest being transmitted fortnightly, alternating with an ATV drama series; but half way through the run, even without full networking, *The Avengers* began to appear in the Network's Top Twenty Programmes.

At the end of 1961, as the last episode of the series was transmitted, production came to an abrupt halt. Equity, the actors' union, had called its members out on strike against Independent Television, and the strike lasted much longer than expected. The production team took the opportunity to stockpile a handful of scripts for the next season, but by the time *The Avengers* could resume production Ian Hendry had been tempted away by a major film contract and the Dr Keel character had to be replaced.

Leonard decided to supply Steed with a female co-avenger instead. He presented Sydney with a short-list of five possible actresses for the part, with Honor Blackman at the top and Nyree Dawn Porter at the bottom. Sydney didn't like the idea of Honor Blackman – "No! Dammit, Leonard. I can't stand that perpetual Rank-starlet-trained-say-everything-with-a-smile kind of acting!" He reversed the order, put Nyree Dawn Porter at the top, and went on holiday. Leonard switched the order back again and cast Honor Blackman. Sydney returned, fulminated mightily, but accepted.

The second series went into production too quickly for the stockpiled scripts to be rewritten. So for her first six shows, Honor Blackman had to play a part written for a man, with only the name changed from Dr David Keel to Mrs Cathy Gale; but she felt so comfortable with it that she asked the writers to continue to write her character that way.

The show was being transmitted live so no stunt doubles could be used. Honor had to learn ju-jitsu for her fights, which she enthusiastically undertook, but the pilot episode revealed more than her enthusiasm so a special wardrobe had to be designed to prevent her bra and panties from stealing the show. Wardrobe Department suggested an outfit made of a material thought likely to be in vogue next season, and Cathy Gale's leather cat-suit and kinky boots were born. The chemistry of Steed and Gale was immediate and the impact of a witty, intelligent action series with a resourceful but still eminently feminine lead was dramatic: without aiming to do so, the series found itself tapping directly into the zeitgeist of the sixties.

At the end of 1962, Leonard succeeded Sydney Newman as Producer of *Armchair Theatre* and John Bryce, who had been story editor for the second *Avengers* series, took over as producer of the third, with Richard Bates as its story editor. ATV had by then been persuaded to alternate series rather than episodes, so *The Avengers* was now a weekly show, making a regular appearance in the Network Top Twenty. But when the final episode of the third season was transmitted at the end of March, 1963, Honor said she didn't want to continue with a weekly television series and accepted the offer to play Pussy Galore in *Goldfinger*.

There were no plans for another *Avengers* series. John Bryce and Richard Bates were both busy with exciting new projects, John as producer of *Redcap* with John Thaw, and Richard as story-editor of *Public Eye* with Alfred Burke. But another possibility opened up when film producer Julian Wintle suggested making *The Avengers* on film instead of a third series of *The Human Jungle*. Howard Thomas jumped at the idea. ABC of America had expressed interest in *The Avengers* but only if it was available on film rather than the fuzzy telerecordings which were selling elsewhere in the world. Howard persuaded the Board to invest the money and *The Avengers* moved from Teddington to Elstree.

Julian cast Elizabeth Shepherd as Steed's new co-Avenger, to be named Emma Peel. She was leathered-up and ju-jitsu-wised and began filming; but half way through the second episode it was clear that there was no chemistry between her and Patrick Macnee, and she left the series. Another production delay. Who to replace her?

Back at Teddington, Leonard produced an *Armchair Theatre* play called "The Hothouse" by Donald Churchill. It featured a young Royal Shakespeare Company actress making only her third television appearance, and Dodo Watts, ABC's brilliant Casting Director, thought she would be ideal for *The*

Avengers role. Julian, Howard and I previewed the *Armchair Theatre* tape and agreed; and Diana Rigg became Emma Peel, the new Avenger. "The Hothouse" came third in the Network Top Twenty, beaten only by the week's two episodes of *Coronation Street*. Happy augury?

The Avengers returned to the screen on 2 October 1965, 18 months after the end of its live and videotape era. Patrick Macnee and Diana Rigg were immediately and most effectively compatible. The quirky creative drive of Brian Clemens made every use of the scale and flexibility that film can offer, and consolidated the style that had imbued the show from its beginning in 1961.

ABC of America bought the series, which became an international best seller and one of the most successful British television programmes ever made. Fifty years later an academic University Conference celebrated it and BBC Radio Three discussed its political and cultural significance. End of story.

But consider: if the rapacity of a programme adviser had not led to the closure of *Police Surgeon*, *The Avengers* would not have come into being in the first place. If a prolonged Equity strike had not led to the loss of Dr David Keel, Cathy Gale would not have been invented. If Sydney Newman had not gone on holiday, Nyree Dawn Porter would have been cast as Cathy Gale. If there had been time to rewrite the opening scripts of the second series, the female Avenger might have been a very different kind of character, sans ju-jitsu, sans leather gear. And if Honor Blackman's departure had not left the programme in limbo at the same time as *The Human Jungle* was coming up for renewal, *The Avengers* would not have enjoyed its extraordinary second life as a film series. "By accident! And serendipity!" Accident and serendipity: the story of so many television programmes – and not a few television careers, my own very much included.

On the Franchise Trail

The April 1964 edition of *ABC TV News*, the company's house magazine, carried a buoyant little paragraph: "If you like to play the game of adding up minutes, Granada, with five days on the air, has something like 460 minutes of programming seen in London, 90 of which are afternoon programmes for schools. ABC has something like 580...Not bad for a two-day 'Regional' Contractor!" Having included the number of minutes devoted to education in Granada's tally, the paragraph might have conceded that 60 minutes of ABC's were similarly dedicated; but, nevertheless, its buoyancy was not inappropriate. ABC was making quite a mark on the network.

By the middle of the sixties, there were weekends in London when more of our programmes than ATV's could be seen on the screen. Still more were being transmitted by Rediffusion during the week. As well as *The Human Jungle* and *The Avengers*, the weekday London company had bought our variety series *Big Night Out*, the situation comedy *Just Jimmy*, starring northern comedian Jimmy Clitheroe, which was produced in our Didsbury studios, and several of the videotaped drama series we were making in Teddington. Those of us who lived and worked in London could now watch very nearly the entire ABC programme output in our own homes.

At the weekend, in addition to *Candid Camera*, *Opportunity Knocks*, *Thank Your Lucky Stars* and Eamonn Andrews's late-night chat show, Philip Jones's Light Entertainment Department had taken over the summer replacement slot for ATV's *Sunday Night at the London Palladium* previously filled by impresario Bernard Delfont. *Blackpool Night Out*, from Blackpool's ABC

Theatre, was ideally situated to feature the stars who filled the theatres of that great northern hub of show business each summer. Its hosts were the popular double act of Mike and Bernie Winters and when, after two seasons, Mike and Bernie moved back to Teddington to star in a networked Saturday night series of their own, *Blackpool Night Out* was re-titled *The Blackpool Show* and Mike and Bernie were succeeded first by Tony Hancock, in a brave attempt to revive his flagging television career and then by Dickie Henderson.

Two now legendary comedians, Tommy Cooper and Ken Dodd, began their long runs of comedy shows for us on Saturday night. And ATV's once all-conquering *Sunday Night at the London Palladium* gradually dwindled and faded, and was replaced by an ABC series of Bruce Forsyth specials on Sunday night, with a 90-minute Christmas Spectacular co-starring Frankie Howerd as an annual bonus.

Michael Redington's Features Department had also consolidated its presence on the network. *Tempo*, back in a weekly transmission slot with Mike Hodges as its producer, reinforced its position as the foremost arts programme on Independent Television, by becoming the subject of a book-length critique by novelist A. N. Wilson. ATV's programme billings department and the London edition of the *TV Times* finally recognised reality and credited *World of Sport* to ABC; and London viewers could now watch the work of David Southwood and Didsbury's outside broadcast crews in a second helping of *Professional Wrestling* on Wednesday evenings by courtesy of Rediffusion, for whom *World of Sport* recorded an additional 45 minutes every Saturday afternoon after its own Wrestling transmissions.

ABC's Religious Adviser Penry Jones, the prime mover of *The Sunday Break* from its inception in 1958, had been snapped up by the ITA as its Religious Programmes Officer and then by the BBC as its Head of Religious Broadcasting. In his place Michael Redington recruited the Reverend Ian Mackenzie from the Student Christian Movement, and the Closed Period rapidly opened up a succession of new ABC projects in the fields of music and discussion which *The Sunday Break* had pioneered.

Hallelujah! was a folk-music series of songs of praise and protest led by celebrated poet and folksinger Sydney Carter. *The Singing People* visited towns throughout our regions to hear the music of local choirs and choral societies. *The Song Break* provided a devotional version of *Sing Along with Joe*, with John Lawrenson and the Salvation Army's Joy Strings presenting music from factory locations ranging from the Royal Doulton Potteries in

Stoke-on-Trent to the Cammell-Laird Shipyard in Birkenhead – needless to say without any Talent, Beauty or Mr Adonis Contests. And Duke Ellington and his Orchestra provided ABC with a great coup with the first European performance of his Concert of Sacred Music at Coventry Cathedral.

New discussion programmes included two series hosted by the eminent broadcaster Robert Kee. An entirely fresh strand of ABC programming for the Closed Period was the dramatisation of literary works concerned with the eternal questions of life, death and morality, ranging from contemporary novels like Anne Holm's *I Am David* and Ann Petry's *The Girl Called Moses* to striking adaptations of C. S. Lewis's *The Lion, The Witch and The Wardrobe* and Bunyan's *The Pilgrim's Progress.*

Michael's other new recruit was George Wedell, Professor of Adult Education at Manchester University, who joined ABC as Adult Education Advisor. The two of them embarked on a series of ambitious co-productions with CBC of Canada, ABC of Australia, Westinghouse Television of America and NET, the American National Education Television Network, studying the political and moral issues facing the world in the sixties, the monetary policy of America and the United Kingdom, and the problem of international crime and its prevention. Another of the Department's adult education series, *First Steps in Physics*, became the first television course to lead to a certificated qualification, the final exam being held under the auspices of the Joint Examining Boards of the United Kingdom – five years before The Open University began its own degree courses via the television screen.

As for Lloyd Shirley's Drama Department, Rediffusion began to devote a regular weekday slot to ABC drama in 1964 with the second series of *The Human Jungle* and a re-run of the Cathy Gale episodes of *The Avengers*. The following year, John Thaw's Military Police series *Redcap* made its London debut with Rediffusion on a weekday, and now Alfred Burke's *Public Eye*, having begun its first series with ATV at the weekend, was snapped up by Rediffusion for its second. Robert Banks Stewart's new thriller *Intrigue*, starring Edward Judd, began its London transmissions during the week; so did the Emma Peel film series of *The Avengers*. Along with us at the weekend, ATV were showing Michael Chapman's new series about the supernatural, *Haunted*, written by Robert Muller, together with *Armchair Theatre* and its two new summer replacement series *Armchair Thriller* and *Mystery and Imagination*. ATV were also playing repeats of *The Human Jungle* on Sunday night, so there were periods in the year when no fewer than three ABC drama series were being seen each week in London. Not bad indeed for a two-day Regional programme contractor.

Armchair Theatre itself not only continued to flourish in Leonard White's hands; it also provided spin-off series for both Drama and Light Entertainment Departments. Early in 1967 it transmitted *A Magnum for Schneider*, an original teleplay by James Mitchell about the dark world of espionage. The lead character was a reluctant professional killer called David Callan, working for a shadowy section of British Intelligence. He was played by Edward Woodward in a performance which won him a BAFTA Award and the star role in a series based on the character: *Callan* was developed and broadcast within months and ran for four seasons, as popular and highly regarded in its time as *The Avengers*.

Two weeks later, *Armchair Theatre* transmitted *Never Mind the Quality, Feel the Width*, a comedy by Vince Powell and Harry Driver about two tailors in business together in London's East End, one of them Irish Catholic, the other Jewish. They were played by Frank Finlay and John Bluthal respectively – a notable change of pace for Frank, whose day job at the time was playing Iago to Laurence Olivier's Othello on the National Theatre stage. It was a Top Twenty success and, as Philip Jones was quick to spot from the studio buzz even before it went on the air, a natural premise for a half-hour situation comedy. That comedy series retained its *Armchair Theatre* title but lost Frank Finlay, who couldn't commit himself to what everybody hoped would be a long run – which indeed it became, with Joe Lynch as the Catholic partner. *Never Mind the Quality, Feel the Width* ran for six years.

Things were coming together very nicely for ABC, and the timing could not have been more propitious. On 20 December 1966 the Labour Government's White Paper on Broadcasting stated that no allocation of frequencies for a fourth television service would be authorised for at least the next three years. Consequently, on the following day, the ITA announced its new round of contract awards on the basis of a single service – but with some significant changes. ITV's crazy quilt was going to be picked apart. No more weekday-weekend split franchises in the North and Midlands: the North would be divided into two separate areas, Lancashire and Yorkshire. And there would now be three major seven-day companies, one each in Lancashire, Yorkshire and the Midlands.

A week earlier, *The Guardian* had anticipated the possibility of Granadaland being divided in two, and Sidney Bernstein's response had been "If the territory of Granada is interfered with in any way we shall go to the United Nations." Just kidding, Lord Hill: a seven day contract in Lancashire was a most attractive prospect, as was each of the other seven day contracts. The only split franchise remaining would be in London, where two companies would operate on a four-and-a-half and two-and-a-half day basis, calculated to make their audience reach and revenue potential roughly equal. So, five majors instead of four, with no changes in the ten regional franchises except for Wales. Contracts would be offered for six years, the maximum possible under the present Television Act. Advertisements inviting applications for all fifteen contracts appeared on 28 February 1967. The closing date was 15 April. Interviews of applicants would begin in May.

Which franchise should ABC go for?

We had acquired experience and prestige from our service in the North and Midlands. We believed Granada was a shoo-in for the Lancashire contract (otherwise Sydney might indeed have gone to the United Nations), but we thought it would be discourteous to our loyal viewers not to apply for both the Midlands and Lancashire franchises – as second and third choices. Like all the applicants, we were invited to state an order of preference, and our first choice was the weekend London contract, although we were also certain that Lew Grade and ATV would make a bee-line for it.

We knew only too well the problems inherent in a weekend ITV franchise and believed that we had managed to cope with them pretty well. We believed that the range and quality of the programmes networked by our little two-day franchise, from sport to adult education, religion to light entertainment, drama to the arts, was second to none. We had transformed British television drama with *Armchair Theatre*. We had introduced ITV's first weekly programme on the arts and taken the responsibility for ITV's fight back against the BBC's monopoly of televised sport. We had opened up adult education and religious programming on ITV. We had introduced two new strands of light entertainment in late-night chat and peak-time hoax and reintroduced a third in the television talent show.

All in all we believed we would make a better fist of the weekend franchise than ATV. So did the ITA, as we discovered sixteen years later when Volume Two of *Independent Television in Britain* was published. I quote: "the company that had been a pioneer of adult education and televised religion, that had produced *Tempo*, *Armchair Theatre* and *The Avengers* seemed made for the job." The history went on to say "ABC's written application and the performance of Thomas and Tesler at the interview on 4 May revealed that their thinking about possible weekend schedule improvements chimed in closely with the Authority's own...There could be little doubt, in the absence of more promising competition bringing in talented new blood, the London weekend contract would go to ABC, with ATV getting the seven days in the Midlands."

In June 1967 we knew none of this Authority thinking, of course. We simply awaited the Authority's decision with quiet confidence. With our record, we would surely be awarded either the weekend in London or at least the seven days in the Midlands.

We lost both.

What happened?

David Frost happened. That's what.

Frost over ABC

Things had come together in the sixties very nicely for David too. He had shot into public consciousness and critical approval with the ground-breaking BBC satire show That Was The Week That Was; he had won the Golden Rose of Montreux for the BBC with a compilation of the highlights from his comedy series *The Frost Report*, in which John Cleese made his television debut and Ronnie Barker and Ronnie Corbett discovered that Two Ronnies could be even more successful than one. His own television performances had won him the 1967 Richard Dimbleby Award and the Royal Television Society's Silver Medal; and now he was capturing the headlines with his hard-hitting interviews in The Frost Programme, broadcast three times a week by Rediffusion, the first British current affairs series to be played live in front of an interacting studio audience. Ground-breaking, award-winning, headline-capturing, hard-hitting David joined with a group headed by ITN's first editor, Aidan Crawley, then MP for West Derbyshire, to form The London Television Consortium. This had applied for the weekend franchise in London with a prospectus which was rich in programme talent completely new to ITV – new because it would be coming from the BBC. Quite simply, the Frost-Crawley bid trumped ABC's.

The Managing Director of its proposed new weekend company was to be my old Television Training Course colleague Michael Peacock, who had launched BBC 2 as Chief of Programmes and was now the highly regarded Controller of BBC 1. Drama, Music and Arts would be headed by the BBC's Head of Music and Arts, Humphrey Burton. In charge of the Children's, Educational and Religious Unit would be Doreen Stephens, Head of the

BBC's Family Programmes Department. In charge of its Light Entertainment would be another old colleague from my producing days at Lime Grove: Frank Muir, who was now Assistant Head of the BBC's Light Entertainment Department (Comedy). He was bringing with him the creators of the BBC's *Steptoe and Son*, Ray Galton and Alan Simpson, as comedy advisers and the guaranteed writers of at least one comedy series a year for the new company. Even the consortium's Chief Engineer would be coming from the BBC: Bill Fletcher, its Chief Engineer, Operations, who was at that point supervising the Corporation's conversion to colour.

Still more talent new to ITV was promised by the consortium, this time from *The Sunday Times*. Clive Irving, the newspaper's former Managing Editor and creator of its Insight feature, would be the new company's Head of Public Affairs, and Dr Tom Margerison, the paper's Science Editor, its proposed Deputy Managing Director. And, as a pair of unexpected cherries on the top, it also boasted two highly capable executives bringing their wide experience of ITV to the group: Rediffusion's own Director of Programmes, Cyril Bennett, and its Director of Sales, Guy Paine, both of them without the knowledge of Rediffusion's senior management.

The presence of Cyril and Guy raised eyebrows among the Authority inquisitors since they also appeared in the immediately preceding interview as participants in Rediffusion's bid for London weekdays, but it was after all for a different franchise and the Crawley group clearly had more to offer than two Rediffusion renegades. What it offered was a new and distinctive look to London's weekend schedule, with a glittering array of leaders of industry and commerce on the proposed company's Board to underpin its ambition with business wisdom, experience – and cash. The Authority found the offer irresistible. Down the Brompton Road came the Band of the Scots Guards once again. "A possible decision" wrote Sir Robert Fraser to the rest of the Authority "is that ABC and Rediffusion be told that the Authority is prepared to offer the contract to a new company, formed by the two companies, in which majority control is exercised by ABC but of which the profits as nearly as possible be divided equally between the two."

This solution was adopted by the Authority at its meeting on 9 June and reported two days later by Lord Hill at the Press Conference called to announce the new franchise awards. "With our principle of programme quality in mind," said Lord Hill, "the combination of these two companies seemed to the Authority to offer the possibility of a programme company

174 | THE BEST OF TIMES

of real excellence." There would be an equal division of profits between the two but the Authority specified that the Board of the new company should have a majority of ABC nominees, and that Howard Thomas and I should be appointed as, respectively, Managing Director and Director of Programmes – the only individuals named or specified in the entire roll call of the fifteen franchise awards. The Authority had expressed a preference for an independent chairman to be appointed, but in the event the role went to Sir Philip Warter, ABC's existing chairman.

So our little two-day regional contractor, the smallest of the majors, was now to be the controlling partner of the biggest, the weekday programme company for London, ITV's prime contract. Lord Hill's Press Conference was held on the afternoon of Sunday, 11 June. The morning was spent advising the applicant Chairmen and Managing Directors of the Authority's decisions. I didn't know where in the running order Howard and Sir Philip would lie, so I sat impatiently by the telephone waiting for a phone call to reveal the outcome. There was nothing on the one o'clock BBC news and the next bulletin would not be until 6 pm – there was no on-the-hour or 24-hour rolling news in those days.

Half way through the afternoon I could stand the suspense no longer; I phoned my Managing Director at his home. "Howard, what happened? What did we get? The weekend in London or seven days in the Midlands?" I could hardly hear what he was saying against the background of clinking glasses, laughter and noisy celebration. "Neither! We've got the big one, London weekdays; it's a merger with Rediffusion, but we've got control; it'll be on the six o'clock news. Got to go. We'll talk tomorrow." Howard hadn't phoned George Cooper or any of the other executive directors with the news either; but none of the others had been named or specified by the ITA. Oh well... Audrey and I drank a little toast ourselves. To each other.

Thames Begins

Except it wasn't Thames; not to start with, anyway. The London Consortium had registered Thames as the name of its own programme company and we were hung up for days considering alternatives. Central was a strong runner but Howard Thomas wanted a name with a closer association with the capital, some iconic landmark perhaps. We were about to settle for Capital Television when our Company Secretary, Cyril Orr, burst in on a meeting with the news that Frost-Crawley had dropped Thames in favour of London Weekend. We scooped it up before you could say "Good old Frostie!"

There followed a year of frenzied activity for ITV, not to say turmoil – no, *let's* say turmoil, for turmoil there certainly was, though its initiator would not be presiding over it. Less than two months after the franchise awards were announced, Harold Wilson, in his continuing feud with the BBC for what he believed was its Tory bias, transposed Lord Hill to the Chair of the Corporation, remarking to Richard Crossman, his Secretary of State for Health and Social Security, "Charlie Hill has already cleaned up ITV, and he'll do the same to BBC". Instead, Herbert Bowden, the Secretary of State for Commonwealth Affairs, was given a life peerage and, as Lord Aylestone, appointed Chairman of the ITA. He arrived just as the turmoil was beginning to bubble.

So much had to be done before July 1968. Preparations had to be made within both the industry and the Authority for the technical switch which would take place the following year from Britain's 405-line VHF (Very High Frequency) standard in black and white to 625-line UHF (Ultra High

Frequency) and colour. New studios and offices had to be built, new facilities installed, the fate of thousands of members of staff determined.

Granada and ATV remained the contractors for the North and Midlands respectively but their franchises had been transformed. Granada had won seven days in Lancashire but lost Yorkshire and half its audience. ATV had acquired two more days in the Midlands but lost its weekend audience in London and its pivotal position in the ITV network. Telefusion Yorkshire Limited had been awarded the Yorkshire contract, re-naming itself Yorkshire Television in the process, and now had to construct a television service from scratch within a year.

Nine of the ten regional companies had retained their original franchises but the tenth, TWW, had lost theirs to Lord Harlech, the former British Ambassador in Washington. He had led a consortium as replete as David Frost's with distinguished names from business, industry, finance, the BBC and the world of entertainment, but with a Welsh accent. The BBC's Wynford Vaughan Thomas was to be its Programme Controller and such artistes as Richard Burton, Stanley Baker, Geraint Evans and Harry Secombe were among the many who had made firm programme commitments to the new company. It would only too quickly have problems of its own.

The outraged Chairman of TWW, Lord Derby, expressed his astonishment to Lord Hill at the loss of his company's franchise before his lordship departed for the BBC. Derby protested that at no time in the past ten years, including the application interview with the Authority, had TWW been told of any inadequacies in its performance and he asked for a second hearing so that the company might be given the opportunity to answer the criticisms the Authority appeared to have. He was refused. Lord Hill explained that the Authority had simply chosen the applicant they unanimously judged the better, but offered TWW an invitation to take a 40 percent interest in the new company. Lord Derby and his Board turned the invitation down.

In February 1968 they sold TWW's programme stocks, film rights, studios and facilities in Cardiff and Bristol to the Harlech consortium for £1.6m, consigned the last five months of their contract to Harlech for another half million, and stormed off. Harlech TV was not at all ready to take up the franchise, so until it was, TWW continued to operate for another three months under the alias of 'The Independent Television Service for Wales and the West'. Three disorientating months those must have been for viewers in Wales and the West, who were welcomed on screen by three different television companies in succession, each of them with the same announcers, announcing the same programmes, carrying the same production credits, all of them TWW's.

John Spencer Wills, the Chairman of Rediffusion, was no less astonished and outraged to lose a successful, efficiently run franchise. In his interview with the Authority, he indicated that the contract should more appropriately have been renewed annually as a matter of course, like the licences for the bus and air services run by its parent company, British Electric Traction. Independent Television was certainly indebted to Rediffusion. In the financial crisis which had threatened to destroy ITV at its very beginning, the company had borne heavy losses but had stood firm and carried on with the rest of the faltering network rallying behind it, in spite of the withdrawal of its partner, Associated Newspapers. It had been expected to retain its weekday London contract without question. That it did not was widely considered a grave injustice. Even Sir Sydney Caine, who had been the ITA's Deputy Chairman in 1967, wrote in an Institute of Economic Affairs paper that he had no doubt the decision had been wrong.

The wound never really healed. Thirteen years later, in a letter to the Authority's Deputy Director General, the now knighted Sir John Spencer Wills wrote "I have never been given a reason for the treatment accorded to Rediffusion Television Limited." The reason of course was the brilliant promise of the Frost-Crawley consortium, as Lord Hill later confided in his Broadcasting Memoirs of 1974. "Even allowing for the fact that promising is so much easier than performing," he wrote, "it was difficult to resist the thought that here was a group which would bring new thinking, fresh ideas and a lively impetus to weekend broadcasting. It had to have its chance whatever the repercussions... Lose Rediffusion? Unthinkable. Throw ABC to the wolves? Indefensible. Put them together and you would have acquired for London ITV such an array of talent as had not previously been dreamed of."

It might have been thought that making Rediffusion the junior partner to a small company from the sticks was an unnecessary additional humiliation, but ABC was not exactly undeserving. It was a programme-orientated company owned by a programme-orientated corporation not a business conglomerate like British Electric Traction – and it did possess seasoned Controllers of both Programmes and Sales which, thanks to Frost-Crawley, Rediffusion did not. Cyril Bennett and Guy Paine were summarily dismissed by Rediffusion the morning after the franchise awards were announced.

Deeply hurt though it was by the Authority's decision, the Rediffusion Board ultimately buckled down to the task of making the partnership work. It wasn't easy, and it didn't happen overnight, but the directors it deputed to the new Thames Board, including John Spencer Wills's son Colin, gradually became collaborative rather than abrasive in the negotiations over the tricky problems of premises, facilities and personnel which followed. Inevitably, together the two companies had too much of all of these. After much debate it was agreed that ABC's London offices in Hanover Square would close and Thames's management would move into Rediffusion's Television House in Kingsway until a new custom-built complex of offices and studios could be designed and constructed.

I found myself back in the building in which I had begun my ITV career: same floor, different office. ABC's Didsbury Studios would be leased to Yorkshire Television while the company's own studio complex was being constructed in Leeds. Some of Didsbury's staff were offered positions in Manchester to help Granada cope with its new weekend responsibilities, but the vast majority was taken on by Yorkshire Television in what would be for them a life-changing upheaval, from one side of the Pennines to the other. It was Yorkshire Television's good fortune to be able to inherit such a skilled and experienced body of staff, not least the multi-capable Outside Broadcast units which had contributed so much to ABC's success, from *Sing Along with Joe* to *Big Night Out*, from Frank Sinatra at the Festival Theatre to Duke Ellington at Coventry Cathedral. Those units would be without their Chief, however: David Southwood married his loyal secretary and went off into the sunset with her to the United States.

Alpha Television, the company set up jointly by ABC and ATV in 1956 to operate the Midlands service of our respective dual franchises, was comparatively easy to deal with. ABC sold its stake in the company to ATV and Alpha's studios and employees were transferred to the now seven-day contractor, continuing to operate out of Aston's converted Astoria Cinema until ATV's new Television Centre was ready for them in central Birmingham. The Thames Board agreed that ABC's studios at Teddington rather than Rediffusion's at Wembley would be the company's principal production centre. There was room for expansion on the Teddington site, its engineering facilities were outstanding and it had a head start in the industry's race to convert to colour. Teddington's research under its brilliant Chief Engineer Howard Steele. Its demonstrations of the respective merits of the available colour systems – including America's Never Twice The Same Colour – had played a key role in the adoption of PAL as the standard system for Europe. The ITA was so impressed by this role that it lured Howard Steele away from us by offering him the job of its own Chief Engineer and Director of Engineering, but he left behind an engineering team second to none, headed now by Stuart Sansom.

The remaining problem was how to deal with Rediffusion's studios and employees at Wembley. Rediffusion wanted to sell the studios to the new weekend contractor, but London Weekend were set on building a brand new studio centre of their own on the South Bank. After an agonising period of brinkmanship, and urged by the ITA, Rediffusion agreed to rent the studios to London Weekend until the new complex was ready and London Weekend agreed to take on the studios' employees – 300 more than the 600 they had planned to recruit.

My job – a most agreeable one – was to construct a new programme department from two existing departments whose strengths were remarkably complementary. It more or less constructed itself. There was no question that ABC's Philip Jones and Lloyd Shirley should be in charge of Light Entertainment and Drama respectively. Philip would prove to be the best Head of Light Entertainment ITV ever had – including myself – and Lloyd would become the unsung hero of ITV Drama, whose creative and innovative record would never be fully recognised. As for Features, Michael Redington had gone off with my blessing to become a theatrical impresario, but it was clear to me that I needed an entirely different kind of creative executive to run a weekday company's Features output.

The Features Department for a weekend contractor like ABC was destined to be a kind of catch-all, its responsibilities ranging from Adult Education to Religion, from the World of Sport to the world of Arts. For a weekday company a different kind of Features Department was required: one with a particular expertise in current affairs and documentaries, an expertise which ABC did not possess but which Rediffusion did. I was a great admirer of Rediffusion's hard-hitting current affairs programme *This Week* and phoned its producer, Jeremy Isaacs, to ask if we could meet.

Jeremy said he lived in Chiswick too and had often seen me walking my dogs in Chiswick House: why didn't we meet there? So on a fine sunny morning we walked round the magnificent grounds of Chiswick House and discussed the future of ITV, Thames Television and J. Isaacs. I offered Jeremy the post of Features Controller. It was not a lengthy negotiation. Would I be prepared to keep *This Week*? Of course. Could I promise the department a monthly documentary slot? Certainly. Did I agree that we should produce a daily London news and current affairs programme? Absolutely. And how would Jeremy feel about emulating NBC's *Today* show and presenting London's news and current affairs from a glass-fronted studio on the ground floor of Television House, with busy Londoners passing by as a living backcloth and Eamonn Andrews as the programme's front man? OK with you? OK with me. Done and dusted.

Thames acquired a brilliant Controller of Features and Jeremy embarked on a remarkable career as a creative executive, his achievements ultimately to be crowned by a knighthood. He also agreed to take on the overall responsibility for Thames's children's programmes as part of his brief and suggested Rediffusion's Lewis Rudd as the Executive Producer to be in charge of them. I knew Lewis's work and was delighted with the suggestion. Two more Rediffusion executives completed my creative set: Grahame Turner, their Head of Outside Broadcasts, and Guthrie Moir, their Head of Religion and Education. That was the easy part.

Lord Hill had pledged at his Press Conference that nobody in ITV would lose his or her job as a result of the franchise changes, and there remained the rest of the staff at Rediffusion's Television House to be re-deployed – directors, producers, programme managers, engineers, secretaries, PAs. Some chose to go to London Weekend. Jeremy Isaacs and Guthrie Moir brought with them most of the members of their respective teams. Grahame Turner's accomplished sidekicks Steve Minchin and Jim Pople came with him to Thames, along with the bulk of his Outside Broadcast Department. With the aim of recruiting the best of the rest, I sent Programme Department's Business Manager Jack Andrews to interview the staff at Television House, but they were caught up in the general mood of distrust and anxiety that had infected the system in spite of Lord Hill's pledge. Jack was refused access to the personnel files; one of the programme directors phoned Howard Thomas to complain that she "had expected to be interviewed by someone at least as senior as Brian Tesler and not his assistant" and after four frustrating days Jack was asked by Rediffusion's Director of Personnel to leave the building.

A Striking Opening

The ACTT – the Association of Cinematograph and Television Technicians – had won a famous victory over ATV in the spring of 1967, achieving premium payments for recording Lew Grade's programmes in colour for export to the United States. It was an infamous victory as far as the ITV network was concerned because of the high price it established for working in colour for us all in due course. Now the union was demanding severance as well as redundancy payments for every member affected by the change in his or her company's franchise, even though it had been accepted that no one would be made redundant and most would be doing the same work in the same job, often in the same studios. A series of wildcat strikes, blackouts and overtime bans forced the companies to concede to these demands but, ominously, the current agreement with the ACTT was due to expire on 29 July, the day on which the new franchises would begin.

The union went into the negotiations for a new agreement feeling that it was on an unassailable roll, in spite of the bleak outlook for the national economy. Sterling had been devalued and the government had introduced a pay policy limiting annual wage increases to 3 percent, which the companies were prepared to meet. But the union claimed an increase of 7 percent, a reduction in the working week from 40 to 35 hours, an annual holiday of four weeks and a number of other benefits, the cumulative effect of which would amount to a rise of 30 percent. It seemed an impossible gap to bridge, but the union was determined to show that it meant business. What better time to show it than on the new franchises' opening night?

In an unforeseen anti-climax, the current ITV franchises expired on 28 July, so that Independent Television's bright new era, with its new seven-day contracts and its new London franchises, would begin not with the start of a bright new week but on a Tuesday. This was not a problem for those regional companies which were already seven-day contractors; not a problem for Harlech, which had acquired Monday the 28th along with the rest of TWW's final five months; not a problem for ATV, which was already the weekday contractor for the Midlands. Not a problem for Granada either: it was already the weekday contractor for Lancashire and had generously sold its last contractual day in Yorkshire to Yorkshire Television for a peppercorn sum so that both Northern companies could start the new era with a new week. But it was clearly a problem for London, and Rediffusion wasn't minded to resolve it. Our partners in Thames insisted on a last hurrah for their company (and a last day's worth of undivided advertising revenue). In London, alone on the network, the new ITV era began on Monday, 28 July with the last day of the old. London's new weekday company Thames crept on to the air on the morning of Tuesday the 29th with a relay of county cricket from Yorkshire, and then crept off again, closing down at 1.30 pm.

Tuesday or not, Howard Thomas was determined to launch Thames with a grand gesture. At 1.55 pm, the station opened up again to transport our viewers to an inaugural lunch for Thames Television at Mansion House. Present were the Lord Mayor, together with his Counsellors and Aldermen, leading figures in the City and the Press, Lord Aylestone and the other Members of the Independent Television Authority, the Postmaster General and Members of the Post Office Board, the Boards of Rediffusion and the Associated British Picture Corporation, and the Board and senior executives of Thames. There were speeches from the Lord Mayor, Lord Aylestone, Sir Philip Warter and Howard Thomas and a live commentary by Andrew Gardner. Just a teeny bit over the top, Howard?

In his autobiography Howard Thomas does admit to its being "a rather pompous opening ceremony", but in a nice theatrical touch it provided him with the opportunity to introduce the music which would henceforth accompany Thames Television's station symbol. A pretty girl in period costume made her way into the gold-plated hall of Mansion House with a tray filled with sprigs of lavender, singing "Who Will Buy My Sweet Lavender?" The music and the symbol were both Howard's bright ideas. Thames's graphics department followed his brief and produced a London skyline which looked magnificently right but was in fact wildly wrong, with celebrated but separated landmarks from Houses of Parliament and Post Office Tower to St Paul's Cathedral and Tower Bridge all nestling closely together; and Johnny Hawksworth orchestrated the "Sweet Lavender" melody into one of the most memorable of all television station jingles. Lucky Johnny Hawksworth: the royalties from those eight little notes would keep him comfortably in cigars for the rest of his life.

Howard Thomas's showmanship paid off splendidly. The Mansion House luncheon was the lead story in ITN's national news; it was covered in the BBC's news bulletins; and it made the front pages in the London newspapers that evening and the nationals next morning. Unfortunately, so did the less than splendid aftermath. No sooner had we all returned to our offices than the ACTT pulled the plugs on the afternoon relay of *Racing from Redcar* from Tyne Tees Television and it did the same fifteen minutes after the beginning of our opening night's big entertainment show, [Tommy] *Cooper King Size*. At 8.15 pm, as the programme's first commercial break was about to start, the nation's screens went dark. We put up a caption stating normal service would be resumed as soon as possible, but it was 10.30 pm before we were back on the air.

It was the beginning of a king-sized battle with the union and the normal service caption would enjoy more screen time than *Coronation Street* that week. The round of ad hoc stoppages, overtime bans and blackouts hit company after company across the network. *London Weekend* didn't get to show even the first fifteen minutes of its big entertainment show on its own opening night three days after ours. Thames's presentation announcer handed over to the station at 7 pm on Friday; LWT's announcer welcomed the nation's viewers and invited them to the first edition of Frank Muir's *We Have Ways of Making You Laugh* – and the nation's screens went dark again.

The ITCA Council – the governing body of the Independent Television Companies Association – had had enough of this ruinous nonsense. It sent a letter to every ITV member of the ACTT warning them that these actions were a breach of their individual contracts and if they chose to continue them they would be deemed to have terminated their own employment. The union's response was to withdraw its members' labour itself. The companies' response to the union's response was to run a centralised emergency service from ATV's little control centre in Foley Street, long used as a switching hub between the London companies and the rest of the network.

It was necessarily a service constructed from the stockpile of whatever programmes were available to us on film or videotape, transmitted by management engineers who were no longer union members and linked from Teddington by Thames announcers who were members of the actors union Equity. London Weekend made a brave fist of contributing a live production of a David Frost programme to the schedule, with Cyril Bennett and other managers operating the cameras and sound booms and Michael Peacock directing in the control room.

George Cooper and Thames's Sales Department master-minded the sale of the advertising time for the centralised service and the revenue was shared out proportionately among the companies, so another caption became familiar viewing for our audiences: "All commercials are being transmitted on the national network and we apologise if certain products are not available in your area." As an unexpected bonus for both product producers and advertisers, the subsequent demand led to a number of new marketing opportunities opening up across the UK. The emergency service was rough and ready but it was more successful than we could have hoped, and we let it be known that there was sufficient material for us to continue it for at least another six months. We lied: we would have run out of the stockpile in six weeks.

The ACTT called the companies' action a lock-out and tried to persuade the other television-related unions representing journalists, electricians and other studio workers to come out in sympathy, to no avail. However, a number of these fellow unions wrote to the companies urging the reinstatement of the ACTT members, and after three weeks of this unnecessary turbulence an agreement was reached: the members would be reinstated, there would be no victimisation, and normal working would be resumed under the terms and conditions of the old agreement until a new one was concluded. It took another ten months for that new agreement to be passed and signed. It provided for rises amounting not to 30 percent but 13 percent over the three years to July 1970.

There would be other labour disputes during the ensuing decade: disruption over working in colour, walk-outs over the operation of new equipment, battles over job demarcations and over-manning. It would be a decade in which the power of the unions increasingly prevailed, to the humiliation and cost of the companies. At the same time, ITV would be hard hit financially on all sides: by the cost of re-equipping for 625 line UHF and colour; by the higher annual rentals required by the ITA to pay for its new network of UHF transmitting stations; by the opportunity BBC 2 gave an increasingly competitive Corporation to put its good works on the second channel and concentrate its popular drama and entertainment output on BBC 1; by the disruption to ITV's screens and schedules which would tempt a hitherto loyal audience increasingly to turn to that BBC output; by a fifth major ITV network company adding to the industry's costs and spreading its advertising revenue more thinly. Above all by the swingeing cost of a Television Levy which for half the decade was applied against the industry's revenue rather than its profits, so that ITV would be paying nearly half its total gross income to the government *before* tax.

And yet, in spite of all this, the decade would also be one in which ITV's programme makers thrived, a decade in which Independent Television's programme output attained its highest level of quality to-date and achieved widely-acclaimed success. Thames would take its proud place in the forefront of both that attainment and that success.

Kick ups at the Hazard Table

There is a particularly vivid cartoon by the great English caricaturist Thomas Rowlandson of a rowdy gathering in the back room of an 18th century gambling house. It's a scene of uproar. Five gentlemen are sprawled round a table littered with cards and dice and money. They are in the middle of a furious row: shouting, swearing, gesticulating at each other, apoplectic with rage; their fists are raised in anger, their voices raised in passion, a chair is being raised by one of them to hit another over the head. The engraving is called *Kick up at a Hazard Table*, Hazard being a gambling game played with dice. More than two and a half centuries before its time the cartoon is a remarkably accurate depiction of an ordinary, everyday meeting of the ITV Programme Controllers Group in 1968.

The Group was an invention of the Independent Television Authority. For the Authority too this was a bright new era. The new franchises enabled it fully to implement the powers of regulation it had been given by the 1964 Television Act, and it was determined to see that the business of scheduling, exchanging and paying for the programmes supplied to the network was put on a thoroughly regularised basis. No more the informal, hugger-mugger negotiations between the chief executives of the Big Four companies, like those weekly meetings of Howard Thomas and Lew Grade in which I had participated until we got to the money bit. Instead, there would be quarterly meetings of a Programme Policy Committee, the PPC, chaired by the Authority's Chairman and attended by all fifteen company chief executives together with the programme controllers of the five major companies, the Editor of ITN and the senior officers of the Authority's programme division.

Among a number of other committees, both formal and informal, there would also be meetings six times a year of a Network Programme Committee, similarly constituted but chaired by a major company Managing Director. And weekly meetings of a Programme Controllers Group, made up of the programme controllers of the five major companies, whose responsibility it would be to supply the programmes constituting the core of the network schedule. The PPC would deal with Independent Television's broad programme strategy; the NPC would approve draft network schedules and deal with other programme matters involving all the companies; and the Controllers Group would structure the schedule and allocate the programme-making responsibilities and prices within it.

It was clear that the Programme Controllers Group would become the network's creative motor, so months were devoted to hammering out its brief by the Authority's programme officers with the chief executives and programme controllers of the five companies. These were Lew Grade and Bill Ward for ATV, Denis Forman and David Plowright for Granada, Ward Thomas and Donald Baverstock for Yorkshire Television, Michael Peacock and Cyril Bennett for LWT and Howard Thomas and me for Thames. It was like old times for Michael Peacock and Donald Baverstock, who had worked together at the BBC, and old times too for Michael and me as old colleagues at both the BBC's Television Training Course and Lime Grove.

A great deal of hammering was required. The Authority now had the power to lay down rules and mandate programme categories, so lay down and mandate it most certainly did. The process proved an obstacle course for the companies to navigate. At least three hours of schools or adult education each week were to be included in each company's schedule. ITN's early afternoon, early evening and *News at Ten* bulletins were mandatory and the timing and duration of *News at Ten* immutable. In addition to the news there was to be a minimum of two hours of factual programming in peak time each week. A weekday play, a Sunday play, a weekday documentary and the two weekday current affairs programmes *World in Action* and *This Week* were mandatory. So was *World of Sport* and, for a specified number of weeks a year, a weekend special dedicated to the arts or sciences. The number of quiz programmes and feature films each week would be limited. Two films could not be shown close to each other. All programme schedules had to be submitted to the Authority for approval.

Early on in this new era, I was invited to speak at a meeting of the Royal

Television Society along with Paul Fox, then Controller of BBC 1, on the differences in programme controlling between our two services. My speech began "Programme controlling for Independent Television is not unlike swimming in the Olympics with both hands tied behind one's back and one's feet loaded down with weights – a feasible endeavour but not without a certain degree of difficulty." I exaggerated, but not by much.

As to programme costs, agreement was reached that Category A programmes, those supplied to the full network, would be allocated points and exchanged without payment between the five on the basis of each company's NAR share – its share of the network's Net Advertising Revenue. Any year-end imbalance would be adjusted in the subsequent year. For the first year those NAR shares would be based on estimates derived from the Authority's calculations. Category B programmes, those not fully networked, would be made available on offer at prices to be negotiated. The regional companies would pay the five majors an annually negotiated sum for an agreed volume of network programmes – usually ranging between 30 and 35 hours a week – which sum they would divide according to their respective shares of NAR after levy payments. Regional programmes acquired for the network schedule would have their above-the-line costs paid in full, together with an agreed proportion of their running costs and overheads.

The Authority's intention was that by July 1968, the five company principals would withdraw and leave the programme controllers in charge of the Programme Controllers Group. Except that Lew – for whom the business of devising, scheduling and selling programmes was meat and drink – did not want to go. At the end of one of our many meetings, Denis Forman and Howard Thomas finally persuaded him to face the inevitable. Lew said he wanted to think about it and left the room. Five minutes later he returned to announce that Bill Ward would be ATV's exclusive representative in the Programme Controllers Group. "But all the important decisions he will come back and check with me."

And so, every Monday morning, in one company Board Room or another, chaired by whichever controller whose Board Room it was, and with Frank Copplestone of the ITCA's secretariat in attendance, Donald Baverstock, Cyril Bennett, David Plowright, Bill Ward and I would meet to decide what the network programmes should be, where in the schedule they should go, and how many cost points they should be allocated. Inevitably, each controller would push his own programmes and try to bag the best slots and best prices for himself, arguing, cajoling, jockeying for position, doing deals, inventing programmes on the hoof when a vacant slot presented itself, putting up his own scheduling proposals, turning down everybody else's – not even *listening* to everybody else's.

To test this, I once put up a proposal in the middle of the hullabaloo which was roundly rejected and said "OK, OK, I'm only putting it up as a suppository". Nobody even *heard* me. It was an *Alice in Wonderland* madhouse, a combination bazaar and battle zone: I used to take a valium before I went into each meeting. To survive, you needed determination, the ability to argue persuasively or at least loudly, a good portfolio of programmes, and a brass neck. Cyril Bennett possessed these qualities in abundance, but he was given a particularly hard time in those Monday morning melees. Sadly, it was a reflection of the hard time his company was being given all round.

It had all begun so well. London Weekend's deputy chairman David Montagu later recalled how, at the end of its formal interview in May 1967, their delegation received what almost amounted to a standing ovation. I myself saw at first hand how highly LWT was regarded by Brompton Road a little before the new era began. Sir Robert Fraser and other Authority dignitaries joined the chief executives and programme controllers of all 15 companies at a lunch given by Roy Thomson, the chairman of Scottish Television, at Thomson House. We waited together in the foyer for the lifts to take the gathering up to the dining room and some of us were left standing with the Authority's Director-General and his team as Michael Peacock and Cyril Bennett were the last to enter the lift in front of us. "There goes the future of Independent Television," said Sir Robert. I knew the problems that lay in wait for a weekend ITV company and thought instead, but did not say, that Michael and Cyril and London Weekend were brave, ambitious – and doomed.

At their interview the Frost-Crawley consortium had asserted that they would give a new look and a distinctive style to ITV's weekend schedules. David Frost's interview programmes would be a key peak-time feature on each of the three evenings. Saturday night would present a series of major specials including Leonard Bernstein and the New York Philharmonic Orchestra, Yehudi Menuhin and Stravinsky's *The Soldier's Tale*, and operas by Benjamin Britten and John Gay. Sunday afternoon was to be devoted to Music and the Arts and a 40-minute current affairs show called *Seven Days*. At the conference following their franchise award, Michael Peacock told the press "The present weekend programmes are bland, featureless and tasteless. You won't have to be a moron to get something out of London Weekend Television." David Frost, in full Reithian mode, explained that they wanted to give the public what they would grow to want: "We have a duty to lead public taste to a higher ground."

The press dubbed the company BBC 3. At a stroke, London Weekend succeeded in alienating both the British public - which was quite happy with its weekend programmes thank you very much and did not consider itself moronic in watching them - and their ITV network colleagues, whose programmes it so roundly decried. In the process it also encouraged the BBC – happy to hit defecting ex-colleagues where it hurt – to move the Corporation's serious weekend programming to BBC 2 and concentrate its popular entertainment and drama programmes in BBC 1's weekend schedule. For two and a half days a week ITV and the BBC switched personalities. The public switched accordingly – and instantly.

In August 1968, ITV's share of the audience in London on weekdays, which included London Weekend's Friday evenings, fell from 54 percent in 1967 to 51 percent; on Saturday it fell from 51 percent to 38 percent, and on Sunday from 67 percent to 47 percent. Hence Cyril Bennett's trials at the Controllers Group kick-ups. The network was not inclined to include London Weekend's more Reithian peak-time offerings in its weekend schedules against BBC programming at its most competitive. Most of the companies moved Friday's *Frost* programme to 11 pm. ATV and some of the regionals dropped the Saturday edition of *Frost* and LWT's Sunday plays entirely: they felt they could attract bigger audiences in peak-time with movies and American film series.

The seven-day controllers preferred to keep their best programmes for weekdays, where the BBC competition was not so aggressive. Beleaguered, Cyril had to battle hard each Monday to secure both network airtime for his programmes and meaningful contributions from the seven-day companies for his weekend schedule. I could lend only moral support to him and the occasional attempt at a helpful suggestion to our colleagues, which was usually ignored. Some of the battles ended with Cyril simply walking out of the meetings, though he never failed to give me a big wink as he strode past me to the door.

He was not helped by the fact that his company was imploding around him, and his fellow controllers knew it. Loss of audience meant loss of advertising revenue and a consequent loss of confidence in LWT's management by its Board. Jeremy Potter, Bernard Sendall's successor as Independent Television's official historian, observed that "the non-executive tycoons who were vastly experienced in business matters knew little about television, while the executives who were hand-picked television professionals knew little of business." Under pressure, a clash was inevitable. "Michael Peacock," Potter continued, "was determined to brook no interference from a Board which he regarded as... cumbersome and televisionally untutored. The non-executive members thought him impossibly arrogant and became alarmed at what they saw as a company floundering from lack of entrepreneurial activity and insight, run by non-commercially-minded people who had been cosseted at the BBC and sheltered from the realities of earning a living."

For LWT the harsh realities of earning a living were exacerbated by the government's decision in its 1969 Budget to increase the levy on ITV's advertising revenue, which with a weakening national economy had already ceased to grow. Something pretty drastic had to be done. Declaring in a press conference that "the first duty of a commercial station is to survive", Cyril re-drew his weekend schedule with Michael's agreement, incorporating a mix of light entertainment, feature films and American film series which resembled the weekend schedules of the old regime rather than the glowing promises of the new. Now there was open dissension between the ex-BBC creative executives and LWT's senior management. Humphrey Burton, expressing the dissidents' view, wrote to Michael and Cyril protesting that "Something has gone crucially wrong with our company... we didn't join forces only to make money, now did we?"

Somebody leaked the company's franchise application to the first edition of *Open Secret*, a periodic pamphlet from The Free Communications Group – a heaven-sent scoop for a brand-new publication. The press picked up the story at once and, contrasting the franchise promises with the new proposals, embarked on a venomous anti-LWT campaign of scorn and derision. "The Scandal of London Weekend!" was the *Evening Standard*'s headline over an article by its television critic, Milton Shulman, whose conclusion was that LWT's first duty was not survival but suicide. *The Sunday Times* Insight team produced a stinging expose of the franchise delinquencies "of Frost and Co at London Weekend." Peter Black in *The Listener* accused Michael Peacock and his ex-BBC colleagues of running out of nerve in not facing up to the network or its own shareholders.

192 | THE BEST OF TIMES

It was the end of the road for Michael, upon whom all the frustration and disappointment felt by the non-executive members of the Board was concentrated. Little more than a year after London Weekend Television first went on the air, Michael was fired. His ex-BBC colleagues Humphrey Burton, Frank Muir and Doreen Stephens resigned in protest, along with Head of Plays Derek Granger, Executive Producer, Features, Terry Hughes, and Executive Producer, Children's Programmes, Joy Whitby. With the company in disarray, Cyril stayed on for a few months and then accepted an offer from the American producer David Susskind to represent him in the UK. LWT began a long and bitter struggle to survive.

As for Cyril, the Programme Controllers Group gave him the fondest of farewells: our battles had only ever been over programme schedules. Quite by chance, browsing through a collection of Rowlandson's cartoons, I had come across a reproduction of *Kick up at a Hazard Table.* I had it photographed, enlarged and framed, and presented it to Cyril at our farewell party. It was inscribed "For Cyril Bennett. To Remember our Programme Controller Meetings 1968–1969" and signed by all of us. It is reproduced, inscription, signatures and all, in volume four of *Independent Television in Britain.* Look on it, dear reader, and marvel.

"Sweet Thames, Run Softly...

A
fter the Thames inaugural luncheon, and the ACTT inaugural strike which followed it, the company moved into its stride with speed. In 1974, half way through the new franchises, the Authority – renamed the Independent *Broadcasting* Authority two years earlier when Parliament handed it the additional responsibility of Independent Local Radio – produced a mid-term Review of the Television Companies' Performance. Thames, it concluded, had "rapidly made a favourable impression on audiences, advertisers and opinion-formers and earned the Authority's commendation as 'a thoroughly capable company'". Rapidly indeed: in the spring of 1969 Thames had more of its programmes in London's weekday Top Ten than the BBC and as many as all the other ITV companies combined.

Initial revenue projections had suggested that seven days in the Midlands would be the most lucrative contract, but in fact it was the London weekday contract which proved the most valuable in both revenue and prestige. The revenue was the work of George Cooper and the Thames Sales Department, whose success in selling the network's entire advertising time during the ACTT strike gave it an impetus it would never lose. The prestige was down to the company's equally gifted team of programme makers.

At the beginning of our franchise, Thames's Programme Department was a mixed assortment of ABC programme makers and Rediffusion programme makers. They had to be melded into a cohesive team of Thames programme makers. As a programme maker myself eight years earlier at ABC, I had been enormously impressed by the collegiate spirit of Sydney Newman's Drama Department. I admired the way its producers and directors and story editors wandered in and out of each other's offices and the offices of the various production departments, talking about their projects, working out creative problems, exchanging casting suggestions and discussing promotion ideas. I had tried to inculcate that spirit in my own department as ABC's Features and Light Entertainment took shape and encouraged it across the whole of Programme Department when I became Controller, setting up a Programme Co-ordination Committee in which ABC programmes were discussed each week by the creative department heads together with representatives from Press and Publicity, Presentation, Engineering and Administration.

The collegiate spirit had prompted a heartening amount of cross-fertilisation across the company. *Armchair Theatre* spawned Light Entertainment's *Never Mind the Quality, Feel the Width*; Reg Collin, the producer of *Tempo*, moved from Features to Drama to take over the production of *Callan*; other Features producers and directors turned their hand to drama within their own department, like Pamela Lonsdale with her outstanding production of *The Lion, the Witch & the Wardrobe*. Studio managers like Mike Vardy became directors, so did cameramen like Ronnie Baxter; administrator Michael Chapman became a producer; designers became directors, like Bob Fuest with *The Avengers* and Voytek with *The Pilgrim's Progress*. Now the task was to transfer that spirit to the new and very much bigger Programme Department of Thames.

Howard Thomas and I began with a weekend conference in Brighton in an attempt to break down the loyalty barriers between ex-ABC and ex-Rediffusion programme makers, and the camaraderie which the conference helped to generate carried over into Thames's own Programme Coordination Committee. I was blessed with a programme team at the top of its form, eager to win both audiences and acclaim, and I was confident enough in my programme heads to let them get on with the job, with me suggesting programme ideas and projects rather than imposing them, tendering advice when they sought it, offering guidance when they needed it. My confidence was fully justified.

In Drama, for example, Lloyd Shirley's department quickly earned both excellent ratings and critical praise with a succession of intelligent, off-beat series of action and detection. The first of them, transmitted strike-free in our opening week, was *Frontier*, set at the time of the 19th century's 'Great Game' of skirmish and espionage on the North West frontier of India. It was swiftly followed by Special Branch, about the anti-espionage and anti-terrorist activities of London's Metropolitan Police. We transmitted new series of *Callan* and *Public Eye*, which had begun their runs in ABC's air-time, joined by adaptations of Edgar Wallace's short stories about a 1920s investigator in the Public Prosecutor's office in *The Mind of Mr J. G. Reeder*. And *Armchair Theatre* enjoyed a successful transition to weekdays along with its companion series *Mystery and Imagination*.

Accompanying them was a stream of ambitious anthologies, including adaptations of classic Restoration comedies in *The Way of the World* and period detective stories by Conan Doyle's contemporaries in *The Rivals of Sherlock Holmes*, as well as a diverse range of mini-series, including Philip Mackie's *Napoleon and Love*, with Ian Holm as the young Napoleon and Billie Whitelaw as his Josephine; *Man at the Top*, the further adventures of Joe Lampton, hero of John Braine's celebrated novel and film *Room at the Top*, played by Kenneth Haigh; and what the official history named as the drama highlight of 1974, the story of *Jennie, Lady Randolph Churchill*, with American film star Lee Remick in the title role.

All this in the first six years of Thames. No, not quite all. As we were beginning to set up the company, Lloyd approached me with an entirely different kind of drama project. He wanted to make a couple of feature films for television: two thrillers, *Rumour* and *Suspect*. I said this was surely out of the question: the production costs under the union agreement for film would be prohibitive, so we couldn't possibly afford it. Lloyd said that he and George Taylor, our Head of Technical Operations, had found a way round that problem. They would make *Rumour* and *Suspect* on 16 mm film, not the standard 35 mm stock for feature films, using an entirely different union agreement. The film laboratories had been interested enough in the proposal to promise particular care in processing the films. Armed with that promise Lloyd and George had persuaded the ITA's technical standards division to give the experiment a trial. As a result, the films would cost no more than regular 75 minute plays on tape. Music to a Director of Programmes's ears.

I said OK, but who would write and direct them? "Mike Hodges" said Lloyd. Mike Hodges? Mike had begun his television career with Lloyd in ABC's Advertising Magazines and moved with him to Features, taking over from Reg Collin as the producer of *Tempo*. I said "But Lloyd: Mike is a features producer. He works with live TV cameras and videotape, he's never made a feature film in his life, he's never even directed a *drama*, let alone written and directed a film." Lloyd said "I know Mike. I know what he's

196 | THE BEST OF TIMES

capable of. I've read the scripts and I'm certain they will work. Trust me; just watch what he does."

So I trusted Lloyd. I watched what Mike did. And, when *Rumour* and *Suspect* were transmitted, so did the British movie producer Michael Klinger, who liked what he saw and commissioned Mike to make a feature film for the cinema. That film was *Get Carter* – still one of the best British crime films ever made. For Mike Hodges, *Rumour* and *Suspect* were the beginning of an international film career. For Thames, out of that little test-bed experiment came Euston Films, the production company set up two years later by Lloyd and George which would provide Thames with *The Sweeney* and *Minder* and many other successful series and plays, opening up a whole new territory for television drama which the industry would be quick to colonise.

In Light Entertainment too, Thames quickly came to contribute the largest share of the ITV network's regular weekday output, because of Philip Jones' exceptional eye for variety and situation comedy. Philip really came into his own with the new franchise. He had a first-rate team of producers and directors to offer his artistes, and now had four evenings a week in which to deploy them, not just Saturday and Sunday. The big variety names who had worked with him at ABC continued to work with him at Thames – Tommy Cooper, Frankie Howerd, Max Bygraves, Bob Monkhouse, Bruce Forsyth, David Nixon, Mike and Bernie Winters. They were joined in new projects by popular artistes like Eric Sykes, Dave Allen, Kenneth Horne, Harry Worth and Charlie Drake. Hughie Green's *Opportunity Knocks*, still the only consistently popular talent show on television, transferred its residency in the Top Twenty from ABC to Thames without breaking step.

In an unexpected example of Programme Department cross-fertilisation, Edward Woodward – Callan himself – sang, danced and cross-talked his way into a series of musical specials for Philip. International stars joined the Thames roster in concert performances of very different kinds: Tony Bennett, Liberace, Victor Borge with his unique mix of comedy and music, and the great Jack Benny. Benny in fact joined us twice for the same show. It was a notable coup to bring him over from the States in our opening weeks for a concert at the Albert Hall with the Royal Philharmonic Orchestra. He appeared in his radio and television persona as a vain, hopelessly inadequate violinist who blithely sabotaged every piece he performed and was soundly outplayed by a little seven-year old girl violinist. Unfortunately, that original concert was seen only by the audience in the concert hall itself: the ACTT had gone out on strike again. Jack enjoyed the evening as much as the Albert Hall audience however, and came back to do it all over again when the strike was over.

In addition to all these, Philip had two new projects to handle. I was telephoned early in 1969 by Benny Hill's agent, Richard Stone, who said "Benny wants to leave the BBC and do something new." Benny had done a one-off show with me at ATV, but had opted only to rehash material already seen in his BBC shows. "He still feels that he let you down with that show," said Stone, "and he'd be prepared to come to Thames to make up for it. But who would produce him?" I said "He couldn't be in better hands than Philip's: let's put the two of them together and see how they get on." They got on just fine, and began a hugely successful working relationship that would last until Philip's retirement 19 years later. During that time *The Benny Hill Show* would win audiences of more than 20 million in the UK and earn Thames vast sums of sales revenue overseas, particularly in the United States where Benny has remained a hero of comedy to this day.

In the same year, Eamonn Andrews walked into my office with a programme suggestion. *World of Sport* was now LWT's responsibility and Eamonn's late-night chat show felt out of place on a week night, so we had been looking for another project for him, a network show to add to the local London interest of the *Today* programme. Eamonn put a piece of paper on my desk, wrote down the words "This" "Is" "Your" "Life" and added an insertion before "Life": the word "Colourful". "Don't you think *This is Your Life* would look great in colour?" he said. Colour transmission had begun in Britain the year before; the rights to Eamonn's hit BBC show had been allowed to lapse by the Corporation when he left to join ABC in 1964; and yes, colour could certainly give the show a new look and perhaps a new life. So we acquired the rights, and Philip began yet another long-lasting creative relationship. For 18 highly successful years until his death, Eamonn presented the show's instant biography of a surprised and unwitting guest reunited with key figures from his or her past, and *This is Your Life* joined *The Benny Hill Show* and *Opportunity Knocks* as a permanent resident of the Network Top Twenty.

The three of them were by no means alone. Two more transmission days gave Philip the opportunity to devote more attention to the programme genre with which he began his ABC career: situation comedy. There were six years between Philip's first ABC sit-com as a light entertainment producer,

Dora Bryan's *Happily Ever After*, and his first as a Light Entertainment head, *Never Mind the Quality, Feel the Width*. In the first six years of Thames, in addition to new series of *Never Mind the Quality*, he launched no fewer than fourteen situation comedies, eight of them enjoying long runs of four to seven seasons: *Father, Dear Father* starring Patrick Cargill; *For the Love of Ada*, starring Wilfred Pickles and Irene Handl; *And Mother Makes Three* and its sequel *And Mother Makes Five*, starring Wendy Craig; *Bless This House*, starring Sid James and Diana Coupland; *Love Thy Neighbour*, starring Jack Smethurst and Rudolph Walker; *Spring and Autumn*, starring Jimmy Jewel; and Man About the House, starring Richard O'Sullivan and Paula Wilcox.

During these first six years, Thames Light Entertainment shows regularly made their way each week into the programme charts with as many as five appearances in the Network Top Ten, sometimes as many as seven in the Top Twenty. *Man About the House* kick-started an extraordinary run of overseas sales success for the department's situation comedy formats: its adaptation for American audiences as *Three's Company* – all 174 episodes of it – is still, decades later, earning hefty sums from syndication in the States.

In 1970 the production resources at our disposal were greatly expanded with the opening of four studios in the new custom-built Thames head-quarters in the Euston Road in addition to the three in Teddington. As *Independent Television in Britain* later observed, "The resulting output was high in both quantity and quality. For a single company its breadth was remarkable." The history goes on to say "These resources were most ambitiously deployed in the production of documentaries and current affairs programmes." In fact, Thames's documentary and current affairs account was opened with a magnificent bonus from the merger with Rediffusion.

That company's distinguished documentary producer Peter Morley had been working for three years on a television history of the life and times of Earl Mountbatten of Burma, with the Earl making available his diaries, letters, photographs and film records, together with himself as the pro-gramme's narrator, in return for the overseas sales rights. Thirteen hours in length, lavishly produced, its black and white archive film and home movies complemented by new interviews and other material shot in colour on locations worldwide, *Mountbatten* had been planned as a showpiece for Rediffusion's new franchise. It became Thames's showpiece, and an irresistible opportunity for our Managing Director to exercise his showbiz flair. Howard Thomas laid on no fewer than three previews of the series at the Imperial War Museum: one for the press, one for Lord Mountbatten's military colleagues, and one red-carpet gala for Her Majesty the Queen and the entire Royal Family with the sole exception of the Duke of Gloucester, who was unwell.

The first home-grown documentary programme from Jeremy Isaacs's Features and Current Affairs Department was scheduled for transmission on the company's opening night and, like our first Light Entertainment special with Tommy Cooper, it fell victim to the ACTT strike. But when the programme aired a few weeks later *What Shall We Tell the Children?*, an incisive report on sex education, was a notable success. It was followed by a remarkably varied run of well-received documentaries, ranging from *Hard Times*, an examination of poverty in Britain, to *The Sun is God*, a celebration of the bicentenary of J. M. W. Turner; from *Annapurna – the Hardest Way Up*, a spectacular record of Chris Bonington's 1970 climb of the South Face, to *May I Have the Pleasure?*, a profile of the Hammersmith Palais de Danse; from *The Day Before Yesterday*, a six-part series charting Britain's fortunes since the Second World War, to *The Hero of My Life*, a dramatised biography of Charles Dickens; and from *Queen of Hearts*, about the life of Eva Peron, which won Best Network International Award at the Chicago Film Festival, to *We Was All One*, about life in London's dockland, which won Thames its first Prix Italia.

"...Till I End My Song"

Our company name was Jeremy's inspiration for one particularly striking programme, *Till I End My Song*, a collage of sights and sounds of the River Thames from its source to the sea, filmed by David Gill across an entire year. In his autobiography, Jeremy quotes Chris Dunkley's review in the *Financial Times*, which praised the programme as being more "audio-visual poem than a common or garden film". It ended with a wedding in a riverside church and a blissful journey by water to the reception in a riverside pub, over which Michael Jayston read Edmund Spenser's wedding song "Prothalamion", which concludes "Sweete Themmes! Runne softlie, till I end my Song!"

This Week, another fine inheritance from Rediffusion, continued to be one of the pillars of ITV's regular coverage of national and international events and issues. In its first six years it examined the domestic problems of health, housing, poverty, education, industrial relations; it produced programmes on trade union ballot rigging, censorship and pornography, the struggle against inflation, the care of children; it interviewed the party leaders at general elections in Britain and the candidates at presidential elections in the US. Its producers and camera crews brought back vivid reports from the trouble spots of the world: Ulster and Londonderry's 'Bloody Sunday'; Czechoslovakia and the crushing of the Prague Spring; Poland and the riots which led to the downfall of Gomulka; the violence in South Africa, Bangladesh and Rhodesia. A 1973 film about the hitherto unknown famine in Ethiopia, prompted the creation of a charitable fund which raised £1.5 million of famine relief, and was nominated in France 'the great documentary of the year'. Jonathan Dimbleby received the Society of Film and Television Arts' Richard Dimbleby Award for his work on the programme.

The happy synergy between Thames's Sales and Programme Departments was financing this vigorous activity in Drama, Light Entertainment, Features and Current Affairs against a background in which the overall growth in ITV's advertising revenue was slowing down and the industry's overheads, Authority Rentals and Television Levy were accelerating.

In December 1969 the Board of Harlech Television informed the Authority that if the levy continued at its present level it would have to abandon the promises which had won it the contract for Wales and the West. In February 1970 Scottish Television could pay neither rental nor levy nor its bills and had to be rescued by the ITA with the postponement of all its due payments. At last, in February 1971, the Government relented and Christopher Chataway, the Minister for Posts and Telecommunications – the first person to hold that office with an inside knowledge of the medium, having been both a newscaster for ITN and a commentator for the BBC – announced a halving of the rates of the levy "to provide Independent Television with the resources it needs" and "enable the companies to improve the quality of its programmes".

The timing was ideal. Peter Batty, a fine freelance documentary producer, had written to me proposing a series about the major battles of the Second World War and I had passed his proposal to Jeremy Isaacs as an idea worth pursuing. Jeremy told me that he and others had been approached by the BBC in the past about a possible follow-up to the Corporation's acclaimed series on The Great War of 1914-18, but its potential cost had led to the idea being dropped. He had remained interested in such a project however, although not as a military history. He wanted to use a combination of archive film and present-day interviews with survivors to take in the whole panoramic sweep of the war. The Second World War had been a total war in which civilians had suffered more losses than had fighting men and women, and he wanted to show how its terrible events had affected ordinary lives.

Financially, such a project had been beyond our reach until Christopher Chataway's announcement. The changes in the levy now made it possible. Howard Thomas and I put it to the Thames Board; the members gave it their blessing; and we announced it before the BBC could revive its own interest in the subject. Peter Batty was commissioned to make six of the twenty-six hour-long episodes and a team of producers, writers, directors, film researchers, film editors and camera crews was assembled in less than two months. Under Jeremy, with Jerry Kuehl as associate producer, work on the series began on 1 April 1971, and the first episode of *The World at War* was aired on 31 October 1973. It was arguably the clearest demonstration of Thames's richness in talent and resources, a remarkably sustained achievement for which Jeremy as producer and everybody associated with the series received and deserved the greatest credit.

The strength and authenticity of *The World at War* has endured in spite of all the additional information that has since been disclosed with the belated cooperation of the Russian authorities, the opening up of the national archives of Germany, Japan and China, and the revelations of Bletchley Park, revealing facts that were then unknown to the world at large. Transmitted across the entire ITV network in peak-time throughout its 26-week run, to audiences averaging seven to eight million and reaching at times as many as ten million, the series has been shown and repeated around the world in over a hundred countries. In Britain, BBC 2 has repeated it half a dozen times; the cable channel Yesterday played it for the first time in 2011; in Japan it was repeated in 2011; in America, on one channel or another, it has never been off the air. In the UK on the Yesterday channel, its entire 26 episodes filled the Christmas Day and Boxing Day transmissions of 2015. It has won both BAFTA and International Emmy Awards. As Jeremy says in his autobiography with justifiable pride, it "demonstrated what a commercial system of public service broadcasting could do".

ITV's record in other areas of public service broadcasting was already notable, particularly in the case of the two companies which had merged to form Thames, with Rediffusion as a pioneer of Schools Broadcasting and ABC of Adult Education antedating the BBC in each case. Now the entire Rediffusion schools unit had moved to Thames, with Guthrie Moir at the head of its team of producers, directors, advisers and education liaison officers, so continuity was guaranteed for its output and its links with the educational world. Thames continued Rediffusion's specialisation in French for secondary schools, its documentaries for school-leavers and its regular presentation of drama, with a particularly well-received production of Macbeth in 1974. Series aimed at stimulating children's creative activity continued with *Finding Out* for junior classes, Seeing and Doing for children in primary schools – 27,000 of which were using it in 1974 – and *You and the World* for slower learners. To help develop the language and number skills of pre-school children, Guthrie's team used fairy stories in *Once Upon a Time* and puppets in *Rainbow*, a much loved attempt at a British version of America's Sesame Street, which went on to win the Society of Film and Television Arts award for Best Children's Programme of 1975.

ABC's major contribution to ITV's Religious and Adult Education programming was inevitably curtailed with the move from the weekend, where they were obligatory, to the weekdays, where they were not, but even folded into Thames's new department of Education and Religion its enthusiasm and expertise were faithfully sustained. The daily late-night *Last Programme* series introduced representatives of non-Christian faiths to the London viewer and in a striking example of inter-company cooperation was carried over into LWT's airtime on Friday night. The department produced major Adult Education series for the network like *Ballet for All*, *Treasures of the British Museum*, *A Place in the Country*, exploring National Trust properties; and its series *Yoga for Health* ran for 65 editions, sold more than 400,000 copies of its support publication and aroused such interest in the discipline that yoga classes throughout the country were reportedly unable to meet the demand for places.

Lewis Rudd's large and versatile children's sub-department carried on his Rediffusion tradition of comedy shows for children with situation comedies like *Robert's Robots* and *Pardon My Genie* and the innovative 'improv' comedy of *Funny Ha Ha*, in which the cast had to improvise on situations suggested by its audience of children. Both ABC and Rediffusion had presented half-hour action and adventure drama series for young viewers in the late afternoon or early evening and the tradition continued with series like *Ace of Wands*, *The Tomorrow People* and *The Incredible Adventures of Professor Branestawm*, adapted from the books of Norman Hunter.

Thames's claim as a network mainstay was staked on the very first day of the new franchises with two programmes which would run until almost the very last. On taking office as BBC 1's new Controller, Paul Fox had cleared out many of the channel's long-running series, including *Sooty*, the show in which the little yellow glove-puppet bear had been delighting young children since 1952. I snapped it up at once even though we had no room for it in any of the studios in either Teddington or Kingsway. But I remembered the pretty little theatre in the West End's Mayfair Hotel which the hotel used for film nights for its guests, and rented it until a Thames studio became available. The other programme was *Magpie*, devised by Lewis and Sue Turner as

ITV's answer to *Blue Peter*, the BBC's long-running children's magazine, offering a twice-weekly mixture of entertainment and information. It won the UNICEF Award at the 1972 Prix Jeunesse for its special edition on the problems of a family with a mentally handicapped child.

With Thames's London base, Grahame Turner's Outside Broadcast Department was a network mainstay in itself, responsible for the coverage of all the royal and state occasions taking place in the capital during the week – the Queen's silver wedding celebration, Princess Anne's wedding, the funeral of the Duke of Windsor, the state openings of Parliament – as well as show business galas like the Royal Film Performances, Miss TV Times Beauty Contests and Society of Film and Television Arts – later BAFTA – Screen Awards. Its everyday job kept it busy too, servicing Light Entertainment's outside broadcast shows like *An Evening with Jack Benny* at the Albert Hall, *Tony Bennett at the Talk of the Town*, *Max Bygraves at The Royalty* and *Frankie Howerd at the Poco a Poco*. Sport, the traditional milieu for outside broadcasts, was in the hands of LWT and World of Sport at the weekend, but Grahame's units provided the coverage for every major sporting event taking place in London during the week for which ITV was able to acquire the rights, from football and horse racing to international boxing. Major local weekday sporting events in the region were comprehensively covered in the department's two weekly sports magazines, *Sportscene* and *Thames Sport*. Thames's Outside Broadcast units might not have travelled as many miles as their ABC predecessors but the department was no less prolific.

Half-way through the franchise period in 1974, the IBA's review awarded Thames good marks for all-round competence and reliability. We had won more national and international awards than any other ITV company. Our revenue from advertising was higher than any other and the revenue from our international programme sales, led by *The Avengers*, *The Benny Hill Show*, *The World At War* and situation comedy formats, was beginning to approach that of Lew Grade's ATV. In audience terms, we were able to respond quickly and efficiently to any scheduling challenge from the BBC, and earned consistently high overall ratings. According to the official history, in 1973-74 four out of every ten of the programmes which appeared in the monthly all-channel Top Ten came from Thames. In its first six years Thames accumulated more programmes in the weekly Top Ten and Top Twenty than any other company in ITV. "The ingredients in this success" says the official history "were popular programming, clever scheduling, and adroit wheeling and dealing in network committees". It is pleasing to see that acknowledged. The company's success would continue healthily for the remaining six years of the franchise period.

But it would be without me.

Meanwhile... in Another Part of the Jungle

The Monday morning meetings of the Programme Controllers Group were now considerably more orderly. They were hardly love-ins – argument and confrontation, like wheeler-dealing, went with the territory – but they were no longer kick-ups: there were no pistols, no raised chairs, no walk-outs. This was partly because Cyril Bennett's successor as LWT's Director of Programmes was a woman, the drama producer Stella Richman, but mostly because it was now graced by the presence of the Deputy Director-General of the ITA, Bernard Sendall, and independently chaired by the amiable bearded Frank Copplestone, now the Director of Programme Planning within the ITCA's Network Secretariat.

Those sixteen months had been hectic in the extreme for London Weekend. The Board had appointed Tom Margerison, Michael Peacock's Deputy, to succeed him. With no experience of working in television before he joined LWT, Margerison inherited a managerial wasteland with no Director of Programmes and no Heads of Drama, Arts, Light Entertainment, Children's Programmes or Current Affairs. His work force was disgruntled and demoralised and his company's advertising revenue diminishing as its audience declined. He rapidly discovered that no one of stature outside the company was prepared to take on Cyril Bennett's role in charge of programmes. Guy Paine, LWT's Director of Sales, suggested an internal candidate, Stella Richman, who had been hired by Michael Peacock to run a subsidiary company set up to make programmes for overseas sales. With no ready alternative, Margerison reluctantly agreed. Two years earlier, when she was appointed Managing Director of that subsidiary, Stella had become the first woman to hold a senior executive position in ITV. Now she was ITV's first female Director of Programmes.

Unfortunately, there was little rapport between her and Margerison, and with both Managing Director and Director of Programmes learning on the job, the pervading atmosphere of distrust and disarray within the company did not diminish. Stella put together a new programme team and a new programme schedule with characteristic energy. She held on to the handful of programme successes which had survived LWT's disastrous first year, like the comedy shows *Please Sir!* and *On the Buses*; she brought back Humphrey Burton as a freelance producer of *Aquarius*, the successor to ABC's *Tempo* and ITV's only regular series devoted to the arts; and she was comforted to find that there was neither distrust nor disarray in LWT's sports team. Jimmy Hill, the former manager of Coventry City, had been signed up by Michael Peacock to run LWT's Sports Department, and with John Bromley producing *World of Sport* and commentator Brian Moore and director Bob Gardam transforming television's coverage of football in *The Big Match*, the department was enjoying popular and critical success on both Saturday and Sunday afternoons.

Stella's reputation in television drama attracted two outstanding programme makers to LWT: Verity Lambert, to produce *Budgie*, a big hit for pop-singer Adam Faith in his first major acting role, and John Hawkesworth, to produce *The Gold Robbers*, a successful thirteen-part crime series. There were disappointments too, however. A sequel to *The Gold Robbers* was abandoned after its first episode; the opening episode of another drama series wasn't good enough to show at its press preview. Simon Dee, the star talk show host bought away from the BBC, was so unmanageable that his producer left the show after three weeks and Stella's new Light Entertainment head, Barry Took, cancelled both host and show after three months.

Despite all this effort and energy, LWT remained stubbornly in the doldrums, the widely acknowledged sick man of ITV. Scenting blood, industry wolves were circling round the company. In June 1970, in a memorandum to Lord Aylestone, Robert Fraser reported that "the leaders of ATV asked me privately last Friday what I thought would be the likely attitude of the Authority if ATV entered into some form of association with LWT, which could include the outright purchase of LWT, followed by its operation as a fully owned ATV subsidiary".

Sir Robert had discouraged the idea of ATV acquiring control of LWT but Lew Grade returned to it two months later. He made another approach to the Authority, pointing out the rocky situation in which LWT now found itself. It was not a well-conducted company, he argued. It was in the hands of amateurs. And in failing to attract the size of audience needed at the weekend, it was a weakness at the heart of Independent Television. Lew clearly missed his own presence at that heart in London. A file note by Sir Robert records that "At various points in the conversation, Sir Lew expressed his disappointment with the Midland contract. He said he felt that ATV had made a mistake in not applying for one of the London contracts. Knowing the mind of the Authority at the time, I told him that he need lose no sleep on that point, for there had been no chance of success."

Next came an approach to the ITA from the Managing Director of Granada, Denis Forman, who suggested an association between Granada and LWT similar to that of Trident Television, the joint holding company which the Authority had approved for Yorkshire and Tyne Tees. By this time Sir Robert had retired and it was the new Director General, Brian Young, who told Denis firmly that a merger of two of the five major companies would in no circumstances be allowed. This approach was followed by the Managing Director of Yorkshire, Ward Thomas, who suggested a merger of the two London companies. When Young pointed out that the London split was necessary to preserve the balance between the five majors, he replied that Yorkshire, Granada and ATV would be prepared to merge in order to preserve the balance.

Really? Did Lew and Denis know about this? Ward confirmed over lunch many years later that this was indeed the case. But the truth of the matter, as Fraser's memorandum to Lord Aylestone made plain, was that "the only association or merger that would make any kind of sense, and stand a chance of giving the authority the weekend schedules it hopes for, would be between LWT and Thames". Whether or not it was with the Authority's encouragement, Howard Thomas asked me to put together some possible seven day programme schedules for London, "just in case". LWT's problems were jeopardising the stability of the network. Something had to give. And what gave, as was so often the case in the early history of LWT, involved David Frost.

A few weeks after Michael Peacock's departure in 1969, David Frost presented an edition of *Frost on Friday* which, in addition to being the first live programme to be broadcast in colour on ITV, introduced the British public to an Australian newspaper proprietor named Rupert Murdoch. He had acquired the *News of the World*, Britain's largest-selling Sunday newspaper, and was now in the process of buying the national daily *The Sun*. Murdoch was under attack at the time for publishing in the *News of the World* the diaries of Christine Keeler, whose liaison six years before with John Profumo had led to the disgrace and downfall of the Conservative Minister for War. Murdoch had been condemned by Britain's premier Roman Catholic cleric, Cardinal Heenan, for not taking into account the many charitable works by which Profumo had since purchased his redemption, and there had been a uniformly hostile response both to his ownership of the *News of the World* and to the newspaper's conduct. More than four decades later, in 2011, the *News of the World* phone-hacking scandal must have been a painfully acute case of déjà vu for its proprietor. Nevertheless, Murdoch's public relations representatives assured him that the programme would be balanced and would give him an opportunity to explain himself to the British public, so he agreed to be interviewed.

Bad call. David Docherty describes what happened after David Frost welcomed viewers to the programme. "After that it was downhill for Murdoch, who found himself at the centre of a censorious whirlwind. The audience were encouraged by Frost to denounce Murdoch's morals, his values, and his lack of responsibility... Frost was tormentor-in-chief; he orchestrated the attack and encouraged the condemnation and censure". At the end of the programme, a furious Murdoch stormed out of the studio. As he reached the front door of the Wembley complex he turned to his entourage and vowed revenge. "I'm going to buy this place," he said.

Enter John Freeman

The transfer of voting shares in an ITV company required the Authority's advance approval. In November of that year the Authority gave its consent to the *News of the World*'s acquisition of the 7.5 percent of LWT voting shares owned by Sir Arnold Weinstock and Rupert Murdoch became a non-executive director on the LWT Board. In the same month, the company's profit for the previous year of £2.92 million was eaten up by its levy payment of £2.99 million, resulting in a loss of £67,000. It had run through its entire share capital. Its £3 million of loan stock was being deployed to secure bank overdrafts of £2.5 million; and the cost of its new studio centre being built on the South Bank was now estimated at £5.5 million. Reciting this litany of woe to the following month's Board meeting, Murdoch pointed out that the company actually lacked the resources to finance its forthcoming programme schedules. However... he would be prepared personally to inject £500,000 into the programme budget in return for new shares and a seat on the company's executive committee.

The ITA's official history notes that out of all the other powerful institutional shareholders represented on the LWT Board, from The London Co-operative Society and Pearl Assurance to the *Daily Telegraph* and Lombard Banking, none had sufficient faith in the company's future to risk additional investment. And since no additional investment was on offer from any outside source, the Board agreed to a rights issue underwritten by the *News of the World*, for which, because they were non-voting shares, the Authority's advance approval was not required. The issue produced 550,000 new shares, the majority of which were duly purchased by Murdoch. "I'm going to buy this place," Murdoch had said; and in a little over a year he had done so.

There is no doubt that Rupert Murdoch's intervention rescued LWT from what the ITA's history described as "slithering toward bankruptcy", the consequences of which would almost certainly have led to extensive structural change for the entire ITV network. Murdoch was almost certainly the best thing that happened to LWT at that stage. He spent considerable time at the company, cut much of the fat and eradicated many of the bad practices which had plagued it. Deputy Chairman Lord Campbell later asserted that Murdoch "salvaged" LWT. He certainly lost no time. Sales Director Guy Paine was fired within three weeks and Bert Hardy, the director of advertising at the *News of the World* was brought in as LWT's acting Director of Sales. Stella Richman was fired a week later. Ironically, the last programme she commissioned before leaving, *Upstairs, Downstairs*, would become one of LWT's greatest successes. The following month Tom Margerison was asked for his resignation. In announcing it, the Chairman and co-founder of LWT, Aidan Crawley, also announced the setting up of an executive committee to run the company, which Rupert Murdoch would chair.

Murdoch was now in effect both LWT's Managing Director and its Controller of Programmes. He instructed the company's Presentation staff that future programme schedules had to be cleared with him and their feature films and American film series chosen by him. He cancelled a series of six planned documentaries; *Aquarius* was relegated to 11.15 pm; Anglia Television's nature documentary series *Survival* was replaced by a quiz programme. Some of Barry Took's light entertainment shows were summarily dropped; others – like *On the Buses* – were scheduled to continue week-in week-out without a break. It was finally too much for Barry, who resigned. As for the other co-founder of the company and his three *Frost* Programmes a week... ah, revenge would be eaten cold, but it would be sweet. Murdoch announced that LWT would not be able to afford to pay David Frost's existing salary so he would either have to accept a substantial reduction for the next series of *Frost* programmes or he could take his talents elsewhere.

The non-Murdoch press erupted with barely concealed delight at this latest LWT scandal. There were demands in the Commons for a full enquiry. Clive Irving, erstwhile head of LWT's Public Affairs Department, sacked by Peacock and Bennett in the previous LWT debacle, joined in the renewed frenzy with a letter to *The Times* claiming that Murdoch had fired Margerison without reference to the full Board and had drawn up the company's new programme schedule without reference to the company's programme staff. He asked for a thorough and formal enquiry into the transfer of power within the company.

Was this at last the point at which the company's contract would be revoked? It was certainly the case that LWT was a very different company from the one which had secured the contract in the first place. The Authority wrote to LWT stating that the sacking of Margerison and the establishment of an executive committee over which Murdoch would preside constituted a breach which entitled it to determine the company's contract. While reserving its right to do so, however, the Authority invited the LWT Board to a meeting to discuss the company's future plans for its management and programme provision, after which the Authority would announce its decision. LWT was given six weeks in which to choose a new Managing Director and a new Programme Controller and to prepare a new submission to the Authority – in effect, the company would have to reapply for its contract.

Re-enter David Frost. He wasn't concerned about the threatened cut to his salary – these were now the golden days when he was famously flying back and forth between London and New York by Concorde to present three talk shows a week for the Westinghouse Television Corporation as well as the three each weekend for LWT. David's concern was for the future of the television company he had helped to create, and it was clear to him that the company desperately needed a new Managing Director and a new Programme Controller whose names would impress and reassure the Authority.

Back in the heady days of 1967, when Frost was putting together a consortium to bid for an ITV franchise, his close friend and colleague Clive Irving had suggested John Freeman as the chairman of the consortium's proposed new television company. It was an inspired suggestion. Freeman was both high-profile and highly respected. Awarded a Military MBE for his service with the Army, he had stood for Parliament immediately after the Second World War and become a junior minister in Attlee's post-war government. Standing down in 1955 to pursue a career in political journalism, he had become Editor of *The New Statesman*; and he was renowned for his courteous but unsparing interviews in the BBC television series *Face to Face*. In 1964, Harold Wilson appointed him British High Commissioner to India, so Freeman had become a well established and highly regarded member of the British Diplomatic Service. Undeterred, Frost had flown to Delhi to try to interest him in the post of company Chairman. Freeman turned him down, but had been intrigued enough to say that he might consider such a position if he were ever to leave the Diplomatic Service. In the event, he didn't leave the Service: he went on to Washington as British Ambassador to the United States. But Frost had felt sufficiently encouraged to include his name as prospective Deputy Chairman in the bid for the weekend London franchise. Without Freeman's permission.

John Freeman's displeasure at this Frost faux pas had however dissolved over the years; he had retired from the diplomatic service and was back in England. The day after the Authority's decision, Frost was back too, back from his weekday Westinghouse shows and ready for the weekend's LWT programmes. He saw at once that, if Freeman had been an inspired suggestion for the company in 1967, he could be its saviour in 1971. Would he be prepared to consider the post of Managing Director? Would the LWT Board be sympathetic to the idea? Frost hit the phones, testing the idea with LWT's two key non-executive directors and Rupert Murdoch. Lord Campbell knew Freeman well and immediately saw the sense of Frost's recommendation. David Montagu, on the other hand, was sceptical. 'I thought, "Oh my God, not another ex-politician who could not run a whelk stall with a pre-paid supply of whelks"' but he went on to say 'Thank God they did not listen to me, because undoubtedly John Freeman saved the company'.

Rupert Murdoch, bitter at the Authority's refusal to let him run the company his way, was still LWT's largest shareholder and he saw the logic of Frost's proposal. He had just one proviso: Aidan Crawley had to resign as Chairman. "Murdoch insisted that I was no longer to be Chairman because I had not defended him. I told him he was being absolutely rotten; however, he insisted that if he was to maintain his investment then there would have to be another Chairman." It was agreed that Crawley would step aside and accept the nominal role of company President. The way was clear for Freeman to become both LWT's Chairman and its Chief Executive. Frost phoned to say the job was his for the asking and flew back to New York and Westinghouse. His Friday to Sunday LWT *Frost* programmes had gone well too. Now that's what you call a productive weekend.

Lord Campbell made the formal offer to John Freeman: "We are in an awful mess, would you be prepared to take over?" Freeman, determined from the outset that there should be no misunderstanding between himself and the company's principal shareholder, insisted that the invitation should come from Murdoch. Rupert called him to indicate his wholehearted support for the offer and agreed that Freeman would be given a free hand in running the company. Freeman was taking no chances: "You do realise that a free hand applies to you as well as to everybody else – I really do want a free hand." He received Murdoch's genuine assent. It was the beginning of a lasting mutual respect. As Freeman said later to David Docherty: "We had a rather odd relationship over quite a long period and became, I hope, friends; I certainly became, and remain, fond of him, and I think he is a decent and much abused man. However, our relationship was based on the fact that I had to prevent him doing what he wanted to do until eventually, and quite inevitably, he decided to focus his attention elsewhere."

At the all-important interview with the Authority on 22 April 1971 Murdoch, Campbell and Montagu were all members of the LWT team, which was headed by John Freeman. They were without their new Programme Controller, but Lord Aylestone had been advised of his name, which was formally announced the following day. Freeman had persuaded Cyril Bennett to return to the role of Director of Programmes. In advance of the meeting, the company had been sent a penetrating questionnaire covering every aspect of its structure and operation and the Authority thanked the team for its comprehensive answers and noted that the offending Murdoch executive committee had been disbanded. In the discussion which followed, Freeman answered most of the Authority's questions himself with conviction and reaffirmed that "London Weekend Television still believes in the ideals it presented to the Authority in its original application." No one was left in any doubt that he had assumed full executive control of the company's affairs.

The Authority was not only satisfied with the company's response, it was mightily relieved by it. In its public statement the following day confirming the contract, it expressed its pleasure that uncertainty about the future of London Weekend Television had been removed and declared that LWT's franchise now had the same security as that of other programme companies throughout the current contract period. The sun seemed suddenly to come out. LWT sold two of its comedy series, *Doctor in the House* and *Doctor at Large*, to Westinghouse Television in America for a gratifyingly large sum; and the government halved the television levy at last, thereby restoring the prospect of profitability to a hard-hit industry, not least to LWT. Serendipity! Chance! Neither development had anything to do with John Freeman's appointment, but to a company starved so long for good news they seemed happy auguries. The staff was proud to have a widely respected and charismatic leader at its head. The company had a renewed sense of direction and purpose; and the industry recognised it. The circling wolves returned to the jungle.

Takeover

There was another wolf on the prowl in the television jungle of the sixties; a big and powerful wolf. It wasn't Thames it was stalking, but when it finally caught and devoured its prey, Thames was swallowed up along with it. Another London company headache for the ITA.

Stuffed with cash from the international success of its Beatles records, the giant electronics, music and recording company EMI – Electric and Musical Industries Ltd – was diversifying into the film and theatre business. It had bought the Grade Organisation, the biggest entertainment agency in Britain, and along with it Bernard Delfont, the country's biggest theatrical impresario. Bernie had sold his own production company to the Grade Organisation and had subsequently taken over as its Chief Executive when his brother Leslie Grade suffered a stroke. Now EMI wanted to move into film production and exhibition. The Associated British Picture Corporation, with its Elstree film studios and extensive chain of cinemas, was an obvious target.

EMI's first move was to acquire the Warner Brothers holding in ABPC. It wasn't difficult. Jack, the last surviving Warner brother, was growing old and infirm and losing interest in the film business which he and his four brothers had founded in 1932. He had sold the Warner studio to the Seven Arts Company in 1967; the following year EMI acquired Warner's 25 percent holding in ABPC. In the spirit of cooperation, the ABPC Board invited EMI to nominate two non-executive directors to join it, and EMI's nominees were John Read, its Deputy Chairman and Chief Executive, and Bernard Delfont, who was now Chairman and Chief Executive of EMI's Film and Theatre

Division. The ABPC directors were inviting a pair of man-eating tigers to sit down at the Board table with them. A fierce struggle for control of the rest of the Corporation began almost at once and ended early in 1969 with a complete takeover by EMI – and a complete clear-out of the ABPC Board.

As a result, since ABPC was the controlling partner in the merger with Rediffusion to form Thames, the television company was now controlled by EMI. Bernard Delfont also happened to be Chief Executive of the Grade Organisation; and the Grade Organisation had retained its ties with its co-founder Lew Grade; and Lew Grade was Chairman and Joint Managing Director of ATV... the plot had thickened. According to Howard Thomas's autobiography, Lew and his fellow Managing Director, Robin Gill, were now giving him a series of mysterious nods and winks intimating that the close link between ATV and EMI was about to extend to Thames: "We could all be together," they assured him, "in running a colossal conglomerate."

The ITA was faced with another London company quandary. Should it allow the control of the weekday London contract to pass into the hands of a company which had not applied for it and which had close connections with another ITV company? Or should it terminate the contract, re-advertise it and start the procedure for the London weekday franchise all over again? At the same time, seeing an opportunity at last to regain lost ground, Sir John Spencer Wills was urging the Authority to adjust the Thames share-holdings by a mere 2 percent so that control of the company might pass to Rediffusion. The Authority's action was firm and astute. It made clear to Sir John its view that a leading entertainment company like EMI was a more appropriate choice to exercise control over a television company than a City conglomerate like British Electric Traction, the owners of Rediffusion. And it laid down stringent terms to ensure that management of Thames would remain in the hands of Howard Thomas and the other former ABC executives; not Rediffusion, and not the Grade Organisation either.

EMI would have to sever all connection with the agency activities of the Grade Organisation. No members of the Grade Organisation could be connected with the Board or management of Thames Television, which ruled out Bernard Delfont. Any nominee proposed for inclusion in the Thames Board would have to be approved by the ITA, and the Authority did not approve the appointment of John Read, on the grounds that it would upset the balance with Rediffusion. The Authority nominated Lord Shawcross, a non-executive member of the EMI Board and former Attorney General in the post-war

Labour Government, to be co-opted to the Thames Board and appointed its independent Chairman. And a new company, Thames Television Holdings Ltd, would be formed to control the majority stake in Thames Television which EMI had inherited with ABPC. The new company's shares would be divided into non-voting (90 percent) and voting (10 percent). EMI would hold all the non-voting shares but only 40 percent of the voting shares. Of the remaining voting shares two independent companies would be offered 20 percent each, and the remaining 20 percent would be offered to the four principal executives of Thames, Howard Thomas, George Cooper, Bernard Greenhead and yours truly.

That share proposal sounded pretty good to me, but Teddy Sommerfield read the small print of the agreement and discovered that the executive shares could only be sold back to EMI and at the price at which they had been bought in the first place. Since I would have had to borrow money to buy shares which would never appreciate in value, I declined them and the amounts were adjusted to 23.5 percent each for the two independent companies and 13 percent to the Thames executives. It was not until two and a half years later, when the Television Advertising Levy was halved and the prospect of profitability for the industry revived, that any corporate investor thought the two 23.5 percent stakes were worth taking up. They were finally acquired by Sir Charles Forte and a property development company, South Bank Estates.

I was personally sorry to see the departure of the ABPC directors. They had always treated my programme department at both ABC and Thames with courtesy and a kind of guarded respect. They were never sure enough of their television ground to question what we were up to, and never withheld finance from any of our ventures. I also owed to the two Warner representatives an odd little excursion as ABC's Programme Controller. The sixties were hard times for Hollywood as well as for ITV and the film studios were turning increasingly to the production of television series for their successes. Britain was a potentially valuable market for these and early in 1963 Warner's asked Howard Thomas to send me over to the States to advise their new TV production boss on the kind of series that would go down well with British viewers. If only I knew!

My trip was to New York not Hollywood, which was something of a disappointment, but the new production boss was one of my TV heroes so I was delighted to go. Jack Webb had been the creator, producer, director and star of *Dragnet*, the most successful TV police drama series of its day, and I was a great admirer of both his own feisty performance as Sgt Joe Friday of the Los Angeles Police Department and the show's crisp, innovative, documentary style. We spent a very pleasant day together. He had been appointed in March; I met him in May; whatever I was able to tell him about the tastes of British viewers turned out to be irrelevant: he was fired in December. I hope it wasn't anything I said.

Having been so comprehensively corralled by the Authority, EMI made no attempt in these honeymoon years to interfere with the management of Thames. Howard Thomas and I were invited to join its Creative Committee, which was chaired by Bernard Delfont, where we were treated with some-times quite embarrassing respect. The most that was ever asked of us was whether this or that feature film could be spun off into a television series or if this or that theatrical production was suitable for television transmission, the answer to both of which queries usually being No.

The only attempt at interference, oddly enough, came not from EMI itself but from its former non-executive Board director, now Thames's new independent Chairman, Lord Shawcross. An edition of *This Week*, our regular current affairs programme, featured a profile of Frank Chapple, the General Secretary of the Electrical Trades Union. Chapple had been a member of the Communist party but now, in the seventies, he was attempting to drive the party's presence and influence out of the union: a suitably dynamic story for our programme. Lord Shawcross, whose own politics had themselves moved very much to the Right from his early Labour Party days, was outraged. He complained to Howard Thomas that the programme had been unbalanced and politically biased, that it had set out to apotheosise Chapple as a heroic figure of the Left and should be condemned. He demanded a private showing of the programme for the full Board so that his colleagues could join him in issuing a severe reprimand to Jeremy Isaacs and his Features Department.

Howard and I couldn't understand the Chairman's reaction to what we both thought was a first-rate piece of television journalism, but we respected his wishes and set up a private showing. The Thames Board sat through the programme, saw nothing untoward in it and rejected the suggestion of a reprimand. But if the diaries of Cecil King, the publisher of the *Daily Mirror*, are to be believed, Lord Shawcross's view of his company's Features output became something of a fixation. In the published entry for 26 October 1973, King wrote: "On Wednesday Hartley Shawcross had lunch with me. He is

Chairman of Thames Television and has been disturbed at the volume of left-wing propaganda put out by the commentators from his station. He had up the man responsible, and questioned him about the bias shown by his department. The man said he was a left-winger himself, as were most of his staff. He would not brook any interference with his work, though of course the directors could dismiss him. If they did so there would be a strike and the station would close down."

"The man responsible" was of course Jeremy Isaacs. But he states categorically that he had had no such encounter and no such preposterous conversation with Lord Shawcross, and I firmly believe him. Whether this was fantasy or overstatement on the part of either King or Shawcross, no whiff of it ever came near Howard Thomas or myself – nor did any future request for a reprimand or a private showing.

The only other intervention by the Chairman was in 1971, on 23 April, the day after LWT's franchise was reconfirmed. Lord Shawcross wrote to Aidan Crawley suggesting that the two London companies might initiate "some joint action on the advertising front" and cooperate with programmes "so as to maintain consistently better ratings than the BBC". Crawley replied in similar vein, inviting Lord Shawcross and his executive directors to dine with John Freeman, Cyril Bennett and himself so that they might consider arrangements "whereby we could schedule programmes broadly on a seven day basis and combine our sales operations, so as to eliminate the mutually destructive competition in which we indulge at the moment".

We dined by candlelight on 2 June at Aidan Crawley's house in Belgravia. According to Docherty, though I don't recall it, the complaint was made that Thames's Sales Department had been bad-mouthing LWT's rival team to advertisers and advertising agencies, and the hope was expressed that the departments could cease hostilities and allow the two companies to build a new partnership based on trust. Other initiatives were discussed, such as sharing OB units, operating a combined master-control unit, and jointly manufacturing, storing and transporting scenery. I confess that I remember very little of the evening, other than that it was courteous and temperate and, with all the candlelight, vaguely Dickensian, and that Cyril and I found ourselves exchanging increasingly wry glances. We knew that the two London companies were *meant* to compete and that a combined, seven-day London operation would have been unacceptable not only to the rest of the network but also to the ITA.

I have no idea whether George Cooper's salesmen had indeed been bad-mouthing LWT's, though I doubt it because they didn't have to. They were running rings round LWT's Sales Department as a result of the several advantages they had enjoyed from the very beginning of the two franchises. These included the head start which had been handed to Thames when it was entrusted to sell network airtime during the 1968 ACTT strike, the disastrous ratings of LWT's early months, and the inadequacies of Guy Paine's ex-Rediffusion salesmen. In their previous weekday franchise, selling air-time had become a mere matter of opening their books on Monday morning and closing them, full, on Monday afternoon. Selling a faltering weekend against their thriving weekday competitor was a very different proposition. In 1968, the potential value of the four biggest ITV franchises had been estimated by the Authority to be roughly equal. The actual figures for the four companies of total Net Advertising Revenue before levy in the financial years from 1968-69 to 1972-73 showed ATV's share to be 22.2 percent and Granada's 20.2 percent. Total London share was around 43 percent, of which Thames was punching above its weight at 25.7 percent while LWT trailed at 17.6 percent.

Our little dinner party broke up in good humour, with mutual assurances of sportsmanlike behaviour between the two companies, which is what ensued. Nothing of substance however came of the proposals for sharing, combining or jointly manufacturing: in one way or another they were all impractical. The relationship between Messrs Thomas and Freeman and Cyril and myself continued courteous and temperate and mutually supportive on behalf of London in our dealings with the rest of the network, but it would have done so anyway. In light of the imbalance between Thames and LWT's respective Net Advertising Revenues, the Authority reduced LWT's rental by more than £300,000 and raised Thames's by nearly £200,000, a move which at Thames we bore with a brave grin.

At the same time, LWT's Sales Department underwent a remarkable transformation for the better, which Thames's Sales Department bore with respect rather than a grin. They would become a genuine challenge; but anything that increased the total amount of advertising revenue attracted to London was to be welcomed. Bert Hardy, LWT's Acting Director of Sales installed by Rupert Murdoch, had brought in Ron Miller from Anglia Television as his Sales Manager and Ron was blessed with a singular flair for the management of advertising airtime. His energy and inventiveness introduced an abundance of ideas for seeking out and exploiting new sources of revenue at the weekend, and the following February he was appointed Director of Sales, with Bert Hardy withdrawing to the LWT Board as Rupert Murdoch's representative.

John Freeman and I found ourselves sitting next to each other at the ITA's monthly meeting of the Programme Policy Committee at Brompton Road, which was attended by the Managing Directors of all fifteen ITV companies and the Directors of Programmes of the five major companies. The big five sat cheek by jowl at the huge circular doughnut of a table, directly facing the Authority's Chairman, Director General and senior officers, with the regional Managing Directors on either side of us. Each of the five major MDs sat alongside his Director of Programmes, so John's jowl was next to my cheek, with Cyril on his left and Howard Thomas on my right. John and I chatted easily together and came to know each other quite well, discovering in the process that we shared a birthday as well as a fondness for the novels of Dashiell Hammett, Raymond Chandler and other masters of American crime fiction. If only I could also have shared his composure, his command, and his clarity of thought and expression!

As for Cyril Bennett, we were of course competitors as well as friends. Scheduling programmes for different parts of the London week as we did, we were competitors principally in the acquisition of feature film packages and television film series, and the film distributors were adept in playing us against each other. Gordon Smith was the canny film buyer for the BBC and when packages and titles were being considered every buyer in ITV was accustomed to being told that "Gordon Smith is interested..." In negotiations with either of the two London companies the customary come-on in turn was "Cyril – or Brian – is interested...".

Cyril and Brian were competitors particularly for action film series which could be played to family audiences in the afternoons. In the sixties and early seventies, 20th Century Fox were turning out a succession of such shows, usually produced by Irwin Allen, "the most successful science-fiction producer of the decade" according to *Science Fiction* magazine. These were series such as *Voyage to the Bottom of the Sea*, *The Time Tunnel*, *Lost in Space*... you get the idea; you probably remember the shows.

I had been beaten to the punch by Cyril on several of these purchases so when the latest series – *Land of the Giants* – was announced I called Bill Saunders, Fox's British representative, and said I wanted first look at it.

"Of course, Brian. I'll send a print over to you right away and I promise I won't show it to Cyril until you've seen it. My bosses are coming over from California tomorrow, so why don't we all have lunch together and you can tell us what you think of it?" So next day Bill Saunders and I met the Joint Vice-Presidents of 20ᵗʰ Century Fox, Herb Lazarus and Alan Silverbach, at Jack Isow's long gone and sorely missed delicatessen restaurant in Brewer Street. We introduced ourselves to each other, shook hands, sat down at the table, and Bill, rubbing his hands together with consummate self-assurance, said "Well Cyril, what did you think of it?" Stunned silence, followed by roars of laughter from Herb, Alan and me and strangled noises from Bill. Cyril Bennett got the series. I got Herb Lazarus as a good and close friend for the next 47 years and counting. I think mine was the better deal.

It wasn't only the American film distributors who enjoyed playing Cyril and me off against each other. The Programme Controllers Meeting at the beginning of Christmas week that year was held at ATV House in Great Cumberland Street. Half way through the meeting, Lew Grade – *Sir* Lew Grade: he had been knighted in 1969 – put his head round the door and said "Cyril, Brian, come to my office after the meeting: I've got something for you." Appropriately intrigued, we made our way to Sir Lew's den at the end of the day where we were each presented with a welcoming cigar, a glass of wine and a Christmas present: a large square box, beautifully wrapped in Christmas paper and ribbon, decorated with tinsel and stars and a large Christmas label inscribed "Merry Christmas from Lew". Overwhelmed, and not a little embarrassed – "But Lew, we've got nothing for you... you shouldn't have... this is so unexpected..." – we picked up our Christmas presents (with some difficulty – they were heavier than we expected) while a beaming Lew said, "Well open them! Open them!" So we did. And they were filled to the brim with the shooting scripts, promotional literature and photographs of the artists and locations of the six feature films which his ITC company was about to put into production. "Merry Christmas! So who's going to buy what?"

Song Ended

Towards the end of 1973 I was called into Lew's office on another occasion, without Cyril Bennett and for a very different reason. ATV was now spread over three complexes, its new Midlands centre in Birmingham, its main production base in Elstree and its headquarters in Great Cumberland Place, and Lew couldn't be in two places at once, let alone three. He had brought over from Australia a dynamic young Australian television executive named Bruce Gyngell to share the load as ATV's Managing Director, but Bruce was returning to Australia the following year. How would I like to be Joint Managing Director with Bruce until he left and then succeed him as sole Managing Director? Of course I was flattered, immensely so, but I couldn't see how Joint Managing Directors could work in a creative enterprise like television. And Howard Thomas was due to retire from Thames at the end of the year and there was a chance that I might be given a shot at succeeding him – as sole Managing Director. So, with thanks and the deepest appreciation, I said No. The following year Lew offered the Joint Managing Directorship to Lord Windlesham.

David Windlesham was an old friend and colleague. He had worked in ITV from its earliest days. He had been Chief Programme Executive for Rediffusion and I had offered him a job at Thames when the company lost its franchise in 1968, but Grampian Television had offered him a much more attractive one: Managing Director. It was a role in which he excelled until the Heath Government tempted him into ministerial office in 1970. During the subsequent four years David was Minister of State at the Home Office, Minister of State for Northern Ireland, Lord Privy Seal, and Leader of the

House of Lords. He retired from politics when the Conservatives lost the General Election of October 1974, at which point Sir Lew smartly offered him the ATV Managing Director job. Timing is all in television.

Those years leading up to the Authority's mid-franchise Review in 1974 were good for ITV – but not good enough. The halving of the Levy in 1971 helped to shore up financial stability and expand programme budgets but, even so, the Director General of the ITA was able to point out to the Minister of Posts and Communications that companies were still spending more money than they could hope to recoup on such distinguished programmes as ATV's productions of Shakespeare and *Long Day's Journey into Night*, Granada's *State of the Nation*, LWT's *Weekend World* and Mahler Festival, Southern Television's operas from Glyndebourne, Thames's *The World at War* and Yorkshire's series on *The Brontës of Haworth*.

What was needed, the Authority felt, was a Levy related to profits rather than one imposed on income irrespective of profit or loss, and it had spent years arguing this case to the Treasury. At the end of 1973 the decision to legislate along the lines proposed by the Authority was finally taken by the Conservative government and accepted by the incoming Labour government the following year, to be enshrined in due course in a new Independent Broadcasting Act.

With a new Broadcasting Act as well as the ITA's mid-term review, 1974 was going to be a significant year for Independent Television. It was also going to be a most significant year for me personally. Early in December Howard Thomas called me into his office. "I've just come back from a meeting with John Read. Lord Shawcross is retiring in February. EMI have offered me the Chairmanship, and I've proposed that you should succeed me as Managing Director. What do you say?"

"What *can* I say! That's wonderful, HT! Congratulations! And it's very flattering to be considered as your successor. Are you sure that's OK with you?"

"Of course it's OK: you know that I've always had that in mind for you" – no Howard, I didn't know – "but who would you have as your Director of Programmes?"

"Jeremy, of course. Jeremy Isaacs."

"Jeremy? ...What about his politics?"

"What *about* his politics? They've never caused a problem. We both agreed that the Frank Chapple business was an aberration on the part of the Chairman. Jeremy will be fine, believe me."

"If you say so – and of course you'll still be in overall charge... Well, you'd better tell Teddy Sommerfield to come and have a chat with me."

Teddy had negotiated my original ABC contract and its subsequent variations with Howard Thomas and they had always got on well so I didn't foresee any problems, but I confess that as I returned to my office it all seemed very unreal. Managing Director? Just like that?

It didn't seem any more real next morning when George Cooper came into the office and said "Howard's just told me you're going to be Managing Director. Congratulations! I'm delighted, and I want you to know that I'm more than happy to serve under you – though it will only be for another four years I'm afraid: my contract provides for me to retire when I reach sixty-two." And it still didn't seem real at the company's pre-Christmas party, when Lord Shawcross came over to the table hosted by Audrey and me, shook my hand and said "Congratulations. You will be a very good Managing Director and I wish you every success".

And, as it turned out, it wasn't real.

In the first week of the New Year Howard Thomas called me into the office again. "We have a problem. John Read says that managing directors of EMI's subsidiary companies have to be engaged directly, not through their own private company and not through their representatives, so you're going to have to drop Teddy Sommerfield as well as your company if you want to take over from me". I said I'd get back to him and went off to call Teddy. "That's nonsense!" said Teddy. "I negotiated a contract with EMI three years ago for Donald Maclean as Managing Director of their Audio-Visual subsidiary, with his services supplied through his own company. And I happen to know that Bernie's contract with EMI is through Bernard Delfont Limited – and he didn't negotiate that for himself either."

I had no intention of dropping either Teddy or my company. Teddy had guided me out of the BBC and into ITV seventeen years ago and acted as my business adviser ever since. It was he who had suggested setting up a private company at the end of 1956 when I was beginning to be involved in activities other than television production, which was why I called the company Multithon. Billy Cotton had asked me to produce his Christmas stage show at the Prince of Wales Theatre and Teddy had arranged commissions for me to write a book about *Ask Pickles* (which fell through when Wilfred decided to write one himself), as well as articles in *TV Mirror* and *She* magazine, a weekly column for *The Star* newspaper and the *Record Mirror* despatches from Broadway.

I went back to Howard Thomas with the information about Messrs Maclean and Delfont and he said he would take it up with John Read. How vigorously he did so I have no idea, but Read was adamant. And so was I. George Cooper came into my office once again: "What's going on? Two weeks ago Howard told me you were going to be MD, and now he tells me that *I* am. What's happened?" I told George and returned the compliment he had paid me a fortnight earlier: "and I want you to know that I'm more than happy to serve under *you*."

In the IBA's official history Jeremy Potter describes the impasse with characteristic elegance: "Thomas and Tesler were locked in a state of mutual astonishment at each other's behaviour in allowing the most important appointment in the largest ITV company to fail for such a trivial reason". That's not in fact quite true. Howard was concerned not to jeopardise his own elevation and to be honest I was relieved not to be embracing mine. I didn't think I was ready for it. I didn't even think I was *right* for it: not yet, anyway... perhaps when George retired in four years' time. With Thames running softly and sweetly I was perfectly happy to continue as its Director of Programmes. Except nobody – not Howard, not George, not EMI – noticed that my contract as Thames's Director of Programmes would expire at the end of 1973.

Howard Thomas was due to take up his appointment in February 1974; George Cooper to take up his in April. On the morning George's appointment was announced I received a phone call from Robert Clark. Robert had succeeded Eric Fletcher as Deputy Chairman of ABPC in 1964 when the good doctor joined Harold Wilson's Government as Minister Without Portfolio. He had led the corporation's fight against EMI's takeover bid and was summarily booted off the ABPC Board when EMI won, whereupon he had crossed the river and bought himself into LWT. As a major shareholder with the reputation of being a seasoned and sagacious non-executive director, he had been speedily invited on to the LWT Board and was now that company's Deputy Chairman. Same job, different riverbank. "I thought *you* were going to be MD," Robert said. "So did I," I replied. "Well, I don't need to know what happened. Just tell me one thing. Are you still under contract?" "No I'm not." "In that case, John Freeman would like to talk to you. Why don't you ring his secretary and arrange a meeting?"

I did so and was invited to call at John Freeman's house in Kew the following Sunday. "It's a lovely day," said John. "Why don't we go for a walk?" He and I walked round Kew Gardens on that brisk, bright January morning and talked about television and the network and, finally, me. "I've been sitting next to you at the PPC for nearly three years," John said. "I like the way you handle yourself at Brompton Road. I like the way you've argued your company's case and protected its interests. I like the fact that you and Cyril are close friends. You've been good for Thames and before that for ABC and I think you could be good for LWT. More important as far as you are concerned, I think LWT could be good for you. I have a proposition to make. I shall be 60 next year and must start thinking about the future of my company when I give up the day-to-day responsibility of management. I should like you to join LWT as my understudy and deputy. And if at the end of two years you have grown to know and like the company and the company has grown to know and like you, I shall stand down as Managing Director and remain Chairman, and you will take over from me as MD. How does that strike you?"

How did it strike me? Like everything else I had heard from John at industry meetings over the past few years it struck me as being generous, perceptive, far-sighted, and wise. He didn't think, any more than I did, that I was ready to be a Managing Director now, but I might be ready in time, and time was what he was offering me. I told him about Multithon and Teddy Sommerfield and he said they presented no problem: some of his senior executives were already contracted on a similar basis. We agreed that I would discuss the proposition with Teddy, who would call him to work out the details.

And this time it seemed real.

John came over to our house in Park Road, Chiswick, for tea the following Sunday and he and I repaired to my study to tie up the ends of the contract agreed by him and Teddy. We shook hands on the deal, and Audrey poured us all a glass of wine to toast the future. The next day I handed in my letter of resignation to Howard Thomas and John Read, giving three months' notice of my departure. I also wrote to Sir Joseph Lockwood, the Chairman of EMI, next to whom I had sat at the Thames Board's farewell lunch for Lord Shawcross. He had been aware of the background to George's appointment and was kind enough to offer me some words of advice. "Don't get mad and leave," he had said. Before he heard it at second hand I wanted him to know that I *was* leaving, but that I hadn't got mad. I was resigning from Thames and EMI with the best of good will and with my sincerest wishes for the success of both companies.

To Howard Thomas I said I was proud to have been one of the founders of Thames and to have contributed to its success. I said I had greatly enjoyed my association with my fellow Directors, my colleagues and a staff which seemed to me to be the finest in the industry, and I had particularly valued my long and happy personal association with himself, not only in Thames but also in the years at ABC. My letter to George was handwritten. I wanted him to know that I was leaving with no ill-feeling whatsoever, and certainly not as a consequence of his appointment which I considered a fine one. I said I was sure that we would remain good friends and colleagues; and so we did, until George died in 2015 at the age of 99.

It was far more difficult to say farewell to the members of Programme Department and all those skilled and talented men and women in the other departments who had helped to make the company a success. I had worked with many of them for fourteen years. Whether ex-ABC or ex-Rediffusion, they were all now totally and dedicatedly Thames and I genuinely believed them to be the finest in the industry. I was very much aware that in saying farewell to them all I was saying farewell to more than twenty years of personal involvement with programmes and programme-making and hadn't the faintest idea of what might await me in my new career. But we parted, Thames and I, on a high and happy note.

At our farewell celebration, Graphics Department presented me with me a set of beautifully drawn cartoons of my Programme Department heads and a king-sized Farewell Card containing 147 signatures and good luck messages. The May edition of the Thames Newsletter reported that "Brian Tesler's farewell party at Thames on Friday, 5 April was as enjoyable and as relaxed as any party tinged with sorrow at losing a loved and respected colleague could be (apologies to readers for that slightly funereal note which Brian would be the first to challenge with a raised eyebrow). Over a hundred of us it seemed gathered in Euston West to drink champagne and hear two witty speeches. The farewell speech delivered by Jeremy Isaacs reminded us that Brian was 'that quiet man on the third floor who worked for Vera Green'" – Vera being my supremely capable secretary – "Brian capped his own response by handing over to Jeremy the key of the executive loo and another key which he said he could not identify, but which he hoped was the key to the company safe."

Though it had not been announced, everybody knew that I had nominated Jeremy as my successor. The Newsletter report was accompanied by a selection of photographs to give a flavour of the occasion, one of which was of Jeremy on one knee receiving the key to the executive loo. Unfortunately, it would be some time before he would be allowed to use it...

Across the River...

((Tesler was not welcomed eagerly at LWT," says David Docherty in his history of the company. "Bennett was far from delighted at being passed over and the senior staff, particularly those who had been recruited by Bennett, felt that Cyril had been slighted."

In his autobiography Michael Grade, then LWT's Head of Light Entertainment, described the mood of the senior staff as "astounded and indignant". I was an interloper, another layer of management interposed between Cyril and John Freeman and, what was worse, I had come from The Enemy, LWT's deadly rival: Thames. I had two years in which to live that down; two years in which to win over the staff, junior as well as senior. I would be helped by the respect in which John Freeman was held – my being there was his idea after all, and his other ideas for the company had worked out pretty well – and by the liking and respect that Cyril and I clearly had for one another. It was Cyril who proposed the welcoming toast at the drinks reception set up to introduce me to the company's executives. The rest was up to me. So I set about learning what made the company tick, getting some sense of the energy and purpose which imbued the men and women who worked in it and, quite frankly, getting them used to seeing me around.

Its impressive new building, Kent House, all eighteen floors of it, towered over the National Theatre and Festival Hall on the South Bank. I explored it in daily forays from my office on the 13th floor, where John Freeman and I shared an inter-communicating suite on either side of the office which accommodated our respective secretaries. I attended Board meetings and sat in on John's meetings with the other executive directors: Cyril, Ron Miller,

General Manager Vic Gardiner, and Finance Director Peter McNally. I had long talks with Roy Van Gelder, the Personnel Manager, about the company's labour relations. Wandering into studios and control rooms during camera rehearsals, I met up again with John Bromley and the *World of Sport* team and many other familiar faces: producers, directors, technicians and artistes with whom I had worked at ABC and Thames, some of them even as far back as at ATV and the BBC.

I was also delighted to find myself involved once more with the British Forces Broadcasting Service, with which I'd spent most of my National Service. LWT's General Manager, together with the company's Engineering Head, Roger Appleton, had made a bid for the contract to supply BFBS with a television service for the British Army of the Rhine. Transmission by satellite from the United Kingdom in the early seventies would have been too costly so Vic and Roger had proposed a process in which programmes selected by BFBS from the daily schedules of both BBC and ITV would be videotaped off air, edited together with continuity links on to master tapes, and trucked to Germany each day to be relayed from the BFBS transmitter in Celle to British Army barracks and homes throughout the Zone. For LWT this would provide a convenient and remunerative way to use the company's presentation suites on weekdays, when we ourselves were not on the air, so I was more than happy to join my new colleagues in making a pitch to the visiting team of Ministry of Defence and BFBS representatives, which to my agreeable surprise included Ian Woolf, my old boss from the radio station in Trieste, now BFBS's Chief Executive.

It was good to see Ian again after 25 years but, ironically, he felt that my presence at LWT presented a problem. He was concerned that our previous working relationship might be thought by the MOD to influence the bidding process. Happily, his colleagues did not agree. What we were offering in terms of effort and facilities demonstrably outweighed what was being tendered by the BBC, our rival bidder, and we were awarded the contract. The BBC's long history of cooperation with BFBS both during and after the war had led it into believing itself the natural and automatic choice, and it had treated the tendering process as a mere formality. We would find the Corporation taking the process very much more seriously when it came up for renewal in three years' time. Meanwhile, I was co-opted on to the BFBS Board of Management as a liaison officer. From Bombardier to Officer in only 25 years: how's that for rapid promotion?

London Weekend Television seemed to me to be in pretty good shape all round, so I was disturbed to learn that this wasn't quite the case with my old company. Apparently, after my departure Howard Thomas had had second thoughts about Jeremy Isaacs as Director of Programmes and, without involving his Managing Director George Cooper, was interviewing Bill Cotton and Stella Richman for the job after office hours at Thames's Euston studios. I learned this because both Bill and Stella were calling me before their interviews to ask what sort of information they should seek from Howard, and then again afterwards to check whether they could rely on the answers he had given them. Bill took to stopping off at Park Road on his way home after his own interviews for some scrambled eggs on toast from Audrey and a reassuring word from me, but neither of them was enthusiastic about the prospect of joining Thames. Bill was a BBC man through and through and Stella, like me, had a private company of her own which she was reluctant to jettison. They both turned the job down and Jeremy finally got it, as he deserved; but the company had been in some disarray for weeks.

LWT on the other hand was doing well now. Its new studio centre, the latest to be constructed in Britain, was ahead even of Thames's Teddington Studios in its design and facilities. Ron Miller, with his friendly giant of a Sales Controller Craig Pearman, was successfully devising ways of attracting new sources of revenue to the weekend. The latest was corporate advertising: encouraging businesses to sell themselves as well as their products to the viewing audience. "We really started to motor in 1974," recalled Ron later. "Sales department changed from being a team of hustlers, good nitty gritty operators, to people that actually were going to lead the way the industry was going." The company's labour relations were now calm, even congenial: early in May the following year, when the ACTT was gearing itself up to call a national strike on the Bank Holiday weekend, the union shop at LWT voted by 305 to 9 to break it even if the pickets were on parade. LWT was the only ITV company on the air that weekend.

As for its programmes, when Cyril was brought back to the company by John Freeman in 1971 he inherited two major successes from Stella Richman's brief reign as Director of Programmes in *Upstairs, Downstairs* and *Budgie*, as well as two popular children's series, *Catweazle* and *The Adventures of Black Beauty*. He and his head of drama, Rex Firkin, introduced three new series, a police procedural in *New Scotland Yard*, a study of the problems of a single mother in *Helen: A Woman of Today*, and a story of life in a woman's prison, *Within These Walls*, starring the popular film actress Googie Withers. They also commissioned a number of notable single plays like *The Death of Adolf Hitler* and an adaptation of Royce Ryton's stage success about the 1936 Abdication crisis, *Crown Matrimonial*, with Peter Barkworth as Edward VIII and Academy Award winner Greer Garson as Queen Mary. The comedy hits from Cyril's previous period in charge, *Doctor at Large*, *Please Sir!* and *On the Buses*, were still attracting audiences and he had commissioned two new successes in *No, Honestly*, a delightful comedy starring John Alderton and Pauline Collins, and *Billy Liar*, written by Keith Waterhouse and Willis Hall from their stage adaptation of the original Waterhouse novel.

LWT's big Saturday night music and comedy spectaculars with Tommy Steele and, especially, Stanley Baxter, were outstanding; *World of Sport* and *The Big Match* continued to provide first class coverage of sport at the weekend; and Sunday morning's *Weekend World*, produced by John Birt and presented by Peter Jay, was recognised as one of the three jewels in the crown of ITV's current affairs programming alongside Granada's *World in Action* and Thames's *This Week*. Cyril had even managed to persuade the entire network at last to carry *Aquarius*, still presented by its original creator and producer Humphrey Burton and still ITV's only regular series covering the arts – although Lew Grade persisted in keeping it out of ATV's weekend schedule, playing the show after *News at Ten* on Mondays.

Like Ron Miller's sales department, Cyril's programme department in 1974 was really motoring, and its achievements were recognised at the British Academy of Film and Television Arts Awards Ceremony early the following year with no fewer than seven BAFTA Awards, more than the BBC and more than all the other ITV companies put together. On its website the BAFTA Archive carries a large photograph of Cyril on that night, cool and quizzical in the middle of his line-up of seven prize-winners: Peter Jay for *Weekend World*, Humphrey Burton for *Aquarius*, Peter Barkworth for Best Actor; Stanley Baxter for Best Light Entertainment Performance; David Bell for Best Light Entertainment Production with *The Stanley Baxter Moving Picture Show*; Bill McPherson, the show's designer, for Best Design; and Lynda Beighton, its make-up mistress, for Best Make-up. The caption reads 'The LWT Triumph'.

As a result, it seemed to me that the IBA was less than fair to LWT in its 1974 Review of Companies' Performance. It acknowledged the company's traumatic beginnings, noted its subsequent programme successes and

observed that it was "showing signs of emerging as a company of considerable promise". But it went on to observe "In the Authority's judgement
the company's interest in religion and adult education had diminished, the
children's department had been run down, drama was uneven, scheduling
lacked skill, presentation was weak, the choice of films and repeat material
left a lot to be desired, and local programming was inadequate".

I believed that the Authority had not taken full account of the problems
intrinsic to what was now the only weekend franchise in the entire ITV
network, problems far greater than ABC's had been during the previous contract period. Like London Weekend, my old company had been contractually
committed to supply the whole range of television programming within its
brief time on the air – sport, adult education, religion, the arts, children's
programmes, local news and current affairs, as well as drama and light
entertainment. But ABC had then been opposed by just one BBC channel,
and alongside it had been another ITV weekend company only too eager to
throw its best and biggest programmes into the competition for weekend
audiences. Now, however, there were two BBC channels operating in tandem
at the weekend and there was no other ITV company alongside LWT to
share its burden. Added to which, no seven-day company was prepared to
schedule its own popular programmes at the weekend: they preferred to
transmit them during the week when the BBC competition was less intense.

The Authority's criticism stung John Freeman. He wrote to ask for clarific-
ation, particularly of its comments on the company's drama output, listing
such examples as *Budgie* and *Helen: A Woman of Today*. The IBA Chairman
wrote back in the bluntest terms. Alongside these successes, he said, LWT
had also made critical and popular failures such as *Tales of Piccadilly*, *The
Adventures of Don Quick*, *The Frighteners* and *Diamond Crack Diamond*.
Moreover, it did not have a record of producing original plays from new or
well-known dramatists. "Can there be some causal relationship between
the uneven achievement of LWT drama and the proportion of full-time to
freelance staff employed in your drama department?" he asked. "Do you
have anything that can, in the normal sense of the term, be described as a
drama department at all?"

It was clear that the Authority was not prepared to cut the company
any slack, presumably feeling that it had cut quite enough in dealing with
LWT's earlier traumas. Rather than embroil ourselves in a full-scale row
which we could not hope to win, I suggested to John that we simply noted

the Authority's criticisms and undertook to repair our shortcomings. The Government had set up another committee of enquiry into the future of broadcasting, to be chaired by Lord Annan, Provost of University College, London, and the Independent Broadcasting Act had been extended to the end of 1979 to cover the Committee's deliberations meanwhile.

Accordingly, in May 1975 the contracts of all fifteen ITV companies were extended, and in extending LWT's the Authority acknowledged the action we had taken: "We have had discussions with the company on possible advantages and disadvantages of alternative ways of planning and organising drama output in order to maximise the prospects of successful achievement in this most demanding area of production. In relation to religion and adult education, the company has... reorganised the administrative arrangements for these aspects of its programming, and has assured us that its efforts in this field will continue to be given full management support." We had won a little time, but we were under scrutiny, and the fault lines in our programme organisation and output had begun to reveal themselves.

Cyril was not a delegator. He preferred to be called Programme Controller rather than Director of Programmes, and he controlled his programmes in great detail. Each of his creative heads reported directly to him, as did the company's Presentation and Scheduling staff, and he involved himself closely in the work of all of them. His was not so much a single programme department as half-a-dozen separate programme departments, their creative heads titled Deputy Programme Controller (Drama), Deputy Programme Controller (Features) and so on, with Cyril in effect the super creative head of each. As early as October 1972 John Freeman had implored Cyril to delegate more and to take some rest. "I doubt if anybody could carry indefinitely the load of day-to-day detail you are carrying," he had written to Cyril, urging him to divest himself of his self-imposed responsibilities and create more time for planning.

To ease Cyril's work-load he had also urged him to appoint a Head of Light Entertainment, a responsibility which Cyril had taken upon himself when he re-joined the company. It had taken Cyril a year or so to decide that the likeliest candidate for that job was Leslie Grade's son Michael, who had been recruited to his father's talent agency from the world of sports journalism by Bernard Delfont after Leslie's stroke. Bernie, preoccupied with his role at EMI, was prepared to let Michael leave the Grade Organisation. But Leslie had been so pleased when his son followed him into the business that Michael couldn't bring himself to tell his father he wanted to leave it. John Freeman offered to tell Leslie himself; and the former cabinet minister, former High Commissioner, former British Ambassador flew down to the south of France where Leslie was convalescing to ask his blessing. How could Leslie say No?

...via Selsden Park...

I had first-hand experience of the detail with which Cyril involved himself. He used to call me down to his office to run a programme idea past me or ask for my views on a script he had commissioned or play the tape of a Stanley Baxter spectacular and tell me that he was planning to change its running order. "I'm going to switch this sketch with that production number: what do you think?" He had got hold of an advance copy of the new John Le Carré novel, *Tinker, Tailor, Soldier, Spy* and commissioned Le Carré – David Cornwell – to adapt it for television. "I've tried to play about with it myself but I don't think this script works: have a look at it, see what you think," he said.

Cyril was right: it didn't work, and neither did a subsequent script by Julian Bond. The project stalled and Cyril lost the rights. But spotting it in the first place was typical of his nose for what *could* work, and commissioning and then attempting to edit the script himself was typical of his assiduity. *Tinker, Tailor, Soldier, Spy* ultimately became a stunning success for the BBC but it took the Corporation another five years to get round to acquiring it and obtaining Cornwell's agreement to its adaptation by Arthur Hopcroft.

Cyril had a showman's intuition for what would work on television and he was capable of making creative decisions which would not have occurred to me at ABC or Thames. He financed *Akenfield*, Peter Hall's pastoral film about life in a small English village before the 1914–18 war, and scheduled it at the beginning of peak time on Sunday night, not only against fearsome BBC opposition but simultaneously with its release to the cinemas. I would never have risked that, but Cyril achieved not only glowing reviews but an audience of 14 million viewers. He involved himself in the minutiae of programmes which I would not have presumed to do, personally commissioning a title song from French cabaret star Charles Aznavour to give a sense of unity to a group of seven single plays from his drama department called *Seven Faces of Woman*. The song, "She", sung by Aznavour himself under the opening and closing titles, reached No 1 in the pop charts and helped to turn a competent television series into a major success.

But apart from appointing Michael Grade, Cyril had made no attempt either to delegate more, as John Freeman urged him to do, or to organise his department in order to relieve himself of some of his day-to-day responsibilities. To make matters worse, his domestic life was in turmoil. Estranged from his wife Shirley, he was living alone in a little flat at the top of an apartment block in Westminster while his children, whom he adored, lived with their mother in the family home in Surrey. In my own days as a Programme Controller, I used to take Valium to keep me calm during Monday's meetings of the Controllers Group. Cyril was taking Valium every day to calm him down, then drinking black coffee all day to fire him up. One of the idiosyncrasies of LWT I discovered on the day I joined was the provision of a Cona coffee maker in each senior executive's office. Cyril's was constantly being refilled.

He was tired and stressed, and because the department's performance depended so much on him, so were its programmes. By the middle of 1976 the triumphant motoring of 1974 had become listless coasting. The department's long-running successes – *Upstairs, Downstairs*, *On the Buses*, *Please Sir!* and the comedy impressionist show *Who Do You Do?* had either ended or had had the life drained out of them, like the *Doctor* series, now in its fifth incarnation in seven years, from *Doctor in the House* through *Doctor at Large*, *Doctor in Charge*, *Doctor at Sea*, to *Doctor on the Go*. Cyril's attempt to prolong the life of *On the Buses* by following its leading character into retirement abroad in *Don't Drink the Water* had failed after a single series. A similar attempt to perpetuate the success of *Please Sir!* with a sequel, *The Fenn Street Gang*, in which Fenn Street School's unruly pupils were followed into their working life, had itself been over-worked with 47 episodes in two years and had lost its audience by its third series.

Anxious to build on new success when it presented itself, Cyril had instructed *Humphrey Barclay*, the producer of *No, Honestly*, to go into production with a second series immediately following its initial run. But the show's stars John Alderton and Pauline Collins, with other commitments to fulfil, had reluctantly withdrawn from it, and a hastily assembled successor *Yes, Honestly*, with a completely new cast, failed. Writers Ronnie Wolfe and Ronnie Chesney had created a prodigious hit for the BBC in *The Rag Trade* and another for LWT in On The Buses. With Michael Grade in charge of Light Entertainment, they created not only the ill-fated *Don't Drink the Water* but also *Romany Jones*, starring the cockney comic actor Arthur Mullard, which ran for four series, though in the words of Mark Lewisohn's *Guide to TV Comedy*, "how it lasted for four series beggars belief". They followed this with a sequel called *Yus, My Dear*, again starring Arthur Mullard, which has the distinction of being No 2 in the Top Twenty list of Worst British Sitcoms in Lewisohn's *Guide*.

Unfortunately, Lewisohn's list contains another six LWT situation comedies, the total of seven being more than from the BBC or any other ITV company. By the autumn of 1976 LWT had produced only two Top Twenty shows in the previous six months while no fewer than eight of the BBC's fifteen Top Twenty shows during that period had been broadcast at the weekend. "Perhaps the answer," commented the London listings magazine *Time Out*, "is for LWT to buy Bryan Cowgill" – the aggressively effective Controller of BBC 1 – "and put him in Cyril Bennett's shoes p.d.q."

Furthermore, the IBA was very much on our case. In May 1976, the Authority's Head of Programme Services, David Glencross, wrote dismissively to Cyril about LWT's summer schedule: "I can't say that I am happy about your Saturday evening schedule in Weeks 22-26 and I can't believe that you regard it as a very distinguished shop window for ITV in London. If we give it reluctant approval I hope that you will not assume that such a pattern would be welcome in future quarters."

That same month, two years after I joined LWT, John Freeman felt that the company and I had become sufficiently accustomed to each other for him to stand down as planned from his role of Chief Executive and hand over to me as Managing Director. At the drinks reception to mark the handover, Cyril once again proposed the Toast: "We welcomed you as Deputy; now we wish you every success as Sheriff."

Next day, when the newspapers printed the story, I received a lunch invitation from Brian Young, who had succeeded Robert Fraser as the IBA's Director General, to congratulate me on my appointment and talk about the company's future direction under its new management. It turned out to be the opportunity for him to admonish me on the company's programming, though in the mildest and most courteous fashion.

"Don't you think you should be spending more time on less financially rewarding programmes?"

"What do you have in mind?"

"Well, for example, in religion and local programmes you certainly do the hours, but we are not absolutely certain that they receive as much of your programme department's attention as they might. Perhaps you ought to take a look at the problem."

When I arrived back at Kent House I discovered that Cyril had been lunched at the same time on the same day in another of the IBA's Brompton Road dining rooms by the Deputy Director General, Bernard Sendall. Bernard – "moaning on about our local programmes" said Cyril – had been nothing like so courteous. We got the message.

Watching the company over the previous two years it had become increasingly clear to me that Cyril's programme department needed some of the camaraderie and cross-fertilisation that had worked so well for ABC TV and Thames. It needed a Programme Coordination Committee of its own. LWT's programme-makers barely knew one another. They spoke to each other in the lifts and greeted each other going in or out of Cyril's office, but there was no departmental meeting, no forum in which to talk about the department's programmes, no wandering in and out of each other's offices exchanging ideas or discussing mutual problems.

In his autobiography John Birt comments that he and Michael Grade had offices on the same floor but had never moved beyond exchanging pleasantries in the corridor. We needed a departmental get-together, a conference away from Kent House in which programme makers from every section of the department could get to know each other, exchange ideas, share problems, develop a sense of solidarity. Some kind of regular programme coordination could be discussed there. It would at the very least give us an opportunity to address the IBA's criticisms and consider ways of meeting them. Cyril welcomed the idea and suggested Selsden Park Hotel in South Croydon as the venue. We settled on three days in November as the date, Thursday to Saturday, and agreed that I should take the chair. Cyril and his lieutenants set about the planning and organisation. A month or so before the event he told me that John Birt had offered to give a paper at the conference, which he thought could be its opening speech; as conference chairman would I sum up at its end?

Two dozen of us assembled at Selsdon Park that bright and crisp Thursday in November: Cyril and I, the creative heads, the key producers of drama, light entertainment, current affairs, sport, religion, adult education and children's programmes – and a sound engineer to record the proceedings. From the very first session the conference fulfilled all my hopes for it. John Birt's keynote speech pulled no punches: I had clearly not been alone in observing the deceleration of LWT's creative drive during the past two years. We were making fewer prestigious programmes, he said, and fewer people were watching them. He recognised the BBC's aggressive weekend scheduling and the fact that the other ITV companies were hoarding their successful programmes for the weekdays but felt that LWT itself had lost the flavour of the moment it had possessed when he joined it in 1972. "Ideas become sterile, individuals become jaded, programmes become predictable". LWT needed to be reinvigorated, and a programme meeting should be instituted at which the creative heads could discuss their programmes and future programme strategy in a constructive and amicable atmosphere.

John was reading from my script, though I disagreed with his explanation of the BBC's success. He attributed this to the intelligence of its programmes – "not intellectuality, not what intelligent producers think the public want" but "intelligent producers making things which they themselves find interesting". The audience's growing taste for intelligent programmes, he believed, had stepped up to meet what the BBC was offering. I would say why I disagreed with it in my summing up at the end of the conference; but I applauded his forensic analysis of the department's problems, which gave Cyril and me an ideal opportunity to open up the debate on what had gone wrong and invite the conference to discuss ways in which it might be put right.

The resulting self-criticism was frank indeed. Cyril acknowledged that he had made mistakes in keeping series alive far beyond their creative life. He admitted that he had taken some soft options in the previous year and was looking forward to rectifying this in the years to come. Michael Grade castigated himself for his failure to develop new programmes and experiment with new ideas, admitting that his department had produced only three pilot programmes in the previous two and a half years and accepting the contumely heaped on such situation comedies as *Yus, My Dear*. As he endearingly says in his own autobiography, "There was nothing much I could do in my response other than plead guilty but insane." Tony Wharmby for drama and Geoffrey Hughes for children's, religious and adult education programmes each took the floor to outline the reasons for their respective departments' lack of success in the previous year.

Having got all that off its chest, the conference set to work over the next two days analysing the difficulties of the weekend franchise and discussing ways in which the different departments could work together to combat them. When Cyril and I reported the IBA's criticism of our religious and local programming and announced that we were putting extra money into the budget to help respond to it, we were greeted by a flood of ideas for new series from every department and an enthusiastic willingness to cooperate in realising them. When we turned our attention to departmental reorganisation the discussion was equally enthusiastic. We agreed to establish two new bodies, a Creative Committee in which programme-makers across the department would meet fortnightly to discuss their programmes, exchange ideas and plan the department's future activities, and a Facilities Standing Committee in which programme makers and the company's supply departments – engineering, design, wardrobe and make-up and so forth – could regularly discuss technical problems and developments.

On the opening day of the conference, when Humphrey Barclay and I happened to walk into the conference room together, Humphrey had looked around and said "Do you know, I've never had lunch with anybody in this room". By the end of the conference he'd had lunch, breakfast, dinner, two days of frank and vigorous debate and a large number of lively lunchtime and late-night sessions at the bar with everybody in that room, and it had clearly had a salutary effect, on Humphrey and on everybody else. In their separate accounts, Michael Grade reported "a new camaraderie among the senior staff" and John Birt "a tangible release of ideas, energy and good cheer".

There was every reason to be optimistic about the future and I wanted to send the conference members away in good heart. In my summing-up I contended that the BBC had become not more adventurous and intelligent in its programming, as John had suggested, but more cynical, turning BBC 1 into a popular entertainment channel at the weekend and relegating its more adventurous and intelligent programmes to BBC 2. As for LWT, I maintained that we were suffering not from old age but from relief. Having climbed out of the abyss of our early years, having reached the top with ratings, prestige, awards both national and international, we had paused to breathe in pure relief, to consolidate; and that had been our mistake. The time to build for the future, I argued, is when you're at the top; if you don't, you will find yourself at the bottom with nothing to get you up again, and the conference had shown us the way to get ourselves back to the top.

John Birt's autobiography says that LWT's programme-makers left Selsdon Park on the Saturday full of hope for the future; Michael Grade's says that my closing speech was clear-eyed about LWT's failures but hopeful enough about its future prospects to send even Cyril away in a reasonably positive frame of mind. My own belief was that the spirit of cameraderie and cooperation aroused by the conference, the cross-fertilisation it had engendered, and the creative and coordinating committees it had given birth to, would galvanise LWT's programme department into excellence again.

Michael's account also observed that Cyril had seemed gloomier by the day during the conference, and John's that Cyril had seemed deflated. When Cyril and I walked to the hotel car park together he seemed to me to be in perfectly good spirits. He thought the conference had gone well and was proud of the constructive way in which his Boys had approached every session. "There's a lot of good stuff to think about," he said. "The tape will be interesting." We got to my Citroen and Cyril's Jaguar, with the estimable Vic Calder, his driver, at the ready, and Cyril asked if I knew the way back. I didn't. "Follow us", he said; "There's a fork where we go right and you go left, straight back to Chiswick. I'll show you where."

I followed them and pulled up alongside Cyril when we reached the junction. He wound down his window, pointed to the direction in which I should go, said "*Gay Ga Zint*" – the abbreviated version of the Yiddish phrase for "go in good health" – and waved goodbye. Perhaps the mood John and Michael attributed to him in their respective autobiographies was coloured by their knowledge of what happened subsequently. That night Cyril fell to his death from the window of his sixth floor flat in Westminster.

...and Into the Forest

A dismal and disheartening forest, alas.

John Bromley phoned me with the appalling news of Cyril's death on Sunday morning. He had no information about how or why it had happened; nor had the early radio news bulletins. I called as many programme heads and senior members of staff as I could reach and we met together at Kent House in a mood of profound and bewildered grief. Cyril had been held in great affection by all of us. How had this terrible thing happened? I warned them that Monday's newspapers would ask the same question and that their speculation would be remorseless. The press knew our programme conference had ended earlier that Saturday, they had been excoriating us for our falling ratings and declining revenue, and *Time Out* had not been alone in calling for Cyril to be replaced. The line they would take was inevitable. And so it proved. The front page of the London *Evening Standard* next day featured a photograph of the mansion block from which Cyril had fallen, with the headline 'In TV you are only as good as your last ratings'. The *Daily Mail* outdid itself with a dotted line to show Cyril's trajectory from the window of his sixth-floor flat to the concrete courtyard on which he had died. In all the papers, if suicide wasn't stated it was implied.

It was essential to pull the company together, to help it survive the trauma of Cyril's death and the insinuations surrounding it. John Freeman and I agreed that I should take over Cyril's responsibilities as Programme Controller until a new appointment could be made, and he announced this decision to the staff on Monday in a statement that was both affecting and steadying. At Cyril's funeral he was a rock, a father figure for the distraught members of the company. When John Birt broke down in tears as the first handful of earth was thrown on to the coffin, John put his arm round him and hugged him into composure. At the inquest, I tried to do what I could to counter the sinister inferences being drawn from Cyril's death. Cyril's psychiatrist stated that there was a dark and melancholy side to Cyril's personality and he had frequently talked of suicide. When the Coroner asked for my comments I said that Cyril was Jewish, as I was, and a dark and melancholy side was inherent in all of us; Cyril was also in show business, and it wasn't at all rare for people in show business to talk of suicide – until their next success.

Cyril's driver, Vic Calder, confirmed that Cyril had planned to go out to dinner that evening with a lady friend, and had asked him to fill up his car and park it in the courtyard of the flats. A statement was read out from the friend in which she said that, unable to get a reply from her telephone calls and fearing that Cyril might have come to some harm, she had asked a mutual friend to call the police. The police had broken open Cyril's door and found the flat empty and the window open. They stated that the sill of the window was unusually low and that the photo frames and ornaments on it had not been disturbed. Shirley Bennett confirmed that her husband had phoned on Saturday to make arrangements to take their three children to the cinema the following afternoon.

Cyril's fully clothed body had been found by a cleaner at the flats at 7.15 am the following morning in the basement of the courtyard. In his wallet were four tickets for the Sunday afternoon performance of *101 Dalmatians*. Would he have deliberately foregone sharing such an opportunity to spend time with the children he loved? The Coroner's conclusion was that on Saturday night Cyril had leaned out over the sill to see where his car was, lost his balance and fallen. The verdict was accidental death.

Coroner's verdict or no, Cyril's death and the manner of it were deeply distressing for the programme department's heads. They were all Cyril's Boys, all appointed or promoted by him; they had reported only to Cyril and they had all loved his congeniality and compassion; he had been their leader and their inspiration. The loss was particularly traumatic for the two youngest programme heads, John Birt and Michael Grade. John, in tears at the funeral, was unused to death of any sort, let alone the death of someone of whom he was exceptionally fond. Michael, plucked from the talent agency business by Cyril, was in tears in his office, where Ron Miller found him contemplating resignation because he felt there was no point in carrying on without Cyril's leadership. They and their colleagues were bereft, trying to make sense of their loss, trying to focus on something or someone to blame for it. When I called them to my office a few days after the funeral to discuss how we should proceed with the department's programme-making, I was dismayed to discover that the focus had become fixed on me.

What was intended to be a straightforward discussion of programme plans and procedures became an increasingly heated four-hour confrontation. With John Birt as their principal spokesman, the programme heads wanted to know how the company would treat Cyril's dependants. They argued for Cyril's office to be demolished, unable to contemplate it being used by anyone else. They wanted to be consulted about his successor. Above all, they wanted to discuss why Cyril had died. All the unhappiness, all the pent-up feelings of loss and isolation, finally burst their dam – and cascaded over me. I was The Enemy again. I had usurped the job Cyril wanted, I was planning to replace him with another outsider, I had been aggressive and insensitive towards him, I had domineered the Selsdon conference and appropriated its concluding speech: no wonder he had seemed gloomy and deflated throughout it.

I heard them out calmly and sympathetically, and then put the record straight. I had known Cyril longer and better than anyone in the room; we had been good friends for eighteen years. I reminded them that I hadn't applied to be LWT's Managing Director: John Freeman had approached me; if he had wanted Cyril for the job he would have approached Cyril. There had never been the slightest question of my replacing Cyril, whether or not with an outsider: he and I had just agreed a new three-year contract which would have been ready for him to sign after Selsdon.

I told them that my only concern had been to give him as much construc-tive support as possible in reinvigorating LWT's programme output. Hence the conference itself, which I had proposed and for which he had asked me to make the concluding speech. If chairing Selsdon could be considered domineering it, I had to plead guilty, but if Cyril had been gloomy and deflated during the conference, it was hardly surprising. Quite apart from the criticism he was receiving from the IBA, the press and the advertisers, his private life was in ruins, and he was separated from the children he adored. He had been carrying a very heavy burden.

Our marathon session finally cleared the air. In his autobiography, John Birt had the grace to say that "During that meeting – and in subsequent days – I gradually came to the realisation that my suspicions of Brian had been unfair, that my behaviour had been immature". In David Docherty's history of the company, Michael Grade is quoted as saying "Afterwards we realised that Brian had held LWT together, even though it was a terrible time for him." Docherty declares that the meeting "was the turning point in Tesler's relationship with the company". Cyril's Boys had been brought round, though it would be some time before they could be considered *my* Boys.

On then, at last, to the matters for which the meeting had been called in the first place. I told the group that I would continue to act as the Programme Department's controller until I could decide on a permanent successor, and I intended to control it through a Creative Committee of programme heads in which we would plan our shows, discuss our programme schedules, share our ideas and sort out our problems together. And I told them that I hoped our meetings would help to cultivate the seeds of camaraderie and cross-fertilisation which had been planted at Selsdon. What I didn't tell them was that I had no intention of importing Bryan Cowgill or any other outsider to take over the department: I was only too aware of their reaction to the last outsider to join the company. I wanted Cyril's successor to come from the department itself and I would use my time as chairman of the Creative Committee to assess the qualities, skills and potential of each of the programme heads until I could identify which it should be.

Audrey saw very little of me during the next three months. My days were spent at meetings. Meetings of the Creative Committee, meetings with the heads of the other divisions of the company, Board meetings, meetings with the IBA, meetings with the other ITV principals and – in a return to the weekly bedlam of Monday mornings – meetings of the Programme Controllers Group. Cyril's driver, Vic, ferried me about and was allocated to me permanently. In the evenings I would be back in my office, reading my mail, drafting replies and memos for my secretary to type up next day, and signing those that had been typed up the day before, in the company of a plate of sandwiches from the canteen, a bottle of wine and the Cona coffee-maker. It was an exacting regime. Though John Freeman agreed with my approach, he was soon writing the sort of notes of advice to me that he had written to Cyril in the past, urging me to choose Cyril's successor and make a recommendation to the Board before the weight of my combined responsibilities began to damage the company's health as well as my own.

My fellow members of the Creative Committee were Cyril's erstwhile Deputy Programme Controllers, in charge respectively of Current Affairs, John Birt; Sport, John Bromley; Light Entertainment, Michael Grade; and Drama, Tony Wharmby. We worked hard and constructively together. Remarkably, perhaps only John Bromley had the street savvy to realise that I was auditioning them. It was by no means an easy procedure. Six weeks into it, in a handwritten note, John Freeman said "My own gut feeling – but it's no more – would put them in the order (i) JB, (ii) TW, (iii) MG". The JB at the top of John's gut-feeling list was John Bromley, and I did indeed consider him seriously: he was the most experienced of the group, he had run a large and efficient department at ABC and LWT for a decade with great panache, and his cheerful commonsense certainly enlivened our committee's deliberations and would have won points with both ITV colleagues and IBA officials. But his experience and expertise appeared exclusively to lie in sport, and I was looking for wider skills.

I considered the other JB seriously too. John Birt's forensic analysis of Programme Department's problems at Selsdon had been impressive and I warmed to his recognition of its need for the sort of coordination committee in which we now found ourselves. But in spite of the fact that he had begun his television career with a comedy show at Granada, *Nice Time*, his skills since then had been invested exclusively in current affairs and continued to be so. He and the presenter of his *Weekend World* programme, Peter Jay, had published their trenchant views of the traditional television approach to news and current affairs in a series of articles in *The Times* which had created a furore among their fellow professionals. They believed that the traditional approach was guilty of 'a bias against understanding', concerning itself more with pictures than explication.

In time, the Jay-Birt philosophy of television journalism would transform the management of news and current affairs in British television to a degree which neither John nor Peter could have anticipated, but for the moment I thought John's energies should be directed towards transforming the output of LWT's Features Department and I proposed that Features be merged with Current Affairs in a single department under his control in order for him to achieve it. We agreed that Barry Cox, producer of *The London Programme*, would take on the responsibility for Current Affairs and Nick Elliott, producer of *Weekend World*, that of Features. I would recognise the long service of the current Head of Features, Geoffrey Hughes, by appointing him Head of

ITV's new teletext system, Oracle, the responsibility for which I had just been handed by the network.

Tony Wharmby was an outstanding drama producer and director but he had only recently succeeded Rex Firkin as Cyril's Deputy Programme Controller (Drama) and he needed to master that assignment before he could be considered for a greater one. That left Michael Grade, and Michael surprised me. I had assumed from his talent agency background that he was essentially a light entertainment man although, alas, an indifferent Head of Light Entertainment. But that could be attributed to his lack of experience and guidance and he had certainly recognised his deficiencies at Selsdon Park. In our Creative Group sessions, however, I discovered that he was interested and knowledgeable in every aspect of television, not just Light Entertainment. I knew he had been a sports journalist – he had succeeded John Bromley as the *Daily Mirror*'s sports columnist when John was recruited by ABC to run *World of Sport* – but throughout our meetings he put forward interesting and informed ideas on drama, politics, current affairs, the arts and every other area of programming. Michael's creative interests had ranged more widely across the television spectrum than anyone else's.

Michael had never produced a programme, but I was not looking for a producer. The staff liked him; he was a good people manager and, thanks to his training at the Grade Organisation, an able negotiator. And in our Creative Committee discussions he was intrigued by the dark arts of scheduling, for which he seemed to have an instinctive feel. After all, I thought, what was so wrong about his being essentially a light entertainment man? Hadn't I been just that at the beginning of my own executive career? I decided to take a gamble on this bright and energetic 33-year old. Years later I would be asked, at celebrations of his subsequently inexorable rise to prominence, to speak on what had made me decide on Michael for the job. I used to say it was because I needed to remove him from the role of LWT's Head of Light Entertainment in which, in series like *Romany Jones* and *Yus, My Dear*, he seemed dedicated to trying to make an international comedy star of Arthur Mullard. I don't think Michael was ever completely certain that I was joking.

In February 1977 we announced that he was to be LWT's Director of Programmes. There followed for young Grade a period of intensive tutorials. When I was in the middle of my research for this memoir I emailed Michael to ask whether he remembered anything of them, apart from accompanying me to the Monday morning meetings of the Controllers Group. "Yes indeed," he replied. "I remember sitting with you in your office rehearsing various scenarios, getting on top of the Category A and Category B programming system, the network arrangements, deficits and surpluses and war-gaming: intense but necessary before I could fly solo on Monday mornings. I guess we must have had up to half a dozen sessions, with me questioning you about personalities, gambits, how does this work? how does that work? etc. We also talked scheduling, exchanging ideas: would this work on Friday night? would that work on Sundays? etc, etc. I was downloading as much as I could from your experience and knowledge. An intense period of cramming!"

Intense it was, but Michael was a quick learner. He saw the sense of establishing a clear line of management in which his programme heads would be Controllers of their respective divisions rather than his Deputies and enthusiastically adopted our Creative Committee as the model for sharing the Department's programme plans, problems and ideas. I approved his suggestion that the company's Forward Planning Committee should be the forum agreed at Selsdon Park for matching in-house technical facilities and resources with programme requirements and was more than happy with his proposal that David Bell, the inventive producer of LWT's Stanley Baxter Specials, should take over Light Entertainment as its Controller.

We agreed to have regular Friday morning sessions in which Michael and I could discuss programme and organisational matters and he could keep me up to date with what was happening on the network. My method of management from ABC onwards had always been to try to put the right person in the right job and then let him get on with it. I thought Michael was the right person for this particular job, and I told him that when he was ready to fly solo I would always be available for guidance and advice; I might suggest but I would not impose, and I would not be looking over his shoulder: as Cyril Bennett might have said, I would not be *kibitzing*. And at the beginning of April Michael formally took up his appointment. In Cyril's old office. Refurbished, not demolished.

Goodbye to All That

On 21 June 1977 LWT became a public company, LWT (Holdings) plc, with a flotation which exceeded expectations at £14 million: analysts had anticipated an opening share price of 80 pence but the shares traded at 90 pence on the first day of dealings and by August their price was 103 pence. Aware of the unpredictability of advertising revenue – 1977 was a particularly good year but booms and busts were both impossible to foresee – John Freeman persuaded the Board to invest some of this new-found cash in diversification rather than keep it in the Bank. Some of it went into purchasing other companies: the publishers Hutchinson in 1978 and the travel company Page and Moy in 1979. Some of it, at exactly the right time, went into the company's programmes.

To the delight of everybody who had attended the conference and the surprise of everybody who hadn't, the creative energy released at Selsdon Park now thoroughly informed a reinvigorated and re-financed Programme Department. Three decades later, *Independent Television in Britain* observed that "At Selsdon, LWT started to reinvent itself. Under Brian Tesler's Managing Directorship LWT was to become the success for which its founders (almost all of whom had by that time left the company) had so earnestly striven". That creative energy was always there; it only needed to be released. And now it was, just in time: the new franchise round was only three years away. John Freeman and I were well aware that if the round had taken place in 1976, which had been the original statutory intention, LWT might have lost its franchise or been merged with another company. A look at the newspaper archives of the day certainly suggests that the odds on LWT's survival would not have been short. Michael Grade and his programme heads had a great deal of ground to make up, and quickly.

Tony Wharmby's Drama Department set to it with a highly successful run of series and mini-series, ranging from the Edwardian glamour of *Lillie*, the story of Edward VII's most famous mistress Lillie Langtry, to *Enemy at the Door*, a series about the German occupation of the Channel Islands during the last war. *The Gentle Touch* was the first British TV drama series to feature a female police detective. Other successes ranged from the hardboiled crime-solving action of *The Professionals* to the charm of Richmal Crompton's *Just William* stories in which the young Bonnie Langford made an unforgettable impression as Violet Elizabeth Bott. Stella Richman came back to LWT to produce this delightful series; Francesca Annis won a BAFTA Best Actress Award for her performance as Lillie Langtry; and both *The Gentle Touch*, starring Jill Gascoine, and *The Professionals*, starring Martin Shaw, Lewis Collins and Gordon Jackson, became long-running Top Twenty Successes. One of Cyril's last commissions, a dramatisation of Andrea Newman's study of jealousy and obsessive love in her novel *A Bouquet of Barbed Wire*, had been such a sensation early in 1976 that Andrea Newman was commissioned to write a sequel, which we broadcast the following year before it was published as a novel.

The single play was not neglected. Michael commissioned groups of six from both Alan Bennett and Dennis Potter, the most highly regarded TV drama writers of the day. Stephen Frears produced the Bennett plays and directed most of them, including the critically acclaimed productions of *One Fine Day*, *Afternoon Off*, *Doris and Doreen* and *Me! I'm Afraid of Virginia Woolf*, in which he cast Thora Hird, Pete Postlethwaite, Patricia Routledge, Julie Walters and other fine performers who would become Alan Bennett regulars in the decades to come. Frears also brought in the celebrated film director Lindsay Anderson to make his ITV debut as a television director with *The Old Crowd*. That, though, became a testing and expensive experience for the company and its production staff.

Alan Bennett later recalled in the London Review of Books the final production day in the studio of *The Old Crowd*, a day fraught with problems. "Michael Grade was unwavering in his support and when Lindsay fell behind in the shooting schedule Grade sanctioned extension after extension; when the studio finally broke it was half past three in the morning." Michael was warmly thanked by Anderson at the end of his contract "for the opportunity of working – and it doesn't happen very often – in such a friendly, supportive and stimulating atmosphere as I've found at LWT... An extraordinary contrast to the atmosphere I've generally felt in British film studios."

Unfortunately it was also an extraordinary contrast to the atmosphere felt on all sides at LWT with the Dennis Potter plays. These had started so well. Disillusioned by their recent experiences at the BBC, where Director of Programmes Alasdair Milne had banned Kenith Trodd's production of Potter's *Brimstone and Treacle*, Potter and Trodd agreed to return to LWT. Their experiences there during the company's stormy beginnings had been no less disillusioning but, hey, this was a decade later and LWT was under very different management. Potter and Trodd had set up their own production company, Pennies from Heaven Ltd – PFH – and the deal was that the plays would be made on film and PFH would appoint its own producers and directors but use LWT's crews and operate within LWT's accountancy and production procedures. Potter would deliver three scripts initially and PFH reserved the right to produce plays by other writers among the remaining three.

The first of the Potters, *Rain on the Roof*, starring Cheryl Campbell and directed by Alan Bridges, came in on budget and without too many problems. With exquisite timing, the second, Blade on the Feather, starred Tom Conti, Denholm Elliott and Donald Pleasence in a study of spies among the British elite just as Anthony Blunt was being unmasked as the fourth man in the Philby, Burgess and Maclean spy ring. Alas, the production itself was not so blessed. LWT's accountancy and production procedures were not those of the BBC.

Variations from planning on the hoof cost money. So switching location at the last minute from Sussex to the Isle of Wight cost money; adding a flashback scene which entailed two nights' shooting in Cheshire cost money, so did a new sequence involving a train and an unanticipated day's shooting in a zoo in Dudley. Its director Richard Loncraine was at this stage of his career more experienced in directing documentaries and commercials than drama, and the production's expenditure veered out of control. The relationship between PFH and the production staff also soured, as the Production Manager's report reveals. "The film production *Blade on the Feather* is affecting all departments, and constant variation from the original planning has a disturbing affect on management and staff. The constant threats of the Producer and Director to walk out of the programme unless they have their own way on trivial issues places all managers in an untenable and debilitating dilemma." Nevertheless, the film was finally completed, wildly over budget but with no blood spilled and, miraculously, with no technicians called out on strike.

The third film, *Cream in My Coffee*, starring Peggy Ashcroft, Lionel Jeffries and Martin Shaw, also overspent; but it was the proposed cost of the next project that finally caused the collapse of the LWT-PFH relationship. *The Commune*, a play by Jim Allen which Kenith Trodd called "a small epic", had a prospective budget of £780,000, equivalent today to £3,250,000. It was a budget too far for Michael, and the LWT-PFH deal was dissolved. However, we had three fine Dennis Potter plays to transmit, Denholm Elliott won a BAFTA Best Actor award for his role in *Blade on the Feather*, Peggy Ashcroft a BAFTA Best Actress Award for *Cream in My Coffee*, and *Cream in My Coffee* itself went on to win a Prix Italia Award for Drama.

Another drama deal, evolving simultaneously with the PFH saga, proved less abrasive and considerably more productive. Agatha Christie, the world's best-selling novelist, author among other work of 66 detective novels and 15 volumes of detective stories, disliked and distrusted television as a medium – not least, perhaps, because in an early BBC TV version of her thriller *And Then There Were None* one of the corpses in the final scene got up and walked off the set in full view of the cameras. By the sixties she was refusing to grant permission for the television adaptation of any of her works but, when she died in 1976, Michael Grade saw the possibility that her Estate might be more amenable. After 18 months of negotiation he received permission for LWT to adapt two of the Christie novels, *Why Didn't They Ask Evans?* and *The Seven Dials Mystery* for television.

These adaptations were given Special Event treatment: all-star casts and generous production values and shooting schedules, and in an innovative move each was transmitted as a single play rather than a mini-series, occupying an entire evening's peak-time viewing: two-and-a-half hours for *The Seven Dials Mystery* and no fewer than three hours for *Why Didn't They Ask Evans?* Their success persuaded the Estate that television could be an effective medium for the Christie catalogue and LWT a congenial production house. Over the years that followed LWT's Drama department would produce many series and plays adapted from Agatha Christie novels and short stories, including the entire Hercule Poirot canon with David Suchet as the definitive Poirot. Of her major creations, only the Miss Marple stories got away from us, scooped up by the BBC for Joan Hickson to play the lead character; but in due course these too would come back to ITV, with Geraldine McEwan and later Julia McKenzie in the title role.

The Entertainment cupboard was by no means bare for its new Controller. David Bell's own Stanley Baxter shows continued, and Michael Grade had set in train before the Selsdon Park conference two new series which would find themselves among LWT's biggest successes. In *Two's Company*, written by Bill MacIlwraith, Elaine Stritch played an American crime-writer living in London and Donald Sinden the very British butler hired to look after her Chelsea home. New York devil-may-care versus British stiff-upper-lip: the chemistry was irresistible. So too was the subject matter of *It'll be Alright on the Night*, the collected fluffs and bloopers of feature films and television programmes from around the world, a regular series which is still a feature of ITV's schedules after 39 years, 29 of them with its original presenter Denis Norden in charge. To these were now added new artistes, new situation comedies and new formats by David Bell, together with his Head of Comedy, Humphrey Barclay, and two new recruits from the BBC, Alan Boyd and Richard Drewett, not forgetting the enthusiastic participation of LWT's Director of Programmes, whose Entertainment background found it difficult to *stay* in the background.

After supporting the mercurial Freddie Starr in his *Madhouse* series, Russ Abbot took the show over and *Russ Abbot's Madhouse* became another long-running success for the department. *An Audience with Jasper Carrott* was the first television series to feature the wry whimsicality of Jasper Carrott, who was spotted by Michael Grade in a concert at Stratford-upon-Avon. *The Cannon and Ball Show* was the first television series for the broad northern comedy of ex-Oldham factory workers Tommy Cannon and Bobby Ball. They capped a run of eleven successive TV series for LWT with a season at the London Palladium which broke all previous box office records. Here's a pub quiz question with which to win wagers: whose box office takings were the largest in the history of the London Palladium up to and including 1988: Danny Kaye, Judy Garland or Cannon and Ball? Go figure.

And Hello to All This

Two years after the Jasper Carrott series, David Bell borrowed its title for the first of a series of confrontations between star performers and the TV studio audience in *An Audience with Dame Edna Everage*, Barry Humphries's Aussie housewife creation. Its success led not only to the long-running series of '*An Audience with...*' which continues to this day on ITV, but also to further successful Edna Everage appearances, including two more Audiences With and an unpredictable sort of anti-chat show called *The Edna Everage Experience*, in which game but bemused celebrities from Sean Connery to Mary Whitehouse, Charlton Heston to Germaine Greer, Edward Heath to Gina Lollobrigida were exposed to the Dame's dauntingly original interview techniques. And Alan Boyd put the final touches to a format brought to LWT by Jeremy Fox, son of the redoubtable Paul, which combined the 'real people' elements of quiz and game shows with the practical jokes of *Candid Camera* to produce ITV's biggest Saturday night success for many years, *Game for a Laugh*. For three of its four presenters, Matthew Kelly, Sarah Kennedy and Henry Kelly, it would be the launch pad for very different careers; for the fourth, Jeremy Beadle, its hidden-cameras and practical jokes would be the engine of a remarkably long-running succession of hit television shows for ITV from *Beadle's About* to *You've Been Framed*.

The Department also produced a succession of fine situation comedies like *Bless Me Father*, written by Peter de Rosa, with Arthur Lowe as a genially mischievous Roman Catholic priest, following up his success in *Dad's Army* with what Mark Lewisohn's definitive *Guide to TV Comedy* calls "one of the hidden gems in Britain's sitcom archives". *A Fine Romance*, written by Bob

Larbey and starring Judi Dench and her real-life husband Michael Williams, won nine BAFTA nominations for itself and two BAFTA Awards for Ms Dench. *Maggie and Her*, written by Leonard Webb, featured Julia McKenzie as a retired schoolteacher and the magnificent Irene Handl as her interfering neighbour. Maureen Lipman starred in *Agony*, a series about the life and travails of an agony-column editor, written by prominent agony aunt Anna Raeburn together with Len Richmond. The Department also came up with two socially groundbreaking series: *The Fosters*, British television's first all-black sitcom, developed by Jon Watkins from the American show *Good Times*, with comedian Lenny Henry in his first acting role; and *Mixed Blessings*, written by Sid Green, British television's first series about a mixed-race young couple. They were not the only social groundbreakers: *Agony* featured British television's first gay couple among its principal characters.

The Department had its disappointments too. Unfortunately, its biggest situation comedy success turned out to be one of them. Leo Rosten's book *The Education of Hyman Kaplan* is set in a language school in the depression years of America, in which immigrants eager to become U.S. citizens learn the language and the American way of life in a very funny collection of stories featuring the eponymous Mr Kaplan.

It had long been a favourite of mine and I suggested to Michael that an adaptation set in a London language school, with its immigrant students attempting to come to grips with England and the English language, might make a successful television series. And so it did. *Mind Your Language*, written by Vince Powell, regularly enjoyed audiences of over 18 million, the biggest for any LWT sit-com. Unfortunately, its premise became less than credible as it developed: the characters began to talk perfect colloquial English until the lessons started and their mispronunciations became no longer part of the gag but the *only* gag. The show was widely criticised by the press and savaged at the Edinburgh Television Festival for purveying racism. Michael pulled it after three series to the general acclaim of the media and other industry executives.

Far worse, because far less deserved, was the fate of Michael's big idea, *Bruce's Big Night*. Bruce Forsyth was the most popular light entertainment artiste in Britain in the seventies, the star of BBC's hugely successful Saturday night show *The Generation Game*. Michael's big idea was to tempt Bruce to return to ITV by offering him the opportunity to be more than a game show host, to allow him to deploy all the talents he had displayed as compere, comedian, comic actor, song-and-dance man and all-round entertainer in ATV's *New Look* and *Sunday Night at the London Palladium* and his big Specials for ABC and Thames; but deploying them in one all-encompassing show filling two whole hours of Saturday night peak time.

It was a bold venture, incorporating game shows, comedy sketches with artistes then new to television like Cannon and Ball, off-beat variety acts like Pam Ayres with her witty little poems and Rod Hull with his aggressive puppet Emu. Also pocket editions of past comedy successes like *The Worker*, starring Charlie Drake, and the continuing saga of *The Glums* from Muir & Norden's *Take It From Here*, starring Jimmy Edwards; together with interviews and song and dance routines shared with major American stars like Sammy Davis Jr and Bette Midler. And it worked – at first. It was top of the London Top Ten on its opening night in October 1978 and sixth in the Network's. I sent down a bottle of champagne to Michael's office to celebrate his success with the first night's ratings.

Alas, the fizz evaporated only too rapidly. The viewers weren't prepared to dedicate two hours of their attention non-stop to a show which darted restlessly from feature to feature. They liked to know where they were with their programmes, and they were used to finding them on the hour or the half-hour; they also liked a variety of programmes for their Saturday night viewing, not a variety of variety. Within weeks *Bruce's Big Night* had lost a third of its audience to the BBC mix of *Doctor Who*, *The Generation Game*, a movie, *Parkinson* and *Match of the Day*, and the tabloid press, scenting blood, began to hound the show and its star. They used one of Forsyth's own catch phrases "Hasn't he done well!" to beat him with. "Hasn't he done badly!" was the cry. The Goliath of *Bruce's Big Night* had been defeated by the David of *The Generation Game*, making a major star out of its new presenter, the lesser known Larry Grayson. At the same time, Forsyth's private life and his marriage to Anthea Redfern, who appeared with him on the show, were raked over mercilessly. The marriage itself, the press declared, was under strain as a result of the show's failure.

If the show was indeed a failure it was so only in comparison with its instant early success. Shortened and moved out of prime time to an earlier slot its audience grew back up to 14 million, but it was too late, and far too expensive for its new slot. The IBA's Annual Report that year noted that *Bruce's Big Night* was a new and ambitious programme which, after a bad start, was picking up audiences until it was sabotaged by a "cynical and bitter" press campaign. Though that wasn't totally the reason, Michael pulled *Bruce's Big Night* after three months. The show that replaced it, the result of a renegotiation of Forsyth's contract, was another game show. Back to square one for Bruce, but *Play Your Cards Right* would run for 255 editions, restoring Bruce's career, reviving LWT's ratings and outlasting *The Generation Game*, Larry Grayson and, in the end, LWT itself. That's show business.

John Birt's newly consolidated Features and Current Affairs Department had the most ground to make up and the most extensive territory to occupy: religion, adult education, the arts, local programmes... As Michael Grade says in his autobiography, David Bell was Head of Entertainment, John Bromley was Head of Sport, Tony Wharmby was Head of Drama and John Birt was Head of Everything Else. The new Department was rich enough in talent to cope, and with Nick Elliott in charge of Features and Barry Cox in charge of Current Affairs it coped so well that I was able to accede to a request earlier in the year from David Frost to give John leave of absence to produce David's celebrated interviews with Richard Nixon. Now, with John's return, he, Nick and Barry had the specific problem of the IBA's criticism of our religious and local programming to address; and they moved quickly to tackle it.

Features introduced *Credo*, a weekly series of reports, investigations and documentaries on religious matters, many of which are as topical today as they were in the seventies, from international terrorism and the morality of political violence to the problem of racism in the UK, the questions surrounding faith schools and religious education, and the attitude of the Church towards women priests, homosexuality, abortion and assisted suicide. *Plus ca change.* Nick Elliott was also the executive producer of some memorable *Credo* mini-series shot as *cine-verite* with no explicit editorial comment, among them a study of the life and work of the Salvation Army; a sensitive chronicle, *Facing Death*, of the weeks leading up to the death and funerals of two incurably ill women from two different social classes, working and upper-middle; and *Wedding Day*, which followed the nuptials of seven young couples from seven different religious and social traditions all the way to their respective marriages.

Current Affairs responded to the IBA's criticism that LWT's local programming didn't receive enough Programme Department attention by applying an abundance of it to *The London Weekend Show* and *The London Programme*, which became eminent examples of their kind. *The London*

Programme, introduced by Godfrey Hodgson, was a hard-hitting investigative series on topical London issues, and *The London Weekend Show*, produced by Janet Street-Porter, a colourful survey of the music, culture and concerns of London's youth. In the drive to serve the cultural and ethnic diversity of the region the Department set up two special units: the London Community Unit, providing advice, information and airtime to community groups across the area, and the London Minorities Unit, under Jane Hewland, which produced series addressing the concerns and interests of London's gay community in *Gay Life* and its black and Asian communities in *Skin*.

Skin brought bright young people like Trevor Phillips and Samir Shah into television for the first time, along with many others who joined the Department as researchers and reporters. Too many others, David Docherty observed, for LWT's older members of staff, to whom "these young, university educated, impudent young men and women appeared in Kent House like an infestation". But there was a job to be done: Features and Current Affairs had a great deal more than religion and local interest to contribute to the company's programme schedules and these young researchers and reporters were an essential part of its greatly expanded output.

Peter Jay had gone off to become the British Ambassador to the United States, but the Current Affairs flagship *Weekend World* thrived under its new presenter, Brian Walden. John Birt and Barry Cox added to its examination of political matters and personalities an equally robust scrutiny of the television industry's programmes and politics in *Look Here*, presented by Andrew Neil and produced by Rod Allen, the publisher and editor of the trade journal *Broadcast*. A new late-night chat show, *Saturday Night People*, presented by Janet Street-Porter, Clive James and Russell Harty, cast a satirical eye on politics, television and anything else that caught the attention of its presenters. It was a happy example of the cross-fertilisation within and between Departments advocated at Selsdon Park, since Janet also presented *The London Weekend Show* for Current Affairs, Clive was the co-presenter of an adult education series for Features and Russell was the presenter of his own long-running LWT talk show, *Russell Harty Plus*.

A particularly striking example of cross-fertilisation was the drama-documentary *Eighteen Months to Balcombe Street*, co-produced by the Heads of Current Affairs and Drama, Barry Cox and Tony Wharmby, with John Birt as Executive Producer and Drama's Stephen Frears as its director. The programme told the extraordinary story of the Provisional IRA gang which had terrorised London with gun and bomb attacks in 1974 and 1975, exploding 40 bombs across the capital, killing 35 people and wounding many more. Norris McWhirter, the Conservative Party publicist and publisher of the *Guinness Book of Records*, was assassinated after he offered a reward of £50,000 to anyone coming forward with evidence about the IRA. The gang had been spotted and chased by unarmed Metropolitan Police officers to a block of council flats in Balcombe Street, next to Marylebone Station, where they broke into one of the flats and held the occupants hostage for six days in what became known as the Balcombe Street Siege. The LWT team covered the whole affair in drama-documentary form and rushed it onto the air, unscheduled, a week after the gang's trial, to great acclaim.

In addition to religion, Features had taken on the company's adult education commitment, and it produced two major studies of Islam and Stalin as well as a succession of lively series including *The Do-Gooders*, a report on the world and work of the British social services; *How to Stay Alive*, a guide to fitness and health with Colin Welland and Maggie Makepeace; and *A Question of Sex*, with Clive James and Anna Raeburn examining the respective qualities of men and women in a contribution to the early debate on feminism.

Most significantly, the Department also made radical changes to its arts coverage. LWT's *Aquarius*, ITV's only regular series on the arts since *Tempo*, had lost its way after the final departure of Humphrey Burton, its original editor and presenter. Cyril Bennett had persuaded Peter Hall, then Director of the National Theatre, to take it over in 1975, with Derek Bailey as its producer, but Hall's inevitable preoccupation with his theatrical activities meant that his contribution was more or less limited to his on-screen presence and he left *Aquarius* early in 1977. Messrs Birt and Elliott took the opportunity to recast the programme as well as the presenter.

They talked to novelist Melvyn Bragg, the editor and presenter of the BBC's book programme *Read All About It*, and found that their thoughts and ideas coincided happily with Melvyn's. All three wanted to widen television's coverage of the arts to embrace popular culture. Where their thoughts and ideas didn't totally coincide with Melvyn's they were impressed enough by his zest and enthusiasm to go along with his. Melvyn wanted the programme to celebrate the arts as well as examine them, and to be given the airtime and resources to do them justice. An hour's running time not the 45 minutes occupied by *Aquarius*; 25 programmes a year not *Aquarius*'s 15; full, simultaneous networking not the current scatter-gun spread; and choice and control of the producers and directors who would work for the series. John and Nick had no difficulty in getting Michael Grade to persuade me and the rest of the Board to agree the airtime and resources, and Michael was able to persuade the network to transmit the programme simultaneously in every region. No mean achievement since several of its editions would run up to two hours in length.

The South Bank Show took to the screen in 1978. In its opening season it won ITV's first Prix Italia Music Prize with a programme on the making and performance of Kenneth Macmillan's ballet *Mayerling*, which Derek Bailey produced and directed. It completed a rare cultural hat trick with two more Italia Music prizes in 1980 and 1981, the years in which ITV was next eligible, with studies of the life and work respectively of William Walton and Benjamin Britten, both programmes produced and directed by Tony Palmer.

The South Bank Show would go on to grace ITV for over 33 years, with Melvyn interviewing and exploring the work of a remarkably eclectic mix of subjects, from Francis Bacon and Andy Warhol to Walt Disney and Jack Vettriano, from Laurence Olivier to Ken Dodd, Margot Fonteyn to Mama Lu Parks, Sir David Lean to Woody Allen, Kiri Te Kanawa and Maria Callas to Bing Crosby and Dusty Springfield, from the Mariinsky Theatre and The Royal Shakespeare Company to the *Carry On* films and the Dance Theatre of Harlem.

The programme would win over 110 national and international awards including two more Prix Italia. When financial difficulties led to its end on ITV in 2010, *The South Bank Show* was mourned by the media pages of *The Daily Telegraph* as "the last bastion of civilisation on ITV". Eighteen months later the bastion was restored and relocated to the Sky Arts Channel, where it still survives. Long may it continue to do so, along with its hugely likeable, multi-talented begetter. I used to accuse Melvyn of running an *atelier* of over-worked apprentices in his loft. How else, I said, could he have sustained his extraordinary output of television programmes, radio programmes, novels, biographies, books of non-fiction, children's books, librettos and screenplays for both film and television, and still manage to put in a full day's work at the House of Lords as Baron Bragg of Wigton in the County of Cumbria, the eminently well-deserved honour with which his contribution to the arts was recognised in 1998? I'm still not wholly convinced that I was wrong.

Meeting and Greeting

I n my new role as LWT's Chief Executive I was of course delighted by
this great burst of creative activity on the part of Programme Department. But I confess that my pride in its achievement was tempered by
more than a little regret. The achievement only peripherally involved me.
I encouraged it, approved it, persuaded the Board to fund it, tweaked it a
little in my weekly sessions with Michael Grade, made a suggestion here,
a recommendation there, offered guidance and advice when it was sought,
but I had to reconcile myself to the fact that I had finally said goodbye to
any significant personal involvement in programme making. For the first
time in more than 20 years I was not a Producer, a Controller or a Director
of Programmes. I tried to rationalise the situation of course. Whenever I was
asked by a journalist – TV executives were still the object of curiosity for
the press – how it felt now to be a Managing Director and not a television
producer, I usually replied that it wasn't all that different: I was casting
executives rather than artistes, handling a company's budget and not a
programme's, and so on; but who was I trying to kid?

Fortunately, the company's budget could afford to fund this great burst
of programme-making, thanks to our Sales Department and its dauntless
Director, Ron Miller, for whom every advertising break in our brief weekend
schedule was precious. Hence his outrage when ATV scheduled its mini-
series about the life of Jesus at 7.15 pm on two successive weekends in 1977:
three hours of it on Palm Sunday and three and a quarter on Easter Sunday.

"But that's the whole of our peak time on both evenings! – we'll never
get advertisers to buy into it, and certainly not at peak-time rates. It's a

religious programme: can't you get ATV to move it into the Closed Period?"

"Sorry Ron. Michael tried to get the Controllers Group to change it but Bill Ward said Lew Grade was insisting on peak time. I called Lew myself and he was adamant. He's very proud of the series, believes it will get great ratings."

"Well can I speak to him? Can you arrange for me to go and see him?"

Yes I could, and did, and wished Ron the best of luck. I would have given anything to eavesdrop on their conversation: the King of Salesmen versus the Young Pretender on opposite sides of Lew's desk in Great Cumberland Place. Incredibly enough, Ron prevailed. He managed to persuade Lew that scheduling *Jesus of Nazareth* at 6.15 pm in the Closed Period, where there was no BBC peak-time competition to oppose it and no commercial break interruptions, would give the series a huge audience which, once hooked, would carry over to the rest of the evening. Before Ron could get back to Kent House to report to Michael and me, Lew was on the phone. "Brian?" "Yes, Lew." "Your boy Miller..." "Yes, Lew?" "He's a very good salesman." "Yes, Lew, he is." "Tell me... Is he Jewish?"

So as far as programmes were concerned I was no longer a Scheduler, no longer a Programme Head, no longer a Producer-Director. I was a Meeter-Greeter. Meeting and greeting Princess Margaret, the Patron of the actors' trade union Equity, when we mounted *A Royal Night of One Hundred Stars* at the National Theatre to celebrate its Golden Anniversary. Meeting and greeting the former Prime Minister James Callaghan and his wife at the gala preview performance of Stephen Sondheim's *Sweeney Todd*, which we were videotaping for a *South Bank Show* documentary. Being presented to Her Majesty the Queen at the Royal Variety Performance and then presenting the cast to her back-stage after the show. Meeting and greeting Laurence Olivier, his wife Joan Plowright and their close friends at the dinner we gave to celebrate both his 80th birthday and the two editions of *The South Bank Show* which Melvyn Bragg had devoted to a study of his life and work.

This was a very special meeting-and-greeting occasion at the Inn on the Park in Park Lane, with Melvyn, Audrey and me welcoming one by one Lord and Lady Olivier, Alec Guinness, Anthony Hopkins, Maggie Smith, Albert Finney, Peggy Ashcroft, Edna O'Brien, Patrick Garland, Tom Stoppard, Frank Finlay, the Chairman and Director General of the IBA and their distinguished partners... For one extraordinary evening I felt like Hollywood's Louis B. Mayer in the golden days of MGM, surrounded, as his publicity used to claim, by "more stars than there are in heaven". Let me tell you that making a speech to that gathering was considerably more daunting than warming up the audience for *Sunday Night at the London Palladium*.

Admittedly, meeting and greeting did have moments of unexpected comedy which would not have been out of place in the light entertainment shows I had produced at the BBC and ATV. The *Royal Night of One Hundred Stars*, which Michael Grade had engaged the great Robert Nesbitt to stage, celebrated 50 years of British show business, beginning with a sequence of music hall songs made famous by great performers of the past like Marie Lloyd and Vesta Tilley and performed by present day stars – Barbara Windsor as Marie Lloyd, for example. Princess Margaret and I were seated in the Royal Box of the National Theatre's Dress Circle, surrounded by dignitaries from Equity, the IBA and LWT. During the opening sequence of music hall songs, I was horrified to hear someone actually singing along with the performers on the stage. I looked round to see who it was, leaned towards Her Royal Highness to murmur my apologies – and discovered that the culprit was herself. "Oh yes," she said. "I know all these. Mummy used to play them for us on the piano after dinner for a good old sing-song."

At one *Royal Variety Performance*, Bernard Delfont, newly appointed President of the Entertainment Artists Benevolent Fund in aid of which the Performance is presented, was due for the first time to introduce the customary line-up of TV executives to Her Majesty at the beginning of the evening. He didn't know the then Chairman of the IBA, George Russell, the then Acting Director General, Lady Littler, the then Chairman of LWT's parent company, Christopher Bland, or the then Director of Programmes for LWT, Greg Dyke. But he did know me, and as we stood in line waiting for the Queen he asked me to go over the names of the others to help him remember who they were. I was happy to do so, and also explained that Lady Littler's husband standing nearby was Sir Geoffrey – at which point Her Majesty arrived. "Sir Geoffrey" was therefore the last name Bernard heard. Unfortunately, in the stress and tension of the moment, all the other names flew out of his head and he went down the line with Her Majesty introducing Lady Littler, Sir Geoffrey Russell, Sir Geoffrey Bland, and Sir Geoffrey Dyke until, to his great and obvious relief, he arrived at the one familiar name he could remember correctly: mine. To this day, George Russell and I still address each other when we meet as "Sir Geoffrey".

As far as programmes were concerned, then, I was no longer a Producer, a Controller, or a Director. I was a Meeter and Greeter. But I was also, as I was about to discover, a Can-Carrier. It went with the territory.

In November 1977, *Weekend World* transmitted a programme about the disagreements within the medical profession over whether the life support systems of severely brain damaged patients should be withdrawn. In its introduction it referred to two recent instances where the decision to switch off had been properly taken and went on to refer to a case due to be heard the next day in Scotland, where a hospital nursing sister was awaiting trial accused of obstructing the air supply to a 13-year old girl in the intensive care unit at Edinburgh Royal Infirmary. Current Affairs Department had taken legal advice as to whether this reference constituted a contempt of court and were assured that it did not. This was not however the view of the Scottish Court. An action for contempt was brought against the programme and the company, and the charge against the nurse was withdrawn pending its outcome.

Where did I, as the company's chief executive, figure in this? Not at all, said our able company secretary, Judith Thomas. Not at all, said Denton Hall & Burgin, our highly regarded legal representatives. The passage in the programme would be understood as being no more than a reference to the allegation in the charge against the nurse. I need not worry about it. I need not be concerned about its outcome affecting the company. I need not even attend the hearing, which was expected to last only a day or two, unless of course I wanted to turn up for the judgement at Edinburgh's High Court as a matter of courtesy, which they felt would be appreciated by the Lord Justice-General, Lord Emslie.

It certainly was appreciated. I did turn up on the final day of the hearing, and the Lord Justice-General was informed accordingly. When he and his two accompanying judges had completed their deliberations they returned to the Court in all their most impressive red, black and ermined finery. Lord Emslie requested LWT's chief executive to stand up wherever he was in the Court to hear him deliver his judgement. I stood; he stared stonily at me; he delivered. The Court did not accept our Counsel's argument that the passage in question was no more than a reference to the allegation in the charge against the nurse. To refer to the case of the 13-year old girl in this context was utterly indefensible and irresponsible and was in the highest degree likely to prejudice the nurse's prospects of a fair and impartial trial. It would convey to the public mind in Scotland and to the minds of prospective jurors that the case was similar to the others to which the programme had referred. Lord Emslie's judgement was a tongue-lashing excoriation, the burden of which was how dare we Sassenachs attempt to impose an English interpretation of the law on the Scottish Courts? And it was directed stingingly, unequivocally, at me. The can was mine. As I say, it went with the territory.

The company was fined £50,000, I was fined £5,000, so was David Cox, *Weekend World's* Editor; the producer, Nick Evans, was fined £1,000. Lord Emslie's parting shot was that the individual fines had to be paid personally, not by the company on our behalf. In today's money, that was the equivalent of £24,500 each for David and me and £4,900 for Nick. The company's fine would be the equivalent of £245,000: not inconsiderable sums. In the event, David, Nick and I coughed up personally and the company gave us the relevant amounts as one-off bonuses. But you can imagine that the affair left me somewhat wary of carrying the can for our intrepid programme-makers.

Whereupon, Michael Grade knocked on my door with a can of quite spectacular proportions.

Snatch of the Day

In the late seventies, years before the advent of Sky and the creation of the Premier League, all television coverage of weekly football was recorded and aired only on *Match of the Day* on the BBC on Saturday evening or in highlights of the previous day's games in programmes such as LWT's *The Big Match* on Sunday afternoons. Under a Concordat Agreement between the BBC, the IBA and the ITV companies set up in 1971 to conduct negotiations for non-exclusive sporting events, the two broadcasting organisations negotiated the contract for this coverage jointly, precluding any attempt by the Football League to play us off against each other to increase the fee.

Michael Grade had learned from a friend on the League's management committee that the mood of the clubs was to reject television coverage altogether when the current agreement expired, on the grounds that the sport was over-exposed and underpaid. Through that friend, he had proposed an alternative, an exclusive deal on behalf of the ITV network which would at once double the fee and halve the exposure. He and John Bromley had worked out all the angles and thought that such a proposal could succeed but they were aware that if it did there would be, in Bromley's words, "blood on the walls" when the BBC learned of it. Did it have my support?

Well, yes it did; but, while tipping my hat to my Director of Programmes' *chutzpah*, I pointed out that we would first have to obtain the support of the Board, the agreement of the other ITV companies to the sum of money involved and the approval of the IBA for what would in effect be a dereliction of the Concordat Agreement. There was reason to believe that this approval might be easier to obtain than we thought. The BBC had with increasing arrogance over the years rejected the proposals made within the Concordat by the IBA and the companies for avoiding the duplication of major sporting events on the two services by adopting some kind of alternation. The BBC's attitude to these proposals had been made abundantly clear only recently at the Broadcasting Press Guild in a speech by its Managing Director, Alasdair Milne, in the memorable phrase 'As far as I'm concerned, stuff them!' With the proposed Football League deal ITV had for the first time a sanction to deploy in the alternation debate. We could use it to break up the BBC's continued intransigence by offering to let them share the football coverage in exchange for their long-term agreement to alternate such events as the Cup Final, the World Cup and the Olympics.

LWT's Board approved the proposal with unanimity and a number of raised eyebrows. In a telephone conference call Michael secured the support of the other major ITV companies and, via the IBA's Director of Television Colin Shaw, the approval of the Authority. His proposal was formally made to the Football League and, after some hard bargaining, on 16 November 1978 the League's management committee agreed to give ITV the exclusive right to televise its matches for three seasons from 1979-80 for the sum of five million pounds, almost twice the figure it might have expected from a renewal of the old joint contract. At a full meeting of the 51 Club Chairmen that afternoon the proposal was approved by 50 votes to one. At 7 pm that evening, at a Press Conference at Kent House, Michael announced the deal to a stunned audience of journalists. The next morning's first editions would all lead with this compelling story of football, television and intrigue, which was immediately dubbed 'Snatch of the Day'.

The first the BBC heard of it was on the Press conference evening, when a reporter from *Broadcast* magazine phoned to ask if they knew that champagne corks were popping down at LWT. And then, as John Bromley had forewarned, blood hit the walls. The BBC reacted with public and private fury. Alasdair Milne appeared on BBC news programme Nationwide to denounce LWT as "the Mafia with chequebooks very much in evidence". The Corporation sued the Football League for breach of contract. The Office of Fair Trading was brought in and ruled that the agreement between LWT and the League was void because its particulars had not been notified to the OFT within the time limits prescribed under restrictive practices legislation. The European Commission was asked to examine whether the contracting parties had flouted the rules of competition as laid down in the Treaty of

Rome. MPs of both major parties in the House of Commons turned aside from denouncing each other to denounce what they called LWT's piracy. The Corporation argued that the Concordat arrangements imposed a legal obligation on the ITV companies to negotiate jointly with the BBC and threatened to apply to the High Court for an interlocutory injunction.

The IBA's response to the BBC was courteous but firm. "It is, of course, true," wrote Sir Brian Young "that the Authority has laid stress on the Concordat, but our experience has been very discouraging: over and over again, the BBC's clear message was that in sport competition rather than co-operation was to prevail. In many statements and public letters you seemed to be saying that might was to be right, and that the possession of exclusive contracts by the BBC in various sports gave it the right to claim superiority and refuse co-operation; the companies have taken you at your word and joined the game under your rules."

There was, however, one unavoidable weakness in our case. ITV's representative on the joint negotiating committee with the BBC was Granada's Gerry Loftus, who worked out of the Granada studios in Manchester. Gerry was the chief negotiator for ITV Sport, the network's central sports committee, but for the sake of security he had been given no knowledge of Michael Grade's negotiations with the Football League. Unfortunately, Michael himself had been given no knowledge of the fact that earlier in the year, when the joint agreement was nearing the time for renegotiation, Gerry had given his assurance in writing to the BBC that ITV was not considering unilateral negotiations with the League. And the much-aggrieved Gerry was now giving heated interviews to the press claiming that Michael had stabbed him in the back and precipitated a full-scale war with the BBC.

In the light of all these allegations of double-dealing and ungentlemanly conduct the IBA's firm position was beginning to shift. The new Chairman of the Authority, Lady Plowden, sent for John Freeman and told him that if the matter was not satisfactorily resolved heads at LWT must roll. Characteristically, John said that if any head must roll it would be his since the matter had arisen on his watch, which steadied the buffs a little. The Authority would not readily have seen one of ITV's most prominent figures sacrificed on such an altar; but it was obvious that something had to be done.

John and Michael and I consulted a leading commercial silk, Sam Stamler QC, who advised us that our chances of winning in a High Court case were good; but in discussions with the Authority and our ITV colleagues we came to the conclusion that the public airing of our differences with the BBC would be both unedifying and extremely costly. Happily, the IBA discovered that the BBC had come to the same conclusion and it was agreed that a privately negotiated settlement between the BBC and ITV was the sensible solution. As chief executive of the company responsible for this brouhaha, I would have to carry the can. The onus was on me to attempt to reach an agreement on behalf of ITV and LWT with the BBC's Managing Director, Alasdair Milne, whose antipathy towards ITV was visceral.

I have no idea why Alasdair disliked us so much. Twenty years earlier he had actually worked for ITV. Originally one of Grace Wyndham Goldie's Golden Boys, a producer in BBC Television's Talks Department and co-founder with Donald Baverstock of the celebrated *Tonight* programme, he had left the Corporation at the birth of ITV to join Associated-Rediffusion, where he produced half a dozen editions of *This Week* but not very much else. He returned to a very successful career at the BBC until 1967 when the new ITV franchises were put out to tender, whereupon he joined a high-powered Scottish consortium to bid for the Scottish Television franchise. It didn't succeed. Perhaps this failure and his earlier experiences at Rediffusion were the reasons for his animosity, but it was certainly deep-seated and long-lasting.

Years after Snatch of the Day, in one of the attempts to revive the spirit of the Concordat, the new Chairman of the BBC, George Howard, organised a private dinner at Broadcasting House with Granada's Chairman Denis Forman and me, in my capacity at that time as Chairman of the Independent Television Companies Association. This was to be an opportunity for us to talk off the record with George Howard and Alasdair Milne who was by then the BBC's Director General, about the possibilities of renewed co-operation between the two broadcasting organisations. I was sitting next to George on one side of the table with Denis on the other next to Alasdair, and half way through our first course, in response to some innocuous remark by Denis, Alasdair flew into a furious attack on ITV in general and Granada in particular. George Howard was appalled. He leaned towards me to ask "Is he always like this?" "I'm afraid so," I replied.

And now here I was, sitting opposite this dark, brooding man, in a small room at the IBA headquarters in Brompton Road on a miserable winter afternoon, charged with reaching an agreement with him which would keep ITV and the IBA out of the courts and, if possible, win some kind of alternation in sports coverage by using the advantage we had gained with the Football League deal. The tension in that little room was palpable; so was Alasdair's hostility. And it didn't help that I was nursing a heavy cold, for which I had been prescribed medication to reduce its explosive coughs and sneezes. It was a gruelling and gloomy afternoon – where was the Band of the Scots Guards when I needed it? – and our disputation trudged on into the evening as it grew darker outside in the Brompton Road and rain started to fall.

But just as I had begun to think I really couldn't take much more of this, Alasdair finally blinked. He grudgingly agreed in principle to share the greatly inflated cost of the new Football League deal and to alternate its recorded television coverage with us on Saturday night and Sunday afternoon with ITV taking over the *Match of the Day* slot and BBC the *Big Match* slot in alternate years. He also conceded in principle the avoidance of duplicated coverage in major non-exclusive sporting events, the details of which would be agreed between his Deputy, Robin Scott, and me. And with the IBA officers who had been waiting patiently in their offices to be summoned as witnesses, we signed the Tesler-Milne Agreement.

I dashed off to join Audrey and a couple of friends for dinner at Drones in Chelsea, in the quiet little room downstairs from the main restaurant. I celebrated the agreement with a glass not of champagne but brandy, which I felt I needed after the stress and tension of my afternoon with Alasdair. Bad call. The brandy, combined with my reaction to the afternoon, together with my cold and the powerful medication I had been taking for it, made me feel light-headed. I excused myself from the table, said I needed some fresh air and made my way up the stairs. I started to walk to the entrance through the restaurant, which was bright and noisy with the chatter of happy diners, but could manage only a few paces before I had to stop and lean with both hands on the table of a startled young couple. "It's alright," I said "I'm not drunk, I'm just..." – and the sound went. I straightened up, saw waiters running towards me silently, in slow motion, and remember thinking "If this is dying, it's really not so bad", and then the lights went out. When I came to I was lying on my back on some kind of couch with a ring of concerned faces looking down on me, and I heard myself saying what I had always thought was just a movie cliché: it appears that it isn't. "Where am I?" I said. Thanks a lot, Alasdair; how was your evening?

Working out the details with Robin Scott was nothing like so difficult, but the IBA wasn't taking any chances. It asked the BBC to guarantee that Robin would not be overruled by his Managing Director. We brought in colleagues to ensure that we touched all the relevant bases: Colin Shaw from the IBA, the Head of the ITCA Secretariat and the Chairman of ITV Sport – sorry, Gerry Loftus, but not you again – and, from the BBC, the Controller of BBC One, its Head of Sport and the Head of Outside Broadcasts. We agreed to put a new joint offer to the Football League of £9.5 million for four years of recorded coverage on Saturday evenings and Sunday afternoons, the days to rotate season by season between the two broadcasting organisations. We agreed that, once our offer was accepted, all legal actions and claims and counter-claims would be withdrawn. We agreed to reduce simultaneous broadcasts in our coverage of the 1980 European Football Championships, the 1980 Moscow Olympics and the 1982 World Cup. And we agreed that the Concordat meetings between the IBA and the BBC should be resumed. On 6 March 1979, Robin and I signed what the official history designates the Tesler/Scott Concordat.

The Football League held out for an additional £500,000 to round up our joint offer to £10 million, prompting more lurid newspaper headlines, and the Home Office felt obliged to assure members of the public who had written to the Prime Minister that the cost would not be passed on to the licence payers: the cost per hour of football coverage in peak viewing hours would still be less than other kinds of programme shown at that time. But we had a deal. The IBA sent me its warmest congratulations. And I was spared another day in court.

The official history of *Independent Television in Britain* devotes five pages to the saga of Snatch of the Day, an indication of how significant it was held to be at that time. In the 308 pages of Alasdair Milne's autobiography, *The Memoirs of a British Broadcaster*, it occupies only a brief parenthesis in his account of Michael Grade's subsequent move to the BBC. Alasdair merely records that "Michael, a younger member of the famous Grade family, had left being Director of Programmes at London Weekend Television (where, it must be said, I had some harsh things to say when he tried to engineer an ITV monopoly of the Football League contracts)." And that's it. Snatch of the Day? *What* Snatch of the Day?

You Win Some...

I TV's fifteen chief executives had more to do than carry the can for their programme-makers. As well as managing our respective companies we fought our company's corner at the ITCA Council and the Network Programme Committee. We fought the network's corner on Authority bodies like the Programme Policy Committee and the Standing Consultative Committee, which met monthly under the chairmanship of the IBA's Director General to formulate the industry's broad policy. And we fought ITV's corner in outside Committees, Councils and Boards whenever we were invited to supply a representative to speak for us. I had my share of all these fights, and more than my share of the outside ones: my colleagues must have thought me either a safe pair of hands or a useful idiot who wouldn't know the difference between an honour and a lumber.

When ITV was invited in 1975 to provide a representative on the Prime Minister's Working Party on the Future of the British Film Industry, which Harold Wilson himself would chair, it nominated me. When the Working Party was succeeded by the Interim Action Committee on the Film Industry in 1975 it nominated me. When the Interim Action Committee was succeeded by the British Screen Advisory Council in 1985 it nominated me. When ITV was invited to nominate a Governor of the National Film and Television School in 1979 it nominated... well, you get the picture. The same picture when ITV was invited to nominate a Governor of the British Film Institute. All these bodies were packed with the big guns of the British film industry, and most of them were trained on the ITV representative. The British film industry's general view seemed to be that television owed it a living and, since the BBC was strapped for cash, the living should be paid by ITV. ITV was attacked at every meeting, for its income, for its programmes, for the audiences it had taken away from the cinema, for its very existence. I finally figured out the difference between an honour and a lumber, and this was a lumber.

My principal antagonist throughout was Alan Sapper, the General Secretary of the ACTT, the Association of Cinematograph Television and Allied Technicians, the Trade Union which had blacked out ITV at the beginning of the current franchises. Like me, Alan was a member or governor of each of these film industry bodies. Also like me, ironically, as a boy he had been a member of the Poplar Grove youth club in Shepherds Bush, where we had known each other 40 years earlier. Television had brought us into contact again. No, not contact: conflict. I used to tell our film colleagues not to be alarmed by our committee room spats: we were simply playing James Cagney and Patrick O'Brien in those Warner Brothers films of the forties. You remember, those movies with the two childhood friends born in the Bronx. One of them, played by Patrick O'Brien, usually grew up to become a priest; the other played by James Cagney usually grew up to become a hoodlum. I played the Patrick O'Brien part.

Alan hated this sort of thing, but it helped to contain the committee-room pressure, and over the years I like to think I managed to modify the views and temper the anti-ITV attitudes of my colleagues, always excepting Alan. I remained a member of the Advisory Committee and a governor of both the National Film and Television School and the British Film Institute until I retired, for my last three years at the Film Institute as its Deputy Chairman.

There were no Cagney-O'Brien brawls at the ITV meetings, though exchanges of view could be noisy and heated. Walking into my first meeting of the ITCA Council at Knighton House in London's West End was like walking into an early meeting of the Programme Controllers Group. A passionate argument had apparently broken out, with each Managing Director expressing his opinion at the same time, all of them trying to shout each other down, until someone could be heard over the clamour thumping the table and calling "Mr Chairman! Mr Chairman!" The clamour collapsed and everybody looked down the table at the caller, who happened to be Lew Grade. "But Lew," said Cecil Bernstein of Granada from the other end of the table, *"you're* the Chairman."

Generally speaking, however, this was a civilised gathering of the 15 company principals, chaired alternately by major and regional chief executives for two years at a time, each of us fighting our individual company's corner but doing our best to hammer out our differences in the common interest, planning joint action on matters of concern and agreeing joint policy in our dealings with the IBA, the Government, the Advertising Industry, the BBC and any other relevant body. It worked, because it had to work. So did the Network Programme Committee, which met six times a year under the chairmanship of one of the major company chief executives. Here, the 15 Managing Directors were joined by the five major company Programme Controllers, the Editor of ITN and the senior programme officers of the IBA to discuss programme matters, resolve problems, approve draft network schedules and receive reports and recommendations from its various sub-committees and working parties.

Chief among those subsidiary bodies was the Programme Controllers Group, all of whose founder members had been superseded by the end of the seventies. Michael Grade now represented LWT. For Granada, Mike Scott had succeeded David Plowright, now the company's joint Managing Director alongside Denis Forman. Charles Denton had succeeded Bill Ward at ATV. Paul Fox had interrupted his distinguished career at the BBC as Controller of BBC 1 in 1973 to succeed Donald Baverstock at Yorkshire Television. Three years later he succeeded Ward Thomas as the company's Managing Director without relinquishing his programme controllership, so he now accompanied himself at the IBA's Programme Policy Committee, where the major controllers sat alongside their chief executives. Eleven years later still, by courtesy of the whirligigs of both time and television, he would be whizzed back to the BBC to continue his Corporation career at an even more distinguished level. Jeremy Isaacs was still the Director of Programmes at Thames, where he had succeeded me. But for how much longer?

In 1977, four months before George Cooper was due to retire as Thames's Managing Director, Howard Thomas signed up the brilliant Controller of BBC 1, Bryan Cowgill, to succeed him. It was a notable coup, in which Howard omitted to involve George, who first learned of his replacement via a leak from the BBC: why did that not surprise me? The Cowgills had bought a house on the river at Chiswick Staithe, and Audrey and I thought it would be a neighbourly gesture to welcome them to both Chiswick and ITV over dinner at Park Road. We hadn't met Jenny and Bryan but we had become good friends with Paul Fox and his wife, who knew them well from Paul's BBC days, so we asked Paul and Betty to join us to help the Cowgills feel at ease.

As it turned out, Bryan needed no help. He was at his ease from the first Campari, talking non-stop about what was wrong with ITV, what he was going to do to change it, the artistes and events he was going to attract to Thames, and the speed with which he was going to transform the company's competitiveness. No social chat, no involvement of the wives, though Paul and I tried hard to change the subject. By the time we got to the coffee Jenny had had enough. "This will go on for the rest of the evening," she said to Audrey and Betty; "Let's leave them to it. Come over to my place; we can have coffee and a chat there." So they crept out, got into Jenny's car and drove off to the Staithe. They didn't say goodbye. We didn't even see them go.

Paul had been just as competitive a Controller of BBC 1 as Bryan but he had learned that no ITV company was an island. ITV was a network of companies obliged by necessity to co-operate with each other in co-ordinating policies and programme schedules, all of which were subject to the IBA's approval. No ITV Managing Director, no ITV Programme Controller had the freedom Paul and Bryan had enjoyed at the BBC. Independent Television was in truth Highly Dependent Television: dependent on the collaboration and good will of 15 companies of differing sizes, attitudes and aspirations and ultimately dependent on its validation by the Independent Broadcasting Authority. Paul and I tried to get these facts of ITV life across to Bryan at that little Park Road dinner party. We failed.

How would he and Jeremy get on at Thames? Soon after Bryan's arrival, Jeremy sought confirmation that, as Director of Programmes, he would retain total responsibility for the programme department and programme scheduling. The pause before he received this assurance from Bryan was ominously long. Bryan was too compulsive a Controller to stay on the sidelines. Every evening after six o'clock he would summon Jeremy up to his office to talk about programmes and schedules. He set about implementing his manifesto at once, spending vast sums of money to buy Morecambe and Wise, the Miss World Contest and a number of sporting contracts away from the BBC.

Sport was his particular interest and he felt that the standard of Thames's sports coverage needed to be raised, so he removed the responsibility for it from Jeremy's Controller of Outside Broadcasts and handed it to an ex-colleague from the BBC, Sam Leitch. As Jeremy recalls in his autobiography, it was sport which caused Bryan to lose his temper with him, erupting in sudden fury over a boxing match that the Programme Controllers Group had failed to snap up. But it wasn't the odd exceptional outburst that Jeremy found difficult to bear. It was the daily routine, the constant presence of Cowgill at his shoulder, and he finally felt it necessary to tell him so. "Bryan, you don't leave me space to work in. I want to leave Thames. I've made up my mind." Jeremy says Cowgill was aghast, and they agreed to leave the matter for a few weeks, deciding to discuss it together with Howard Thomas the following month.

During those weeks, however, another developing problem for Jeremy came to a head. In the previous year, six of the ten ITV programmes about the troubles in Northern Ireland had come from Thames's *This Week* team. Roy Mason, the Secretary of State for Northern Ireland had written to the Chairman of the IBA complaining about *This Week*'s critical reporting of the conduct of the security forces and the Royal Ulster Constabulary, and the Authority in turn had expressed its concern to Thames about the cumulative effect of these programmes, asking for a more "all-round picture". Now *This Week* notified the Authority that it proposed to deal with a forthcoming report by Amnesty International containing allegations of the ill-treatment of suspects held for questioning by the RUC, which would vindicate the programme's investigations of the previous year.

The members of the Authority ruled that the programme should not be broadcast until the report was made public and the Secretary of State had had an opportunity to comment on it in Parliament. On the afternoon of *This Week*'s planned transmission Roy Mason duly released to the House of Commons the government's formal statement in response to the Amnesty report. But, against the advice of their own programme staff, the members of the Authority decided that the ban should nevertheless remain in force, a decision which David Glencross, the IBA's Deputy Director of Television, criticised in a note of protest to the Director General. ACTT members across the network refused to transmit a substitute programme, with the result that at 9.30 pm that evening ITV screens throughout the network were blank until the commercial break at the end of the *This Week* slot.

In the furore that followed the next morning the BBC asked if they could see the material Thames had been barred from screening. Jeremy told his team to give it to them and let them use it if they wanted to. And use it they did. The furore rose to a crescendo, the press proclaiming that Jeremy had given the banned film material to the BBC in a fit of pique, offending Roy Mason, the IBA and his own Board in the process. It was against this background that Jeremy went to discuss his future with Howard Thomas and Bryan Cowgill. He told them that he hadn't changed his mind, that he still wanted to leave. They asked him to reconsider but, as Jeremy says in his autobiography, "I doubt they meant it". They certainly didn't fight to keep him.

Remembering his response to my nomination of Jeremy as Director of Programmes in 1974 when I was to become Managing Director, Howard must have thought he was at last justified in asking "What about his politics?" And Bryan was at last free to be Director of Programmes as well as Managing Director. He had the job he really wanted, and he held on to it for eighteen months before pressure from the IBA and the Thames Board finally obliged him to appoint Jeremy's successor. And Jeremy himself? He left Thames on 1 September 1978, less than a year after Bryan Cowgill's triumphant arrival. It is one of television's ironies that his career in the industry would outlast and out-lustre his boss's.

Jeremy first told Bryan that he wanted to leave Thames over dinner during a Film Purchase Group trip to Los Angeles. This Group, which reported to the NPC, was made up of the five major company Programme Controllers with a major company chief executive as its chairman. It had the enviable annual task of accompanying the network's film buyer, Leslie Halliwell of Granada, on his trips to Los Angeles each spring for a week of screening the new shows commissioned by the American networks for the forthcoming autumn. Delegations from the BBC and broadcasting organisations from all over the world were in town on the same mission.

Our Group would stay at the Beverley Wilshire Hotel and be driven each day to one of the Hollywood film studios, where it would be greeted in the projection theatre by the studio's Vice President in charge of International Sales and his London representative, and regaled with the traditional Hollywood refreshment table groaning with pastries, fruit, orange juice and coffee. It would be shown the pilot films for the new series and taken to lunch in the studio commissaries in between screening sessions. Back at the hotel the Group would compare notes with Leslie Halliwell, give him its recommendations for the series it wanted him to buy and discuss where in the network schedule they might be played. And Leslie would go off and negotiate.

This unassuming, self-effacing man with an encyclopaedic knowledge of the cinema was universally respected in the film industry and a brilliant negotiator, so the Group seldom failed to get what it wanted at a price the network could afford. The Group's members would have the late afternoons, the evenings and the weekend to themselves, to sit by the hotel pool, meet friends, take in a movie months before its release in Britain, do the Universal studio tour, grab a Reuben's at Nate 'n Al's deli restaurant, and *shop* – when the Group first began to attend the screenings the exchange rate was a mouth-watering $2.80 to the pound. Yes, dear reader, it was hard, back-breaking work, but the valiant members of the Group bravely buckled down to it unfailingly, every year.

I was one of its members on many occasions, as Programme Controller or designated chairman, and the reader can imagine the thrill for this mov-iegoer from childhood to walk through the hallowed gates, the sound stages, the back lots and the commissaries of the legendary studios of Hollywood's past. MGM, Paramount, Warner Brothers, Universal, Disney, 20th Century Fox... Even the projection theatres themselves reflected their glamour: after all, this is where Preston Sturges and Billy Wilder and John Huston had sat and screened their daily rushes. Our own screenings were nothing like as glamorous – we were not watching Greta Garbo or Barbara Stanwyck or Hedy Lamarr – but they could certainly be entertaining, off-screen as well as on, particularly when our group contained both Paul Fox and Mike Scott.

The studio's London representatives were usually left in charge of us, and after five minutes or so of every pilot Paul, as part of his negotiat-ing technique, would cross and re-cross his legs, sigh deeply and mutter "Jesus Christ!" And every time a pilot featured a typical blonde, long-legged, sun-tanned Californian beauty, the susceptible Mike was unable to prevent himself from crying out "*Jesus Christ!*" With this litany of "Jesus Christ!" and "*Jesus Christ!*" emanating from us, the delegation from the Japanese broadcasting organisation passing by must have thought this was not a projection theatre: this was a devotional chapel.

It was also the case that the London sales representatives left in charge of us often knew as little about the pilots we were being shown as we did and had to busk their replies to our questions. Our favourite busker was Ray Lewis. Ray had succeeded Bill Saunders as 20th Century Fox's London rep and was uncomfortably aware that he was as gaffe-prone as his predeces-sor, but he battled on with an air of desperately smiling confidence. On one occasion Ray screened the pilot of a new Fox police series which began most effectively with a pair of detectives, male and female, closing in on a violent criminal gang. They made a tough and attractive duo, with a good line of terse raillery between them, and I called out, "Nice casting, Ray." "Yes," said Ray, busking, smiling, confident as ever, standing to one side of the screen, "The network's thrilled with them. They're going to be as big as Cybill Shepherd and Bruce Willis. We're really going to town with their publicity." Whereupon, in the shoot-out behind him on the screen, the female detective was summarily shot and killed.

In the spring of 1979 the Film Purchase Group returned home in time to vote in the General Election of 3 May, which booted out James Callaghan's Labour Government and brought in Margaret Thatcher and the Conservatives. Twelve days later the Queen's Speech included the announcement that her Government would extend the life of the Independent Broadcasting Authority and that the Authority would be responsible for supervising an additional independent television channel, thereby ending the uncertainty which had surrounded the subject since 1962, when the Pilkington Committee concluded that there would be scope for a fourth channel in due course.

Two major challenges now awaited the companies: the battle to persuade the IBA to allocate the additional channel to ourselves as ITV 2, and the battle to win back our existing contracts when the Authority awarded the new ITV franchises to begin in 1982. We were pretty confident about both. We were in good nick, after all: delivering big audiences, winning many national and international awards, beating the BBC's two channels in the ratings, increasing our advertising and overseas revenue. In the financial year ending April 1979 ITV's revenue increased by 21 percent, with, I'm happy to say, LWT outperforming the rest of the network with an increase of 28 percent. The road ahead was challenging but clear. What could possibly block it?

An immense, unanticipated, additional battle, that's what. Seventy-five days of blank screens, lost audiences, lost programme production, lost advertising revenue. Seventy-five days – ten and a half weeks – of the technicians' strike of 1979.

That's what.

...You Lose Some

The seventies in Britain were years of severe economic hardship. Determined to keep their members' earnings ahead of inflation, which reached a peak of 24.2 percent in 1975, the trade unions battered Government and industry throughout the decade with the withdrawal of labour or the threat of it. A pay strike by the National Union of Mineworkers in 1972 forced the Conservative Government to impose a three-day working week to conserve electricity.

Prime Minister Edward Heath called a General Election in 1974 to decide who ruled Great Britain, Government or the unions. The electorate chose Government but not his, and threw him out. The Wilson Government which succeeded was obliged to apply to the International Money Fund for an emergency hand-out in 1976. In 1978, with the rate of inflation down to 10.1 per cent, Government, with James Callaghan now in charge, attempted to control it further by imposing a ceiling on pay rises of 5 percent. Not a chance. A storm of official and unofficial strikes and stoppages blew a hole in the pay ceiling of both public and private sectors in what was swiftly dubbed the Winter of Discontent, a winter which culminated in the disgrace of unburied dead piling up in mortuaries and uncollected refuse bags piling up in the streets. Government and industry capitulated. The refuse collectors won a pay rise of 11 per cent, the grave diggers 14 per cent, the car workers at Ford 17 per cent, the lorry drivers working for BP and Esso 20 per cent...What would the television unions demand when their national agreements expired in July?

Trade union leaders were powerful and privileged individuals throughout the decade. Their dealings with Government were notoriously conducted with beer and sandwiches in Downing Street. With industry they were more often conducted with champagne and lunches in the Board Room. From my years at ABC and Thames I still remember the Board Room lunches after the Annual General Meetings of our parent company, the Associated British Picture Corporation. Honoured guests always included George Elvin, Alan Sapper's predecessor as General Secretary of the ACTT, together with the General Secretaries of NATTKE, the National Association of Theatrical Television and Kine Employees, and EETPU, the Electrical Electronic Telecommunications and Plumbing Union. Between them, the three unions represented every technician who worked in film or television so it wasn't surprising to find their General Secretaries being honoured by a Corporation which possessed studios, cinemas, and film production and television subsidiaries. In the year of Thames's transmission of *Mountbatten*, Lord Louis himself was also an honoured guest, but you would have been hard put to distinguish who was treated more royally.

As far as the General Secretaries were concerned, ITV was a highly profitable industry and their members were entitled to a piece of the action just as much as ITV's shareholders and executives. The ACTT had already bitten off sizeable chunks of this action with its network blackouts at the beginning of the 1968 franchises and its refusal in 1970 to work in colour without a generous settlement for all its members, including those such as sound engineers for whom colour added not a whit of extra effort or expertise.

Since then, along with NATTKE, the EETPU and the NUJ (the National Union of Journalists), the ACTT had been nibbling away at individual companies, with disputes over such issues as overtime, manning, wage parity, job demarcation and "custom and practice". Women make-up artists went on strike at Thames to protest against the employment of men in their traditionally female occupation. Yorkshire Television suffered a stoppage over who should purchase a pork pie to be used as a prop in a drama production. Granada's *Disappearing World*, a celebrated documentary series about the lives of remote tribes and civilisations, was allowed to limit the size of its camera unit on location in the jungles of Latin America only if the remaining members of the crew flew out with it, with no function to perform, to take their ease in a first class hotel for the duration of the shoot. As a result, the series became too costly to be sustained so *Disappearing World* disappeared.

ITN's NUJ members demanded more money to stand in front of the new lightweight Electronic News Gathering (ENG) cameras; ACTT members refused to work the cameras without special payments for all cameramen, whether they operated the ENG equipment or not, so the new technology had to stay on the shelf. "£2 million pounds of unused equipment lying unused?", Alan Sapper is quoted as saying; "Good, that's a victory for us."

Favourable legislation gave the unions great power throughout British industry, particularly in Independent Television. Here, they operated closed shops, so managements couldn't bring workers in from outside to meet peaks of demand. Any additional work had to be carried out by existing staff on overtime, and overtime was voluntary. The principle of "golden hours" was introduced early in the decade to protect staff from having to work unsocial hours and to compensate them with extra overtime if they were obliged to do so, at rates rising to five or six times the normal. If a statutory ten-hour break between shifts was breached, increasingly more punitive rates were applied, rising to as much as eighteen or even thirty-five times the normal, depending on the circumstances and the ingenuity of a company's workforce. And ITV workforces were nothing if not ingenious.

In LWT's videotape editing rooms the technicians scheduled their voluntary overtime for the convenience not of the directors who wanted to supervise the editing of their programmes but of themselves, usually managing to extend editing sessions into the golden hours after midnight, thereby breaching the ten-hour break between shifts in the process. I was startled one morning to see a large photograph of myself in a *Daily Mail* article under the headline "The Hundred Thousand Pound a Year TV Man". Taking inflation into account, £100,000 in 1979 was the equivalent of more than £450,000 today but the lucky man wasn't me. He was an LWT videotape engineer. The photograph was of the hapless Managing Director who was paying him £100,000 a year in salary and overtime. No wonder the running joke in the industry was What's the difference between an Arab oil sheikh and an LWT videotape engineer? Answer: the Arab oil sheikh doesn't get London weighting.

LWT's union shops were masters of overmanning too. Shortly after the Conservatives came to power, Brian Walden interviewed Mrs Thatcher at 10 Downing Street for *Weekend World*. It was a straightforward two-camera job, but our ACTT shop insisted on covering it with a full camera, lighting and sound crew, and demanded an equally full crew on stand-by. Over 100 LWT technicians were accredited with Number 10's security officials for this simple operation, an egregious example of union strength and management weakness.

But what could we do? What could any ITV chief executive do? Agreements with the unions had been freely entered into. Union customs and practices were underpinned by legislation. Battling a union was likely to provoke a withdrawal of labour, prompting union members in other companies to come out in sympathy. The network could be off the air in a trice, and being off the air meant losing advertising revenue which could never be recouped. The BBC actually saved money when its staff went on strike; ITV lost it for ever. And the IBA couldn't help us: it had no position in a dispute between a company and its workforce. Its only concern was the preservation of the public service and it looked to companies to settle disputes before they could spread to the rest of the network and disrupt it.

This was the melancholy background against which ITV sat down with the television unions at the beginning of July to negotiate the agreement for 1979-80. And we muffed it. With inflation now at 13.4 percent, the unions requested an increase of 25 percent. No doubt they expected the companies to offer a point or so above the rate of inflation and would have looked to settle somewhere between the two. But with consummate misjudgement we offered 9 percent, a figure recklessly below the rate of inflation. We were rewarded with instant rejection, ad hoc industrial action, bans on overtime, and a one-day national strike by NATTKE and EETPU.

A rapidly revised offer of 15 percent to these two unions was made to their national officers, who agreed to recommend it to their members. Encouraged by this reaction we made a similar offer to the ACTT. 15 percent was possibly too little, though it might have succeeded had it been offered earlier, but it was certainly too late now. Thoroughly riled, the membership of all three unions voted for rejection, and management and unions embarked on an inexorable descent to disaster. Walk-outs, stoppages and general disruption resumed. Managements suspended without pay any members of their workforce not working normally. In response, the ACTT called their members out on strike. NATTKE and EETPU members refused to cross the ACTT picket lines and were themselves locked out. By 23 August the entire network was off the air except for ITV's smallest company, Channel Television, whose workers were persuaded that another strike could put it out of business. The longest black-out in the history of Independent Television began.

It lasted 75 days. Everybody suffered. Everybody except the BBC and the electricians. Electricians had little difficulty in finding casual work for their skills outside television; and without any opposition the BBC enjoyed record audiences for both its channels, although bizarrely the ratings books recorded a small regular audience prepared to watch the Disruption of Service captions and listen to the accompanying music rather than turn away from its favourite ITV channel. By the end of October, when the battle-weary companies and union officers finally sat down to discuss the end of hostilities, it was clear that the damage caused by the strike had been extraordinarily far-reaching.

Off the air for ten and a half weeks, the ITV companies lost millions of pounds of advertising revenue. The Treasury lost large sums in taxation and levy. Advertising agencies lost work and commissions and were obliged to cut staff: some of the smaller agencies never fully recovered. Members of ACTT and NATTKE lost their earnings, and were obliged to take casual work where they could find it: more than a few ITV executives found themselves being waited on in cafes, pubs or bars by their own out of work cameramen and vision mixers. *TVTimes* journalists lost their jobs. Half the television bookings for actors, writers, musicians, singers, dancers, variety artistes disappeared overnight. According to Equity, their members alone lost £3 million pounds' worth of television work.

To get the unions back to work we found ourselves obliged to agree pay rises not of the originally requested 25 percent but, over the next 18 months, of between 40 and 50 percent. In exchange, the unions accepted the introduction of ENG, which enabled the companies to retain a modicum of dignity, but we had lost three months of programme production, ITV's autumn schedule was in shreds and it would take many weeks to win the audience back from BBC programmes which had enjoyed a deliriously extended free run. The settlement represented an almost total surrender by the companies, a public and costly humiliation. Bloody, and decidedly bowed, we girded our loins for the next battle: to persuade the IBA to allocate the newly announced fourth television channel to us.

We lost that one too.

It had seemed a simple matter of natural justice. The BBC had been awarded the third television channel; it was only right that ITV should be awarded the fourth. The television manufacturers had taken it as read: the fourth programme button on their new sets was already labelled ITV 2. Even Sir Hugh Greene, now no longer Director General of the BBC or a member of its Board of Governors, argued in a Granada Guildhall Lecture that ITV should in fairness have two channels because the BBC had two. It wasn't just the desire for balanced competition that animated us. A second channel for ITV would provide more scope for our programme-makers, more network opportunities for the regional companies, more efficient use of the studios and facilities we were all required to operate. And for LWT, competing with the BBC at its most aggressive and with a slew of non-competitive programme obligations to incorporate in its brief weekend, it would be heaven-sent.

Lord Annan's Committee of Enquiry had published its Report on the future of broadcasting in 1977, and though it had complimented the IBA on the improvement in ITV's programmes over the past decade, it considered that an ITV 2 controlled by the IBA would provide only more of the same. It proposed instead that the fourth channel be placed in competition with ITV and controlled by a newly created Open Broadcasting Authority, with the IBA responsible merely for the channel's transmission.

There had followed years of widespread debate in the Press, in the House of Commons, in a Government White Paper, in papers submitted by organisations and individuals, by the IBA, the ITCA and the advertisers. Years of conferences and consultations in which the ITV companies and the various pressure groups had argued opposing cases which boiled down essentially in favour of either a complementary ITV 2 with a proportion of its programming provided by independent producers or a competitive fourth channel for freelances and independent producers with a proportion of its programming made available to ITV.

An announcement had finally been made in the Queen's Speech of May 1979 that the Open Broadcasting Authority idea had been jettisoned and the fourth channel would be the responsibility of the IBA, news which had been greeted by the ITV companies with a heartfelt sigh of relief. Unfortunately, some of the ideas put forward in the years of debate following the Annan Report had made their way into the Broadcasting Department of the Home Office, and when the Government's proposals for the fourth channel were announced by Home Secretary William Whitelaw four months later, they were greeted by the companies with not a sigh of relief but a sharp intake of breath.

The new channel was to be a single national service, with no regional variations. The IBA would indeed be responsible for it, but its programming would not be complementary to ITV's. Instead, it would be required to be "distinctive" and expected to find new ways of serving minority and specialist audiences. The ITV companies would not be allowed to dominate its planning or scheduling. The largest practical proportion of its programmes would come from outside the existing system. And though there would be no competition for advertising revenue, the price for the companies' continued advertising monopoly would be the total funding of the new service, to the tune of £18.2 million to cover the financial year 1981–82 and £85.4 million for 1982–83. A subscription, the IBA called it.

Was this the end of the battle for ITV 2?

The IBA had listened to all the post-Annan arguments, and the Home Office had now laid down the parameters within which the Authority's detailed proposals for the fourth channel should be formulated. Those proposals were submitted to the Home Office in November and adopted three months later in the Broadcasting Bill. A new subsidiary, the Channel 4 Television Company, would be established with its own Board, whose non-executive directors would be chosen by the Authority and whose independence would be subject only to the Authority's ultimate control.

The new channel was to have its own distinctive character, with ITV's present programme mix roughly reversed so that about a third of its programming would be intended for the wider audience, though in a style different from that of some of the popular programmes now seen. The other two-thirds would be aimed at those who wanted something not currently provided, though not exclusively of minority appeal. There would be a regular provision for ITN news bulletins, an hour a week of religious programmes, and 15 percent of the channel's output would be devoted to education. The channel's overriding concern would be with the quality of its programmes, with no prescribed rights for any provider to contribute them, though the contribution from independents and regional ITV companies was expected to be given greater emphasis and the role for the major contractors diminished.

So, again, was this the end of the battle for ITV 2?

Yes; it was.

Two down; one to go.

...And You Lose Some More

My two years as Chairman of the Independent Television Contractors Association began in 1980 so the financial hot potato of the Channel 4 subscription fell steaming into my lap. I wrote to Sir Brian Young on behalf of the companies to warn him that if the subscription was too high some of us would no longer be viable and would seek to hand back our contracts. Sir Brian was unmoved. I wrote again, acknowledging the Authority's absolute right to decide the subscription but pointing out that the companies had a legal duty to their shareholders. They were not in business to go out of business.

I put forward a solution which the companies believed would safeguard the needs and rights of both parties. I proposed a 'yardstick', a percentage of our total Net Advertising Revenue, our NAR, which we and the Authority would agree each year, by which the new channel could be sustained and the companies could remain viable. The Director General commended the proposal to the Authority, which not only agreed it but borrowed £30 million to enable us to pay our fourth channel subscription by instalments if needed. Together we settled on 14 to 18 percent of NAR as the band from which the annual subscription rate would be chosen.

This new channel would be a heavy burden on the ITV companies until any revenue generated by it could begin to flow, but there was at least some consolation. Channel 4 would not be competing for our audiences and advertising revenue. Our programme makers would have an opportunity to widen their scope by offering new kinds of programmes to it. And we would have a presence at its heart. A panel of Consultants appointed by the IBA would become its Board, with Edmund Dell, former Labour Minister and City financier, as its Chairman, and filmmaker Richard Attenborough its Deputy Chairman. Four of the Consultants would be chosen from within ITV: Joy Whitby, Yorkshire Television's Head of Children's Programmes; William Brown, Scottish Television's Managing Director; David McCall, Chief Executive of Anglia Television; and yours truly, the only Chief Executive from a major ITV company.

In its account of the composition of the Consultants' Group the IBA's official history describes Bill, David and me as "three of the more free-thinking ITV Managing Directors", and Michael Darlow's book about The Independents acknowledges that "Tesler was known to many of the pro-gramme makers in the Channel 4 Group and was felt to be 'one of the good guys'". But the non-ITV Channel 4 Consultants considered none of us a good guy. All four of us were ITV 2 wolves in Channel 4 clothing, intent on frustrating their purposes. They were a formidable group: Anthony Smith, Director of the British Film Institute; the Hon. Mrs Sara Morrison, a leading member of the Annan Committee; the independent television producer and director Roger Graef; and two educationalists: Anne Sofer, Chairman of the Inner London Education Authority's Schools Committee, and Dr Glyn Tegai Hughes, who had just finished his time as the BBC's National Governor for Wales. For months the Board Room atmosphere was reminiscent of my earlier experiences at non-ITV Boards and Committees, but this time it wasn't a lumber. Being appointed founder-Directors of this totally new kind of television channel was a signal honour, and the four of us very much wanted the channel to succeed. It would offer our frustrated programme-makers creative opportunities which a single over-crowded network could never provide and, quite simply, the greater its success, the less of a drain it would be on ITV's finances.

We were consultants for longer than had been expected. The Broadcasting Bill was held up for three months in its passage through the House of Lords by a little local difficulty in Wales. The Principality had been promised a separate Welsh language fourth channel by both Labour and Conservatives in the run-up to the 1979 General Election, but the successful Conservatives had reneged on their manifesto promise. The final Bill provided for Welsh language programmes to be carried only as occasional opt-outs on the fourth channel in Wales, just as they already were on the BBC and the local ITV channel HTV. Plaid Cymru and its sympathisers were incensed.

In an outbreak of civil disobedience, more than 2000 viewers refused to pay their licence fees, television transmitters were attacked and programmes disrupted by sit-ins in the studios of both BBC and HTV. And in April 1980 Gwynfor Evans, the 68 year-old President of Plaid Cymru, announced a hunger strike. He would begin to starve himself to death on 1 October if the Government did not change its mind. Willie Whitelaw left the Government's response to the last minute but he wasn't prepared to risk the consequences. Towards the end of September I was called out of a meeting of the consultants to take a phone call from the Home Secretary. Why me? I soon discovered why. I was the senior ITV representative on the Board and "We can't let poor Gwynfor die," said Whitelaw "There will be *two* fourth channels, one of them exclusively for Wales, and I'm afraid ITV will have to pay for both."

The amendments tabled in the Lords provided for a new, autonomous Welsh Fourth Channel Authority, responsible for supplying the transmitting body the IBA with its programmes, all of them to be broadcast in the Welsh language. The programmes would come from the BBC free of charge, and from independent producers and the local ITV company on commercial terms. The finance for the service would come from the IBA, which would collect it in rentals from the ITV companies. It would cost us a further £20 million in 1981–82. As compensation, an embarrassed Willie Whitelaw persuaded the Treasury to raise the ITV companies' free slice before paying the Levy from 2 per cent to 2.8 per cent of revenue. The Welsh Fourth Channel – Sianel Pedwar Cymru, or S4C for short – is still alive and well today, the most expensive television service per viewer in the world. Perhaps if John Freeman or Sidney Bernstein had threatened a hunger strike in 1979 we might have had an ITV 2 after all...

The first and most important task for the Consultants was to choose the channel's Chief Executive. There were 25 applicants for the advertised position, seven of whom were short-listed and three called back for a second interview. Sadly, the early Minutes of the Consultants Group were among the IBA documents lost or destroyed when the Authority moved its headquarters from Brompton Road to Foley Street so there is no surviving written record of their names. Having played no part in the sieve process I am unable to identify them, but I knew the three finalists – two of them very well indeed. Jeremy Isaacs had been my Controller of Features at Thames, and John Birt was my current Controller of Features and Current Affairs at LWT. The third contender, Paul Bonner, had been editor of the BBC's Community

Programme Unit and Head of its Science and Features Department. He had been urged by Roger Graef to apply, though he thought there was little point because, he said, "we all know it ought to be Jeremy Isaacs". But he had so impressed the Board that after the interviews he was offered a job which hadn't been advertised, the post of Channel Controller, deputy to the Chief Executive in all programme matters.

Jeremy and John were clearly the leading contenders for the top job. Earlier in the decade, after the Pilkington Report had concluded there could be scope for an additional ITV channel, each of them had submitted a paper to the Ministry of Posts and Communications outlining their respective views on how such a channel might be structured and financed. (John's was composed in collaboration with another outstanding features producer, David Elstein.) Each of them had foreshadowed remarkably closely the structure, finance and remit of the channel they were now applying to run.

John had prepared exhaustively. Together with LWT's Head of Research, Sue Stoessl, and Rod Allen, the producer of LWT's series on the media *Look Here*, he had researched, studied, analysed what Channel 4 should do and how it should be done. He worked out its organisation, its costs and its scheduling in great detail and prepared a 50-page proposal for the channel, including a programme schedule for an entire year, catering to a wide range of minority interest groups. Several of the Consultants were astonished by his prospectus. Roger Graef felt that it "chilled the blood of every single member"; Anthony Smith recalled that "it was rejected, by some almost with contumely. It was felt that someone who had composed so meticulously 'magisterial' an application would not be suitable for the kind of broadcasting organisation we all wanted Channel 4 to be."

John himself acknowledges that in preparing his manifesto he had become too immersed in its detail: "My passionate conviction made me zealous. My application was over-earnest." In discussing our candidates after the interviews, the Consultants in general felt that John lacked humour and warmth. I was able to correct that impression from my personal experience, pointing out that I knew him to be a warm person with a fine sense of humour, capable of a geniality and amiability which, alas, the interview had failed to demonstrate. But John had at least one firm advocate: the Chairman himself. Edmund Dell was very favourably impressed by him.

Jeremy had become a successful independent producer after his departure from Thames. Jeremy Isaacs Productions had been commissioned to make a major series for the BBC on the history of Ireland and a feature-length film for ITV of *A Sense of Freedom*, the story of the convicted murderer Jimmy Boyle. In August of the preceding year, Jeremy had been invited to give the MacTaggart Memorial Lecture at the Edinburgh International Television Festival. His elegant survey of what lay ahead for British television in the coming decade had expanded persuasively on his earlier views of how the fourth channel should be formed and organised, and his *tour d'horizon* became a *tour de force*, widely interpreted as an application for the channel's top job. His formal application now spelled out his priorities if he were to be given it.

Jeremy's Channel 4 would respond to offers from programme-makers from every sector; it would encourage innovation across all its programmes, enable the widest possible range of opinion, accord a high priority to the arts and make, or help to make, feature films for television which could be sold to cinemas abroad. It would also develop its educational commitment to the full, make programmes of special appeal to particular audiences, and maintain a flexible schedule to enable a quick response to changing needs.

All of this chimed well with the stipulations of the Broadcasting Bill, the requirements of the IBA and the hopes and aspirations of the future Channel 4 Board, but some members still had their doubts. Roger Graef reflected on Jeremy's speech at Edinburgh, in which he had appeared committed to ITV 2 as the fourth channel – "whether the channel should actually be called ITV 2 (though in my view it should be and will be)... it is an ITV 2 that we shall have". And in answer to a question about guaranteed access for independent producers he had spoken of a quota of only 15 percent. Edmund Dell felt that he was over-confident, convinced that the job was his and surprised to be called back for a second interview. He thought Jeremy was "extremely Old Labour" and feared for the political balance of the channel if he were appointed – an echo of Howard Thomas's "What about his politics?"

My own concern, also felt by Glyn Tegai Hughes, was to do with the maverick action which had precipitated his departure from Thames. I asked him if he thought he had grown up since he gave the BBC his *This Week* interview with the IRA which the IBA and his own Board had told him he could not show. I know that Jeremy considered my question patronising but also at the back of my mind was the memory of the BAFTA Awards Dinner at which we won five awards for Thames, when I caught Jeremy at our table tearing up little pellets from his dinner roll during the speeches and flicking them at diners at the surrounding tables. I felt my concern about his growing up was justified, but he answered my questions honestly and positively and there was no reason for me or any of the others to doubt his word.

The ITV members of the Consultants Group felt that John and Jeremy were equally capable of handling the job, but clearly what the new channel needed most was someone who would appeal to the independents. This was going to be the independents' channel; John had no experience of the independent production sector; Jeremy was the independents' darling. In the end, the general view was that John was a manager and Jeremy a leader. If some members of the Board had doubts about Jeremy's management of detail and financial matters we would supply the necessary managers to support him. In addition to Paul Bonner, his deputy as Channel Controller on programming matters, we would appoint a deputy on all matters other than programming. In due course, thanks to another inspired suggestion by Roger Graef, this would be Justin Dukes, the Managing Director of the *Financial Times*, who would join us as Channel 4's Managing Director and Deputy Chief Executive.

Channel 4 was entering new and uncharted territory. With no studios, no producers or directors of its own, the channel would be dependent on the independents. As its leader it needed a charismatic Chief Executive who had the respect of the independent sector. Edmund Dell held out as long as he could against the rest of us for John, but in the end he conceded that the Chief Executive should be Jeremy.

It was a grudging concession. Edmund was never fully reconciled to Jeremy's appointment. After the interviews he wrote to John Birt to say that in his view John had been the outstanding candidate; and a dozen years later, at a seminar on *The Making of Channel Four* held by the Institute of Contemporary British History, he said that he'd asked John to show his application to Jeremy and thought that Channel 4 would have been a better channel if Jeremy had bothered to read it. He and Jeremy never hit it off and the tension between them would bedevil the Board's future deliberations. But now the race was on to meet the deadline of 2 November 1982 for the channel's launch, a little more than two years away, and there was a great deal of work to do.

Jeremy, Paul and Justin set about devising the structure of the channel, finding premises for offices and staff, assembling the management team, appointing the editors who would commission the programmes, planning financial and contractual systems, setting up presentation suites and transmission facilities, devising the channel's style, and organising the design of its logo. Above all, they began firing up the creative ambitions of an independent production sector which at the time, without a major market for its programmes, was still very much in its infancy. Jeremy held an open meeting at the Royal Institute to tell independents and would-be independents what the channel's programme needs were likely to be. Almost 600 of them turned up, overflowing the Lecture Theatre, the lobby outside it and the Sobell Theatre below. Sound feeds were hastily organised so that Jeremy's speech could be heard by all of them. It certainly fired them up. The channel was swiftly inundated with programme proposals. The challenge for the channel would lie in choosing the right ones.

Meanwhile, Bill Brown, David McCall and I, together with the other ITV Chief Executives, were facing a challenge of a very different kind. We had lost the battle with the unions, lost the battle for ITV 2 and were now engaged in the battle to win back our franchises when the new contracts for 1982 were allocated. For some of the franchises the specifications published by the IBA in January 1980 incorporated a large amount of tweaking, particularly the two London contracts. An hour and three quarters of Friday's airtime were to be transferred from the weekday London franchise to the weekend. Ron Miller's calculation of the potential advertising value of these additional minutes was between £25,000 and £30,000 a week, around £1.3 million a year, the equivalent of more than £5 million in today's money. It was recognition at last of the disparity between the two franchises but a little more recognition would have been welcome. Why not the rest of Friday?

Several of the IBA transmitters were to be reassigned for the new franchises and London's Bluebell Hill was among them. This was due to be transferred to the South of England, making an already large and profitable region larger and more profitable still. The South would be designated a dual franchise and required to provide a production base in its South East as well as its South. But the transmitter's transfer would reduce the London Region's coverage by an estimated 6 percent, more than cancelling out the value of the weekend's additional airtime and delivering a double whammy to the weekday company. The Midlands too would become a dual franchise, required to provide a production base in the East Midlands as well as the West. And in addition to the existing 15 there would be a franchise for a brand-new breakfast television service.

Who would compete for breakfast television? How would the existing ITV companies fare in the battle for their own franchises? Who would the challengers be? Would the structure and make-up of the network we had consolidated since the awards of 1968 suffer serious change? The applications for all 16 franchises were announced by the IBA on the afternoon of Friday, 4 May 1980; 43 of them. According to the press, "The Great ITV Gold Rush" had begun.

...And Then You Lose Some More Again

It turned out to be more of a Canter than a Rush: there wasn't all that much gold to prospect. The economic forecast for the nation was the opposite of rosy. The financial effect of the previous year's technicians' strike together with the additional burdens of Channel 4 and S4C meant that ITV could no longer be considered a licence to print money. And none of the present incumbents appeared to be there for the taking — which might not have been the case a few years earlier as far as LWT was concerned.

There were no rival applicants at all for the three smallest companies, Grampian, Border and Channel. Only one faced Granada, Yorkshire, Anglia, Ulster and HTV. And only one challenger faced Thames and LWT — the same one. Hughie Green had formed The London Independent Television consortium, which was applying for both contracts with a proposed seven-day service for Londoners, which wasn't on offer, although it said it would accept either franchise if awarded only one. ATV, Tyne Tees, Scottish Television and Westward Television, the contractor for South West England, faced two challengers each. Only the South of England and Breakfast contracts excited anything resembling a Rush, with eight applicants competing for the Breakfast franchise and seven for Southern's. Breakfast television was seen as a new and promising prospect with no incumbent to dislodge and no track record to beat. The already prosperous Southern franchise, enlarged by the addition of the Bluebell Hill transmitter, promised even greater prosperity.

I don't know how the other companies handled the 12 months which followed the publication of the specifications, but LWT was taking no chances. We were all conscious of how close LWT had come to losing the franchise in 1969 and how precarious our position would have been if the present franchises had ended in 1976. John Freeman had recruited Jeremy Potter to the Board, an old friend and colleague from his *New Statesman* days. Jeremy had been Managing Director of Independent Television Publications, publishers of the *TVTimes*. His job now was to oversee, co-ordinate and write our franchise application, working with us to focus our programme strategy, build our case and persuade not only the IBA but our audience that we deserved to retain our franchise. He would make such a good fist of it that a few years later the IBA would commission him to write Volumes Three and Four of the official history of Independent Television in Britain.

Until the IBA published the applications in May we didn't know who would be opposing us, so our nerves were a little taut, our sensibilities a little tender. We held a Programme Department conference at Brighton early in the spring to take a long hard look at our present and planned programme output, in the course of which I'm afraid I looked a little too hard at the output of Tony Wharmby's Drama Department. I thought it had missed a serious trick or two with several of its recent productions and said so in some detail. In his history of LWT, David Docherty records that after the session in which I analysed what I considered its faults, Tony rushed to his hotel room threatening to resign. Happily, Michael Grade and colleagues were able to dissuade him – Tony was too fine a drama producer for us to lose. It would have been kinder if I had taken Tony to one side to give him my analysis of his Department's output, and it has been on my conscience ever since.

John Birt's Features and Current Affairs Department came particularly well out of our discussions, with Barry Cox proposing a new kind of local current affairs programme to occupy an hour of Friday evening's proposed extra airtime. This would in due course become *The Six O'Clock Show*, one of the most watched regional programmes in British television, a bright and original mix of news, features, current affairs and light entertainment hosted by Michael Aspel, Danny Baker and Janet Street-Porter. It would give one young current affairs researcher his first show as a producer and his first real opportunity to make a name for himself. The name? Greg Dyke.

A month later the IBA published the contract applications and we learned that our only opposition was to be Hughie Green's London Independent Television. We pored over its proposed creative and management personnel and the programmes it was offering and thought that, on the whole, it was unlikely to prove a threat to either Thames or ourselves. It appears that Brompton Road thought so too. The IBA staff believed that the quality of the programmes which LIT might provide was extremely uncertain. One internal memo commented that "London Independent Television, on paper at least, hardly hangs together as a group with any clear identity, yet it is applying for the major franchises in the ITV system." But we didn't let up: who knew what the detailed terms and conditions in the contract might be? We held public meetings in town halls and local theatres across London with the aim of getting the public firmly on our side; and we attended the IBA's Final Public Meeting in Caxton Hall at which we, Thames and LIT faced the public and each other in open forum.

The Interviews were held in November 1980 in the big Conference Hall at Brompton Road. The venue needed to be big. Applicants were allowed eleven representatives and four consultants and faced the full panoply of the Authority: twelve Members and ten of their most senior officers from the Director General to the relevant Regional Officer plus the IBA Secretary. As in the interviews 17 years earlier when the original ITV contracts were reviewed, the procedure was forbiddingly formal, with questions put by each of the Members in turn to the Chairman of the applicant group, but LWT's group had no need of a Scots pipe band to rescue it. John Freeman fielded the questions brilliantly, indicating which of us would answer them, with a few introductory remarks in each case to give us a precious half-minute or so in which to focus our answers. There were no hiccups. None of us had to kick ourselves – or anyone else – on the way out. But no one in the serried ranks of the Authority raised his mortar-board either.

On Sunday, 28 December the Chairmen and Managing Directors of the applicant groups were each summoned at an appointed time to the Authority's offices at 70 Brompton Road. Those representing the current contractors were received at quarter-hour intervals in the morning by the Authority's Chairman, Lady Plowden, and its Deputy Chairman Lord Thomson (who was due to succeed Bridget Plowden as Chairman four days later) together with the Director General Sir Brian Young and the Deputy Director General Anthony Pragnell. We were each in turn handed a letter from the Chairman advising us of our fate, and then taken to the Chairman's office for congratulations or commiserations as appropriate. The successful companies were handed a letter from the Secretary setting out the terms and conditions of the offer. The new applicants were received and handed their letters in the afternoon; the successful few met the Chairman; the rest were bidden farewell by Authority staff. The names of the winners were announced at a press conference that afternoon. We were one of them.

How did the franchise battle go for the other companies?

We lost two of them at the very outset. Westward Television had been damagingly weakened by Board Room struggles for control; its application in May had to be amended in November just before its Final Interview, where it was still without a designated Managing Director. It lost to Television South West (TSW).

Southern Television lost to a consortium put together by James Gatward, an accomplished and ambitious independent drama producer designated Managing Director of its proposed television company Television South (TVS). We shall meet him again in these pages.

The industry was stunned, Southern was outraged. The Authority explained that Southern had been 'overtaken' rather than 'rejected'. When the company asked in what way it had failed, Lady Plowden said it was not a question of failure: Southern was 'a victim of the system'. The official history records that "On the arguments and reasoning which lay behind the extinction of this fine company the lips of the members of the Authority remained resolutely sealed."

Other colleagues were wounded, one of them grievously. At the end of 1974, the IBA Chairman Lord Aylestone had given my old ATV boss Lew Grade notice that he was expected to retire on his 70th birthday in January 1976. It was 21 months later, in September 1977, before *Lord* Lew – he had been granted a peerage in 1976 – finally acceded to the Authority's pressure. Lord Windlesham was appointed the company's Chairman and Managing Director. Bill Ward also retired and was succeeded as Director of Programmes by Charles Denton, a fine documentary producer who had risen to become the company's Head of Documentaries.

When the terms and conditions of the new dual-franchise contract were published the company had reacted smartly, re-forming itself as ATV Midlands, with regional public figures appointed as Vice-Chairman East Midlands and Vice-Chairman West Midlands respectively, each half of the region with its own General Manager. But the problem of its London-based ownership and control remained. ATV Midlands was still a wholly owned subsidiary of ATV Corporation, now re-named Associated Communications

Corporation (ACC), a vast entertainment conglomerate controlled from London by Lew Grade and Jack Gill, its Chairman and Deputy Chairman.

The contract was formally offered to ATV Midlands, but with some stern provisions. ACC would be permitted to hold no more than 51 per cent of the new company; the remaining 49 per cent would have to be allocated within the region. The role of Chairman had to be separated from that of Managing Director and only one of them could be an ACC nominee. The non-executive directors of the company were to be divided equally between ACC nominees and others. There were to be separate area Boards for the West and East Midlands, but here again the regional Chairmen and General Managers could not both be ACC representatives. And the name ATV Midlands was disallowed; the new, substantially different, dual-franchise company had to have a new name.

ATV limped from the battlefield mortally wounded, its identity lost after nearly three decades. The new franchise-holder called itself Central Independent Television. Having set it up, Lord Windlesham left not only the company but the industry. His successor as Chairman was a Birmingham businessman. Bob Phillis, Jeremy Potter's successor as Managing Director of Independent Television Publications, was appointed Managing Director.

On 1 January 1982, when Central went on the air for the first time, ATV ceased to exist as a broadcaster. Its Elstree studios were closed down and eventually sold to the BBC. Six months later, having fired Jack Gill and lost control of ACC to Australian business tycoon Robert Holmes à Court, Lew Grade resigned from the company he had founded and went on to continue his pursuit of the holy grail of feature film success. He would never return to ITV, the industry he had helped to create and which he had enlivened so colourfully for so many years.

Yorkshire and Tyne Tees, the companies jointly owned by their holding company Trident Television, retained their franchises. But the Authority required Yorkshire Television to support the role of its Managing Director and Programme Controller, Paul Fox, by appointing a Joint Managing Director with particular responsibility for the company's industrial relations. It also required radical changes in the control of the two companies. Yorkshire Television and Tyne Tees Television would have to be owned and managed separately, their shareholdings opened up to people living in their respective areas, including those who had supported their rival consortia. The Authority required firm proposals to that end within two months, after which it would reconsider the offer of both contracts.

The deadline was not met. Trident held out for as large a degree of control as possible, even threatening court action on the grounds that the Authority was exceeding its powers with its requirement. The Authority gave the companies a final deadline, the end of March, at the same time inviting any other interested parties to submit their proposals by the same date, and two groups took up the invitation. Trident knew it was beaten and withdrew its resistance. In alleviation, the Authority agreed that an advertising sales agreement could continue to operate between Yorkshire and Tyne Tees, to be reviewed after an initial two years.

As for the Joint Managing Directorship, Paul Fox went so far as to engage an *Assistant* Managing Director, Tony Preston, to handle the company's industrial relations, and the Authority accepted the compromise. When it suggested that he should reside nearer his franchise area than his home in Hampstead, Paul moved up the road to Radlett. The Authority accepted that too. Persuasive person, Paul.

The London companies' wounds had been inflicted before battle was joined. We sustained no further injuries but both smarted from the cut in our audience coverage by the transfer of Bluebell Hill. Thames also suffered from the cut in its Friday airtime which, to no avail, George Cooper complained was 'totally unfair and unacceptable'. Most of the other companies suffered flesh wounds of varying severity. Only two were unscathed. Border was praised for its performance and the strong local identity it had achieved in its region. And although the members of the Authority had, in the official history's words, been continually exasperated by Granada's waywardness, Granada was still one of their favourite companies and the offer of a new contract once again paid tribute to the distinction of its contributions to the network.

Who were the other favourites? Thames and London Weekend Television seemed not to be among them, although in announcing LWT's award the IBA noted with approval the emergence within the company of 'diverse good qualities over recent years'. The official history restricts itself to saying that it would have been a bold act on the Authority's part to eject either of the established contractors in its largest region in favour of an untried applicant. The cruel irony of that statement, in light of the way the Authority would act in the next round of franchise awards, will echo through the years, but in 1980 the history merely records that there was a general acceptance that Thames and London Weekend Television, the Authority's controversial creations of 1967, had earned a second innings.

So the franchise battlefield was strewn with casualties. Westward and Southern slain outright, ATV mortally wounded, Trident dismembered; only Border and Granada erect among the walking wounded. The press reaction to this turmoil was severe. The franchise process was no better than a lottery, the Authority was guilty of erratic judgements, it was a lay body passing judgement on professionals, there was no way of knowing the particular reasons in particular instances why the Authority had chosen some applicants and rejected others...and so on.

And there were certainly questions to be asked. If Southern had not failed, why was 'this fine company' not allowed to continue? Why did the Authority place so much emphasis on local ownership and control when it was programme makers who were relevant to a company's performance, not shareholders? Where were the Midlanders among the new shareholders of Central? Neither of its rival consortia had taken up the offer to invest in the company; in the end, its major shareholders were Robert Maxwell, Sears, Ladbrokes and D.C. Thomson, the Scottish publishers of comic books, none of them any more associated with the Midlands than ACC. In an unpremeditated comment about the franchise awards during his speech at the Royal Television Society Conference in Cambridge later that year, Lord Thomson said 'there must be a better way'. It was a phrase which would come to haunt him.

There would certainly be a *different* way, which not many of the participants in the next franchise round would consider better. But that's another story, a decade away. We haven't yet completed the roll call of winners and losers of this one.

Breakfast, and Back at the Ranch

The members of the Authority faced an embarrassment of riches with the applications for their 16th franchise, breakfast television. Not for the first time they chose the richest. And not for the first time they chose wrong.

The applications were packed with prestigious names. AM Television sported as its Chairman Christopher Chataway, the former Conservative minister responsible for broadcasting. Harold Evans, the editor of *The Sunday Times*, was its full-time executive in charge of news coverage, and its team of leading professionals included David Elstein, Jonathan Dimbleby and Sarah Hogg. The ITN bid boasted a Board packed with broadcasting experience, combining ITN's Editor and chief executive, David Nicholas, with four of ITV's biggest guns – John Freeman, Sir Denis Forman, Bryan Cowgill and Paul Fox.

Daytime Television's senior executives included the general manager of Visnews, the editor of *The Times*'s business news, the editorial director of LBC and Independent Radio News, and the Press Association's editor-in-chief. Good Morning Television featured experienced newsmen like Julian Pettifer and Peter Hardiman Scott on its Board but was entertainment-orientated enough to include Ned Sherrin and Tim Rice among its other executives. Morning Television's Chairman was Robin Scott, former Deputy Managing Director of BBC Television, and its chief presenter was David Dimbleby. Daybreak Television was chaired by Stuart Young, later to be Chairman of the BBC, with an Executive Programme Committee including Alan Whicker, Drusilla Beyfus and Mike Brierley and a strong ATV element of professional expertise on its Board, with Francis Essex as its Managing Director and Dennis Basinger, the Controller of ATV's Elstree Studios, in charge of its proposed studio complex on the Elstree site.

But the most star-studded application, featuring more broadcasting experience than any other applicant apart from ITN, was TV-AM, a consortium inspired and organised like the original 1967 London Weekend consortium by David Frost. David had put together what was swiftly dubbed a dream team of the foremost television presenters of the day: Anna Ford, Robert Kee, Michael Parkinson, Angela Rippon, Esther Rantzen and David himself. Esther Rantzen subsequently withdrew because of her pregnancy, leaving a quintet which gave the press an even better tag to play with: they were now the Famous Five, all of whom would appear exclusively on screen for TV-AM and serve on the company's programme committee alongside two members of the Board: Director of Programmes Nick Elliott – a sad loss for LWT – and Director of Features Michael Deakin, producer of *Johnny Go Home* and other documentaries for Yorkshire Television.

TV-AM's Board also included former Labour cabinet minister Sir Richard Marsh and businessman Timothy Aitken, whose company Aitken-Hume, jointly owned with his cousin Jonathan, was TV-AM's largest shareholder. It had not yet appointed a Managing Director but its Chairman was Peter Jay, whose remarkable career encompassed twelve years' experience in television, most notably with LWT's *Weekend World*, ten years as Economics Editor of *The Times*, six at the Treasury and two as British ambassador in Washington. The thesis he had developed five years earlier with John Birt about 'the bias against understanding' in television news, had now developed into 'a mission to explain' and the Famous Five and their Board Room colleagues were dedicated to making the news more meaningful, merging it with current affairs in order to explain its context and implications. But at breakfast-time? With the company's programme policy run by the company's programme makers? With no Managing Director, no chief executive in charge?

The IBA record had shown that the Croydon audience at the Authority's final public meeting on breakfast television favoured a service with elements of entertainment and a light and cheerful treatment of its news. The official history makes it clear that the Authority's programme staff tried to remind members of the near-collapse of LWT at the beginning of the 1968 franchises and warned them of the dangers of awarding a contract to another group 'too studded with stars for its own good'. The IBA's final decision was a pretty close-run thing. Lady Plowden and the Director of Television and his staff were in favour of Christopher Chataway's AM Television; another member's preference was for ITN. Lord Thomson himself thought that a breakfast-time franchise could wait: TV-AM would be competing for ITV's advertising revenue and there were major contract changes as well as the financial impact of Channel 4 and S4C to be absorbed before the system could sustain another drain on its revenue.

But, by a single vote, TV-AM's idealism won the day. As the IBA's staff had warned, and as time would demonstrate, it was a risky call, made riskier by the decision to delay the start of the service for two years to clear the way for Channel 4's launch in the autumn of 1982. The delay would give the BBC all the time it needed to prepare a competitive breakfast-time service and get it on the air weeks in advance of TV-AM. And theirs would be a service short on idealism and long on entertainment.

Meanwhile, back at the LWT ranch, Programme Department had been making plans not only for its additional Friday airtime but also for the new programme-making opportunities of Channel 4. Aware of John Birt's bitter disappointment at not winning the Channel's top job, Michael Grade had come to John's rescue by giving him a different kind of Channel 4 challenge. He had appointed John as the LWT link with the channel, taking responsibility for co-ordinating all our programme offers. In its first year Channel 4 commissioned 194 hours from us: £6 million pounds' worth of programmes. For years we would be its largest programme supplier, producing series of programmes on books, music, art and history, and factual magazines for the black and Asian communities with *Black on Black* and *Eastern Eye*.

We created major entertainment series like the ground-breaking 90-minute *Saturday Live*, situation comedies like *No Problem*, drama series like *A Married Man* from Piers Paul Read's novel and *Mapp and Lucia* from E. F. Benson's gloriously funny saga of middle England rivalry. Also game shows like *Babble* and *Tell the Truth*, Clive James's oddball chat show *The Late Clive James*, mock trials of Richard III and Lee Harvey Oswald with leading British counsel for Prosecution and Defence, a series of three hour-long interviews by Brian Walden of James Callaghan on the former Prime Minister's newly published memoirs... I say three but there were in fact only two and a half. The third programme was about defence. Mr Callaghan declined to answer Brian Walden's questions on Labour and the Bomb and

Brian called the interview to a halt. I don't recall how Channel 4 filled the missing half hour.

The channel's budgets for individual commissions were less than lavish and John was concerned not to lose money for the company in fulfilling them, so with Chris Turner from Accounts Department he set up a system by which, for the first time in British television, the total cost of programmes could be assessed. Not just the direct cost of their performers, writers, musicians, sets and so on but also the indirect cost of the facilities and support services employed in making them, together with an estimated proportion of the entire company's staff and overheads. The total sum of all these costs was hair-raising and there was no way that Channel 4 could pay it, but armed with that information John was able to ensure that our programmes were sold at a fair price, and the exercise was an invaluable marker for the future, when total costing of programmes would become the norm for the entire industry. With the Channel 4 link to supervise and his Features and Current Affairs Department to run, 1981 was a busy year for John. It was about to become significantly busier.

Michael Grade signed a new contract with us at the beginning of the year. It didn't call for much negotiation. John Freeman and I were delighted with his achievements and his autobiography indicates that the delight was reciprocated: "I had no desire to be anywhere else in TV: John Freeman and Brian Tesler were a joy to work for and I had an excellent team supporting me. I was well contented." Whatever contract I placed in front of him, he said, he would sign without a quibble, and I made sure that the contract was quibble-free.

Sadly, however, Michael's personal life was not equally well contented. His marriage had ended and its settlement had plunged him into financial crisis. His house had gone to his ex-wife and their two children, he had failed to build up any significant capital and he had a huge overdraft to cope with at the bank. So when he received an offer from the American production company Tandem to run its TV business in Hollywood, with a starting salary of $250,000 a year, he found it difficult to resist. He came to me with his predicament.

Tandem, later to be named Embassy Productions, specialised in situation comedy. Its founder and President, comedy writer Norman Lear, an old friend of his, was retiring and wanted him to take over as President. It would be a new beginning for Michael, a different kind of creative challenge and

Steamboat Shuffle 1960.
Above: designer and future TV and film director Bob Fuest's preparatory sketch for the boat.
Right: the show in action.
Below: ABC programme heads in 1960. Sydney Newman, Supervisor, Drama; David Southwood, Chief of Outside Broadcasts; and BT, Supervisor, Features and Light Entertainment.

Sammy Davis Jr Meets the British 1960. *Above:* Sammy leading the kids across the Battersea Funfair campus, a camera dolly moving out of the shot to a different position. *Below:* Sammy and Lionel Blair doing their "Shall We Dance?" number back in Teddington Studios .

Candid Camera 1960. *Above:* Bob Monkhouse viewing the dailies; Jonathan Routh is on the right of the screen he is watching. *Left & Below:* The celebrated car with no engine stunt.

ABC TV NEWS ▼

Thank Your Lucky Stars 1961. *Left:* the cover of ABC house magazine *ABC TV News*: Light Entertainment Controller Philip Jones *(inset)* and the cast of the Merseyside edition of *Thank Your Lucky Stars*, ITV's entry at 1964's Golden Rose of Montreux Festival of Light Entertainment. The Beatles are in the back row, presenter Brian Matthew in the centre of the middle row, Cilla Black in the front.
Below:
The Avengers 1961. Leonard White giving a direction to Patrick Macnee.

ABC TV NEWS

THE HOUSE MAGAZINE OF ABC TELEVISION & IRIS PRODUCTIONS — No. 13   AUGUST, 1962

THE BEST PEOPLE READ . . . . . .

This is Sinatra! 1962. "The best people read ABC TV News". The Trainee Director on the cover of the August 1962 edition of the house magazine is BT's son Simon who, at seven months, seemed to have acquired all the control-room gestures and facial expressions of a budding TV director. *Below: World of Sport* 1965. The studio production team, with front row L to R John Bromley, Eamonn Andrews, producer Geoffrey Gilbert, executive producer Lloyd Shirley and director David Wickes.

Tempo 1961.
Above: Peter Sellers as the magnificently bad Scottish poet William McGonagall. *Right:* Editor Kenneth Tynan with Truman Capote.

Left: with the Archbishop of Canterbury, Dr Michael Ramsey, and Dr Tom Murchison, Moderator of the General Assembly of the Church of Scotland, for an ecumenical gathering at Thames to view our documentary on the Russian Orthodox Church.

ITV'S CHRISTMAS PROGRAMMES

Above: "Hello!..." ITV's first Programme Controllers Group, at its press conference for Christmas 1968. L to R: Frank Copplestone, seconded from the IBA as Chairman, Bill Ward for ATV, BT for Thames, Cyril Bennett for LWT, David Plowright for Granada, Donald Baverstock for Yorkshire TV.
Right: "...and Goodbye!" The Rowlandson cartoon presented to Cyril Bennett when he left the Group in 1969.

Above: Thames's Programme Department 1968. L to R: Guthrie Moir, Controller, Religion & Education; Grahame Turner, Controller, Outside Broadcasts; Sue Turner, Producer, Children's Programmes; Kim Mills, Deputy Controller, Drama; BT; Geoffrey Lugg, Head of Presentation; Muir Sutherland, Programme Coordinator; Lloyd Shirley, Controller, Drama; Philip Jones, Controller, Light Entertainment; Jeremy Isaacs, Controller, Features & Children's Programmes; Patrick Downing, Head of Design.

1970. *Above:* Howard Thomas and BT, poised to nail Good Luck horseshoes to the front door of Thames's new Studios building in Euston. *Left:* Sir Brian Young, Robert Fraser's successor as ITA director-general, meets Mike and Bernie Winters at Teddington Studios.

Above: Thames's BAFTA winners 1972:
L to R: Patrick Downing, Howard Thomas,
Benny Hill, Jeremy Isaacs, BT, David Bell
and Philip Jones.
Left: with friend and colleague Philip Jones.
Below: 1974. Leaving Thames. BT's nominated
successor Jeremy Isaacs is presented with the key
to the executive loo. Thames's new Managing
Director George Cooper is behind Jeremy.

Left: LWT's BAFTA winners 1975. From L to R: David Bell, Bill McPherson, Stanley Baxter, Cyril Bennett, Linda Beighton, Peter Barkworth, Humphrey Burton, Peter Jay.

Above: With Cyril Bennett, Ron Miller, John Freeman and a cake presented to LWT by a major advertising agency to mark the success of one of Ron's ingenious sales schemes. Cyril's expression suggests that he knows it was his programmes that made the success possible, but for how long?
Left: with Audrey and Bryan Cowgill.

Above: Succeeding Howard Thomas as President of the Television and Radio Industries Club in 1970. Between us and on the extreme right are two distinguished previous TRIC Presidents, Lord Hill and Norman Collins. Behind us are two of our distinguished fellow guests, Robin Scott and Huw Wheldon.
Left: John Freeman, who rescued LWT's franchise, revived its morale, rebuilt its strength and ran it with consummate skill for 13 years.

Top: Visiting us: Lord Thomson, new Chairman of the IBA/ITC, meets
members of LWT's Programme Department and other colleagues. L to R in
the front row: John Birt, Humphrey Barclay, Michael Grade, Judith Thomas
(Company Secretary), Lord Thomson, Sue Stoessl (Head of Research), BT; in
the background John Blyton (Controller, Programme Management), Roy van
Gelder (Head of Personnel), Vic Gardiner (General Manager).
Middle: Visiting them: The IBA gives a reception to mark the Prix Italia Award
for *Cream in my Coffee.* L to R: Lord Thomson, author Dennis Potter, producer
Kenith Trodd, BT, Peggy Ashcroft, Lionel Jeffries, Martin Shaw. *Bottom:*
John Freeman and BT in Brompton Road on the way to hear the ITA decision
regarding LWT and the 1982 Franchise Renewals.

1982. *Top:* BT with two future lords a-leaping: Michael Grade leaping out to the States, John Birt leaping in to Michael's shoes as Director of Programmes.

Above: The board of London Weekend Television Ltd in 1982. Back row L to R: Robin Scott, Peter McNally, Ron Miller, Vic Gardiner, Peter Cazaly, Jeremy Potter, Roger Harrison, Roland Freeman, John Birt. Front Row L to R: BT, Judith Thomas, John Freeman, Heather Brigstocke, David Montagu. *Left:* with the man who originally launched LWT, David Frost.

LWT IN VISION

magazine for the staff of LWT   Spring 1987

SUCCESS!

LWT (Holdings) shares soared again when news of the company's half-year results were released on 19 March. Pre-tax profits doubled from £6.13 million to £12.7 million in the first half, with LWT's performance comfortably outstripping the rest of ITV.

'We have had an outstanding first half,' said Holdings chairman Christopher Bland. And the company's results were greeted as 'spectacular' by City experts as shares surged ahead at the news.

* Fair Shares — see page three.

IT'S GREG!

Greg Dyke is back at LWT. The former current affairs editor returns as Director of Programmes following John Birt's move to the BBC as Deputy Director-General. And with Alan Boyd taking Greg's job at TVS, Marcus Plantin is LWT's new Controller of Entertainment.

Announcing Greg's appointment, Brian Tesler, Chairman and Managing Director of LWT, said: 'It is good to welcome Greg Dyke back to LWT, where he first made his programme mark. That experience, together with his subsequent success as the director of programme departments outside the company, equips him admirably for his new role at LWT.'

Greg, a 39-year old Londoner, said: 'I am delighted to be returning to LWT as Director of Programmes. I spent six happy years with the company and find the new prospect an exciting challenge. I have very much enjoyed my time with TVS and would like to thank the board and all my colleagues there for the friendship and help they have given me over the past three years.'

Greg worked for six years in LWT's Current Affairs and Features depart-

1984. *Top:* A Toast to John Freeman on his retirement. Ron Miller, BT, Jeremy Potter, Peter McNally, Vic Gardiner, John Birt, Peter Cazaly, John Freeman.
Above: A more private toast: Audrey and BT with John and his wife Judith.
Left: LWT's staff magazine breaks the news of Greg Dyke's return as Director of Programmes.

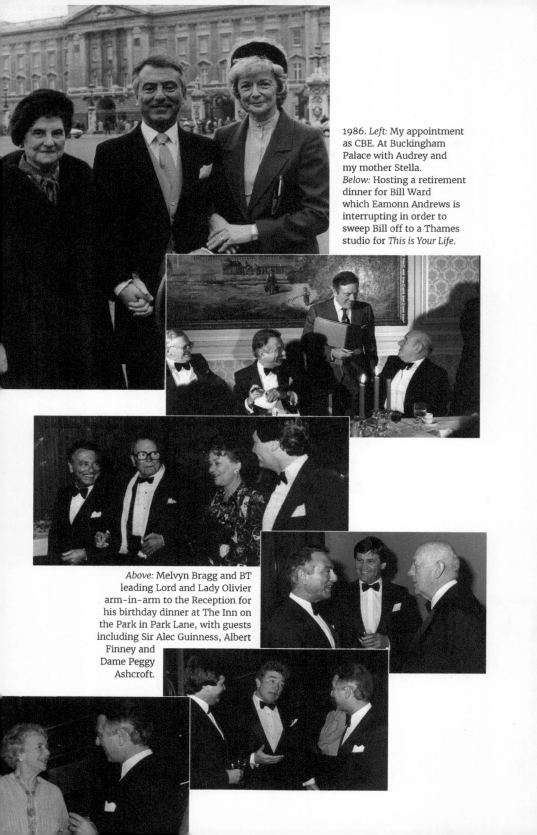

1986. *Left:* My appointment as CBE. At Buckingham Palace with Audrey and my mother Stella.

Below: Hosting a retirement dinner for Bill Ward which Eamonn Andrews is interrupting in order to sweep Bill off to a Thames studio for *This is Your Life*.

Above: Melvyn Bragg and BT leading Lord and Lady Olivier arm-in-arm to the Reception for his birthday dinner at The Inn on the Park in Park Lane, with guests including Sir Alec Guinness, Albert Finney and Dame Peggy Ashcroft.

Above: Backstage at the Royal Variety Performance
1987, presenting Shirley Bassey to H.M. The Queen.
Left: Screen shots from television coverage of the
launch night of SuperChannel, introduced by the
Prime Minister the Rt Hon Margaret Thatcher,
who also visited the control room.
Below: with Princess Diana: "We nearly lost you there!"

Diana. 1994.

Above: Celebrating LWT's 1992 franchise win: L to R: strategist Tony Cohen, Director of Corporate Affairs Barry Cox, Finance Director Peter McNally, BT, Chairman Christopher Bland, Group Chief Executive Greg Dyke, Chief Accountant Tony Kay and financial associate Neil Canetty-Clarke.
Right and below: Two colourful contributions to the volume of tributes presented to BT on his retirement in 1994: Bob Monkhouse's cartoon and a collage from fellow aficionado of American crime fiction Christopher Bland.

Just another old clown you launched & kept afloat...
MUCH LOVE... BOB (monkhouse)

T. JEFFERSON PARKER

LAGUNA HEAT

KILLER'S PAYOFF

ELMORE LEONARD

SIDESWIPE

CHARLES WILLEFORD

ED McBAIN

SHOTGUN

AN 87th PRECINCT MYSTERY

to celebrate our shared appreciation of the finest aspects of American literature — its violence, sex and bad language. Chris Bland a much needed opportunity to resolve his financial problems. How could I deny it to him? LWT certainly couldn't begin to match the salary, let alone its annual bonuses and its promise of unlimited first-class air tickets to visit his children or bring them out to visit him. We agreed that I would release him from his contract at the end of the year, which would give me time to find his successor. Did he have any suggestions? "It has to be John Birt," he said.

Five years earlier, when I appointed Michael Director of Programmes, I had indeed considered John as a possible alternative. His performance at the Selsdon Park conference had been impressive, particularly in his forensic analysis of Programme Department's problems, but he was not the all-rounder I needed at that time. His programme skills had been exercised almost exclusively in Current Affairs and I thought they would be more effectively employed in regenerating LWT's Features and Current Affairs output. But as co-ordinator of our Channel 4 offers he had been working closely for nearly two years with every section of Programme Department. He now knew the other departmental programme makers as working colleagues. More important, they now knew John.

John and his Department had been viewed since Selsdon Park with a degree of suspicion and even active dislike because of the vast growth of Features and Current Affairs. I had been aware of it myself: in my introductory words at the Brighton Conference in 1980 I remarked that the Department seemed to be seen by some as a cross between a cuckoo in the nest and The Incredible Hulk. But I believed that the shared experience of the past two years had abated the suspicion and de-activated the dislike.

I thought that, though he lacked the instinctive flair that had made Michael so effective as Director of Programmes, John's assiduity and analytical skills could make him an adept successor, though I hadn't reckoned on his having to be one so soon. First, I thought, I really ought to try to succeed where Howard Thomas had failed in persuading Bill Cotton to join Independent Television. I might have realised that I would get nowhere. Bill and I enjoyed a happy lunch-hour recollecting the past and speculating about the future but, however tempting he found the prospect of our working together again, he could not be moved. The barnacle on the soul of the BBC could not be prised away.

On the day he returned from his summer holiday, Michael Grade brought John up to my office. We told him that Michael was leaving LWT at the beginning of 1982 to work for Tandem Productions in Hollywood and that I wanted John to succeed him as Director of Programmes. "This is all happening years earlier than I planned," I said. "I had hoped that in due course Michael would succeed me and you would succeed Michael, but his departure has fast-forwarded the whole process. If you think you are up to it, I'd like you to take over now." It was clearly a bolt from the blue for John; I'd never seen him so taken aback. "Go away and think about it for a few days," I said "and then come and tell me if you'd like the job. Michael recommended you for it: he'll fill you in on what it entails; and I'm happy to answer any questions you might want to ask before you make up your mind."

A few days later, when he returned to the office, John had only two questions to ask. The first was "Why me? I'm a totally different person from Michael." I told him that most television executives were different from Michael. I knew he didn't have Michael's instinct for programmes and programme schedules but I believed that, underpinned by research and analysis, he would come to the same conclusions intellectually that Michael would have reached instinctively. It might take him longer, but he'd get there in the end. John accepted my offer. His only other question, as he left my office, was "Will I be ITV's youngest ever Director of Programmes?" "How old are you?" "Thirty-seven." "Sorry, John. Michael was thirty-three. And so was I."

At Michael's last appearance at the LWT Board as our Director of Programmes I asked the Chairman if I might say a few words about his tenure now that it was so nearly concluded. Michael was leaving us on a conspicuously high note. Our programme department was in a most healthy and efficient state. Our overall ratings performance was better than it had been for years. Our programmes were earning an unprecedented number of international awards and record overseas sales. All this, I said, had been achieved directly or indirectly by Michael's hard work, his creative ability and the entrepreneurial dash he had brought with him from the light entertainment agency world which he had inhabited before Cyril Bennett made an honest man of him.

How odd it was, I said, that this fugitive from the Finsbury Park Empire should have made us the most respected producers in ITV of programmes about the arts, religion and current affairs. Thanks to Michael, according to that week's edition of *Time Out* magazine we were even the producers of a series which was "a dangerous development towards the techno-revivalist nightmare apocalypse". That series – in case you, dear reader, like the Board, fail to recognise its description – was Bruce Forsyth's *Play Your Cards Right*. Michael handed over to John at the end of December. There is a happy photograph of the three of us celebrating the occasion on the windswept terrace of the 15th floor of Kent House, with Michael and John, the once and future Lords, on either side of me. They would work together again in the course of their remarkable careers, but never so harmoniously.

Barry Cox took over John's Features and Current Affairs Department with ease. David Bell and his lieutenants Alan Boyd and Humphrey Barclay continued to run Light Entertainment with their customary brio. Tony Wharmby wanted to return to production – I hoped not because of my comments at the Brighton Conference – and resume a career as producer, director and writer of drama both in Britain and America, where he would become particularly successful; but, happily for LWT, Nick Elliott had had a change of heart about his role at TV-AM. "As time went by," he says, "it became clearer and clearer that we had no structure, no money, too many stars and a muddled set of ideas. So I rang Peter Jay and quit."

We offered him the job of running Drama Department as well as the Arts programmes he had previously controlled. John was confident of Nick's suitability for the job because he knew that drama had been Nick's abiding interest since his University days with the OUDS and the ETC. But for at least one member of the Department his appointment was another instance of aggrandisement on the part of Features and Current Affairs and Nick was greeted with hate-mail vicious enough for an ex-policeman to be called in to investigate it. In a sequence that could have come out of a TV detective story, the ex-cop failed to nail the person responsible but Nick's PA stayed late one night and tested all the typewriters in the Department until she found a type-face matching the hate-mail. The culprit was confronted, admitted his guilt, and was invited to leave.

As for the programmes, John had inherited enough from Michael to give him time to put his own stamp on the Department's output. It was already there of course on Features and Current Affairs but light entertainment programmes like *An Audience with…*, *A Fine Romance*, *Cannon and Ball*, *Game for a Laugh* and *It'll be Alright on the Night* still had years of life in them. It was the same in Drama with *The Gentle Touch*, *The Professionals*, and more Agatha Christie adaptations – this time, *Partners in Crime*, the novels featuring amateur detectives Tommy and Tuppence. There were also two of Michael's last drama commissions, the wartime romance *We'll Meet Again* and a run of *Saturday Night Thrillers*. Unfortunately, however, John also inherited one of ITV's unpredictable cycles of advertising revenue booms and busts – at the wrong end of the cycle.

The ITV companies had recovered surprisingly swiftly after the technicians' strike of 1979. In the financial year containing the strike ITV's revenue decreased by 4.5 percent – though, thanks to the hard graft of our Programme and Sales Departments, LWT's revenue actually went up by 2 percent. By the end of 1980, however, ITV as a whole had bounced back spectacularly and in the financial year 1980-81 LWT's own revenue increased by 23.5 percent. We were able to introduce an Employee Share scheme in which an allocation of shares would be made to all staff members each January from a five percent share of the previous year's profits. My copy of the Spring 1987 edition of the LWT house magazine reminds me that we were the first ITV company to introduce such a scheme and that by 1987 we had distributed over 1,169,000 shares to the staff with a value at that time of around £10 million.

Rupert Murdoch sold his own LWT shares in the spring of 1980. Perhaps he was insuring himself against the possibility of LWT losing its franchise, but the shares he had bought in his 1970 bid to take over the company turned out to be a sounder investment than he or anybody else could have imagined: he sold them for £4.8 million pounds. His timing turned out to be sound too. We retained our franchise at the end of 1980 but, together with the other successful franchise-holders, we were hit hard by the contractual obligation to finance Channel 4 and S4C: in 1981-82 there would be a pump-priming requirement of £38.2 million pounds, followed by another £85.4 million in 1982-83 when advertising revenue from the two channels would have had only a few months in which to flow. But now, before they had even begun to go on the air, the pump was about to become comprehensively clogged.

Back at the Other Ranch

I n March 1982 the IPA – the Institute of Practitioners in Advertising – wrote to the British Actors' Equity Association to propose that fees and residual payments for performances in commercials on Channel 4 and TV-AM should be related to the size of their audience, and in light of the audience projections for the new services, these payments would amount to 25 percent of the rates on ITV.

Equity considered this proposition totally unacceptable and in the negotiations which followed sought a figure nearer 75 percent. Neither side was prepared to budge; the negotiations broke down; and a month before Channel 4 was due to begin transmission Equity instructed its 30,000 members not to work on any commercials for either of the new channels unless they were paid the full ITV rates. Deadlock. A deadlock which lasted nearly two years, the longest-running dispute to-date in the history of independent television in Britain. It nearly did for TV-am. What would it do to Channel 4?

Preparations for the channel's launch had been hectic enough without this new distraction. Thanks to a happy find by Deputy Chairman Richard Attenborough, the channel had its own premises: a 1970s office block in Charlotte Street with a little cinema in the basement which had been converted into the channel's one and only studio. Two years of punishingly hard work by Jeremy Isaacs, Justin Dukes, Paul Bonner and their teams, and two years of nudging, prodding, cheering and chivvying by the Board, had created from scratch a new kind of television channel.

It was a publisher rather than a producer, its programmes conjured up by a team of Commissioning Editors - a new kind of television executive - and delivered to the screen by a new kind of computerised transmission system – except that the system wasn't working properly and our overstretched engineering staff had to operate it manually on opening night. The last thing we wanted as we went on the air for the first time, at 5.15 pm on Tuesday 2 November 1982, was a succession of blank screens where the commercial breaks were meant to be; but that's what we got.

Jeremy had decided on a low-key first night without any celebratory opening ceremony or gala variety special. The schedule was to be typical of the programme-mix viewers could expect to see regularly on the channel, a combination of different kinds of programmes and different takes on familiar kinds. Opening night featured a handful of shows which would become some of Channel 4's signature programmes. A game-show as an alternative to the afternoon's children's programmes on ITV and the BBC, but a brain-teaser of a game-show in *Countdown*. A soap opera, but a gritty, down-to-earth soap-opera in *Brookside*. A nightly news broadcast in *Channel Four News*, but one which would be able to cover its subject-matter in depth across an entire hour for the first time in British broadcasting.

There was a challenging new feature film, *Walter*, directed by Stephen Frears with Ian McKellen as its mentally handicapped lead character: the first of many feature films to be financed by the channel under the banner of *Film on Four*. A comedy series, *The Paul Hogan Show*, was bought in from Australia rather than America and introduced British audiences to an Australian performer who would become an international comedy star. And there was a British comedy show, *The Comic Strip Presents...* "Five Go Mad in Dorset", spoofing the adventures of Enid Blyton's Famous Five in the first of a series of half-hour comedy films starring members of the Comic Strip cabaret company new to the television audience, among them Dawn French, Jennifer Saunders, Ade Edmondson and Peter Richardson.

Interspersed among these were some of the channel's shows for minority audiences: a discussion series about books in *Book Four*; an educational series in *The Body Show*, demonstrating exercises to improve fitness in people of all ages; and a late-night revue, *In The Pink*, celebrating women's lives in an anthology of music and poetry devised, performed and produced exclusively by women.

The newspaper headlines next morning were broadly favourable – 'A night to remember' in *The Guardian* and 'Four's Friendly Image' in *The Daily Telegraph* – though *The Sun* gave the opening night only '4 Out Of 10'.

The reviews were rather more mixed. Nancy Banks Smith in *The Guardian* thought the channel was "trendy enough to make your teeth peel"; Peter Ackroyd in *The Times* wrote of the channel "There is a tendency, perhaps, to excessive wind"; while Chris Dunkley in the *Financial Times* attacked what he considered "the feminist fanaticism of *In The Pink* and its unhealthy odour of hatred". But Herbert Kretzmer in the *Daily Mail* declared Channel 4 "A lusty, noisy and decidedly provoking infant" and wished "the brat" good luck.

The dispute between Equity and the advertisers had been well publicised and most reviewers thought it would be transitory so the empty commercial breaks at this stage were given no more than passing comment. When the eagerly awaited ratings became available, the channel's first-night audience figures proved to be varied but not unreasonable: *Book Four* and *In The Pink* had been watched by a million viewers, *Channel Four News* by 1.2 million, *Brookside* by 2.8 million, and *The Comic Strip Presents...*, *The Paul Hogan Show*, *Countdown* and *Film on Four* by 3.3 million, 3.4 million, 3.6 million and 3.7 million respectively. The channel's share of the viewing audience for its first six days was 6.6 percent, an encouraging figure. Could it be sustained? Would it grow?

In the weeks that followed, the mix included more series destined to be among the channel's long-running signatures: the cult pop music series *The Tube*; lectures from speakers of all political persuasions in *Opinions*; the channel's magical animated film for Christmas, *The Snowman*; the innovatory game-show *Treasure Hunt* in which, with cryptic clues supplied to them by the producers, contestants had to direct its helicopter-borne 'skyrunner' Anneka Rice to wherever in Great Britain the prize-winning treasure was hidden. The mix included more fine editions of *Film on Four*, opera matinees from the Metropolitan Opera House in New York, outstanding drama productions of Shaw's *Arms and the Man*, the Royal Shakespeare Company's *Nicholas Nickleby* and a series adapted from *The Irish RM*, Somerville and Ross's comic masterpiece.

It also included more series targeted at minorities: *Tom Keating on Painters*; a weekly discussion on cultural issues in *Voices*; an overview of world music in *Sleevenotes*; a radical slant on news and current affairs in *The Friday Alternative*; two consumer programmes, *For What it's Worth* and *Well Being*. There were also two political programmes: *A Week in Politics*, examining the week's goings-on in Parliament and political life, and *Union World*, a less than lively round-up of topics concerning the trade unions - even Arthur Scargill, the President of the National Union of Mineworkers, said he would rather watch the test card.

Alas, the channel's audience share did not grow. Nor was its 6.6 percent sustained. It wasn't helped by the hideously barren advertising breaks, filled with stand-by captions, an endlessly repeated handful of commercials minus actors in either vision or voice-over, a few filmed seascapes and pastoral scenes, even a return to the channel's own version of the ancient BBC Pot-ter's Wheel. "At times, Channel 4 was virtually unwatchable," acknowledged Sue Stoessl, the channel's then Head of Marketing, in an interview decades later. By the end of January 1983 the channel's audience share had slumped to 3.7 percent. Some of the programmes, including its flagship *Channel Four News*, were achieving audiences of 250,000 or less, a figure that didn't even register in the ratings.

The newspapers, the tabloids in particular, had begun to scent blood. A *Daily Mail* headline above a viewer's letter read 'Channel Bore'. *The Sun*, under the headline 'Channel Swore', devoted itself to counting the swearwords heard on the channel since opening night: 173 of them by the beginning of December, by no means all in the grittily naturalistic *Brookside*. Chris Dunkley in the *Financial Times*, still pursuing what he considered the channel's feminist fanaticism − "the late sixties attitudes of the Guardian's Women's page" − now, under the headline 'Dangers In Benign Fascism', repeated what he had told several members of Channel 4's staff to their face: the channel's arrival, "far from ushering in a brave new world of liberality and multicultural broadcasting... seems to have meant institutionalising policies hideously similar to those of the Third Reich and the South African government". Over the top, certainly, but Dunkley could not be discounted: he was an influential and highly regarded television critic.

On Boxing Day, the *Star* ran a story that ITV chiefs had decided at a secret conference that Jeremy Isaacs had to go. This was not at all the case − it wasn't for ITV chiefs to decide anyway − but the Channel 4 Board had certainly discussed the channel's programming and the precipitous decline of the audience's interest in it. Maggie Brown's book *A Licence to be Dif-ferent: The Story of Channel 4*, quotes a Minute from the Board's December meeting in which I said "Channel 4 needs to attract wider audiences. It needs more popular programmes and popular series. It is important to ease the tone, to make the audience understand that minorities are not always earnest and depressed." She notes that, in agreeing, Anthony Smith added that Channel 4 gave him the feeling of watching a series of videotapes. She also reported Jeremy's concession that he would try to make the channel more popular but was anxious that it remained distinctive. So were we all, Jeremy; so were we all.

Twenty years later, following up the *Star* newspaper's story, Maggie Brown interviewed commissioning editor John Ranelagh, who had devised the channel's commissioning system under Jeremy's instructions and doubled as Secretary to the Board for the channel's first two years. John recalled packing up after a Board meeting and being asked by Edmund Dell to stay but not to make any notes while the non-executive members of the Board informally discussed the channel's problems. He remembered being delegated to tell Jeremy that he "really was on notice and had to do something". He recalled subsequently meeting Jeremy in the lift with Bill Brown and saying "Something's got to give, Jeremy"; and that Jeremy's face was "frozen in a furious grimace". Bill Brown told him to calm down, saying "We're not going to fire you, but we are not afraid to if it comes to it".

I confess that I remember nothing of this episode. I have found no reference to it in the official history or any of the books written by Jeremy and others about Channel 4, and, sadly, cannot ask for corroboration from Bill Brown, who died in 1996. Perhaps this was the 'secret conference' to which the Star referred and which had somehow been leaked to the newspaper. But certainly there was deep concern about the channel's unpopularity, and at its January meeting the Board decided to call a weekend conference with the executive and commissioning staff in a determined effort to get to grips with it.

We gathered at the Berystede Hotel in Ascot on Friday, 28 January. Edmund Dell's opening remarks set the conference's agenda: what had we done that we shouldn't have done and why were our programmes not getting the size of audience they deserved? He asked me to provide a professional critique of the situation. I'd had advance warning of this but not enough time to prepare a written piece so I ad-libbed from notes I had put together from my own observations, from comments made by other Board members, from technical reports I had seen from LWT's Presentation Department. I found myself saying for the first and only time in my life that we were drinking in the Last Chance Saloon. Forty years later that seems to me to be as far over the top as Chris Dunkley had been in the *Financial Times*, but it didn't then.

I thought there were three reasons why we were losing our audiences. The first was that we were going out of our way to be different at all costs. Some of our programmes and scheduling decisions were barking mad: weird, out of the way, off the wall, perversely minority orientated. It was simply wrong-headed, for example, to screen programmes like *Union World* and *A Week in Politics* on Saturday night, the big night for family viewing. The second reason was that there were no fixed points in our programme schedule, no landmarks other than the *News* at 7 pm. Audiences couldn't make dates to see programmes they might like because they had no idea what was going to happen or when.

The third reason was so counter-productive as to be self-destructive: we seemed determined to be so different from ITV that we were deliberately avoiding common programme junctions with it. If ITV programmed on the half hour or the hour, we would doggedly *not* schedule our programmes on the half hour or the hour, but at quarter past or quarter to, with the exception again of the *News*. That was certainly a demonstration of independence, but it was also a demonstration of tactical idiocy: ITV was committed as well as obliged to promote Channel 4 and hand audiences over to it, but how could it do so if the audiences would be handed over half way through a Channel 4 programme. The channel was designed to provide a choice of alternative viewing, and there were minorities within the mass audience eager to know what might be available to them, but how could the channel give them a choice if its programme junctions were not common with ITV's?

I went on to say much of what I had already said at Board meetings following the launch. The channel was too heavy, too serious. We needed to ease its tone. It needed an astute eye on the possibilities of complementary scheduling. There were not enough entertaining programmes, particularly at the weekend. What Channel 4 needed to schedule as an alternative to ITV's Saturday night entertainment was not minority programmes about politics but a different *kind* of Saturday night entertainment. Two years later Channel 4 did exactly that with *Saturday Live*, which gave the world of alternative comedy its entrée to prime-time television and made stars of among others Ben Elton, Harry Enfield, Stephen Fry and Hugh Laurie. Ironically, *Saturday Live* was commissioned from LWT, so my own company was dutifully handing over 90 minutes of its night-time audience to Channel 4 every Saturday night. At least by then Ron Miller was selling the advertising time on both channels...

In his book about the early years of the channel, *Storm Over 4*, Jeremy says "We left Berystede in good heart and good order. There would be more emphasis on how we presented ourselves, on entertainment. You gotta accentuate the positive, the song said. There would be no betrayal of trust." Years later, he remembered the Ascot conference as a critical meeting and his speech at the meeting's end a vital speech for the channel's future, "a speech in which I said I will make those concessions but we absolutely must not abandon the notion that this channel is trying to be distinctive." Indeed. Jeremy's vision for the channel remained intact. All that the Board and I were trying to do was enable that vision to be more easily realised. Three days later, on 1 February 1983, we were helped from a quite unexpected quarter. TV–am went on the air for the first time. The press had fresh meat to feed on and Channel 4 could, like the song said, accentuate the positive, eliminate the negative and latch on to the affirmative, without trying to accomplish it all in the glare of the media spotlight.

The Berystede Rebound

A period of intense activity followed. The channel's videotape editors worked all hours throughout February, editing programmes to lengths which could be more easily scheduled to meet ITV's programme junctions. Sue Stoessl joined the scheduling team of Jeremy Isaacs, Paul Bonner and Programme Planner Eric Flackfield at regular Monday morning meetings in which they analysed and responded to the weekly audience figures as they came on line from Audits of Great Britain. In the process, entertainment programmes and their place in the schedules were given more attention. The channel had acquired *Cheers*, the best of the new American situation comedies, and astute scheduling on Friday nights made it an instant success. This, in turn, encouraged the use of other American comedy shows like *Bewitched* and *The Mary Tyler Moore Show* and re-runs of past ITV situation comedy successes to bolster evening transmissions of educational programmes which were themselves beginning to attract larger audiences than the minorities for which they were intended. As a result, programmes about gardening, fishing and cooking began to be scheduled in peak-time.

The Board accepted Jeremy's recommendation that, to tighten the channel's editorial control, ten of the Commissioning Editors should in future report to Paul, whose title should be changed from Channel Controller to Programme Controller. Jeremy would retain the responsibility for actuality, fiction and the arts, and he was asking Justin, the Managing Director, to set up a comprehensive system for governing the entire commissioning procedure. In the process, it was decided not to renew the contracts of two of the Commissioning Editors.

It was also decided that Paul should become a member of the Board, an appointment which was handled rather less than felicitously by the Chairman. Jeremy had no quarrel with the appointment in principle, but thought it should wait for the new system to be in place. Edmund Dell decided not to wait but told Jeremy of his intention only the night before he announced it at the Board. This was an indication of the disharmony between the channel's Chairman and its Chief Executive which its Deputy Chairman, Richard Attenborough, would work hard to moderate in the years to come. At least Edmund told Jeremy in advance, even if only at the last minute. Justin, the channel's Managing Director, wasn't told at all: he learned of the appointment indirectly, from the IBA's Secretary.

Channel 4's style of on-air presentation was also given a long, hard look. In the channel's pre-transmission planning period, Roger Graef and other members of the Board, striving for *difference* wherever it might be introduced, had pressed for an on-air style in which non-professional presenters with a mixture of regional and ethnic accents introduced the channel's programmes informally in vision. By the time we assembled for the Ascot conference it was clear that the audience was finding this approach, in the official history's phrase, "highly resistible". It was giving the channel an untidy, amateurish look. Paul Bonner and the channel's Head of Presentation, Pam Masters, were now instructed to replace this approach with viewer-friendly voices introducing our programmes out of vision, accompanied by stylish graphics which emphasised the station's identity. The on-screen transformation was completed the following summer when the IPA-Equity dispute ended and the channel's commercial breaks could be fully populated at last.

Ron Miller populated them with his customary ingenuity. Channel 4's Commissioning Editor for Sport was Adrian Metcalfe, lured away from ITV where he had been one of the founding members of the *World of Sport* team. Faced with the problem that the most popular sports in the UK were already under contract to the BBC or ITV, Adrian had the bright idea of introducing some of the most popular American sports to Channel 4 viewers, and Ron went to town with American football. For the channel's transmissions he converted LWT's Studio One into an American bar complete with a giant TV screen, serving the advertising company representatives Red Eye, Budweiser and Jack Daniels with pastrami on rye, burgers and hot dogs, and bringing in a hip little swing band to add to the the atmosphere. Entrance was by invitation only, non-transferable and much sought after in the industry.

At half-time Ron's lads would set up the following year's ad-break chart and invite the buyers to reserve their bookings. They were rewarded with a complete sell-out every time.

The poor performance of *Channel Four News* was a matter for urgent action. In the channel's planning period some members of the Board had resented what they considered the imposition of ITN as its news provider and felt that its approach would not be distinctive enough for the channel. I remember Roger Graef furiously protesting that Four's news had to be different in every way, even if it meant its presenter wearing a tu-tu. (You *were* joking, weren't you, Roger?) Now Anthony Smith was proposing to the Board that we should give notice to ITN of terminating its contract. Weeks of intensive argument and negotiation ended instead with the programme's complete overhaul. *Channel Four News* would be given splendid new presenters in Peter Sissons and a young Trevor McDonald; and ITN agreed a commitment to reach an average nightly audience of 750,000 viewers.

The programme's agenda would include nightly news analysis, weekly reports on industry and the economy, weekly reports also on world affairs from foreign perspectives, and regular items on science, new technology and the arts. Crucially, *Channel Four News* would be assigned a significantly strengthened team under Stewart Purvis, one of the brightest young editorial minds at ITN, and the Board was given the right to determine the contract if, after a year under his editorship, it was felt that the programme was not being produced to the Board's satisfaction. There was never a need to impose this sanction. Within months, Channel 4 News reached its target of 750,000 viewers and began to look like the distinctive news programme we had all hoped for from the beginning.

The Authority's reaction to the criticism from viewers and the press was a canny one. Reluctant to quash initiative in the new channel and eager to encourage innovation and experiment in the form and content of its programmes, the IBA was nevertheless bound by the Broadcasting Act to ensure that nothing was included which offended against good taste and decency. It adopted an approach which David Glencross, who succeeded Colin Shaw as the Authority's Director of Television, characterised as being one of "repressive tolerance". It let a few mistakes get on the screen initially but over the first few months benchmarks were mutually agreed.

The Authority's audience research demonstrated that swearing and coarse language were high on the list of things causing offence to the channel's viewers – not just in *Brookside* but also in the channel's drama programmes, in its *Film on Four* productions and in its bought-in feature films. There was also a problem with the sexual content of some of the art-house films bought in from the continent. The channel experimented for a brief period with a red triangle in the top left corner of the screen to warn viewers. For art-film devotees this practice was a joke, for the ordinary viewer a mystery and for the prurient something of an advertisement, and it was summarily dropped.

Instead, Jeremy reined in the Commissioning Editors, instructing them to ensure that only sexual content or expletives defensible in artistic terms reached the screen. And Paul, in consultation with Pam Masters, Eric Flackfield and Programme Manager Joyce Jones, set up a panel of retired staff from the Purchased Programmes and Presentation Departments of both BBC and ITV to preview the channel's bought-in material from home and advise on whether and where it could be scheduled in the light of the IBA's regulations.

Feature films of a different kind were beginning to give the channel a noticeable ratings boost. Jeremy had commissioned Leslie Halliwell, ITV's buyer of feature films and television series, to put together seasons of feature films of the thirties and forties from packages acquired for ITV. After the introduction of colour television in 1968, the network had had little use for black & white classics. It was a task tailor-made for a master movie buff like Leslie, who lovingly devised packages billed as 'Golden Oldies' for transmission in off-peak hours: Universal Studios's original *Frankenstein* and *Dracula* films in sequence, and seasons built round the work of film-makers like Frank Launder and Sidney Gilliat, musical stars like Jeanette MacDonald and Deanna Durbin, comedians like Bob Hope and Max Miller, actors like Humphrey Bogart and Charles Laughton.

He also compiled series like *What the Censor Saw*, *Yesterday's Britain*, and several seasons of British films about the Second World War. Wherever practicable these series and seasons were introduced by individuals associated with the films in some way. Launder and Gilliat looked back on their own careers for example, and Sam Goldwyn Jr introduced a season of his father's work. It was a particular pleasure for me to see such seasons introduced in this way in the schedules. I wondered if viewers in the North and Midlands would remember that ABC Television's schedules had beaten Channel 4 to the idea by more than two decades. Leslie's film seasons were popular enough for his Channel 4 commission to be extended from compiling packages of golden oldies from films already purchased to trawling the archives of the film studios of Hollywood and Britain for treasure that was still buried. Leslie filled 300 off-peak slots a year with these delights and when he died in 1989 Jeremy paid tribute to his "unsurpassed contribution" to the channel's success.

Golden oldies certainly played a part in increasing the channel's audience share and more and more viewers were beginning to discover Channel 4 for themselves, tempted by an evening's showcase of the channel's work across the entire ITV network and encouraged by the alternatives now offered to them at ITV's programme junctions.

Three months after the media spotlight's glare switched to the problems of ITV's new Breakfast TV channel, Miles Kington was able to write in his column in *The Times* that "people are now beginning to say nice things about Channel 4. How varied it is, how good the film and book items are, what wonderful repeats and films they have, how refreshing the pop music programmes are, how unusually interesting their news coverage is..." By June 1985, when David McCall and I completed our five-year terms on the Board, total TV broadcasting hours had increased by 25 percent with their extension into breakfast-time and the previously unused hours of the afternoon. Nevertheless, Channel 4's share of the total viewing audience had increased from the disquieting 3.7 percent of January 1983 to a healthy 6.8 percent, and it was also beginning to pay its way. In its financial year ending 31 March 1985 the channel's share of the combined ITV and Channel 4 ratings was 12.5 percent; the share of ITV's revenue with which Channel 4 was financed was 12.3 percent.

June 1985 saw quite an exodus from the channel's Board. Roger Graef and Sara Morrison left along with David and me. Bill Brown and Joy Whitby had finished their four-year terms the previous year. Of the founding Board only Edmund Dell, Richard Attenborough and Glyn Tegai Hughes remained. At the farewell Board dinner I thanked Jeremy, Paul and Justin for the ride, hair-raising though it had been at times, and wished "what was left of Channel Four" continued success. Edmund Dell departed the Board two years later, and Jeremy two years after that. Channel 4 remains today a great independent force in British broadcasting, long after most of the ITV companies which funded it have ceased to exist. Its concept and the imagination and drive that brought it to life and sustained it in those early years were Jeremy's, and they remain a tribute to his achievement.

Life in the Red

C hannel 4 had been able to weather its early squalls, those deserted ad-breaks and deserting audiences, secure in the knowledge that it was in no danger of running out of funds: the subscription levied on the ITV companies by the IBA would underwrite it rain or shine. The other brand-new ITV franchise-holder had no such protection and encountered nothing but squalls from its outset onwards.

At its final IBA interview, the TV-AM consortium explained that rather than incur the expense of building new premises it proposed to acquire and convert Keith Ewart's independent studios in Wandsworth. Unfortunately, unable to agree terms with Mr Ewart it was obliged to build from scratch after all. And build it did, on a site in Camden, North London, an ambitious, exotic and expensive complex unlike any other in British television, whose "building and landscape elements", its publicity declared, were "landmarks in a journey of the sun's travels", from "a Japanese inspired pavilion used for hospitality" through "the temple-like forms of the Mediterranean and Greece" to "the desert plants and mirror glass architecture of the North American West". It was a striking and costly contrast to BBC *Breakfast Time*'s location in the old Lime Grove studios, now 20 years more ramshackle than when I had worked in them but still eminently efficient.

TV-AM, or TV-am as it was now less stridently titled, had also told the IBA that it proposed to work with ITN in providing its contractual service of national and international news but here also it was unable to reach agreement, this time on principle as well as on terms. ITN wasn't prepared to be a mere agency, supplying news stories for TV-am to process, and

TV-am wasn't prepared to surrender blocks of its limited airtime to ITN for variations of *Channel Four News*. So while Breakfast Time had the BBC's world-wide news-gathering resources at its disposal, TV-am was forced to rely on expensive independent agencies in putting its news service together.

In spite of these set-backs and the on-screen effect of the Equity-IPA dispute, TV-am's audience peaked at an encouraging 1.3 million viewers at its launch on 1 February 1983. Unfortunately, by the end of the week the figure had fallen by two-thirds to 400,000. The BBC's Breakfast Time, comfortably settled in with a two-week head-start, averaged 1.5 million throughout the same week and by the end of the month was enjoying an average audience of 1.6 million viewers against TV-am's 300,000. That should have surprised no one. The IBA's public meeting on breakfast television at Croydon three years earlier had indicated quite clearly that the British TV audience would prefer a light and cheery treatment of its early morning news, and Breakfast Time was more than happy to provide it in the relaxed and affable company of its presenters, Frank Bough and Selina Scott.

The audience certainly sampled TV-am's mission to explain the news, via the high-powered professional expertise of Anna Ford and Angela Rippon, the first two members of the Famous Five to take up presenter duty. But, having sampled it, the audience disobligingly turned away. With disastrous ratings, empty advertising breaks and costs spiralling out of control – Jonathan Aitken was quoted as saying "I think we were losing a million pounds a month" – TV-am's costs had to be cut, more capital had to be raised, new investors had to be found, and the IBA had to be asked to waive its rental 'on a temporary basis' – a temporary basis which in the event lasted for two years.

The TV-am Board was in turmoil. It had neglected to find a Chief Executive in the three years since the award of its contract, simply adding the Chief Executive's role to Peter Jay's responsibilities as Chairman. That was perfectly agreeable to Peter Jay. Unfortunately, it meant that there was no one else to carry the can for the company's desperate plight and six weeks after TV-am went on the air, under pressure from his Board, Peter Jay resigned. The turmoil didn't end with his resignation. Two other Board investor-directors resigned. Lord Marsh was appointed Peter Jay's successor as Chairman and Jonathan Aitken as Chief Executive, but Aitken was a serving MP and the IBA wasn't prepared to have a Member of Parliament as Chief Executive of one of its franchise-holders. He too had to go, although the IBA generously suggested that his appointment could be an acting one until his replacement, cousin Timothy Aitken, a founder-member of the original consortium, was able to succeed him.

Four weeks later, Timothy arrived as Chief Executive and within days had begun cutting costs by sacking Anna Ford and Angela Rippon. Anna Ford famously took her revenge at a subsequent social gathering by hurling a glass of wine at Jonathan, thus revenging herself on the wrong Aitken; but by that stage, who was counting?

Like the rest of the industry, LWT watched this chaotic sequence of events with horrified sympathy – except for the bright young editor of LWT's *Six O'Clock Show*. "There was something about the chaos that I quite fancied," Greg Dyke said later, "so I wrote to Jonathan Aitken and said I thought there'd been a complete cock-up in the way he'd launched it but if he was looking for someone to take it all over, I wouldn't mind." Aitken must have been overjoyed. When John Birt told me we were losing Greg I was surprised to hear it – and more surprised 20 years later when I learned that we had lost him for a comparatively trivial reason. Apparently, Greg said later, we had just refused to provide him with a company car. "I was pissed off, having run their most successful show of the year." He got his company car all right with TV-am: a battered BMW that had clearly seen better days; he picked it up at the end of his first day with TV-am and was stopped by the police on his way home on suspicion of driving an un-roadworthy vehicle. I was sorry to lose him, but we had more serious matters to deal with at Kent House. We couldn't have given Greg a company car without giving one to all our other successful producers and editors, and we couldn't have afforded that. We were running out of money too.

The British economy had by now entered another of the recessions that dogged it throughout the seventies and eighties and ITV was hit hard by it. Advertising expenditure across the network was less than buoyant. The competition from the BBC had never been so strong, especially at the weekend. The ITV companies were handing out vast sums of money to fund Channel 4 in exchange for the right to sell Channel 4's advertising air-time, but the Equity-IPA dispute had ensured that there *wasn't* any Channel 4 advertising air-time. The entire network was feeling a draught and when the network felt a draught LWT caught a cold. In the financial year ending July 1982 LWT suffered a shortfall in its projected advertising revenue of £3 million. After programme costs, the Levy, taxation and our share of the fourth channel subscription, we were £556,000 in the red, the equivalent in today's money of £1.8 million.

The seven-day major companies were maximising their monopoly of the advertising revenue available in their regions by scheduling their strongest programmes during the week, when the BBC was less competitive. There was no such monopoly for the two London companies: Thames and LWT had to fight each other for their share of whatever the advertising agencies were prepared to spend on the region, so we also had to fight for our share of the strongest programmes from our seven-day colleagues. When Cyril Bennett and I were rival Directors of Programmes we spent much of our time at the Controllers Meetings trying to dodge the least promising programme offers from our seven-day colleagues and manoeuvre the most promising into our own half of the week. Dodging and manoeuvring were not going to be easy for John Birt in his first year as LWT's Director of Programmes.

He set about it with the meticulous research and analysis I had expected of him. Thoroughly briefed by a team of bright young executives led by his Head of Programme Planning, Warren Breach, he turned up at the Monday morning meetings armed with plastic bags bulging with files of facts and figures, unyielding in his focus on the needs of the weekend. To the annoyance of his seven-day colleagues, he refused programme offers and moved programmes out of peak-time when his research indicated they wouldn't work there. With my blessing, he even argued that LWT was prepared to quit the barter system of programme exchange and propose instead a system of willing buyer/willing seller if they didn't offer a better balance at the weekend.

Paul Fox rang me to complain about his intransigence: "You really must do something about your boy Birt. He never compromises. We had our disagreements with Michael Grade but Michael always compromised in the end. John never does!" In the battle of dodges and manoeuvres, Cyril Bennett and I each used to win some and lose some, and so did our respective successors; but in spite of John's efforts, LWT's win rate was now practically zero. In the face of the BBC's fierce weekend competition and their own financial pressures, the strongest peak-time drama and entertainment programmes from Granada, Central and Yorkshire continued to go into Thames's four-and-a-half days. With our own financial resources already stretched, how could they be replaced?

I set up a task force to work out what economies could be made across the company, and my regular Friday morning sessions with John, in which we would normally discuss programmes and problems and share information on what was going on in the industry, now became deadly serious planning meetings. We analysed our current and future programme schedules in the light of the total costing system which John and Chris Turner had devised to monitor the cost of our Channel 4 offers, and came up with some highly disturbing facts. That post-Selsden response to the IBA's call for improvement in our local and minority programmes had been too enthusiastic: the programmes on the fringes of the weekend schedule were consuming more of the company's resources than our entire output of programmes in peak-time – exactly the opposite of what was happening at the weekend on BBC 1.

What's more, the below the line costs of our drama and situation comedy output were doubling the direct costs of their artistes and writers, making them more expensive per hour than any other type of programme except the big light entertainment specials like *The Stanley Baxter Moving Picture Show*. Each of these consumed vast amounts of company resources, studio days and production man-hours to produce a single hour of entertainment, fine though that single hour might be. These were acutely serious problems. How should we tackle them?

John and I worked out a four-strand strategy. We had to persuade the IBA to let us reduce the number of our minority and local programmes in the short term so that we could switch their resources to peak time programming. We had to slow down the commission and production of dramas, drama series, situation comedies and entertainment spectaculars and divert their resources to a less expensive form of peak-time entertainment. Because the costs of programmes were not written into the company's accounts until they were transmitted we had to put any expensive newly completed series into stock rather than on the air. And since the company itself couldn't afford to make enough peak-time programmes to match the BBC's output at the weekend, we had to talk the seven-day majors and the bigger regional companies into joining us to fill in the gaps.

Just like that, as Tommy Cooper might have said.

I wrote to the IBA's new Director General, John Whitney – needless to say I omitted to remind him that the last time we met he was operating the teleprompter for me on *Bath Night with Braden* at the BBC. I explained our predicament and sought the Authority's approval of our proposal to ease it by cancelling or postponing some of our local, drama and current affairs programming in the coming financial year.

A conveniently timed Channel 4 conference gave me the opportunity to buttonhole the IBA's new Director of Finance, Peter Rogers, who was now also a fellow director of the channel, and during a break in the proceedings the two of us walked round the conference centre gardens while I enlarged on LWT's financial problems and asked Peter what he thought the Authority's response to my letter might be. It was 40 minutes before we got back to the conference. Peter told me that the Authority was not happy with our requests. The members felt that if they accepted a reduction in our local programmes there would be a long queue of other companies seeking the same treatment. Any reduction in our peak-time programme supply would oblige the other network companies to increase their own output, in financial circumstances which were no less difficult than ours. And in any case LWT had had a long and very successful run. "What's wrong with one bad year?" Peter asked.

I argued that if we didn't take action now there would be more than just one bad year, our peak-time contribution to the network would be even less, and our local output would begin to look more like London Talking Heads than London Programmes. In the end, after a further exchange of correspondence, the Authority met us most of the way. We could drop some programmes, but we would have to add three more editions of our new local chat show *Sunday, Sunday* with Gloria Hunniford.

In July, at the annual meeting of all the company Programme Controllers with Members and Officers of the Authority, John attempted to apply to the network the logic which had led LWT to the programme strategy we were pursuing. In a paper entitled *Competition and Change*, stuffed full of pie-charts, statistics and estimated total costs, John argued that ITV spent twice as much on off-peak local, religious, adult education and other minority interest programmes than it did on peak-time and proposed a reduction of 11 percent in their amount across the network, the freed expenditure to be reallocated to the majors for investment in peak-time programmes. Another approach, John suggested, could be to ease the obligations on the regionals to make local programmes and ask them instead to carry a greater share of the Channel 4 subscription, thereby freeing resources with which the majors could increase their provision of peak-time programmes.

John's presentation was roundly rejected by Members, Officers and Programme Controllers alike. A memorandum about it sent by the Television Division to Authority Members commented "When examined in detail, neither his general argument nor the figures on which it is based carry conviction". By the end of the decade, many of John's ideas would eventually be accepted. But we couldn't afford to wait that long.

Having failed to persuade the Authority and the network to re-balance ITV's programme output, John now concentrated on re-balancing LWT's. Nick Elliott's Drama and Arts Department was hit even harder than Features and Current Affairs. *The Gentle Touch* ended its long run in 1984, as did *Partners in Crime*, our adaptation of Agatha Christie's Tommy and Tuppence detective stories. Another action series, *Dempsey and Makepeace*, was in production and began transmission in the same year but it was shot on film on location with American co-funding so made little demand on Kent House resources. Gratifyingly, it boosted the company's finances instead: Tony Wharmby's production and the chemistry between Michael Brandon and Glynis Barber as its Anglo-American police-detective team made it a big seller overseas. But for nearly three years the only new projects for Drama and Arts were commissions for Channel 4: a mini-series adaptation of Piers Paul Read's novel *A Married Man* starring Anthony Hopkins, and two series of the delicious *Mapp and Lucia*. *Marlowe*, a film series adaptation of Raymond Chandler's short stories about his fictional private detective with American actor Powers Booth in the lead, was made but put on hold to avoid its cost going into our books with its transmission. LWT's output of new drama for the ITV network in the next programme year hit an all-time low of seventeen hours. Ten years earlier it had been sixty-five.

In light entertainment, out went productions like *The Stanley Baxter Moving Picture Show* and *Russ Abbot's Madhouse*, which tied up artistes, studios and editing suites for too many days at a time. In came shows that could be transmitted live or produced as close to transmission as possible: all-star variety like *Live from Her Majesty's*; chat shows like *Aspel & Company* and *Sunday, Sunday*; more series featuring the ironic wit of Clive James; and game shows like *Punchlines* and *We Love TV*. And also more of what came to be called 'people shows' like *Game for a Laugh*, with members of the public as their voluntary or involuntary stars. Two of these shows, *Surprise! Surprise!* and *Blind Date*, both featuring John's fellow Liverpudlian Cilla Black, would in due course become two of the network's biggest long-running successes.

Existing shows which were undemanding of resources, like *Alright on the Night* and *An Audience With..*, continued their runs, as did established successes like *Cannon and Ball* and the Judi Dench-Michael Williams situation comedy *A Fine Romance*. One new situation comedy, *Me and My Girl* starring Richard O'Sullivan, managed to force its way into the weekend schedule to begin a run of five successful seasons.

With some scheduling sleight of hand this re-balanced output could help to provide a successful and financially manageable programme mix. The sleight of hand was supplied by the ingenious Warren Breach. Thames and LWT Planners traditionally divided up the London rights of the network feature film packages acquired by Leslie Halliwell by picking their first-runs alternately, the second runs going to whichever of them missed out on the first, which naturally enough bore the bulk of the movies' cost. With his Birtian aptitude for research and analysis, Warren gave his Thames opposite number, Tim Riordan, a more or less free run of the adult movies in the packages and went for the films likely to win big audiences in the afternoon and early evening. He had worked out that the Thames predilection for adult movies scheduled at 9 pm was in fact counter-productive: the films were always interrupted by *News at Ten*, after which their audiences usually tended to tail off. With no *News at Ten* at the weekend LWT didn't have that problem so the second runs we acquired were not only cheaper: they could be played without interruption in their peak-time slots, amounting to first showings for those viewers who had seen not much more than half their running-time on Thames.

Warren also persuaded Tim that rather than fight for the big, all-star American mini-series like *Winds of War*, *North and South* and *Return to Eden*, which were usually produced in two 90-minute episodes, they could be transmitted to the benefit of both Thames and LWT by scheduling them across Sunday and Monday evenings. Warren's proposal, which gave LWT audiences the first impact of both the programmes and the publicity associated with them, was endorsed by their Central and Yorkshire colleagues – ah, the camaraderie of the Programme Planners!

I don't know how Tim got it past his Managing Director, Bryan Cowgill. Bryan was as fiercely competitive with LWT as he was with his former colleagues at the BBC. I have a particularly vivid memory of the evening at the Dominion cinema in Tottenham Court Road when Thames premiered the first of a series of "Thames Silents" commissioned by Channel 4. The Silents were magnificent restorations by Kevin Brownlow of classic silent movies, with an added musical sound-track by composer Carl Davis. The one we were about to see was Douglas Fairbanks's *The Thief of Bagdad*, and for this red-letter occasion the accompaniment was to be live, with Davis conducting a huge symphony orchestra.

The specially invited audience filled the dress circle of the cinema and I was there as a member of the Channel 4 Board, way over on the right with the rest of our contingent. I can still see Bryan and the Thames party in their pomp, working their way down the centre aisle, greeting dignitaries and celebrities, until they reached the rows reserved for them. I can see Bryan beaming, looking round the auditorium before taking his seat and suddenly catching sight of me way over on the side. And I can still see him exclaiming to a colleague so furiously that I could almost hear as well as lip-read him saying "*What the fuck is **he** doing here?*"

All we needed now was an effective contribution from the network to take up the slots we couldn't fill ourselves. Separately or together, John and I embarked on a whistle-stop tour of the seven-day majors and major regional companies, calling on them in their London offices or their respective regions, sometimes by taxi, sometimes by train, once by plane, to try to convince them that the network and not just LWT needed to field a strong weekend schedule against the BBC, and that they should join us in delivering it.

All aboard!

On the Whistle-Stop Express

I took a train up to Tyne Tees Television in Newcastle to meet the company's Managing Director Peter Paine and Programme Controller Andrea Wonfor. Andrea wondered if a co-operative regional presence in Sunday's Closed Period, a sort of religious *Down Your Way* in opposition to the BBC's *Songs of Praise*, might help to get the evening off to a good start. I thought it was a splendid idea and urged her to pursue it with John. The two of them developed Andrea's idea into *Highway*, a travelling road-show visiting a different region of the ITV network each week with a mixture of hymns, chat and local interest. The whole operation would be supervised by Tyne Tees Television but each edition would be produced by the relevant regional franchise-holder. That would certainly reduce the size and expense of the party doing the travelling, but the show would need the right star personality to carry it as the presenter and an executive producer experienced and powerful enough to co-ordinate what would be a major creative and logistical enterprise.

Andrea phoned one day to say that she was stumped: could I suggest somebody capable enough for these roles? I told her: get Bill Ward out of retirement. "He'll run it and he'll know just who to present it." Bill jumped at the opportunity to get back into production and persuaded the great Harry Secombe to present the series. And for the next ten years, until the Closed Period really did close, *Highway*'s audience of some eight million gave ITV's Sunday evening schedule exactly the jump-start it needed.

Yorkshire Television already provided the weekend with two game shows, 3-2-1 and *Winner Takes All*, and Paul Fox, wearing both his Managing

Director and Programme Controller hats, now generously promised weekend slots for three big new Yorkshire shows in development. These were Alan Plater's serial *The Beiderbecke Affair*, Rik Mayall in *The New Statesman*, a satirical political comedy by Laurence Marks and Maurice Gran, and a comedy drama series called *A Bit of a Do*, based on books by David Nobbs and starring David Jason. John and I got an equally sympathetic hearing at Central Television from Managing Director Bob Phillis and his Director of Programmes Charles Denton. The second series of their current drama success *Auf Wiedersehen Pet* would be scheduled on Friday evening; Central's new game show *The Price is Right* would go straight to Saturday; and Sunday night would be enlivened by a new satirical puppet show they had in development called *Spitting Image*.

Like Yorkshire's contributions, Central's new shows would be of immense help in re-building the network's weekend schedule. John and I fared less well at Granada's Golden Square offices where we met David Plowright, now the company's Managing Director, with his Programme Controller Mike Scott. Two years earlier, when David was still Programme Controller, Michael Grade had turned down David's proposal of a Sunday night slot for *Brideshead Revisited* and it still rankled with him. Admittedly, however, we were guilty of considerable chutzpah in asking for a third episode of *Coronation Street* for Friday evening while also suggesting that Granada might like to revisit its golden days of comedy shows like *The Lovers*, *Bootsie and Snudge* and *The Army Game*. These might appeal to viewers in the south of England as well as the north, instead of their current run of parochial comedies like *The Wheeltappers & Shunters Social Club*.

David didn't throw us out of his office but he didn't accede to our requests either. Many years later, he confessed to "getting a little cross" with John at our meeting. When John had worked in current affairs at Granada, he and his current affairs colleagues were apparently forever asking David "why the hell do you tolerate the schedule being dominated by light entertainment?" and now here was John asking for more of it. As for *Coronation Street*, like our own *Weekend World* it was sacrosanct, not to be touched. Mike Scott did supply us with *Albion Market*, an alternative continuing drama series ("soap-opera" was a dirty word at Granada), set in a covered market in Salford. Scheduled at 7 pm on both Friday and Sunday, it was, alas, no *Coronation Street*, and after a year of declining audiences its stalls were folded and its caravans moved on. *Coronation Street* itself did eventually expand to a third episode on Friday but not until 1989, by which time Andrew Quinn had succeeded David as Granada's Managing Director.

Three of the major regional companies, Anglia Television, Scottish Television and HTV, were delighted at the opportunity to join the majors on the network and came up with a number of first-rate drama series which would enjoy long-running success at the weekend: three years for HTV's Robin Hood series *Robin of Sherwood*, ten for Anglia's adaptations of the Superintendent Dalgleish novels, and a remarkable twenty-eight for *Taggart*, the detective series from Scottish Television.

But what of TVS, run by its ambitious founder and Managing Director James Gatward? It certainly had the resources to make programmes for the network: the South and South East region was among the richest in ITV, with a share of Network Advertising Revenue which had already overtaken Yorkshire's and was within reach of LWT's. The entire industry knew that James felt TVS was big and rich enough to join the big five and be recognised as a sixth major, so why wasn't it offering to make big rich programmes for the network? I discovered why from James himself when I flew to Jersey for an industry conference.

We had learned that Greg Dyke was unhappy at TV-am. Over the past twelve months the company had teetered constantly on the edge of financial disaster because of the paucity of advertising revenue but he and Senior Editor Clive Jones had turned its ratings round by a combination of luck, inspiration and sheer hard work. TV-am was now regularly equalling and frequently beating *Breakfast Time*'s audience of 1,400,000, but it still needed new funds if it was to remain solvent while the Equity-IPA dispute dragged on. And at last it had got them.

Just as LWT was saved financially in 1970 by one Australian media tycoon, Rupert Murdoch, fourteen years later TV-am was saved by another: Kerry Packer, the owner of an entire empire of Aussie publishing and broadcasting. His investment in TV-am brought the company back from the edge. It also brought back to British television the ex-Deputy Chairman and joint Managing Director of ATV, Bruce Gyngell, who was appointed by Packer as his nominee on the TV-am Board.

Within months Lord Marsh had stepped down from its Chairmanship, with Timothy Aitken succeeding him, and Bruce Gyngell had been appointed Managing Director. A hands-on Managing Director, whose hands fell inevitably, and heavily, on editorial matters. Hence Greg's discontent. John and

I were concerned that the BBC might scoop him up. Could James Gatward be persuaded to offer Greg a job which would not only keep him inside ITV but also energise TVS's programme-making for the weekend?

I got on well with James. I'd liked his work when he was a drama director, we had Walthamstow in common, both of us having been brought up there, and he had been part of the crew on my Sammy Davis Jr show at ABC, as a scene-shifter. That's how this founder and chief executive of one of ITV's richest companies had started out in British television. It wasn't difficult to find an opportunity during one of the conference breaks for the two of us to take a walk round the conference gardens and talk about what was happening in the industry. I told him what his fellow regional majors were planning to supply to the network in the shape of drama and light entertainment at the weekend. Why didn't he join them?

He told me that his problem was that drama and light entertainment were not among the strengths of his Director of Programmes, Michael Blakstad, who had been a leading member of the BBC's Science and Features Department and whose particular expertise was in documentaries. I suggested that if Michael ever left TVS James ought to consider Greg Dyke for the job. He was known to be unhappy at TV-am; it was important to keep creative people like him in ITV and ensure that they didn't go to the BBC; and Greg certainly knew what would work for LWT at the weekend.

It wasn't a deal, explicit or implicit, but a few months later Michael Blakstad left TVS and Greg was appointed his successor. He brought Graham Benson into the company to handle its drama and John Kaye Cooper its light entertainment. Within a year TVS was beginning to make its way on to the network's weekend schedule with the game show *Catchphrase* and an ambitious comedy series starring a bright new comedian and impressionist called Bobby Davro. These were accompanied by drama series like the splendid *Ruth Rendell Mysteries* and *C.A.T.S. Eyes*, a spin-off from LWT's The Gentle Touch which continued the crime-solving career of Jill Gascoine as Maggie Forbes.

These new shows from the majors and major regionals didn't hit the screens all at once of course: they filtered through as they became ready for transmission and as the weekend schedule required them, filling the gaps which LWT couldn't itself fill. They dovetailed neatly with LWT's own re-balanced programme output and together they provided a weekend schedule as full of entertainment as BBC 1's. Was it too full? We were still producing

Weekend World, the network's only weekend current affairs programme, as well as *The South Bank Show*, the only regular network series on the arts, which won a BAFTA, an Emmy and a Prix Italia RAI Prize during this period of financial constraint.

Barry Cox and his Current Affairs department were still producing *The Six O'Clock Show* and first class documentary series like *The Making of Modern London*, and *Breadline Britain*, which explored the problem of mass unemployment and drew high praise from the IBA, in addition to single documentaries like *From the Shadow of the Gun*, about Northern Ireland, which won a silver medal at the New York International TV and Film Festival. Our Channel 4 commissions – the largest among the ITV companies – continued to range across the whole spectrum of programme-making. But for nearly three years LWT's principal peak-time contribution to the ITV network was almost exclusively that of out-and-out entertainment: people shows, variety shows, game shows, chat shows...

Our Press Department proclaimed LWT 'The Channel of The Entertainers' in a publicity campaign which incorporated newspaper cartoons and photographs by Lord Snowdon of LWT stars from Cilla Black and Bruce Forsyth to Melvyn Bragg and Brian Walden – who bore the tag of 'Entertainer' with admirable grace. An animated *Entertainers* on-air promotion film by Pat Gavin won a British Design Award as well as awards at the Design and Marketing Festivals of Chicago and New York and the Animation Film Festival at Annecy in France.

John and I were very much aware that with this emphasis on entertainment we were running the risk of appearing to take the company down-market. With game shows alone, for example, LWT was producing almost 40 hours a year by 1985; in 1979 it had been 15. We were aware that the austerity cuts and production changes were unpopular across the company's creative departments and that our studio workforce was less than happy with what was for them a very different work pattern – Gavin Waddel, LWT's ACTT Shop Steward told David Docherty "Morale is very low here...There [has] been a sharp decline in drama on the shop floor, and the workers don't like this".

But there was not a word of criticism from the IBA or the LWT Board. And the new regime worked. It worked while the Equity-IPA dispute was being settled at last, in October 1984, with Equity artistes being paid 55 percent of the ITV rate for appearing in commercials on Channel 4 and 37 percent for TV-am. It worked as advertising revenue began to flow from Channel 4's airtime and Nick Elliot was able to commission new drama projects for the network again. It worked as Ron Miller's Sales Department developed a new strategy of targeting specific sub-demographic sections of the audiences for both ITV and Channel 4. It even worked through yet another financial downturn for the network in May 1985. This was pronounced "the worst crisis to hit the ITV companies in at least a decade" by Colin Shaw, who had left the IBA to become Director of the ITCA's Planning Secretariat and discovered life at the coal-face was rather harsher than it had seemed from Brompton Towers.

With the gradual easing of financial restraint, John Birt wanted to follow up the huge success of Jayne Torvill and Christopher Dean in the 1984 Sarajevo Winter Olympics. Wearing his Arts hat, Nick Elliot worked with the Olympic ice-skating champions, director Tom Gutteridge and composer Carl Davis to devise and produce a spectacular ice-skating fantasy called *Fire and Ice*, which won the Bronze Rose at the 1985 Rose d'Or Entertainment Festival in Montreux. Switching to his Drama hat, Nick invited Linda Agran, Script Executive at Euston Films, to join his Drama and Arts Department and new LWT plays, series and mini-series gradually returned to the weekend schedule. Three original plays shot on film made an impressive impact: *Blue Money*, a thriller starring Billy Connolly, won the Grand Prize at the 1985 Banff Television Festival; *Dutch Girls*, a comedy by William Boyd, was the highest-rated ITV drama of 1985; and the success of *London's Burning*, the action-packed film written by Jack Rosenthal about London's Fire Service would lead to the award-winning *London's Burning* series, which ran for fourteen years from 1988.

Nick's single plays were accompanied by a mini-series dramatisation of Frances Hodgson Burnett's novel *A Little Princess* starring Maureen Lipman, which won 1987's BAFTA Award for Best Children's Drama, and *Drummonds*, a drama series about a boys' boarding-school of the fifties, with Richard Pascoe as the school's headmaster.

A thoroughgoing review of ITV Sport by working parties comprised of Programme Controllers, Heads of Sport and representatives of Channel 4 concluded that after 20 years it was time for Saturday afternoon's *World of Sport* to be dismantled, moving Racing to Channel 4, handing responsibility for the Football Results to ITN and leaving wrestling to stand alone as a separate programme while the network pursued a policy of live and exclusive sport. An invigorated ITV Sports Committee out-bid the BBC for exclusive coverage of British Athletics and then joined forces with the Corporation to negotiate a new joint contract with the football authorities.

There was a particular piquancy in the ensuing negotiations because Michael Grade was in the thick of them once again, having been persuaded back from America to become Controller of BBC 1. This was no re-run of 1978's Snatch of the Day however: this time the BBC and ITV were united, and Michael worked closely with John Birt in briefing their respective negotiating teams. Both services were determined to jettison the edited recordings of *Match of the Day* and *The Big Match*, securing live coverage of League games in their stead. And the Football League, arguing that live football would greatly increase ITV's profitability and the size of the BBC's audience, was equally determined to make both services pay heavily for it. With the prize of live coverage within their grasp, the BBC team and John's network colleagues were prepared to pay over the odds for a deal. But John, resistant as always to compromise, told John Bromley, now Chairman of the Network Sports Committee as well as LWT's Controller of Sport, that if the League refused ITV's offer he would immediately take football out of next year's LWT budget, and Michael stood firm with him at the BBC. As a result, when the 1985-86 season began there was no football at all on British television, live or recorded, for three long months. And the League blinked. This time, even Paul Fox appreciated John's refusal to compromise.

With live football and athletics on Saturday and Sunday afternoons, together with LWT's re-balanced schedule of drama, arts, light enter-tainment and current affairs and the programme contributions from the seven-day majors and major regionals, ITV's weekend was strong again. And Ron Miller's new sub-demographic targeting strategy made brilliant use of it. In September 1985 the trade journal Campaign commented that LWT was "undoubtedly the star performer vis-à-vis advertising. LWT consist-ently sells more of and commands a higher price for its airtime than any other station". In November 1986 LWT's share of London's advertising revenue reached 47 percent. With only two-and-a-half days on air each week against Thames's four-and-a-half, that was a remarkable figure and I sought confirmation of it from Ron. Yes, it's true, he told me, and went on to say "In one month in the eighties we reached 49.3 percent... ...I cried!"

Stand By Operation Evergreen

John Freeman retired from the Boards of LWT and LWT Holdings on 31 January 1984, a little more than a fortnight before his 70th birthday. This modest, courteous, extraordinary man had joined a failing LWT, rescued its franchise, revived its morale, re-built its strength and run it with consummate skill for thirteen years. Now he closed the door on his career as a television executive just as, one by one, he had closed the door on all the other careers in his remarkable life – on politics, on journalism, on television in the *Face to Face* interviews, on colonial governorship, on diplomacy – never to open any of them again. I am proud to say that he and I remained good friends, celebrating our mutual birthday together whenever we were both in the same country, until he died at the end of 2014, just a few months short of his own 100th.

Characteristically, John had planned his succession well in advance. In 1982 he invited on to the Holdings Board the recently retired Deputy Chairman of the IBA, Christopher Bland, with the understanding that Christopher would be a serious contender for the future Holdings chairmanship when the time came. In the same year he put down a marker for the future chairmanship of the television company by announcing my appointment as its Deputy Chairman. And the day after John retired Christopher became Chairman of the Holdings Board and I the Chairman and Managing Director of LWT.

John had persuaded the directors of the Holdings Board to accept this potentially unwieldy arrangement because he wanted the TV company to run with its own separate chain of command right to the top; answerable to the Holdings Board, but not to anyone else. Christopher and I were two very different people in both background and experience. He was a young, dynamic businessman who had also been involved in Conservative Party politics as a member of the GLC, the Deputy Chairman of the Inner London Education Authority and the Chairman of the Bow Group think-tank. He had served two terms as Deputy Chairman of the Independent Television Authority, later the Independent Broadcasting Authority, and was currently Chairman of the Hammersmith and Queen Charlotte's Hospitals NHS Special Health Authority, for services to which he would be knighted in 1993. And I had spent my entire professional life in television. But we respected each other and got on well, even before we discovered that we shared the fondness for hardboiled American crime fiction that I had also shared with John Freeman. What *was* it with LWT Chairmen and crime fiction?

We chaired our respective Board Meetings on alternate weeks and sat on each other's Board as members. He asked so many questions at both Boards about the television company's programme-making and scheduling problems that John Birt suggested it would save time if we invited him to join our weekly Friday morning meetings, where he could hear about them at first hand. Good call, John: there were problems on the horizon that would need more than a Board Room discussion to tackle.

There were changes across the river at Thames too, though nothing like as tranquil. The American drama series *Dallas*, a huge success for the BBC on Thames's weekday patch, was due for renewal and Bryan Cowgill was determined to acquire it for Thames's own schedule. He authorised a deal with its distributors Worldvision at $60,000 an episode, nearly twice the amount being paid by the BBC and $16,000 more than the Corporation had hoped to pay for the renewal. In order to act with both speed and secrecy Bryan had not sought the prior agreement of his Board or the ITV Network's Film Purchasing Group. When he reported his purchase to the ITCA Council the consensus of his colleagues was that they could not show a series which had been bought outside the agreed film purchasing system at a price which they would not have sanctioned and which would set a regrettable precedent for future purchases.

Three days later the secrecy was blown and the press went to town with headlines even rowdier than they had been for Snatch of the Day – "Cowboy Cowgill: Thames TV Boss outguns the Beeb" cried the *Daily Star*. John Whitney summoned Bryan to the IBA where he told him that if ITV was not going to network the series it should be handed back to the BBC. At a specially convened meeting of the Thames Board Bryan's initiative achieved broad support, albeit grudgingly on the part of Rediffusion representative John Davey who felt that an acquisition of this nature should not have proceeded without the Board's prior consideration. It was agreed to try at Chairman and Managing Director level to gain the acceptance of the series by the seven-day ITV companies.

There followed a succession of meetings with those companies to win their acceptance – which it failed to do. Then meetings with the Authority's Chairman and Director General to ascertain whether the Authority would be prepared to mandate acceptance – which it wouldn't. Followed by meetings with the BBC about renegotiating its *Dallas* deal with Worldvision – which it wouldn't at the Thames price. Finally, meetings with Worldvision's boss Kevin O'Sullivan about reassigning the series to the BBC – which he wouldn't at the BBC's price, and condemned the anti-trust nature of the ITV-BBC 'gentleman's agreement' not to poach each other's programme acquisitions.

In the middle of this sequence I received a phone call from the Thames Chairman asking if I could come over for a chat. I knew Hugh Dundas well from my time on the Thames Board and liked him enormously but it was an oddly deja vu experience to find him questioning me about Bryan in the same words that George Howard had used about Alasdair Milne: "Is he always like this?" Hugh asked. I explained that it was Bryan's freedom to act unilaterally at the BBC that had enabled him to become a supremely effective Controller of BBC 1 and freedom was a hard habit to break. It had worked brilliantly for both Thames and ITV when he bought Morecambe and Wise, Mike Yarwood and Miss World away from the Corporation because the network could accept these programmes as part of Thames's offers in ITV's system of programme exchange. But film purchases could not be treated in that way: they had to be paid for in hard cash and the network had to agree both their purchase and their price. Bryan's pursuit of *Dallas* demonstrated that in film purchasing you acted at your peril if you acted unilaterally; in the end Dallas would have to go back to the BBC.

And in the end that's what happened. But at what cost! Worldvision eventually sold the new series of *Dallas* back to the BBC at the price Thames had contracted to pay, which was £500,000 more than the BBC's offer. Thames had to subsidise the Corporation with £300,000 of that difference; the remaining £200,000 was collected from the seven-day ITV companies and handed over to the BBC by the ITCA. But there was more than a financial loss for both Thames and the network. On 12 July 1985 Bryan Cowgill was obliged to resign. He never returned to the industry, and ITV lost a senior executive whose competitive skills would have been invaluable in the new era of television broadcasting about to confront us.

Bryan's successor as Managing Director was Richard Dunn, the company's Director of Production, whose very different skills had been demonstrated most effectively the previous year. Thames's management had produced a roster for a night-time service to be run by six staff members on time-and-a-half rates. The ACTT however wanted 32 staff members to run such a service, to be paid "golden hours" rates – six times the normal figure – and called its members out on strike. At ACAS the union negotiators settled on terms nearer Thames's proposals than their own but the station had been off the air for eight days, and that was not acceptable.

Richard, a polite but determined pragmatist, saw that the Government's Employment Acts of 1982 and 1984, which put an end to 'closed shops' and secondary picketing, had removed the broadcasting unions' most potent weapon in the battle with management over restrictive practices: there was no longer the threat of industrial action spreading from company to company across the network. He decided to take the ACTT on again in a subsequent dispute about the use of portable electronic cameras instead of film cameras for Electronic News Gathering. The new cameras were lighter and easier to handle but the union was demanding extra payments for their use, which Richard flatly refused.

With Fred Atkinson, his head of engineering, Richard put together a hastily trained team of managers, office-workers and other non-unionised staff. When negotiations at ACAS broke down and the ACTT called its members out on strike again, the station was off the air for only 36 hours before a management service of feature films and taped programmes, complete with commercials, was up and running, put together by his Head of Programme Planning Tim Riordan. When the Thames chapel of the National Union of Journalists came out in sympathy with the ACTT, management was even able to provide a local news service, courtesy of two temporary news readers – Director of Public Relations Donald Cullimore and Head of Sport Ronald Allison. They were obliged to deliver it the old-fashioned way – heads down, read the script, look up at the camera – because the teleprompter operators were on strike too. But Thames's audience remained loyal; so did the advertisers; and a deal with the union was reached within a fortnight, with no premium payment whatsoever for the use of the new cameras. The rest of the network watched, admired and took note.

At Ulster Television, non-broadcast managers were sent on technical courses to learn how to operate cameras and sound and lighting equipment in readiness for any future management service. At Border Television, Managing Director James Graham turned the area secretary of the Electrician's Union from troublesome poacher to trouble-shooting gamekeeper by persuading him to become Border's Head of Industrial Relations. At Kent House, John Birt and I decided to explore the possibilities of an operation similar to Thames's should one become necessary, perhaps by beaming in a programme service from outside the UK in the event of an all-out technical strike. John asked Warren Breach, his redoubtable Head of Programme Planning, to come up with an idea. Warren proceeded to do so – in spades.

Looking for a facility outside the UK from which we might be able to transmit such a service, he consulted Les Rowarth, LWT's Controller of Production Engineering, who identified three non-unionised facility houses in Amsterdam, Toronto and New York. These were likely to be sympathetic and capable of feeding a programme service by satellite into LWT or direct to the IBA transmitters. So off to Amsterdam, Toronto and New York went Les and Warren, together with LWT's Director of Programme Organisation, Sydney Perry, whose budget would have to pay for the operation. They checked out the three facilities, found them all amenable and put all three on a modest retainer. Warren's next task was to devise the strike-breaking schedule itself. By happy chance, he had secured the first-run London rights to all three episodes of *Evergreen*, a blockbuster American mini-series from NBC. This would form the peak-time centrepiece of an initial strike-bound weekend. It would also provide the code name for the entire project. Operation Evergreen was born.

Supporting *Evergreen* in the first weekend of Warren's schedule and filling two further peak-time weekends were first-run and repeat runs of films and film series whose London transmission rights we owned, from *South Pacific* and *New York, New York* to *Murder She Wrote* and *Hawaii Five-O*, prints of which were held at the Independent Television Film Centre in West London. Warren asked the Centre's General Manager Ken Fletcher, an old friend and colleague, to ship them to Nexus, the facilities house he had signed up in New York, and arranged for NBC to send a print of *Evergreen* to join them there. Then off he went again to the Big Apple, this time accompanied by Presentation Assistant Vincent O'Brien.

At Nexus, Warren and Vincent worked through the night for a week putting three weekend peak-time schedules together on reels of videotape, complete with promotion and continuity announcements written by the two of them and delivered over continuity footage by an English actor residing in New York; commercials would be inserted by management at the time. On the belt and braces principle, to guard against future breakdown or sabotage, copies of the completed reels were put under lock and key at Nexus, sent to the facility houses in Toronto and Amsterdam and freighted back home to Ken Fletcher, who stored them in his house in Dulwich. LWT was primed and ready for any new confrontation with the unions.

The tectonic plates on which Independent Television had rested for 30 years were beginning to shift. The following year they were given an almighty shove by a Research Professor at the Heriot-Watt University of Edinburgh named Alan Peacock.

The Peacock Explosion

I ronically, the shove wasn't intended for ITV at all. In the spring of 1985, the BBC, which had managed to irritate Mrs Thatcher and her Government in several previous ways, went one irritation too far by asking for an increase in its licence fee, and Home Secretary Leon Brittan set up a Committee to consider alternative means of financing it. Professor Peacock, who had been a Chief Economic Advisor at the Department of Industry, was appointed its Chairman with a brief 'to assess what would be the effects of the introduction of advertising on the BBC's Home services, either as an alternative or a supplement to the income now received through the licence fee'.

After months of deliberation, however, the Committee decided that advertising was not the answer to the BBC's financial problems. The problem lay in the interdependence of the two systems, what its members called the comfortable duopoly of BBC and ITV. The Committee concluded that to retain its workforce, stay on the air and maintain its profitability ITV paid its staff more than was necessary, exerting pressure on the BBC to follow suit, which resulted in over-manning, indulgent working practices and a waste of resources throughout the entire industry. Competitive suppliers had an incentive to be cost-conscious; duopolists did not. The solution? Multiply the sources of supply and increase the competition.

The Committee's deliberations were inspired by its concept of consumer sovereignty. It believed that broadcasting was not for broadcasters: it was for its consumers, the viewers and listeners. A multiplicity of broadcasting systems, programme channels and payment methods would give consumers a multiplicity of choice, and the ensuing competition would compel suppliers to be efficient and cost-effective.

In spite of the Committee's disinclination to scrap the television licence fee in favour of advertising, this was a concept which fitted well with the Government's entrepreneurial philosophy. It did not fit at all well with ITV's, however. The Committee's conclusions would impact far more heavily on ITV than the Corporation it had been set up to examine. It recommended that funding by licence fee should continue, indexed to inflation until it was practicable for it to be replaced by subscription. To this end, all restrictions on pay-per-view should be lifted and all new television receivers fitted with encryption encoders. It also recommended that Channel 4 should be allowed to sell its own advertising time, that within ten years 40 percent of the output of both BBC and ITV should be sourced from independent producers, and that ITV franchises should be put out to competitive tender.

Two double whammies for ITV at one stroke. Fitting all television receivers with encryption decoders would accelerate the growth of cable and satellite competition. Selling its own airtime, Channel 4 would become a competitor for ITV's advertising revenue instead of a source of it. Reducing ITV's programme output by 40 percent could not be achieved without an extensive down-sizing of staff and production facilities. And competitive tendering meant that a deep pocket could trump any dedicated programme maker in the next franchise round. Those tectonic plates were shifting rather uneasily now.

ITV had seen none of this coming. We all thought that if we behaved well, performed reasonably, produced worthwhile programmes without frightening the horses in the street, the old regime would continue, give or take a little adjustment: a rearrangement of the network perhaps, rolling contracts possibly, new procedures, new requirements, new responsibilities. After the disappointments of the 1980 franchise awards, the incoming IBA Chairman, Lord Thomson, had said "there must be a better way" to award ITV contracts. Unfortunately the IBA hadn't come up with one. The Peacock Committee believed it had.

At the press conference in 1986 to announce its publication Alan Peacock said that the report could not be shelved because it raised issues which went far beyond the immediate interests of the government, but its initial reception by government seemed cautious rather than enthusiastic. Presenting it to Parliament, Home Secretary Douglas Hurd said it was "essentially a holding statement" which would receive "careful study". The Shadow Home Secretary, Gerald Kaufman, said it should be put in the waste paper basket. The press was generally dismissive. The trade paper *Broadcast* called it a dead duck, "the first Peacock to end up in a pigeon hole". Yorkshire TV's press release was terse: "Leave well alone – that's the message from Yorkshire TV to the Peacock report." Alan Sapper, the ACTT's General Secretary, described the recommendation that BBC and ITV should take 40 percent of their programmes from the independents as "a poisonous pie" which threatened up to 50,000 jobs.

As it happened, two days before the Report's publication IPPA, the Independent Programme Producers' Association, had launched 'The 25 percent Campaign', seeking a commitment from the BBC and ITV that within five years 25 percent of their programmes would come from independent producers. Michael Darlow and his IPPA colleagues could now argue that their proposal was more reasonable than Peacock's, offering more immediate action to the government and a less demanding requirement to the broadcasters. It was an argument which they would passionately pursue at the meetings, debates, seminars and conferences that followed in the ensuing months.

At a Royal Television Society Symposium Douglas Hurd made it clear that the Home Office had certainly not shelved the Report's recommendations: they were being gone through with great care. Studies on deregulation and the feasibility of subscription had already been commissioned and a technical study had been set up to establish the practical possibilities of pay-per-view. Hurd told our ITCA representatives at a Home Office meeting that there was a desire among his colleagues to loosen up the system. In a House of Commons debate he stated that the days of the status quo were numbered. And to give the government more time to examine the franchise system and consider the introduction of changes to the award of ITV contracts the Broadcasting Act of 1981 was amended early in April 1987 to extend the current contracts by three years. They would now expire on 31 December 1992.

The independents were not the only passionate lobbyists during this period. James Gatward, now both Chairman and Chief Executive of TVS, matched them in passion and persistence. Not content with access to the network for his programmes through LWT at the weekend, James was determined to make his company a sixth Major. He had tried two years earlier at a private dinner to persuade the five established Major companies to recognise the justice of his case. There we had been, the five Managing Directors, Bryan Cowgill for Thames, Paul Fox for Yorkshire, Bob Phillis for Central, David Plowright for Granada and I for London Weekend – "the five old warhorses" as he would later call us – having a cocktail or two before going in. James had said, "Just before dinner I'd like to make you a little presentation." For the next half hour, with graphs and statistics, he proceeded to demonstrate that as the equal third largest company in ITV, earning more than Yorkshire TV and almost as much as LWT, TVS ought to be accepted as the sixth Major or possibly replace Yorkshire as the fifth. His presentation was received with polite interest and only a few harrumphs from our Yorkshire member, but it made for an uncomfortable dinner.

I wrote to James, for whom I had great sympathy, to point out that his arrangement with LWT was clearly the best he could achieve under the present contracts. The change he was proposing would require the formal consent of not only the other Majors but also the other regional companies, all of which would be affected in one way or another. I couldn't see Granada and Yorkshire going to the Authority in its enthusiastic support; could he? Perhaps as a result James's subsequent pitch to the Authority was angled rather differently. He proposed that under the present contracts TVS should become a Major company at the weekend, remaining a regional during the week. Then at the next contract-round the South and South East franchise should be for a seven-day Major, required to produce the majority of its product for the weekend.

He had been no more successful with John Whitney and his programme staff than he had been with the five old warhorses. Now, in the post-Peacock lobbying furore, James was making his pitch straight to government. He phoned me to ask if I would like to join him at lunch with Douglas Hurd: "Just the three of us." "Really? Do you know the Home Secretary?" I asked. "No," said James. "But he's the Member for one of our constituencies and I asked if he'd like to talk about his local television service over lunch." Never short of chutzpah, James. How could I resist?

The lunch was in TVS's London offices, with Douglas Hurd non-committal and James non-stop, deploring the position in which the Home Secretary's local TV station found itself. Bigger and wealthier than at least one of the five major companies, with two state-of-the-art production centres, it was denied major company status as a guaranteed provider of network programmes. Mr Hurd, who must have wondered what the chief executive of one of the very companies denying network status to TVS was doing at this lunch, asked for my view. I said I thought James had a legitimate case and LWT had done what it could to give his programmes a place on the network at least at the weekend. But changes in the system such as he envisaged were in the hands of the IBA and would have to wait until the prospectuses for the next franchise round were being drawn up. We all parted perfectly amicably, but I couldn't help wondering on my way back to Kent House whether Mrs Thatcher's response to her Home Secretary's report of the conversation might not be "Splendid! If these companies have so much money with nothing to spend it on, let them spend it on buying their franchises!" Be careful what you lobby for, James...

The fact is that a good deal of this lobbying was successful. The IBA was very conscious of the pressure from TVS and the other large regional companies to change the system of programme provision and payment. Decades later in the official history, David Glencross would recall that by 1986 the Authority had come to believe that the Controllers Group with its guarantees and the regional companies in the role of supplicants did indeed look rather odd now that there had been some equalising up both in revenues and programme-making capacity within the system. In May of the following year, in announcing its plans for extending the current ITV contracts to the end of 1992, the IBA would state that it was seeking to loosen up ITV's arrangements "in regard to programme exchange between the majors, the supply of programmes to the network by the ten regional companies, and the exchange of programmes between the weekday and the weekend".

Meanwhile, in December 1986, only four months after IPPA launched its Campaign for 25 percent, the Home Secretary wrote to the Chairman of the IBA to say "We should like to move towards a position where, on the ITV system, independent productions took up around 25 percent of the air time devoted to originally produced material. We also believe it to be right if independent productions came to share a similar share of the production budget." He hoped that an early start could be made "and that we can look forward to a target of this kind being achieved within four years." It was time to warn the staff at Kent House of the upheavals that lay ahead. And to take the dust covers off Operation Evergreen. Just in case.

John Birt and I worked out a strategy over the New Year. Barry Cox would draft a speech for me to record on videotape. Copies of the tape would be

352 | THE BEST OF TIMES

handed that evening to department heads, who would play them to their respective departments at a synchronised time the following morning. Accompanied by John, Ron Miller, Finance Director Peter McNally, Director of Production Peter Cazaly and Company Secretary Judith Thomas, I would address an open staff meeting that day at which we would hear the staff's reaction to the tape and answer their questions. But not yet. Another significant event was looming, another subject on which I would be asked questions by another, very different, inquisitor.

The Times They Are A-Changing...

O nce Channel 4 was on the air there was room in the bandwidth then available to the UK for only one more terrestrial channel. True multiplicity would have to wait for digital technology. Nevertheless, the technology of the day made it possible for a number of additional channels to be delivered directly to the home by cable and high-powered satellite and ITCA's Council set up a Cable and Satellite Working Party to examine its potential. Similarly, at the BBC Bill Cotton was appointed Managing Director of Satellite Broadcasting. Like ITCA's Council, Bill had nothing but working parties to manage, but the Conservative government had been attracted to the economic and industrial possibilities of electronic technology from the moment it came to power and throughout the eighties it encouraged a steady crescendo of cable and satellite activity.

In 1982 an Information Technology Panel set up by Mrs Thatcher reported that there was no reason to delay the introduction of new cable services and it expressed the view that valuable possibilities could lie in programme provision via satellite. In 1983 the Hunt Committee of Inquiry into Cable Expansion and Broadcasting Policy endorsed the licensing of cable operators and recommended competition for their franchises. The Cable and Broadcasting Act of 1984 established a Cable Authority to implement the industry's expansion and regulate its services. And in 1986 the cable industry had been given a hefty boost by the Peacock Committee's recommendation that restrictions on pay-per-view should be lifted and all new sets in the UK market fitted with decryption equipment.

Direct Broadcasting by Satellite – DBS – enjoyed a more chequered progression. Five high-powered DBS channels were available to the UK and in 1982 Mrs Thatcher's Information Technology Panel recommended an early start for their services. The Government promptly awarded two of the channels to the BBC, with the requirement that the satellite delivering them should use British technology only. British Aerospace, British Telecom and Marconi joined forces to supply that technology in a consortium they called United Satellite, or Unisat. Unfortunately, Unisat's costs were too high for the BBC to accommodate by itself so in a spirit of entente, cordially reciprocated by ITV and the IBA, the Corporation proposed a Tripartite Working Party in which Unisat, ITV and the BBC could explore the project's possibilities together. By the middle of 1984 the Tripartites had been joined by Consolidated Satellite Broadcasting, Granada TV Rental, Pearson plc, Thorn-EMI and the Virgin Group, forming a most impressive consortium known as the Club of 21. Unfortunately, Unisat's costs remained too high and a year later the project was abandoned and the Club of 21 dissolved.

In its determined pursuit of a viable DBS service the Government then turned to the marketplace. It amended the Cable and Broadcasting Act to give the IBA sole responsibility for the provision of high-powered Direct Broadcasting by Satellite in the UK, and authorised it to invite applications for a 15-year, three-channel DBS contract free of any obligation to Unisat. Some of the consortia teaming up to bid for the contract were joined by ITV companies, London Weekend Television among them. Our consortium was led by Michael Green's Carlton Communications company and our application made it to the final shortlist of three from which the Authority made its selection in December 1986. We were beaten to the contract by the British Satellite Broadcasting consortium, but by then LWT was working on another satellite project with its ITV colleagues, a project which seemed to offer commercial prospects more promising than the one we were to lose.

In July 1985, a month before the Council of 21 abandoned its pursuit of high-powered DBS, Bryan Cowgill, at that time Chairman of Council's Cable and Satellite Working Party, presented a paper to his fellow members which indicated that Intelsat, a medium-powered communications satellite cheaper and with a wider footprint than Unisat, could deliver a service to cable stations throughout Europe without waiting for the direct-to-homes technology of DBS. Moreover, such a service could conceivably be sustained by advertising rather than subscription and pay-per-view. Unfortunately, in that same month the *Dallas* debacle removed Bryan from both the Working

Party and Thames Television, but his paper had a galvanising effect on his colleagues. BBC and ITV programmes were already selling well on the continent. Research proved the success not only of the commercial television stations in Europe but also of the commercials shown on the state broadcasting networks. The Working Party's advertising consultants Saatchi & Saatchi concluded that a pan-European market for a satellite service combining the best of both BBC and ITV programmes could not merely be sustained by advertising, but could make a great deal of money from it, and they produced a highly optimistic revenue forecast for such a service.

LWT's media expert Rod Allen, the producer of *Look Here*, was co-opted onto the Cable and Satellite Working Party to work on a business plan for a Best of British TV satellite channel together with colleagues from Trident and Central Television, the ITCA Secretariat and the accountancy firm Peat Marwick. Their deliberations echoed Saatchi's research, appearing to offer breakeven for the service within two years. The group reckoned, in the words of its Peat Marwick representative, that "it could be a nice little earner".

Inspired by Ted Turner's Atlanta SuperStation in the States, which distributed its programme output by satellite throughout the USA, Rod suggested that ITV should call its service SuperChannel. The Working Party was sold on both idea and title and proceeded to sell them to the ITCA Council. Members of Council enthused their respective Boards and, caught up in the excitement of what promised to be the high-risk, high-reward possibilities of the project, company after company agreed to participate in financing it. Ironically, the only standout was Thames, whose now departed Managing Director had inspired the project in the first place. Richard Dunn's Board put its money into hardware instead and Thames became a founder-investor in the European consortium which was building another medium-powered satellite called Astra.

There was a great deal to do. ITV had to set up a SuperChannel Board, appoint a chairman, a managing director, a sales director, a director of programmes. We had to lay our hands on a transponder to connect us to Intelsat. We had to get the BBC on-side, find a studio, control room and offices to house the staff we would need to compile and deliver our service, and negotiate deals with cable stations throughout Europe to take it. Looking back, it doesn't seem possible that all this could be accomplished with any kind of speed but SuperChannel was on the air not much more than 18 months after Bryan Cowgill's paper was presented to the Working Party.

Those of us who were involved in it were flying on zeal and adrenalin and everything seemed so *feasible*. Did we move too fast? Should we have been more measured, more circumspect?

Council nominated a handful of its Chief Executive members as Super-Channel's non-executive directors. A proposal that Christopher Bland be appointed chairman was vetoed by Granada's representative, David Plow-right, on the grounds that Christopher lacked a background of programme making and scheduling, and I was appointed in his place. As SuperChannel's Managing Director we recruited Richard Hooper, then running Prestel for British Telecom but previously a radio and television producer for the BBC and one of the founders of The Open University.

Next task, the big one: find a transponder. Rupert Murdoch had one but he was using it to transmit his own programme service, Sky Television, to cable operators in Europe and Super Channel would be a direct competitor. Richard Branson had one, delivering Virgin Communications' Music Channel to the continent. Perhaps an arrangement of some kind would be possible with him?

Christopher Bland had had dealings with Virgin before and he agreed to go with me to talk to Branson at his home in Holland Park. In an unusually domestic meeting in his sitting room, interrupted by his 5-year old daughter Holly who wandered in from time to time to discuss other pressing matters with daddy, we roughed out a provisional plan which Christopher and I agreed to put to our colleagues.

The ITV companies would invest some £40 million in a merger with The Music Channel, in effect acquiring all of it save the portion retained by Branson as Virgin's investment. The Music Channel would then trade as SuperChannel, its daily Music Box programmes available to us wherever and whenever we required them. Branson proposed his business partner and brother-in-law Robert Devereux as Virgin's representative on the SuperChannel Board and Charles Levison, the Music Channel's chief executive, as its Managing Director. We readily accepted Devereux, who had set up Virgin's successful entertainment division, but pointed out that SuperChannel already had a Managing Director. A compromise was finally reached in which, subject to Richard Hooper's agreement, he and Levison would be joint Managing Directors. It was a cumbersome arrangement, but we needed the transponder and Richard Hooper generously did agree. The SuperChannel Board endorsed the terms discussed with Branson, and in collaboration with Hooper and Levison we recruited Carol Haslam, a senior Commissioning Editor from Channel 4, as SuperChannel's Director of Programmes and Michael Schlagman from the Direct Mail Trade Association as its Sales Director.

All the other requirements fell swiftly into place. Limehouse Studios at Canary Wharf supplied our play-out point for the channel. Virgin supplied offices, editing suites and a small presentation studio at its premises in Rathbone Place in Soho. Negotiations began with the European cable stations. The BBC, still in beneficent entente mode, agreed to supply its programmes to the channel in a memorandum of agreement drawn up with BBC Enterprises, the Corporation's programme sales division. And on 30 January 1987 SuperChannel was launched to the potential audience of 9 million viewers in 14 different countries served by the cable stations we had by then signed up. Or, rather, *Super Channel* was launched: the two halves of its title, one above the other, fitted the screen much more effectively than stretched out as *SuperChannel* in one long line. Sorry, Rod!

SuperChannel Goes on Air

There is a half-hour compilation of moments from the launch party at Limehouse Studios on YouTube, which gives some sense of the evening's excited optimism. Anne Diamond welcomes our European viewers in front of a map which lights up as she names their respective countries and reads out the good wishes from their cable stations. Benny Hill and the cast of the BBC's *'Allo 'Allo!* say 'allo to their new audiences. Wayne Sleep dances his own welcome in the character of the Master of Ceremonies he was currently playing in Cabaret in the West End. We see Denis Norden introducing *It'll be Alright on the Night*, Jeremy Beadle fronting a compilation of the best of *Game for a Laugh*, and a snatch of *Spitting Image* puppets behaving indecorously.

We see trailers for that evening's play *Romance on the Orient Express* and the star-packed two-hour edition of the Music Channel's *Music Box* show from Cannes which will follow it. There's John Suchet introducing ITN's coverage of European and international news, business and weather which he will be presenting each evening in *SuperChannel News*, and Paul McDowell and David Cass trailing the weekend sports coverage we plan to present in *SuperSport* – both services blazing the trail for the Eurosport and Euronews channels of today.

Our guest of honour is the Prime Minister. As the channel's chairman I greet her as she arrives in her limousine, introduce her to Richard Hooper, Charles Levison, Carol Haslam and Michael Schlagman and invite her to address our European audience. SuperChannel is exactly the sort of entrepreneurial activity dear to Mrs Thatcher's heart and she is in buoyant mood.

"I am delighted to be here this evening at this super party for SuperChannel, to celebrate the launch of a service which will give our friends all over Europe the very best of British," she says. Mrs Thatcher was not known for her love of ITV, but this time we seemed to be doing the right thing. "It is going to be financed by advertising," she says. "I think if you have got something good you had better shout about it otherwise no one will ever know about it, and so this not only gives us British television in Europe but it will also enable British manufacturers to market their products over a very much wider area".

The full text of the Prime Minister's speech is still available on-line. "This whole venture is an example of the latest technological change and a great example of European cooperation," she says. She even goes on to provide some good-humoured programme promotion for us. To those who are watching, she declares "I would like to say I think they have a treat in store in some of the programmes they are going to see. I had a list of them: I wonder if I can remember them: Eastenders, Van der Valk...All Creatures Great and Small...and as a kind of foundation course in British humour, Spitting Image. Now I am not quite sure what they will make of that, but I am quite sure they will learn a great deal."

After the speech I take the Prime Minister into the studio for a performance by the National Youth Jazz Orchestra. The studio has been dressed and lit to resemble a night club and there are Mrs Thatcher and I sitting together at a cosy little table for two to watch the show, for all the world as if we are on a date. As the compilation ends she is asking me questions about SuperChannel, but now that the channel's launch is over I am very much aware that in a fortnight or so I will have to be in another studio in another part of London, having to answer questions of a very different kind.

At Kent House, John Birt, Barry Cox and I have settled on the date for our showdown with the staff. The three of us work on Barry's draft for my speech. I videotape it on 17 February, and at 9 am the next morning it is played back by each department head to the members of his or her staff. It pulls no punches. The staff hear me say that licences have now been given to the satellite and cable operators who will be our future competitors for audiences and advertising revenue, but more immediately it's clear that the independent producers have won their fight to gain access on both BBC and ITV and by the end of the present franchises the IBA and the Home Office will expect 25 percent of ITV's annual production to be supplied by independents. Losing so large an amount is bound to affect the size of ITV's workforce: it makes no sense for companies to maintain the staff levels to produce 100 percent of ITV's output if they are allowed to produce only 75 percent. At LWT this will have a serious impact on our own plans for the future. None of us wants enforced redundancies, but absorbing overtime and not replacing members of staff when they leave might not be enough to match the size of our workforce with the size of our future output.

The reduction in that output will create spare capacity in our studios and I tell the staff that we must make use of that spare capacity by encouraging the independents to produce their programmes here at Kent House. We will be competing with other ITV companies in the same boat. We will also be competing with outside facility houses – and outside facility houses pay their staff less than we pay our own. We will have to make ourselves as cost-effective as any of those houses if we hope to attract business from the independents. We will have to match their prices, offer a service in whatever form is required, using the full range of our facilities or only part of them, supplying our studios fully crewed or only partly crewed, bringing in key specialists from outside wherever necessary. We will have to improve our efficiency, reduce our manning levels, create greater flexibility across our entire programme-making process.

I said that I saw these developments as a challenge to everyone who worked at LWT, whether in management or in the unions. I told them that our production and programme-making skills were second to none, our record in industrial relations was a good one, and I could not believe that, to preserve our future security and stability, we would not be able to achieve local agreements to enable management and unions to move forward together into this new era of broadcasting. I believed we could make our production costs so competitive and our working practices so flexible that the independents would be eager to use our facilities. I believed we could make our unit costs so attractive that the satellite and cable services which threatened our future audiences and revenue would become keen customers for our programmes. I said we had talked about providing for the future long enough. Now we had to act – or the future would leave us far behind.

Ignore the rhetorical flourishes. The meat of what John, Barry and I had put into the speech was pretty raw. Absorbing overtime? Reducing manning levels? Changing working practices? Matching the flexibility and cost-effectiveness of outside facility houses? How would the union shop stewards react to this wildly heretical agenda? We phoned department heads to ask what kind of reception the tape had received from their staff members that morning. Stunned silence for the most part, apparently. But there were two and a half hours before the mass meeting at noon; what kind of fire-storm would build by then?

Answer?

No kind of fire-storm. Not even a spark. John Birt, Ron Miller, Peter McNally, Peter Cazaly, Judith Thomas and I filed onto the platform set up in Studio One to face a sombre, receptive staff, shop stewards and all, wanting to know more about the problems and opportunities facing the company and the difficulties we would need to overcome in winning a new franchise. Perhaps those local agreements would not be so difficult to achieve after all. LWT's management team could begin to analyse what was needed and how we might secure it....

And then my Director of Programmes, a key member of that team, tells me he is leaving that team. John Birt has accepted an offer to join the BBC as its Deputy Director General.

In yet another attempt to sort out the irksome BBC, Mrs Thatcher and Douglas Hurd had appointed Marmaduke Hussey as the Corporation's new Chairman, and the day before SuperChannel went on the air Hussey summarily dismissed his Director General, Alasdair Milne. Some commentators attributed the Prime Minister's buoyant mood at the SuperChannel launch to this coup rather than to SuperChannel's entrepreneurial enterprise. Writing in *The Guardian* more than a quarter of a century later, Maggie Brown remembered asking Mrs Thatcher at the launch party what she thought of Milne's departure and Mrs Thatcher, "triumphant, flushed", had simply cried "Talk to the Chairman of the BBC!"

The Chairman of the BBC had proceeded to promote Alasdair's Deputy, Michael Checkland, to succeed him and Michael, with accountancy rather than programmes as his background, had sought a programme man as his own Deputy: a programme man with the editorial skill to knock into shape the BBC's news and current affairs departments, which were badly out of control. He had chosen John Birt. I couldn't fault his choice, but I deeply regretted it. It was not simply because John was an important part of the management team working on the local agreements we intended to put to the unions — Roy Van Gelder and the other managers in the team could handle those — but because I had very different plans for him.

I was 58, two years away from my retirement as LWT's Managing Direc-tor. The company's Articles of Association required Executive Directors of the Board to stand down at 60 though they could remain on the Board as non-executives until the age of 70. My own intention was to retire at 65, as my service agreement provided. Taking a leaf out of John Freeman's book I had planned my succession well in advance and discussed it with Christopher Bland. I wanted John Birt to succeed me as Managing Director. Christopher had been happy to agree and suggested that nearer the time we should send John to the Harvard Business School to equip him for what looked like becoming a much more business-oriented television industry than the one to which we were accustomed. Michael Checkland's offer had put paid to that plan but at least I had two years in which to consider an alternative. My immediate problem was finding a new Director of Pro-grammes, and quickly.

Some months earlier, when I told John what I had in mind, we had dis-cussed who should succeed him as Director of Programmes when the time came. The likeliest internal candidates would clearly be the Controllers of our principal creative departments, Drama's Nick Elliott, Entertainment's Alan Boyd and Current Affairs boss Barry Cox. But there was one external candidate who already had the necessary experience for the job. Our scheme to keep Greg Dyke within ITV in 1984 had paid off and Greg had become a very effective Director of Programmes for TVS. He knew LWT well from his six years in its Current Affairs Department, he had personal, hard-won experience of network practices and politics, and he was not only aware of the problems that faced our own Director of Programmes, he had been help-ing to solve them with TVS programmes for the past three years. He would have been our first choice in two years' time. He was my first choice now.

Christopher Bland was prepared to go along with me but he didn't know Greg and wanted to have a look at him first, so I phoned Greg early one morning and asked if he could come up to London that afternoon to meet us. He didn't ask why; he just said yes. That afternoon, when he joined Christopher, John and me in my office, I asked him why he hadn't asked what the meeting would be about. He said that if the Managing Director of LWT rings you at 7.30 am and asks you to meet him, it's got to be worth saying yes. I said I hoped he would think so. We explained what was happening with John and the BBC and told Greg that we wanted him to replace John as LWT's Director of Programmes.

In his autobiography Greg says he knew immediately that he would take the job, but there was a problem. He and his family were now firmly settled in Southampton; his partner Sue was lecturing in sociology in a local college and their older children were happy at their school. If he took the LWT job they would all have to be uprooted again. Greg went back to Southampton to discuss the problem with Sue, and Christopher and I set up our interviews with Nick, Barry and Alan.

Alan, who featured in *Broadcast* magazine's front page story of 27 March under the headline 'Dyke And Boyd Tipped In Race For LWT Job', remembers his interview being tough but fair. Nick says that by the time he was interviewed he was under the impression that Greg's appointment was a foregone conclusion. Barry remembers his interview with little pleasure and thought we were simply going through the motions. The fact of the matter is that all three were genuine prospects as Director of Programmes but their potential was trumped by Greg Dyke's years of experience at TVS and our immediate need. Greg managed to square the move with Sue, and I was able to go with my original choice for the job – two years earlier than I had thought I would be doing. We said goodbye to John Birt at the end of May and Greg was appointed to the Board in July.

Alan, Barry and Nick realised their potential, as I always knew they would. Alan succeeded Greg as Director of Programmes at TVS. Barry was invited on to the LWT Board as its Director of Corporate Affairs. And, in the enormous reorganisation of LWT and ITV which took place in the ensuing years, Nick would become Managing Director of LWT Programmes and subsequently Director of Drama for the entire Network. 1987 was little more than six months old; and if you think it already sounds like the year of great change for LWT and ITV, in the words of the great Al Jolson *you ain't heard nothin' yet!*

Breaching the Bastion

D ouglas Hurd's welcome to the Peacock Report in the House of Commons may have been cautious, but his Leader's was decidedly not. Mrs Thatcher set up a Cabinet Committee chaired by herself to structure the government response to the Report's conclusions, and to assist her Committee in its deliberations she held a Seminar in September 1987 at Number 12 Downing Street.

She was accompanied by the members of the Committee and a number of advisors from 10 Downing Street. Professor Peacock, now Sir Alan, was there to speak on 'The Peacock Report 14 Months Later'. Guests invited from ITV to observe but not to speak were the new Chairman of Thames Sir Ian Trethowan; David McCall, Chief Executive of Anglia Television; Bill Brown, Managing Director of Scottish Television; and David Nicholas, Editor and Chief Executive of ITN. No one from LWT or any of the ten other ITV companies was invited, but in an ironic little touch Michael Grade and John Birt were both there, representing the BBC: my Directors of Programmes certainly got around. Jeremy Isaacs represented Channel 4 and John Whitney was there for the IBA. Completing the list were representatives from the independent production sector, cable and satellite executives, an advertising industry representative and the Home Office's consultant on subscription television. Also a surprising wild card: the Managing Director of Carlton Communications, Michael Green, who had failed to take over Thames in 1985 in a bid for the London weekday franchise and failed again in 1986 to win the IBA contract for DBS.

In his memoir *The View from No.11*, Nigel Lawson, a key member of the Cabinet Committee, described the Seminar as generating "neither heat nor (despite one or two eloquent contributions) light; merely the deafening sound of axes being ground". One of the eloquent contributions came from the wild card. The gist of what Michael Green had to say was "I have built a £600 million business related to broadcasting, but I am still an outsider. What do I have to do to become an insider?" That of course was exactly what Mrs Thatcher wanted to hear. She didn't actually go so far as to declare "Bid for it, Mr Green! Bid for it in the forthcoming auction for ITV franchises!" but she had clearly embraced the Peacock Committee's conclusions with enthusiasm. Summing up one pivotal session, she reiterated the Report's argument that it was the monopoly powers of the BBC and ITV that had led to excessive pay demands and restrictive practices by the unions, holding back new developments and acting against the interests of the consumers. "Television," she famously said, "was the last bastion of restrictive practices."

She was fingering television as a whole and not just Independent Television, but we knew that ITV was the primary culprit and we knew that if we were to get ourselves into shape for the next franchise round those restrictive practices would have to go. It was also clear that the Peacock Report was by no means destined for the waste paper basket as Gerald Kaufman had suggested. The impending franchise trail was going to be a long and bumpy one.

Some of its road signs were already in place: Douglas Hurd made known his colleagues' desire to loosen up the system and declared that the days of the status quo were numbered; the government had commissioned studies on deregulation, subscription, and pay-per-view; the IBA had announced that it was seeking to loosen up ITV's arrangements for the supply and exchange of programmes within the network. It was just that it took time for the 15 companies to see those signs: not all of us were travelling at the same speed.

Now at last, however, we lumbered into action. ITCA, the Independent Television Companies Association, gave itself a more user-friendly image by changing its name to ITVA, the Independent Television Association, and began by addressing the reformation of an ITV networking system which had been operating broadly unchanged since the franchises of 1968. In October, Greg and I and all the other Managing Directors and Programme Controllers met in Jersey for our annual Strategy Conference and hammered out some of the basic principles of a new system.

The Regional companies would be guaranteed 50 hours of networked drama per year, and the major companies' guarantee of 42 hours of network programmes per week would be reduced initially to 35 hours and progressively reduced further thereafter. The hours released by this process would go into what was dubbed a 'flexi-pool' by Steve Morrison of Granada whose idea it was, and would be competed for by all 15 companies. The flexi-pool would be operated by a new Network Controllers Group: the old Programme Controllers Group being augmented by two Controllers from the major Regionals – STV and TVS to begin with – and their own planners would join those of the Network. A Controller would head each of seven flexi-pool Sub-Groups: one to deal with the system's finance and six responsible respectively for recommending Drama, Entertainment, Factual, Children's, Sport and Daytime programmes to the Network Controllers for their approval and subsequent commissioning or producing.

It sounded straightforward enough, but the devil was in its realisation. With 15 different companies, each with its own priorities, the network needed more meetings and more strategic conferences before it could agree on how to handle the financial and organisational implications of the principles, and both Government and IBA grew impatient with the time it was taking. A White Paper on 'Broadcasting in the '90s', published the following year, acknowledged the efforts being made to bring greater efficiency and competition to the network but declared "The Government believes that a more radical approach is needed".

John Whitney proposed just such an approach by putting a set of unmistakeably radical propositions to managing directors at the Standing Consultative Committee meeting of September 1989. Among them were the abolition of *all* guarantees, including regional drama, and the idea of a single Network Commissioner and Scheduler supported by a central unit owned and funded jointly by all the companies. They were discussed and, ultimately, the reformation of ITV's networking system would indeed be radical, but not until the IBA's Invitation to Bid for the new ITV contracts was published in 1991, which concentrated the companies' minds wonderfully.

We moved much more swiftly in our attack on restrictive practices. The abolition of union closed shops and secondary picketing by the 1982 and 1984 Employment Acts enabled the ITV companies to tackle the unions in their own manner at their own pace without provoking industrial action across the network. It had provided a new Secret Weapon for the companies to deploy: a viable Management Service. Thames had won a battle with the ACTT in 1984 by staying on the air with a programme service produced and transmitted by Managers, office-workers and other non-unionised staff. And TV-am – not part of our network but operating under the same union agreements – had been transmitting a Management Service ever since November 1987, when Managing Director Bruce Gyngell reacted to a one-day strike over manning levels by locking out his ACTT employees until they agreed to take no further industrial action.

With TV-am's Managers, Executives and Secretaries acting as Camera-men, Video Engineers and Lighting and Sound Technicians the Service's technical standards were perhaps not of the highest order but the audience seemed to like it and by January 1988 TV-am was recording the highest weekly reach ever achieved in its five-year history. The following month the company dismissed the 289 locked-out technicians and announced that it was replacing them with just 70 non-unionised personnel. Nineteen months later, in September 1989, the sacked technicians finally threw in the towel and called off the dispute. That year Bruce received a Christmas card from Margaret Thatcher saying 'Carry on the good work.'

A Management Service was now the elephant in the background of every negotiation between the companies and their union shop stewards. Granada, Yorkshire and Thames led the way in what Brian Appleyard described in a full-page *Times* article on ITV's industrial relations as "quiet and steady renegotiations of union agreements intended to strip out the worst abuses gradually over a period of years". At LWT, we moved the elephant to the foreground and decided that the best way to strip out the abuses was to confront all our union shops at the same time and let them know that a Management Service was very much in our minds.

Our own Secret Weapon, Warren Breach's Operation Evergreen, was primed and made ready. We checked that Warren's tapes were set to go in Amsterdam, engaged in a little judicious leaking of our plans, supplied teach-yourself-Dutch books to our managers to be carried about casually or left lying on desks, and on Tuesday, 22 March 1988, launched what Appleyard called "the most dramatic piece of *perestroika* yet seen in the commercial sector....a bold and unprecedented step from an ITV company".

We released what we called The Document to our workforce. My video speech the previous year had outlined the challenges that faced us and emphasised how necessary it was to ensure we could make programmes as efficiently and cost-effectively as any production house in the United Kingdom. Now The Document laid out how we intended to achieve that aim.

We were withdrawing from ITV's National Agreements with the ACTT, the EETPU, the NUJ and BETA, the Broadcasting and Entertainment Alliance formed by a merger of NATTKE and the BBC's 'house' union the Association of Broadcasting Staffs.

In their place we were laying down new local agreements to modernise the company's working practices. From now on, management would decide crew size and manning; the maximum overtime rate would be twice the usual hourly rate; there would be no payment for hours not worked, no inefficient job demarcations and no procedures inhibiting the introduction of new equipment; and management would have the right to sub-contract outside the company wherever necessary. We would enforce no compulsory redundancies but generous terms would be offered to those who chose to leave voluntarily. After three months of consultation and negotiation, the new agreements became operative at the beginning of July, without any disruption from our union shops. And Warren Breach and his fellow planners finally scheduled *Evergreen* one weekend across the entire network.

By the end of the month, which was also the end of LWT's 1987-88 financial year, the permanent staff of the company had been reduced by 300 through voluntary redundancies, natural wastage and unfilled vacancies, and we had established our studios as a separate profit centre, LWT Production Facilities, with Peter Cazaly as its boss. Peter put a spirited young executive Penny Lent in charge of selling our facilities to the independent market in competition with the other studios and ITV companies, and Penny got off to a spectacular start: in the next financial year almost half our studio production hours would be taken up by independent producers.

LWT's strategy as a Group was now to concentrate on its core business – making and transmitting programmes, selling advertising time on air, and marketing its shows internationally. We began to dispose of our holdings in the travel company Page and Moy and the publishing group Century Hutchinson and embarked on the decentralisation of the component elements of our television business, giving each of them its own managerial and profit responsibility.

LWT Production Facilities was not the first of these. Earlier in the year we had parted on friendly terms with RPTA, the company responsible for many years for selling LWT's product overseas, and set up our own sales organisation, London Weekend Television International Ltd, with Sydney Perry as its Managing Director. The other parts of the business would devolve in due course. We were on our way to making the company more efficient in our preparation for the new franchises. More efficient, and more lean: by the starting date of the new franchises our television company staff numbers would decrease from 1,468 in 1986 to 723, without the loss of a single day through industrial action.

Superchannel Blues

Meanwhile, in another part of the forest, my other concern – SuperChannel – was going through a much more difficult time. A great deal of money was going out, and nothing like enough advertising revenue was coming in. Did we, after all, move too fast in getting SuperChannel on the air in 18 months? Should we have indeed been more measured, more circumspect? I'm afraid the answer is Yes. The stunning array of programmes Carol Haslam had bought from BBC Enterprises and ITV programme sales divisions didn't come ready-cleared for satellite transmission to Europe. Urgent negotiations had to begin for their clearance with the Actors Equity Union, the Musicians Union and the Writers Guild.

We managed to agree terms with the Musicians and Writers in time for the launch but not, unfortunately, with the Actors. Equity was concerned that the sale of BBC and ITV programmes to SuperChannel would undermine their direct sale to the stations themselves, which would be more rewarding for its members. It refused to agree a blanket clearance and decreed that individual agreements would have to be concluded with each actor in each programme before it could be transmitted.

Would the negotiations with Equity have succeeded if they had been given more time? Perhaps. But how much more? Equity had taken all of two years to reach an agreement on residual payments for commercials on Channel 4 and TV-am, seriously jeopardising the stability of both channels in the process. Now it jeopardised SuperChannel's. Six hours of peak-time programming a day had to be withdrawn from transmission at the last minute and Carol Haslam's ingenious schedule, packed with goodies for our continental viewers, was demolished at a stroke. She worked hard to put together something resembling it but not every member of the cast of every programme would be traceable, not every member of every cast would agree the residual payments they would be offered, and SuperChannel's schedule would never be the same.

Even so, this was not SuperChannel's biggest problem. Saatchi & Saatchi's vision of a rich pan-European advertising market had been a chimera. There was no pan-European advertising market: Europe was a number of different, quite separate, individual markets. There wasn't even a pan-European trademark for everything that was being sold to them: products were often marketed under different names in different countries. European commercial television and the commercials broadcast on individual state networks may have been successful, but the advertising consultants who extrapolated from that success a lucrative pan-European advertising market for the best of British television had seriously misjudged it.

They had failed to factor in the fortunes of Sky Channel. Rupert Murdoch's satellite service to Europe had been haemorrhaging money ever since it began and in 1987 was still losing at the rate of £10 million a year. Certainly, it was offering a different kind of programming – the best of American and Australian rather than the best of British – but if Sky Channel had failed to grow a pan-European advertising market in five years how could Super-Channel, with a weakened schedule, be expected to do so in five months?

Hang on a minute, thought Rod Allen and I at one of our strategy meetings. If the two channels were having difficulty in growing the market separately, perhaps they could grow it together? Perhaps a single channel, combining Sky Channel's mix of American and Australian with what remained of Super-Channel's best of British, could achieve it? If the two channels merged they would not only win themselves more time in which to do so, they would also stem their individual losses and halve their costs in the process. We wondered how Rupert Murdoch might react to such a proposition.

I had met Murdoch with John Freeman when I joined LWT as John's deputy in 1974. Rupert was still a major shareholder then, and whenever he was in London John and I would call on him at The Sun's offices in Bouverie Street to report on the company's progress. We'd talk about programmes and ratings and the state of the industry and then repair to his private dining room for lunch, where we would be joined by the newspaper's editor Larry Lamb. Now, when Rod phoned Murdoch's office to request a meeting, we were invited to join him for supper with Sky's Managing Director Jim Styles, in his private dining room at the Gray's Inn Road offices of *The Times*. And a very pleasant evening it was.

The four of us discussed the barely existent pan-European advertising market and the problems that both Sky Channel and SuperChannel were experiencing with it, and Rod and I made our pitch for a joint approach to tackle them. Rupert listened intently, nodded sagely, observed that it was an interesting idea to which he would give serious thought, and said Jim would get back to us the following week with his response. Jim didn't.

Murdoch had clearly concluded that too much of News Corporation's time and treasure had been spent on trying to breathe life into an unresponsive European market. He had been curious to see whether SuperChannel's own experience reinforced that conclusion, and it did. He hadn't been interested in joining us or anybody else in persevering with Europe: he was going to turn his back on it. Literally. Instead of beaming programmes to cable stations in Europe Sky would beam them directly to homes in the United Kingdom.

At a press conference the following year he announced that Sky was forming a Sky Television Network with three additional channels: Sky Movies, Sky News and a channel dedicated to Sport. The Network would move from Intelsat to the higher-powered Astra satellite beamed to the UK, and because its transmissions would be up-linked from Luxembourg they would be outside the IBA's DBS remit. Like LWT, Murdoch had been one of the unsuccessful bidders for the IBA's DBS franchise in 1986, and he had subsequently been rebuffed by the victorious BSB Consortium in an attempt to join it. Now he would have his own United Kingdom DBS service and could begin the relentless, massively expensive process that would lead to the prominence it enjoys today.

Oh well... Perhaps SuperChannel could find another partner? Right on cue came a call from Patrick Cox, the son of ITN's founding Editor Geoffrey Cox. The American network NBC was contemplating a satellite venture into Europe and had commissioned Patrick to explore the market's possibilities. He'd appreciate it if I could mark his card in the light of SuperChannel's experiences. "With pleasure," I said, "and perhaps there's a way in which SuperChannel and NBC could work together in developing the market?" We arranged a lunch date at which such ideas could be discussed and I went home to Chiswick that weekend, happily working out how SuperChannel's fortunes could be transformed by such a collaboration. What should we call it? "NBC SuperChannel" of course; why not? Sounded good to me... That Sunday I was enjoying my morning bath when Audrey walked into the bathroom with a telephone in her hand. "It's Robert Maxwell, calling from Capri," she said, and I found myself renewing the acquaintance of yet another Media Mogul.

I'd met Maxwell the previous year through the Television and Radio Industries Club, an amiable organisation established in 1931 "to promote mutual understanding and good will among those engaged in the audio, visual, communications and allied industries". The Club's membership was and remains principally drawn from these industries but its annually appointed Presidents are usually radio and television executives or performers. In 1979 I was invited to succeed Howard Thomas in the role and was honoured to do so: the long list of past Presidents also included Norman Collins, Sir Robert Fraser and two past Chairmen of the Authority, Lord Hill and Lord Aylestone; among those succeeding me would be Robin Scott, Bill Cotton and Michael Grade. And in 1986 the Club had invited Robert Maxwell to be its President.

Maxwell's first duty was to preside over a Club dinner at Grosvenor House at which the speaker would be Frank Chapple, the controversial leader of the Electricians' Union. We put on a good show of support for our new President. The outgoing President, John Whitney, Director General of the IBA, was there with his wife Roma, so was Lord Thomson, the IBA's Chairman and another previous TRIC President, with his wife Grace. I was there with Audrey as both a previous President and a recently appointed Companion of TRIC alongside John Whitney and David Frost.

There was an excellent turn-out of members. The Thomsons and Whitneys and Audrey and I were chatting in a group when the new President arrived with his wife Betty and made a bee-line for us. After a chorus of introductions all round – "Call me Bob!" he said to each of us – he looked round the room and studied the rest of the gathering. "Not many raisins in the mix," he commented. "Raisins?" I asked. "Yes," he said, "Where are all the television stars, all the big names?" "Well, Bob," I explained, "there are two other organisations, BAFTA and the Royal Television Society, and producers and television stars usually belong to one or other of those." "Well," said Maxwell "Why don't we just buy one of them up?"

Now his secretary was saying "Mr Tesler? I have Mr Maxwell for you." He must have thought she was putting him through to my office because there he was, bluff as ever, booming "Brian! Good to know you're also hard at work on a Sunday morning!" – yes indeed, Bob, you on your yacht and I in my bath – "Morning Bob," I said, " What can I do for you?" "I understand you've been talking to NBC about collaborating in a satellite channel for Europe?" "Well yes, I've had a bit of a chat with Patrick Cox. What about it?" "You should understand, Brian, that when you talk to NBC you are talking to Robert Maxwell. They don't make a move in Europe without consulting me." "Thank you for telling me that, Bob; so...? "So don't bother with Patrick. I'll call you as soon as I get back to London and you and I can tie this up in my office in half-an-hour over a cup of coffee." "That's excellent, Bob. I look forward to your call." I never heard from him again. A few months later the American music channel MTV launched its pan-European satellite channel in direct competition with the Music Box element of SuperChannel. Half it was owned by Robert Maxwell.

I did bother with Patrick of course. Disappointingly, I learned from him that NBC's plans were nowhere near advanced enough to be of assistance to SuperChannel, and SuperChannel's shareholders were getting restive. Our brave new enterprise, which had started out with such promise, cheered on by the Prime Minister herself, was suffering losses of £1 million a month. The shareholders had understood that SuperChannel was a high risk-high reward enterprise, but they'd had enough of the risk; where was the reward?

Richard Hooper and Charles Levison made a funding call for another £20 million to sustain the Channel. Faced with demands from the shareholders for an economy drive, the call was reduced to £12.3 million but, at a stormy Extraordinary General Meeting in August, even this amount was rejected and only a little over £8 million subscribed. Carol Haslam agreed to be bought out of her contract as part of the economy drive and went on to become a successful independent producer. The channel limped along without her as effectively as it could with shareholders breathing down its neck, but in May 1988 the Boards of Central Television and LWT Holdings refused to contribute any further finance. I advised the SuperChannel Board of LWT's decision with the heaviest of hearts. In the circumstances, I said, it would be wrong for me to continue as the channel's Chairman; and I resigned.

That summer Charles Levison returned to Virgin Entertainment, Richard Hooper left to become first a consultant and then a regulator – Chairman of the Radio Authority and Deputy Chairman of Ofcom no less – and Robert Devereux took over from the two of them as SuperChannel's sole Managing

Director and de facto Chairman. Virgin bought up the defectors' holdings, paying £125,000 for LWT's 11.2 percent – the Holdings Board wrote off its investment of £5.1 million – and Branson invested a further £10 million in the company, becoming its biggest shareholder.

But SuperChannel's fortunes failed to improve. Within a year it was sold to Beta TV, a television company with a successful music channel in Italy. The new owners had no more luck with it than the old ones: five years later, financial difficulties prompted its sale to – wait for it! – NBC. Yes, in 1993 Europe finally did have a satellite service called NBC SuperChannel. Where were you in 1987, NBC, when we needed you?

Sadly for the American network, it turned out to be a case of where were *we* when NBC needed us in 1993. The producers of hit American drama series – NBC itself included – were mostly interested in the more rewarding business of selling their programmes direct to individual European countries rather than to a satellite operator, so NBC SuperChannel couldn't schedule anything like as much American fiction as it needed. In 1987 we could have supplied enough British fiction to take up the slack.

With its American content more or less limited to NBC's own news broadcasts and chat shows, in 1996 NBC SuperChannel changed its name to NBC Europe and filled the rest of its schedules with European product. It didn't help. The channel folded two years later and was sold by NBC's parent company General Electric to a German network. A sad end to a bright beginning. But SuperChannel's story was by no means unique. In the 11 years since its launch there had been many other bright beginnings and sad endings in television's exponentially expanding universe.

Not least, alas, in ITV...

The Day Job

Freed from the responsibility of SuperChannel, I could concentrate exclusively on my day job; and the day job was going very well. In the twelve months to 30 July 1989 – normally the end of LWT's financial year but we were in the process of changing that to 31 December – the company achieved its best-ever profit: £30.8 million, a third better than the equivalent figure for 1987-88. It was an achievement made possible by our reductions in staff and production costs and outstanding performances from both Programme and Sales Departments. The Board actually had to increase the size of the Sales Department to keep pace with the enterprise with which Ron Miller and his division were exploring new areas of growth, but we were still employing fewer people in Sales than any of the other major ITV companies.

Greg Dyke had proved as dynamic and resourceful a Director of Programmes as I had hoped, revitalising our schedules, spotting programme winners, persuading seven-day colleagues to favour the weekend in their offers. He had inherited a fine creative team. Marcus Plantin, the producer of the BBC's *The Two Ronnies*, brought in by Alan Boyd to handle some of Light Entertainment's biggest shows, was the obvious and natural successor to Alan and had taken the Controller's baton without missing a beat. Cilla Black's two programmes, *Blind Date* and *Surprise! Surprise!*, continued to feature in ITV's entertainment Top 20, alongside new series of two of our most popular situation comedies: *The Two of Us*, starring Nicholas Lyndhurst and Janet Dibley, and *Me and My Girl*, starring Richard O'Sullivan. They were joined by *Beadle's About*, a spin-off from *Game for a Laugh* starring Jeremy

Beadle, and *You Bet!*, a new game show hosted by Bruce Forsyth. Michael Aspel's *Aspel & Company* also enjoyed its most successful season, the high-light of which was a rare and revealing interview with Elizabeth Taylor.

Two of Light Entertainment's programmes achieved particular distinc-tion. Gareth Hale and Norman Pace began the first series of their sketch show *Hale and Pace* in 1988 and the following spring won the Golden Rose of Montreux Light Entertainment Award – a rare achievement for ITV. And *The Dame Edna Experience* became a cult show as well as a popular success, with a Show Business Personality of the Year Award for Barry Humphries – sorry, Dame Edna – from the Variety Club of Great Britain and a Best Entertainment Award from the Broadcasting Press Guild for the show itself, together with Gold Awards from both the Chicago and the San Francisco Television Festivals.

The Department's production skills were thoroughly exercised by a suc-cession of major entertainment events for the network: the Royal Variety Performance, the BAFTA Awards, a Royal Gala in Aid of the Prince's Trust, and ITV's first network *Telethon*, a marathon 27-hour live broadcast which attracted £22 million for charitable causes – the equivalent of £50 mil-lion today – for which we provided the studio, the facilities and the core production and administration teams.

In a major switch of our resources to drama, Nick Elliott delivered three of ITV's top drama series of the late '80s: *London's Burning*, developed from the 1986 one-off by Jack Rosenthal; *The Charmer*, a thriller adapted from Patrick Hamilton's novel, starring Nigel Havers; and *Wish Me Luck*, the story of the heroic women of the S.O.E. in World War II, starring Kate Buffery.

These were part of a great surge of creative activity from Drama Department, which also included *Troubles*, a two-part dramatisation of J. G. Farrell's novel shot in Ireland and starring Sean Bean and Ian Charle-son; *Bust*, a new series about a Jack-the-Lad forced into bankruptcy – a role tailor-made for its star Paul Nicholas; and three co-productions with American companies: *A Shadow on the Sun*, the story of Kenyan adventurer and aviatrix Beryl Markham, directed by Tony Richardson and starring Stefanie Powers; *Queenie*, a mini-series based on Michael Korda's *roman a clef* about the life of Merle Oberon, the film-actress wife of his uncle Alexander Korda, filmed in India and England with an international cast including Claire Bloom, Sarah Miles, Kirk Douglas, Topol and Joel Gray; and *Ticket to Ride*, the pilot for a comedy thriller co-produced with the ABC

Television network, starring Anthony Andrews and Margaret Whitton, which was picked up as a series by ABC, the first order for a peak-time network series to be obtained by a UK television company. Anthony Andrews had committed to another project by then so the lead male role was taken over by Christopher Cazenove. In addition, production began on the first series of *Agatha Christie's Poirot* and the first of Drama Department's feature film commissions, an adaptation of Evelyn Waugh's novel *A Handful of Dust*.

Wearing his Arts Department hat, Nick also presided over *The South Bank Show*'s 10th Anniversary Season, which was celebrated in a notable series of events in both Britain and America. The Tate Gallery showed ten *South Bank Show* films on British artists, which were accompanied by a series of lectures introduced by the Director of the Tate, Sir Alan Bowness, who pronounced *The South Bank Show* "the finest arts programme there had ever been". A lecture by Melvyn Bragg introduced a substantial *South Bank Show* season at the National Film Theatre. A photographic exhibition was devoted to the show at the Festival Hall. And in New York, the Museum of Broadcasting opened its International Festival of Film and Television with *The South Bank Show*, presenting no fewer than 37 of its editions during the Festival's run, accompanied by associated seminars and discussions. Melvyn and his programme finished a triumphant Season with a Grand and three Gold Awards at the International Television Festivals of New York and Chicago.

David Cox, LWT's Controller of Features and Current Affairs, had left the company in 1987 to begin his career as a journalist and consultant on educational and ecological matters. He was succeeded by Jane Hewland, one of the Department's brightest producers, who set to work with Greg to renew and refresh the company's features and current affairs output. The Brian Walden interviews had become the most highly regarded component of the now 16-year old *Weekend World* so they brought the series to an end and replaced it with *The Walden Interview*, a lively encounter by Brian each week with the major politicians of the day. They also retired *The Six O'Clock Show* and introduced a new early evening current affairs series, *Friday Now*, which added investigative consumer journalism to its predecessor's look at the quirkier side of life in the London region.

The Department introduced a local news service in the shape of regular LWT News bulletins throughout the weekend, commissioned from the independent production company Screen News Limited; and with Trevor

Phillips as its new presenter *The London Programme* went from strength to strength, winning the Royal Television Society's Regional Journalism Award for the third time in four years with its 1988/89 season.

The Department's portfolio of local programming continued to include Gloria Hunniford's *Sunday, Sunday* chat show. *South of Watford*'s exploration of trends in the cultural life of the region won a Silver at the Chicago International Film Festival, and its widely acclaimed history project *The Making of Britain* ended its run with 12 programmes about Britain in the 20th Century.The Department also began a new series, *Network 7*, devised for the younger members of the audience by Jane together with Janet Street Porter, with the mission statement that "News is Entertainment and Entertainment is News". The programme was transmitted live for two hours between noon and 2 pm on Sunday afternoons and won a BAFTA Award for Originality.

Among Jane's documentary and feature series for the network were *Educating Britain*, which contrasted the state of schooling in the UK with the achievements of other countries; *Men of Violence*, examining the problem of violence with the clinical psychologist Oliver James; and *The Trial of Sir Roger Hollis*, an engrossing three-hour courtroom examination of the case of the late Roger Hollis, who had been accused of spying for Russia when he was the head of MI5. The proceedings were presided over by former Judge Bernard Gillis, with prosecution and defence barristers presenting and challenging the testimony of former officers and intelligence experts from Britain and the United States.

In Sport too, the Programme Department was flourishing. Together with David Elstein, his counterpart at Thames and a fellow newly-appointed Director of Programmes, Greg pulled off a notable coup in 1988, beating the BBC and British Satellite Broadcasting to a contract for exclusive live coverage of Football League matches for the following four years.

Meanwhile the two newest divisions of LWT's core business were also doing well. Before the end of the financial year LWT Production Facilities, re-named The London Studios, would be producing more transmission hours for independent producers, ITV Sport and other broadcasters than for LWT itself; and LWT International's success would be recognised by the presentation of the Queen's Award for Export Achievement, only two years after the subsidiary was established. Whoever succeeded me as Managing Director would inherit a company in particularly good nick. And it was time to decide who that individual should be.

White with Green Edges

I n February 1989 I would be 60, the statutory age at which the company's executive directors were required to stand down. Bill Cotton had just retired as Managing Director of BBC Television at the age of 60, another statutory requirement, but had been succeeded by the 62-year old Paul Fox, prompting Bill's celebrated line at his retirement dinner that he was making way for an older man. This particular older man had previously persuaded the IBA that Radlett (the Hertfordshire village in which he lives) was part of the Yorkshire Television area and had also talked the network into allowing him to sit on both the ITVA's Council of Chief Executives as Yorkshire's Managing Director and the Network Programme Controllers Group as Yorkshire's Director of Programmes. Paul was clearly Television's Special One, a status to which I could not begin to aspire, so I reminded the Holdings Board of my forthcoming birthday.

Our Company Secretary Judith Thomas pointed out that the statutory requirement for the retirement of executive directors was the age of 60, not the day upon which that age was reached. I would be 60 for an entire year, so the Board decided to appoint a sub-committee to search for a successor, comprising Christopher Bland and me, together with Roger Harrison, the longest-serving non-executive director of both Holdings and Television Boards. There was clearly no hurry, and as we left the Board Room Christopher said "You've got enough to do with the White Paper on Broadcasting coming up. Why don't you let Roger and me talk to the head-hunters? We'll take our time and draw up a short-list for you to interview and then the three of us can decide which is the most promising." That was fine with me.

I already had a good idea of who I wanted as my successor but it would be interesting to see how he stacked up against the short-list.

As for the White Paper on Broadcasting, we had already had a foretaste of what that might contain. An all-party Home Affairs Committee had published a report in July on The Future of Broadcasting, the recommendations of which were distinctly Peacockian in flavour. The report endorsed Peacock's system of competitive tendering for all ITV franchises; it recommended that the encryption device to facilitate subscription proposed by Peacock be incorporated in every UK TV set by 1990; and it adopted Peacock's proposal that a significant proportion of programmes on both BBC and ITV should be made by independent producers, setting a target of 25 percent to be reached by 1992. It had even transformed one tentative suggestion by the Peacock Committee into a full-blown proposal. Peacock had suggested that there might be a case for a single transmission authority for all television programmes; the Home Affairs Committee set the BBC to one side and recommended that a new Authority should replace both the IBA and the Cable Authority, becoming the sole regulatory body for all *commercial* television, however transmitted – including a new fifth channel.

The Committee also emphasised that the principles of public service broadcasting should remain an integral part of the new broadcasting environment. Both the IBA and the ITVA praised this aspect in their otherwise qualified responses, the IBA stating that it would need to consider the proposals for a new authority, and the ITV Association expressing its concern about the undefined nature of the proposal for competitive tendering. Both bodies were holding back for the White Paper itself. Not so the influential media commentator Raymond Snoddy.

In the *Financial Times* of 30 July 1988 Snoddy saw the Committee's recommendations as "The rehabilitation of a much-maligned report" and quoted Professor Peacock himself as saying "I think we have had a very good run for our money. We have stirred the pot and given a point of reference and departure." Snoddy's view was that the Peacock Committee recommendations, bolstered by those of the Home Affairs Committee, would "form the basic template for the most dramatic changes in British Broadcasting since the introduction of commercial television more than 30 years ago." And he was right.

The White Paper on *Broadcasting in the '90s: Competition, Choice and Quality*, published on 7 November 1988, was pure Peacock. It declared that the purpose of the government's proposals was to place the viewer and listener at the centre of broadcasting policy and enable the individual to exercise much wider choice. This echoed not only the Peacock Committee's concept of consumer sovereignty but also its conclusion that a multiplicity of broadcasting systems would give consumers a multiplicity of choice. The White Paper proposed kickstarting that multiplicity with a new fifth channel and also a sixth channel if it was technically feasible. And the Peacock recommendation that 40 percent of original programming on BBC and ITV should be provided by independent producers became a minimum of 25 percent in the White Paper, as it had done in the Home Affairs Committee Report, but it would now be a statutory requirement.

Peacock's suggestion that there was a case for a single transmission authority for all commercial programmes, which the Home Affairs Committee had adopted in July, was now a firm proposal. A new agency, the Independent Television Commission – the ITC – would licence and supervise the entire commercial television sector, replacing both the IBA and the Cable Authority. The ITV system itself would be superseded by a regionally based Channel 3 with positive programme obligations – the same system but with a new and deliberately down-graded title. And there in the White Paper, unbeaten, unbowed and unchanged, was the Peacock Committee's recommendation for the competitive tendering of franchises. There should be a quality threshold of specific programme requirements for applicants to pass but, having passed it, the applicant submitting the highest tender in each case would be awarded its new Channel 3 franchise.

Was there the remotest possibility of a get-out clause in any of this? *Broadcasting in the '90s* was described as a White Paper "with green edges". Green papers are consultation documents issued when a government wishes to obtain comments and views, so in this case comments on the proposals were indeed expected. There was not much doubt what those comments would be from the companies.

In March 1989, in the press conference to report its full and considered response, the ITV Association was careful to welcome the White Paper's encouragement of competition, choice and quality but felt that it was flawed in several key respects. The Association opposed a statutory requirement for independent production since it was already aiming at a 25 percent target by 1992 on a voluntary basis, but it considered the most damaging and inappropriate proposal was the auctioning of contracts which, it pointed out, had only been recommended by the Peacock Committee on a split vote with a majority of one. Auctions, it argued, would discriminate against incumbents, who had to sustain the cost of the studios and staff they had been required to assemble in the first place, while publisher contractors would need only to bid the highest sum; and the quality threshold as outlined in the White Paper would be easy to cross. If there had to be bidding it should be concerned with programme quality not money.

The IBA's full and considered reponse was also published in March 1989, but by an unfortunate accident of timing it was preceded at the end of November 1988 by the Robert Fraser Lecture at the Banqueting House in Whitehall, which was to be Lord Thomson's valedictory address on retiring from the Authority. At the last franchise round in 1980 Lord Thomson had been the incoming IBA Chairman and the experience had prompted him to advocate "a better way" of awarding ITV franchises. In the intervening years he had failed to find one. Now, too late, he explained that he would have abolished the whole concept of a franchise round and allowed the IBA to roll contracts forward if a company's programme-making was satisfactory. If it was not, he would have permitted newcomers to take over contracts subject to IBA approval. He firmly opposed the auctioning proposal and said he thought the government was running the risk of knowing the price of everything and the value of nothing. It was a personal view but it was regretted within the IBA because it appeared to demonstrate unwillingness on the part of the Authority itself to adjust.

However, five days after Lord Thomson's lecture, on 3 December, George Russell was appointed Chairman of the IBA and Chairman designate of the ITC. He was a successful businessman with a comprehensive knowledge of the commercial television sector having been a member of the Authority from 1979 to 1986. With Russell in command the IBA took a much more positive approach to the government's proposals. It chose not to challenge the principle of competitive tendering, proposing instead an expansion of the White Paper's commitment to quality.

As well as the quality of the applicant's response to the threshold's programme requirements it advocated an assessment by merchant bankers of the quality of the applicant's money. The bid should first be based on a percentage of what the applicant estimated its Net Advertising Revenue would be and only then on a lump sum in a sealed envelope. The assessment of the bid should consider how realistic the estimated income from an applicant's programme proposals would be and how it would be used to meet each requirement of the licence. The Authority firmly stated its belief that over the course of a licence period it was not the highest bid but the soundest business plan which would yield the greatest value to the Exchequer and provide the finest programme service to the viewer.

At the press conference to announce the IBA's response the intrepid Ray Snoddy asked George Russell what he would do if the government were to limit the licence awards to the highest bidder. The Chairman replied "If I am faced with a straight envelope tender, which I cannot believe in, if that actually happens, I do not think I could continue in the job."

His reply caused consternation in the Home Office. Having hand-picked Russell for the job, it would be most embarrassing if within a matter of months he were to resign from it on a key point of government policy. At a hurriedly called press briefing, Timothy Renton, the Minister for Broadcasting, praised the IBA submission as "ingenious" and "highly constructive". In an interview with *The Guardian*, John Wheeler, the Chairman of the Home Affairs Committee, said George Russell had "done a first-class job in setting out practical plans while marching in tune with the government's views. I think he's cracked it." A few months later, in June, Douglas Hurd announced that a franchise bid would be based not only on a substantial strengthening of the quality threshold but also on the financial requirement of a pre-determined fixed percentage of Net Advertising Revenue, plus a lump sum to represent the competitive element of the bid: exactly the Authority's formula.

What was LWT's reaction to all this? We had no quarrel with the statutory requirement of 25 percent for independent productions: we were already a leading ITV commissioner of independent productions, particularly of drama; and because a major company's network programme obligations were tied to its share of the network's Net Advertising Revenue, our obligations increased whenever Ron Miller's department raised our share so we needed independent productions to help us fulfil them.

As for the quality threshold, we had every confidence in the quality of our programmes and programme makers, but would we be wise to rely exclusively upon it? Quality could also be promised by prospective contractors. They would soon be circling present incumbents and the BBC to lure talented managers and producers away to provide it; and if independent producers could make programmes of quality for us they could also make them for prospective contractors. All in all we believed it would not be wise to rely on quality alone. We should also be putting money in our purse: we needed to have the financial resources to outbid any competitor if it became necessary. And we needed to reassure the IBA of continuity in the management of the company, most particularly in its senior management when I stood down from the Managing Directorship.

So how were we getting on in the search for my successor?

Making Way

In the middle of all the Reports and responses, press briefings and press conferences, I wandered into Christopher's office to ask how the short-list of my potential successors was going. "It's not," said Christopher, "It's gone. We interviewed the people the head-hunters sent us and one of them was so good we scrapped the rest and stopped the search. He's really first class; wait till you see him!"

"That sounds great, Christopher. What does he do? Is he in television?"

"No, he runs Halfords in Coventry."

"Halfords? The bicycle people?"

"Yes; the company was in a bad way until he was made Managing Director, and he transformed it, turned it around."

"But we don't need turning around, Christopher: we're already round. We're in good shape, we're in the middle of our most successful year ever, we're about to fight for our next franchise, and from what you say he doesn't know anything at all about the television business."

"Yes I know, but he's a great business *manager* and he'd be exactly right for the way the industry is going. Look, see for yourself. I'll arrange a meeting for you and you can interview him, just you, and you can tell Roger and me what you think."

Intrigued and curious, I agreed. Christopher arranged for this remarkable paragon to come and see me, and a few days later my secretary Andrea Turner knocked on my office door and ushered him in. I'm afraid I don't remember his name but as we shook hands I thought him a little cold-eyed, a little distant, not immediately congenial: perhaps having to undergo yet another interview had put him under a strain? We sat, he declined my offer of a coffee, I tried to put him at ease with some general chatter, and we finally got down to business.

"I hear great things about you and what you've done for your company," I said. "Of course, television's a very different world, but I'm sure you've done a little homework and know something about the ITV system and LWT's place in it."

"No," he said, "not at all. I've done no homework. I know nothing about the television industry or LWT's place in it. I don't need to know. I'm a manager. I manage companies, and all companies function in the same way. I can pick up anything I need to know about television while I'm managing the company."

The rest of the interview remains a blank for me. I can't think what else there could possibly have been to discuss though I like to believe I remained courteous and polite to the end. After we shook hands and said goodbye I stormed down the corridor to Christopher's office where he and Roger were waiting for my reaction.

"Well?" they said, "What do you think?"

"Christopher, Roger, you can't be serious about this man," I said. "He knows nothing about television. He knows nothing about the company. He says he doesn't need to know, he'll pick up whatever he needs as he goes along. He's cold and humourless and I can't see Ron or Greg or the other Department heads taking to him, let alone the staff. He's not a leader, he's a manager. We don't want a businessman, we want someone with business *nous*. We want someone who knows the industry, knows about television and the problems this franchise faces; we want someone the company will get along with and be happy to follow."

"And if you're right, where do we find such a someone?" Christopher asked.

"Right here," I said, "here in the company."

"In the company? Like who?"

"Like Greg!" I said.

Christopher said "Bollocks!"

"It's not bollocks, Christopher," I said. "Greg knows the company inside out, the company knows him, and will follow him. He knows how ITV works, he has a good relationship with the IBA, he knows the problems we face in winning back our franchise, and if you're talking about turning companies around, remember he managed to turn TV-am around. If you think his business *nous* isn't adequate let's send him to the Harvard Business School: we were going to do that with John anyway."

"Look," said Christopher, "this fellow clearly got off on the wrong foot with you. Roger and I will talk to him and put him straight. Will you see him again in a week or so's time, give him another opportunity to show just how good he would be for us?"

With the greatest reluctance I said yes. I couldn't imagine it happening, I thought it would need a complete personality transplant on this man's part, but maybe I had put him off in some way; maybe he deserved a second chance.

The following Monday, Greg came back from a Controllers Meeting, charged into my office and exclaimed "What's going on?" "What's *what* going on?" I asked. Greg said "The first thing Andy Allen said to me at Controllers this morning was 'I had dinner with your new boss last night' and when I asked him what he was talking about he said 'Last night: dinner with my mate – he runs Halfords in Coventry: he told me he's going to be your new Managing Director when Brian steps down. He's looking forward to it. It's all cut and dried.' So what's going on?" Greg said. "Shouldn't you have told us what was happening?"

"But it's not happening," I said. "I've interviewed the man and that's all – unless... come with me, we'll have a word with Christopher" and the two of us bustled down to Christopher's office. "Christopher," I said "You need to hear Greg's account of what happened at Controllers today."

A now rather bemused Greg repeated his story and I told him to go back to my office and wait for me. When he'd gone I put it to Christopher.

"Is that true? Have you and Roger told the Halfords man that he's got the job, that he's going to be Managing Director?"

"No, of course not: we were waiting for you to see him again."

"Well it's surely out of the question now," I said, "How could we possibly appoint someone who shoots off his mouth, takes a major appointment like this for granted and is indiscreet enough to boast about it to people in the industry?"

Christopher didn't hesitate. He said "I agree with you... We'll go with Greg."

And I returned to my office, at a considerably gentler pace.

"It's OK," I told Greg. "Nobody from Halfords is going to be your next Managing Director. I've told Christopher who I want as my successor, and he's agreed with me." "And who's that?" Greg asked. "You" I said. "*Me!* Why me?" "You can thank Napoleon," I said.

The story goes that when Napoleon needed to promote one of his officers to General he asked his *aide de camp* to bring him the candidates from which he should choose. 'Bring me the lucky ones,' he apparently said, 'I want only lucky generals'. "I think you're one of the lucky ones," I told Greg, "and with the new franchises ahead of us we need all the luck we can get. It'll take a little time: Christopher has to consult Roger, we'll have to get it through the Board – they expect to discuss a short-list of potential successors – but we'll send you to the Harvard Business School to give your business skills a bit of a shine and you'll take over from me when you get back."

And that's what happened. Roger agreed with Christopher and me; we saw Greg and gave him the good news; we ascertained that the next Advanced Leadership Course at the Harvard Business School would begin in September and continue for three months; and we presented our recommendation to the other members of the Holdings Board. They applauded our choice and agreed that Greg should take over the Managing Directorship of the television company in the New Year, after his return from Harvard. Because that would be very nearly six months away we decided to make no advance announcement to the public or to the company, though we would advise the IBA in confidence.

It was not the only confidence we were about to share with the Authority. By now the company had disposed of the last of its non-television investments, selling our interests in both the publishing group Century Hutchinson and ITP, the publishers of *TVTimes*, for a total of £31.3 million. We were free to concentrate on our television business and we were rich with cash. What's more, because debt was cheaper than equity we could borrow more cash if we needed to, and Christopher had come up with a brilliantly simple plan for the use of it which, if it won the approval of the company's shareholders, would enable us not only to bid higher than any prospective rival for our franchise but also, by removing the temptation for key programme-makers and managers to be lured away from us, would enable the company to maintain both the quality of its programmes and the continuity of its management.

Christopher's plan was for a radical reorganisation of the company's capital in what would formally be known as a Scheme of Arrangement. We would buy back some 60 percent of our investors' holdings, significantly reducing their exposure to the risk of losing the franchise and increasing their potential returns if the franchise was won. By radically lowering the equity capital on which the company had to provide a satisfactory return LWT would be better able to finance a competitive franchise bid. To succeed in that bid, we knew we needed to retain and motivate our senior managers, and Christopher's plan incorporated a Management Incentive Scheme designed to achieve that aim.

The key members of the four separate business areas of the company – creating the programmes, making the programmes, selling the airtime and selling our programmes overseas – would be given the opportunity to buy, or to exchange existing shares and options for Preferred Shares in the new, slim company's remaining equity. The value of those Preferred Shares would increase in a series of ratchets as the market price of the shares rose, with a maximum conversion rate of four times their value if they reached a specified figure by the end of June 1993.

Christopher believed that the Scheme's potential rewards would provide a double incentive, spurring on the efforts of the management team to make the company as lean and efficient as possible, and cancelling out the temptation for any members of the team to be attracted to a rival bidder. The Holdings Board agreed and approved Christopher's plan in its entirety. We gave Greg the job of consulting his fellow Executive Directors in order to compile a list of those who should participate in the Management Incentive element, and we went on to consider when we should announce the Scheme to the public. Fortuitously, a most appropriate opportunity was only weeks away. LWT's franchise had begun on Friday, 2 August 1968. We had already planned to celebrate the company's 21st Anniversary on Wednesday, 2 August 1989, and we now decided to publish the Scheme the following day, in advance of which Christopher undertook in confidence – confidence No. 2 – to advise Shirley Littler, the Deputy Director General of the IBA, of our plans.

Meanwhile, to mark the Anniversary I sent a letter on behalf of the Board to every member of the company, thanking them for their personal contribution to LWT's success in the past 21 years and enclosing a £10 House of Fraser gift voucher for each year of service they had completed. As a permanent memento of the occasion, every member of staff would also receive a framed limited edition lithograph of Kent House and its Thames setting by the celebrated young artist Caroline Nisbett, specially commissioned for our Anniversary. And as well as celebrating the company's past I took the opportunity in an article for the Anniversary Edition of the house magazine to reassure the staff about the company's future.

I said I was aware that some members might be confused or worried by press reports of the proposed broadcasting legislation, particularly the process of auctioning the new franchises. I wanted them to know that whatever the outcome of that process LWT was intent on remaining a broadcaster. Getting our Channel 3 franchise back was our number one priority and we would do everything in our power to achieve it. If we failed we could bid for the new Channel 5, which would be put up for offer subsequently. If we failed to win any terrestrial licence we could rent one of the transponders on the Astra satellite and continue to broadcast to the UK. The transponders were not expensive. In fact, at £2.5 million a year they compared very favourably with the £30 million we were currently paying in IBA rentals and levy. In congratulating the staff on LWT's 21 years of achievement I told them I was wishing them not only a Happy Birthday but also Many Happy Returns: LWT was determined to celebrate its future anniversaries as a broadcaster.

I could not know how severely that determination was to be tested.

We celebrated our Anniversary with a party on a Thames riverboat for our friends in the network and at the IBA. Christopher's advance notice of our scheme to Shirley Littler had prompted a paper from its Secretariat which the Authority was due to consider at its next meeting. Here and there, amid the festive cacophony of music and chatter as our boat made its way to the Thames Barrier and back, quiet little conversations were going on between Christopher or Greg or me with various senior officers of the IBA, which raised an eyebrow or two among our other guests.

The eyebrows were raised a little higher the next morning when the details of the Scheme were published. LWT was proposing to buy back £135 million pounds' worth of shares from its shareholders. To facilitate the purchase it planned to borrow no less than £95 million, £50 million of which it undertook to pay back by the end of its current contract, 31 December 1992. Figures worth raising an eyebrow at.

The Authority's meeting was a fortnight away and Christopher and I went to Brompton Towers the day before to elaborate on the details of the Scheme. The only reservation at that meeting was expressed by IBA's Finance Director, Peter Rogers, who thought the Authority needed to be reassured that LWT's preoccupation with financial matters during the remaining two years and four months of its current contract would not have a damaging effect on the quality and diversity of its programmes. I was able to write to the Authority the next day to reassure them. Our programme budget would remain constant in real terms for the remainder of the present contract period, and our programme plans for the new contract period would of course be subject to the full scrutiny of the IBA – or, by then, the ITC – in our franchise bid. The Authority approved the scheme on those terms.

However, LWT's shareholders still had to be persuaded of the virtues of the scheme, and we needed 75 percent of them to approve it. I take the liberty of quoting the official history's summary of what ensued because it only too accurately foreshadowed what my future role in the company was to be. "The combination of the confidence that Bland aroused in City circles, the verbal skills and charm of Brian Tesler, about to move up to an emeritus position within LWT, and the firecracker impact of Greg Dyke, who would take over the role of Managing Director in time to manage the bid, was ultimately unbrookable." So there we were in the future incarnation of LWT, Christopher, Greg and I: Business Man, Action Man – and Front Man.

Greg delivered the list of those who had been chosen to participate in the Management Incentive Scheme – 44 of them – and flew off to his Business School course at Harvard. Christopher wrote to each of the fortunate 44, explaining how the scheme would work. It was a long and comprehensively detailed letter – five pages, with seven appendices – listing each individual's entitlement of Management Shares in the new company, how it could be taken up by paying cash or exchanging existing shares or share options for them, offering a facility through Barclays Bank for those who needed to borrow to finance their cash subscriptions and making available a tax "surgery" with representatives of the Company's auditors and solicitors to explain the tax implications of the proposals to those who needed to know.

Christopher's letter also demonstrated how the ratchet would work. Subject to the Company's performance, indicated by the market price of its listed shares after the publication of its financial results for the six months ending 30 June 1993, the team's Management Shares could convert into as much as four times the number of listed shares. As an example of the Scheme's potential rewards: if the price at which the Management Shares were acquired was 80p, which it was expected to be, and the market price on conversion in June 1993 was 268p, each member's initial investment would have increased by more than 13 times its value. And there would be a second opportunity to convert in December 1993 if any member of the team chose to wait until after the publication of the financial results for the following six months.

What did the members of the Management Team have to do in return? They would have to undertake not to compete with the Company in its franchise renewal application and to stay in LWT until the Management Shares converted. If they left of their own volition before that date they would have to sell back their Management Shares at the original purchase price. If they left for reasons of illness or retirement they would be able to sell the shares at market value plus any accrued value of the ratchet. If they left after the new franchise began on 1 January 1993 they would be able to keep their Management Shares.

Christopher and I gave the Management Team time to consider the Scheme, consult the tax "surgery" and seek their own legal and tax advice if they needed to, and then called a mass meeting of its members to discuss the project and answer any questions they might have. Features and Current Affairs producer Robin Paxton put up his hand. "Yes, Robin," said Christopher. "That example in your letter about the ratchet," said Robin. "Let's face it. The Company's listed shares will never get as high as 268p." "Bollocks," said Christopher, "Next question." Not even Christopher could have imagined just how high those shares would in fact go. Or why.

In the end the trigger share figure became 278p and the favoured 44 became 55. All but one of the 55 signed up as a team. The single exception was Controller of Features and Current Affairs Jane Hewland, who came to see me to explain why she wished to decline. It was a meeting charged with emotion. Jane said she loved the Company, had always enjoyed working for it and had no intention of joining any other whether it was in competition with us or not, but she couldn't commit herself to us for the length of time the Scheme required. She wanted to set up her own independent production company and this seemed the moment to do it.

I told her how sorry we would be to see her leave. I respected and admired her ambition and thought she could enjoy a very successful career as an independent, but why not not stay with the Team, reap the Management Scheme's rewards and use them to finance her enterprise? No: Jane was tearful but adamant: this was her opportunity; she didn't want to wait another three years to take it. A sad goodbye, then, but I'm happy to say that her courageous gamble paid off: Hewland International has been a successful independent production company now for decades.

At an Extraordinary General Meeting on 17 November our proposals for the radical reorganisation of the Company's capital were approved. Instead of the 75 percent benchmark we needed, the Scheme was approved by 82 percent of the shareholders by value. We were free to press on with the equally radical reorganisation of the company's structure. At the end of December Greg returned from his Advanced Leadership Course at the Harvard Business School and two months later, on my 61st birthday, I handed the Managing Directorship of the television company over to him, just as, 14 years earlier, John Freeman had handed it over to me.

Back on the Franchise Trail

The Broadcasting Bill was published on 7 December 1989. It triggered eleven months of scrutiny, discussion and debate in the Commons and the Lords, accompanied all the way by briefings from the IBA, representations from the ITV Association, and intensive lobbying which ranged from The Voice of the Listener & Viewer on behalf of the audience to The Campaign for Quality Television on behalf of the programme-makers.

David Mellor piloted the Bill through Parliament, having succeeded Tim Renton as Minister for Broadcasting. After 1,356 amendments, what began as the 1988 White Paper writ large ended as an Act which Richard Dunn, Chairman of the Committee co-ordinating ITVA's franchise strategy, felt able to describe as "a mass of compromises, mostly for the better." Richard was addressing a *Financial Times* conference on 'The New Shape of Independent Broadcasting' a few weeks before the Act received its Royal Assent in November 1990 and, in anticipation, he expressed his belief that "The Act will be better than the Bill, which was better than the really shoddy White Paper."

It was certainly more workable than either. Channel 3 licences would run for 10 years, renewable for further periods of 10 years. The ITC would regulate with a lighter touch than the IBA, whose powers to preview programmes and approve schedules in advance were abandoned. The auction process was modified by enabling the ITC to apply "exceptional circumstances" if it considered the quality of an applicant's programme plans exceptionally higher than that of the highest bidder. The programme quality threshold for applicants was strengthened by giving the ITC the power to lay down programming guidelines, including "a suitable amount" of children's and religious programmes and a high quality regional news service.

The quota for independent producers on both ITV and the BBC would become statutory, but remain set at 25 percent. Channel 4 would be run by a new non-profit-making Channel 4 Corporation and sell its own advertising, but would no longer have to be wholly financed by the ITV companies. There would be a funding formula to protect both parties: Channel 4 would pay the companies 50 percent of any advertising revenue it earned over 14 percent of total terrestrial NAR. If it earned less, ITV would pay the Channel up to 2 percent of total terrestrial NAR. A fifth terrestrial channel would be licenced, but not a sixth. And if, after a year of the new franchises, the financial position of any of the six smallest companies needed to be shored up, it would be permitted to merge with any of the nine largest.

It could have been worse. Losing the right to sell Channel 4's advertising was a blow, especially to LWT, which had benefited so greatly from Ron Miller's ingenious marketing of the channel. And the prospect of both Channel 4 and a new fifth channel joining DBS as competitors in the advertising marketplace was clearly daunting, but ITV could live with it. It would have to. It would also have to live with the dreaded auction process, which the Association had tried so long and hard to eliminate.

That particular sword of Damocles had hung over ITV's head from the moment the Peacock Committee handed it to Mrs Thatcher in 1986, and there was never any chance of its being put back in its sheath. Now, any company which hadn't yet attacked its cost base to prepare for the rigours of competitive tendering set to work to do so. And the companies had something else on which to concentrate their minds. The Act contained a statutory requirement for a new Channel 3 networking system which would take control away from the five major company programme controllers and open up the schedule to all 15 companies as well as to the independents. If we failed to produce a suitable arrangement voluntarily the ITC now had the power to impose one on us.

Two months later, on 15 February 1991, the ITC issued its Invitation to Apply for the 1993 franchises, and at Kent House LWT's reorganisation process went into over-drive. By 15 May, the deadline for the receipt of applications, London Weekend Television had been subsumed within LWT (Holdings) plc, which was now the holding company for four separate profit-and-loss businesses, each with its own Managing Director: LWT

Programmes Ltd, London Weekend Television International Ltd, The London Studios Ltd and – in a new incarnation of our Sales Department – Laser Sales Ltd. Laser was Ron Miller's idea, a merger of the Sales Departments of LWT and TVS, based at Kent House and jointly owned by the two companies, with Ron and his TVS counterpart John Fox as joint Managing Directors, in the process both Departments achieving significant overhead savings by combining their respective administration and computer operations. Not one to miss a trick was Ron. The Managing Director of the International Company remained Sydney Perry, and Marcus Plantin was translated from LWT's Director of Programmes to Managing Director of LWT Programmes Ltd.

As for London Studios Ltd, Peter Cazaly had retired, taking his Management Shares with him, and the company's new Managing Director was Mike Southgate, one of Greg Dyke's Young Turks. Previously a junior member of LWT management, Mike had left the company in 1985 and joined TVS, frustrated by the power wielded by LWT's union shops. Greg had brought him back to LWT. Now, although London Studios had become the leading London supplier of studios, equipment and skilled staff in a highly competitive market, a total costing exercise had demonstrated that it was still losing £16 million a year and Mike was charged to make the company break even by the time the new franchises began in 1993. He would only just fail to meet the deadline – but he would not miss the target.

All four Managing Directors sat as executive directors on the new Holdings Board with Christopher Bland as Chairman, me as Deputy Chairman and Greg as Group Chief Executive. How the wheel turns! I was back as a Deputy again and the wearer of divers other hats: Chairman of LWT Programmes, London Weekend Television International, The London Studios and a new entity, the Programme Advisory Board. Just like old times, but this time with absolutely no lumbers.

The Advisory Board had been set up in 1990 to guide us on our way to the new franchises. Its participants were members not just of the great and the good but also of the feisty and formidable: Baroness Brigstocke, formerly High Mistress of St Paul's Girls' School; Baroness Flather of Windsor and Maidenhead, the first Asian woman to receive a peerage; ex-Parliamentary Consultant Roland Freeman JP; Kate Hoey, then – and still – the Labour Member of Parliament for our constituency, Vauxhall; Robin Scott, ex-Controller of BBC 2, ex-Deputy Managing Director of BBC TV and co-signer of the Tesler-Scott Agreement in the saga of Snatch of the Day; Anne Sofer,

Chief Education Officer of Tower Hamlets; Business Consultant Linbert Spencer; and Tom Webb, Managing Director of the London Tourist Board. Our meetings, which were attended by Marcus Plantin, his Programme Department Controllers and Barry Cox, the company's Director of Corporate Affairs, were, shall we say, spirited and salutary – and great fun.

Our Franchise Committee met together for the first time at the beginning of February 1990: Christopher, Greg, Peter McNally and me together with Chief Accountant Tony Kay and two more of the company's bright Young Turks: Tony Cohen, who had worked as a researcher on The Six O'Clock Show and after a year at the London Business School was now Greg's strategist, and Neil Canetty-Clarke, a young merchant banker who had joined LWT on a placement in 1989 and in 1992 would succeed Peter McNally as Group Finance Director. Greg and his sub-committee of number-crunchers had the job of demonstrating the quality of the Group's business plan in our franchise application.

My job was to demonstrate the quality of LWT's programming. I worked with Press & Publicity Department's Nick Roberts on a 64-page colour brochure entitled *LWT Programmes and Programme People.* With 279 photographs and reproductions of on-screen programme titles the brochure reviewed the strength of the company's programming past, present and future and highlighted its current staff and independent programme-makers, together with their recent productions, their future programme plans and the artistes featuring in them.

We had a good story to tell. Since 1980, this little two-and-a-half day company had won over 250 national and international awards, among them twenty-eight BAFTA Craft, Production and Performance Awards – more than any other ITV company – and thirteen Royal Television Society Awards, including three for Technique – more than any other ITV company – and three Royal Television Society Awards for Regional Current Affairs with The London Programme – more than any other regional programme on ITV or the BBC. We had won four Prix Italia Awards: a Drama Prize, two Music Prizes and a Friuli-Venezia Giulia Prize – again more than any other ITV company – three of them with the South Bank Show, which itself had won more awards than any other programme in any category. And we had won more Rose Awards at the Montreux International Festival of Light Entertainment than any other ITV company, equalling the number won by the BBC with its two seven-day channels.

The day before the brochure was published it was announced that Pat Gavin's opening titles for *The South Bank Show* had won an additional Prix Italia for LWT, the first time the Jury had given an award to a title sequence. We managed to get that item of news printed on a wrap-around for the brochures before they were distributed, but the news that *A Night on Mount Edna* had won a Golden Rose at the 1991 Montreux Festival arrived too late to be similarly treated, which was a pity: it would have been nice to say that it was Dame Edna who had edged the company's Montreux tally ahead of the BBC's.

There was one other contender for the weekend franchise: London Independent Broadcasting, a consortium made up of the record company Polygram, two British film companies Working Title and the Palace Group, and the successful independent production company Mentorn Enterprises, run by Tom Gutteridge, who had directed our 1985 Montreux prizewinner *Fire and Ice*, founding Mentorn in the same year. He was an old friend of Greg's, who made it his business to find out what Gutteridge and his consortium were up to.

Greg also had a little unfinished business of his own. He hadn't forgotten the unhappy circumstances leading to his departure from TV-am: "I left," he would say in his autobiography twenty years later "because Gyngell wanted me out and I couldn't be bothered to fight him." Now, he and his sub-committee had come to the conclusion that, since it would always be cheaper to run a breakfast service off the back of an existing broadcaster rather than run it as a stand-alone business, TV-am could always be outbid, so why not go for the breakfast franchise too? An unused studio in Kent House and LWT's crews and transmission facilities could provide the essential working elements of an application, and though the tendering rules would not allow us to own more than twenty percent of another franchise, we could lead a consortium to bid for it. The Franchise Committee agreed and Greg went off to put a consortium together under the banner of Sunrise Television.

It didn't take him long. A couple of phone calls to old mates like Gus McDonald at Scottish Television and Etienne de Villiers at Walt Disney's British company brought in their respective organisations in due course and they were soon joined by The Guardian Media Group, with some additional equity held in reserve for whichever other old mate became available once the smoke of the franchise battleground had cleared. And yes, the three joining participants were more than happy to accept Kent House as the company's production and transmission base and to share the costs of its office, studio, production and transmission facilities. Whatever the outcome of the bid, as Sunrise's landlord LWT would make money from it from the very beginning.

There was also a third competitor for the franchise: Daybreak Television Ltd, headed by Sir Paul Fox, who had just concluded his three-year contract as Managing Director of BBC Network Television, for which he had been awarded his knighthood. This impressive consortium contained ITN, The Daily Telegraph, Clive Hollick's media group MAI and the British arm of America's NBC Network. Like Sunrise it could easily outbid TV-am because its service would run off the back of another broadcaster – in this case ITN, which would come equipped not only with studio space, production staff and transmission facilities but also with a ready-made worldwide news-gathering organisation.

You would have thought that Daybreak was a shoo-in for the breakfast franchise, but you would have neglected to take into account Mrs Thatcher's implacable auction process. TV-am also had a ready-made news-gathering organisation and there were no exceptional circumstances for the ITC to consider. If the programme and business plans of the three candidates passed their respective quality thresholds the prize would have to go to the highest bidder. TV-am could not match whatever Daybreak and Sunrise were capable of bidding – interviewed eight years later Bruce Gyngell said "it wasn't worth having a licence if we had to pay too much for it". And somehow, somewhere, someone still unknown today, leaked the size of Daybreak's bid to Greg...

Greg's private-eye probe into the competition for LWT's weekend franchise was equally illuminating. He didn't discover what London Independent's bid was going to be, but he didn't need to. Having talked to people who had been offered the job of Managing Director and to programme-makers and finance executives who had beeen approached by the consortium he felt that LIB was inadequately financed and that its business plan would fail the quality threshold. It seemed to me that its programme plan would also fail: it appeared to have no television programme-maker or production executive on board in any key position other than Tom Gutteridge himself.

Nevertheless, as Greg reminds me, he and his number-crunchers spent two days in Hever Castle in Kent processing all the information at their disposal and reached agreement on a bid "up towards £30 million" before

Christopher phoned him to say we should bid "really low". The Franchise Committee and the Board finally agreed a figure that was certainly low, but not insultingly so: we submitted the perfectly respectable bid of £7,585,000.

The Channel 3 licence awards for 1993 were to be announced by the ITC on Wednesday, 16 October 1991 and the company secretary of each applicant would be advised of the results by fax. At 10 am that morning, the fax machines of the thirty-seven applicants for Channel 3 licences and the three for breakfast-time whirred into action and disgorged the results. LIB's business plan and its bid of £35,406,000 hadn't even been considered: its application had failed the programme quality threshold. LWT won back its franchise for London's weekend with an offer of just a fifth of its rival's. And the breakfast licence? TV-am had bid £14,125,000, Daybreak had bid £33,261,000 and the Sunrise consortium – surprise! surprise! – had just pipped it with a bid of £34,610,000. When Christopher, Greg and I walked into the LWT restaurant that lunchtime to meet the assembled staff, we were given a standing ovation.

Went the Day Well?

Not for some.

In the end, not even Mrs Thatcher believed that the auction process was a better way to award television franchises. In a private letter to Bruce Gyngell she wrote "When I see how some of the other licences have been awarded I am *mystified* that you did not receive yours and heartbroken. You of all people have done so much for the whole of television – there seems no attention to that. I am painfully aware that I was responsible for the legislation." Yes, Prime Minister: Bruce's success in his union battles of 1988 didn't qualify as 'exceptional circumstances' in 1991. Your legislation made it possible for him to be trumped by a bid more than twice the size of his own. And trumped he was.

Exceptional circumstances were certainly considered in the case of Thames however. One of its rival contenders, CPV-TV, failed the programme quality threshold and was rejected, much to the displeasure of its founder-members, David Frost and Richard Branson. But the other contender, Michael Green's Carlton Television, passed both programme and business quality thresholds and its bid of £43,170,000 was very much larger than Thames's £32,794,000, presenting the ITC with a genuine dilemma.

Thames and Carlton both offered programme plans of high quality. Thames was an established broadcaster with a fine track record. Carlton was an unproven outsider but the track record of its contracted independent producers was also fine. Thames had delivered before, and there was no reason to think it wouldn't do so again. Carlton's independent producers had also delivered before and there was no reason to think that they wouldn't continue to do so either. Carlton Television itself had not delivered, but Carlton Television had never been given the opportunity. Could the Commission conclude with any certainty that the difference in quality between the two companies' future programming would be substantial enough to trigger the exceptional circumstances clause?

In the official history, David Glencross, by then the ITC's Director General, confirms that its use had been "firmly explored" and that it was a most difficult judgement to make, but "At the end of the day we felt that we couldn't apply it, we didn't have sufficient justification for applying exceptional circumstances for Thames or indeed for anybody else." The highest bid had to win therefore, and the London weekday franchise was awarded to Carlton.

There was much speculation about the reasons for Thames's defeat, but none of it was germane: Thames lost because in this egregious auction process it had bid as much as it could afford and what it could afford was not enough. At LWT, we believed that Richard had been unable to bid any higher because he had failed to attack the company's cost base rigorously enough, but he had been dealt a difficult hand by his shareholders. Just as Thames had begun to put its franchise application together in March 1990, BET and Thorn, who owned 95 percent of the company's share capital between them, announced that they were seeking to sell their Thames holdings in line with their strategy 'to concentrate their resources on their core businesses'. Shareholders who wish to sell their companies are not inclined to fund large-scale redundancies in order to attack their cost base.

Thames had not been in line with its shareholders's strategy for some years. In 1985, the year in which Richard succeeded Bryan Cowgill, Michael Green made his first bid for Thames and had found BET and Thorn-EMI willing sellers: they signed the bill of sale without telling their new MD that his company was about to have a new owner. When Richard discovered what was going on he drew it to the attention of the IBA and Green's bid was rejected by the Authority in the light of its responsibilities under the existing Broadcasting Act. The Broadcasting Act of 1990 had radically revised those responsibilities but not even Michael Green was prepared to make a bid 12 months before the new licences were to be awarded, and BET sold its stake to Thorn-EMI instead.

As a result, when the Thames franchise committee met to put the final touches to its application the company was owned by a single shareholder who was intent on selling it, who had ultimate control of the level of its bid, and who was represented on the committee by its representative on the company's Board. I didn't envy Richard those meetings.

Interviewed by ITN, the BBC and Channel 4 News that fateful Wednesday, Richard confessed to being devastated by the loss of Thames's franchise but, pragmatic as ever, he had prepared an alternative future for his company. Thames closed down for the last time on 31 December 1992 but it continued to be a major supplier of programmes to ITV in a new life as an independent producer. Pearson bought it six months later and it produced a profit of £13 million for its new owner in its first year. Under its current owner, Fremantle UK, Thames remains one of British television's leading independent production companies, with *The X Factor* and *Britain's Got Talent* among its current successes. Tragically, Richard himself was able to enjoy only the early years of its achievement: he died of a heart attack in 1998, a great loss to the industry.

Thames and TV-am lost their franchises because they bid too little. TSW and TVS lost because they bid too much.

TSW's business plan didn't convince the Commission. In its judgement the company would be unable to sustain its proposed service throughout the licence period and it awarded the South West licence to Westcountry Television, whose £7.82 million pound bid was less than half TSW's.

The TVS story was a sad and ironic one for its founder and Managing Director, my accommodating colleague James Gatward. Frustrated by the refusal of the major companies to accept TVS as a sixth major and unwilling to wait and see whether the forthcoming licence round would provide an opportunity to realise his ambition, James decided to make TVS an international major instead. In 1988 he restructured his company, establishing TVS as the television subsidiary of a media group he named TVS Entertainment and doubling its size by buying one of America's most successful television studios, MTM, for £190 million.

It was a high price but it looked like a good deal. Named after its actress founder Mary Tyler Moore, MTM was valued by Wall Street at $500 million. Producing hits like *Hill Street Blues* and *The Bob Newhart Show* it had a turnover of $200 million a year with an annual profit of around $50 million, principally from the syndication of its product to the 1300 regional TV stations throughout America. Unfortunately, the syndication market in America collapsed the following year, and with it went MTM's profitability.

The effect on TVS Entertainment was toxic. James was obliged to issue a profit warning to the City, cutting its predicted 1989 profits by a third. The Group's share price plummeted, its Chairman Terry Boston left and the non-executive shareholders brought in a new Chairman, Rudolph Agnew, from Consolidated Goldfields. Agnew removed James from the Group Board, installing him as Executive Chairman of the television subsidiary with the responsibility of concentrating on TVS's franchise application, but the Board had lost confidence in James and, after a final showdown with Agnew in February 1991, he left the company he had founded with its application uncompleted.

Agnew took over the application and decided to blow his rival contenders out of the water with the highest possible bid. Which the ITC thought was too high. It wasn't persuaded by TVS's business plan, considered its proposed programme contribution to the network modest in relation to its size let alone to its ambitions, and felt that its financial difficulties with MTM had not only influenced its programme proposals but would remain a risk for the future. It awarded the franchise to Meridian Television, whose bid was lower than TVS's by £23.24 million.

Elsewhere, companies gambled, took chances, crossed fingers. Granada's sole rival failed the programme quality test, which was just as well because David Plowright had planned to rely on the exceptional circumstances clause and bid only a modest £9 million. Tyne Tees took no chances and retained its franchise with a bid three times higher than its only rival bidder. Yorkshire Television's £37.7 million bid seemed extravagant to the ITC, as did HTV's £20.53 million, which put their respective business plans very much at risk, but both finally passed the business quality test "with reservations". Scottish Television and Central Television were unopposed and retained their franchises with what they understood to be the minimum acceptable sum of £2,000. Border Television also planned to bid the minimum until it heard that 'someone' was interested in its small North West regional franchise and raised its bid to £52,000. It turned out to be unopposed after all and ended up with a franchise costing 26 times more than it had originally planned.

At Anglia, MD David McCall knew his company faced strong competition, not least from. David Frost and Richard Branson, who were making their third bid for a franchise with their CPV-TV consortium. He admitted in a subsequent interview that Anglia's projections had suggested that with a bid of "over £15 million or £16 million you'd almost be better selling off

406 | THE BEST OF TIMES

the assets and handing it all back to shareholders" but he went the extra mile anyway and bid £17.8 million. Had he stayed with its projections he would have saved his company more than two million pounds a year: its only rival to pass the quality tests bid £14.078 million.

Anglia was CPV-TV's third quality test failure, the others being with bids for the South and South East and London weekdays. It was a considerable blow to Richard Branson's pride and a quadruple whammy for David Frost: with TV-am's defeat he had also lost his Breakfast franchise. It was the first time he had come away from an ITV round of franchise awards empty handed.

The three remaining incumbents, Channel, Grampian and Ulster, bid what they could only just afford, which turned out to be very much lower than those of their rivals. Fortunately for each of them, the rivals all failed the quality threshold and they retained their franchises.

End of roll-call.

All in all, sixteen Channel 3 licences had been put up for auction. Thirty-six different organisations had made a total of forty applications. Twelve incumbents had retained their licences. Four had lost them. Three new licence-holders would join the ITV network, and the fourth, Breakfast Television's new owner, would change its name from Sunrise to GMTV because Sky Television's breakfast show was already called Sunrise – didn't anybody notice that beforehand?

The auction process was intended to expose the comfortable monopolistic world of ITV to market forces, to dismantle the last bastion of restrictive practices, to open up a cosy old system to new blood, and to siphon off the system's vast profits to the Treasury. Now that the hurly-burly was done and the various battles lost and won, what in fact had been achieved?

Not a triumph for the Treasury, certainly. Only six of the sixteen licences had been won with the highest bids; eight had been won with the lowest. The quality thresholds for which George Russell had held out and which David Mellor had piloted so skilfully through Parliament, deprived the Treasury of very nearly £100,000,000. But the process left some of the successful contenders perilously insecure.

The IBA had demerged Trident Television a decade previously; within months the ITC would find it necessary to allow Yorkshire and Tyne Tees to merge once again in order to shore up the weakened finances of both companies. And all too soon another winner would discover it had paid too much for its prize. GMTV would lose two million viewers within six weeks of going on the air and within six months would be reporting financial losses of £10 million. It would take ten years, two reprimands from the ITC and a dramatic reduction in its licence fee before it would begin to make a respectable profit.

And the last bastion of restrictive practices? That bastion had already been undermined by the Employment Acts of the eighties with their bans on union closed shops and secondary picketing. Companies had been dismantling the bastion brick by brick ever since. By 1991 ITV's workforce had been reduced by 40 per cent and the unions were no longer running the system. We were all grateful to Mrs Thatcher for enabling us to achieve this. Why couldn't she have just stopped there?

As for new blood, the two previous franchise award rounds had introduced just as much of it. In the 1968 round, Harlech Television, LWT and Yorkshire TV had made their debut, as had Thames's new blend of old blood. In the 1982 round, TVS, TSW and TV-am arrived, as well as a regenerated ATV in the form of Central Television. How ironic that the new blood of 1982 was now being swept away by the new blood of 1991. And how deeply sad that 1968's new blend of the old was being swept away with it.

I was acutely sorry for Richard Dunn and the men and women of Thames who had contributed so much to the success and esteem of ITV. Richard was the most courteous and generous of rivals. We had never worked together but he was aware of my own connection with the company and on my 60th birthday in 1989 – my last as LWT's Managing Director – he threw a dinner party for Audrey and me on Thames's new riverside boat, MV Sir Thomas More, and presented me with a silver salver engraved 'To Brian from your friends at Thames'. That Thames generosity of spirit didn't end with its franchise. The company's staff association continues to thrive today as the Association of Reunited Thames Staff – ARTS. I was honoured to be invited to speak at its 25th Anniversary in 2010, able at last to pay a personal tribute to all that they had achieved.

ITV should not have lost Thames. Michael Green should have bought it when he had the chance in 1990. Thames would have survived the change of ownership, just as it had done when EMI bought out ABPC in 1969. It would have cost Green considerably less than it did in the auction a year later. Richard would have been given his wholehearted support in attacking the company's cost base, and with Carlton's financial resources Thames could have seen off any contender in the auction process. Michael Green thought that this is what he should have done too. "I definitely think we should have bought Thames second time round," he said later. "I think it's the biggest single mistake I've made in business – so far."

But now, and for the next fifteen months, all twenty licence-holders, the victorious and the vanquished, would sit together round the discussion tables of ITV and the ITC in an attempt to hold the present network together and plan its restructure for the future. They would also have to fulfil the statutory requirement for a networking system which would open up the programme schedule to all 15 companies as well as to the independents. Their deadline for this new networking system was 1 January 1993, the beginning of the new licence period.

And they would fail to meet it.

Ready, Steady, Whoah!

In the ITC's Invitation to Apply for Channel 3 Licences, applicants were asked what kind of commercial arrangements for networking they would like to see. We were provided with 21 paragraphs of clear and uncompromising guidance. There would have to be a distinct separation between the commissioning and provision of programmes. Networking arrangements could be organised through a company established for the purpose, through a trade association employing separate commissioning and scheduling staff, or through any other arrangement, provided the ITC's Programme Guidelines were observed and there was no conflict of interest between the commissioning of programmes and their supply. So no more kick-ups at Controllers. Goodbye Guarantees! Farewell Flexipool!

By the time the applications had to be submitted on 15 May 1991, both majors and regionals had warmed to the concept of a separate Network Commissioner and Scheduler supported by a jointly owned central unit. Nobody remembered that this was the proposal to which we had all given a cold shoulder two years earlier at the Standing Consultative Committee meeting when John Whitney suggested it as a response to the Government's call for a more radical approach to ITV's networking system. The ITC generously refrained from reminding us.

A fortnight later, Greg Dyke succeeded Richard Dunn as Council Chairman and nominated Granada's Managing Director Andrew Quinn as chairman of a Work Group to devise the structure and functions of a central commissioning and scheduling organisation. The Group moved with admirable speed. Rather than change networking systems in the middle of a programme year, it proposed that the Controllers Group, enlarged by its regional representatives and retitled the Network Scheduling Group, should continue to commission and schedule on the present financial basis up to the beginning of autumn 1993, at which point it would disband, while the Central Scheduler commissioned and scheduled for autumn 1993 onwards under a new system of negotiated prices.

The Network Programme Committee should become ITV's Broadcast Board, each member representing his or her company's broadcasting function and not its programme makers. A study should consider how the central scheduling organisation might relate to a new trade association over which Council would preside. And a division of the programme budget between weekday and weekend should be worked out by the two London companies for the seven-day Majors to approve.

The proposals were agreed by all the successful companies and in due course by the new licensees, though not every company saw the need to separate its broadcasting and production functions in order to supply a representative to the Broadcast Board. The ITC suggested a compromise. The Broadcast Board had to be seen to ensure that the Centre was not pressured by production representatives to take programmes from the companies rather than the independents, so the larger companies would have to separate their broadcasting and production divisions, but the smaller companies could be scrupulously monitored instead.

Greg was impressed by Andrew Quinn's handling of the Work Group's business and offered him the job of Director of the Network Centre, but dramatic developments had taken place at Granada Television and Andrew was needed there to steady a deeply unhappy staff. David Plowright, who had succeeded Denis Forman as Chairman, had pulled off a significant coup in retaining his company's franchise with a bid of only £9 million. Three months later he had been asked by his parent company to resign.

Market forces had hit Granada with a vengeance. The television company was part of the Granada Group and the Group's other interests – in TV rentals, bingo halls, motorway services, the newly formed BSkyB – were floundering. A 1990 profit of £121 million had shrunk to £57 million in 1991, the Group's shares were under pressure, and its shareholders' criticism had forced the resignation of Derek Lewis, its Chief Executive. He had been replaced by Gerry Robinson, the Chief Executive of Compass plc, a major company in the catering industry. Robinson had arrived in October 1991, the month in which the new franchise awards were announced, and had lost no time in telling David Plowright what was demanded of the Group's television subsidiary: higher profits, more redundancies and a big cut in programme costs.

Plowright insisted that cuts would make it impossible to deliver the programme plans promised in the company's franchise application, but the two men were talking two different languages: Plowright was speaking Programmes, Robinson was speaking Profits; and the Granada Board was listening to Robinson. In January 1992 David sent a memo to members of Granada TV staff: "I regret to have to announce that I have been asked by our parent company to resign as Chairman of Granada Television." The following month this uncompromising, highly respected programme maker and executive departed the company to which he had given 35 years of his professional life.

Promoted to Chief Executive in his place, Andrew Quinn was left to pick up the pieces and hold the company together during the storm of protest that followed, external as well as internal: petitions from Granada staff in Manchester and London; protests from the company's programme executives and the casts of Granada's Coronation Street and The Adventures of Sherlock Holmes; letters in the press signed by 67 leading actors including Sir Alec Guiness and Anthony Hopkins and 70 leading writers, directors and producers including John Mortimer and Michael Frayn. Famously, John Cleese sent a fax to Gerry Robinson "Why don't you fuck off out of it, you upstart caterer?" Questions of a more decorous nature were asked in the House of Commons, along with an early day motion signed by northern MPs.

Gerry Robinson and the Granada Group Chairman Alex Bernstein were summoned to meet the ITC Chairman and its Chief Executive. George Russell and David Glencross were seeking assurance that the commitments made by Granada in the bid for its Channel 3 licence would be honoured. Assurance was duly given and in a press statement issued the following day George Russell acknowledged the widespread concern caused by David Plowright's resignation but expressed his confidence that Granada Group would give Granada Television the wholehearted backing it needed to fulfil the terms of its licence.

In an attempt to achieve the sort of savings that might satisfy Gerry Robinson, Andrew Quinn had embarked on a carefully considered series of cuts and redundancies. Granada Group's profits for the first half of 1992 were higher than they had been for the whole of 1991, but whatever Andrew came up with Robinson pressed for more. At the same time, Andrew was also being pressed by Greg Dyke, who was asking him again to take on the role of Chief Executive of the Network Centre, negotiations with an alternative candidate having fallen through. This time Andrew said yes and his appointment was announced at the end of July.

The ITC had published its approval of Channel 3's Networking Principles two months earlier. Of prime importance to the Commission was its obligation to ensure that Channel 3 complied with its Programme Guidelines on balance, violence, sex and bad language. The trouble was that the Commission had legal sanctions over the licensees which would enable it to fulfil that obligation but not over the ITV Network Centre, so it declared that the Centre would only be able to contract programmes from independent producers through the licensees.

The independents were outraged. They complained that the ITC's declaration was anti-competitive, as were Channel 3's proposed Network Supply Contracts and Terms of Trade Agreements, and they were also infuriated by the delay in operating the new commissioning and scheduling system. Their trade association, now retitled PACT, the Producers Alliance for Cinema and Television, took their case to the Director General of the Office of Fair Trading, whose approval of ITV's networking arrangements was required by the Broadcasting Act.

Unfortunately, the OFT's Director General had come to the end of his term of office. His successor had to be given time to settle in before he could be fully briefed for this, his first major case, and his Report was unlikely to be ready for some months. This was July 1992 and the new Network Centre had to be in place by 1 January 1993. It was at this point that Andrew Quinn chose to leave the problems at Granada to become the Director of a Network Centre which existed only on paper. The words "frying pan" and "fire" come to mind.

Andrew couldn't afford to wait for OFT clearance. He had less than six months to put the Centre together and make it work. First, he needed an executive – the *right* executive – to direct the commissioning and scheduling of all Channel 3's networked programmes, local programmes remaining in the hands of the individual companies. He and Greg went straight to their first choice, LWT's Director of Programmes, Marcus Plantin, and persuaded him to leave his company and take on the massive new responsibility of

Network Director. Next, Andrew together with Marcus set about recruiting commissioning editors and staff and building the Centre's organisational structure, in which enterprise they were fortunate enough to be joined by Paul Bonner.

For the past five years Paul had been Chairman of the Network Controllers Group, now about to be superseded by the Network Scheduling Group, so he was available, and his wide experience as programme-maker and executive at the BBC, Director of Programmes at Channel 4, and Director of ITV's Programme Secretariat as well as Chairman of Controllers would prove invaluable, as it would later in the decade when he was commissioned to write the final volumes of *Independent Television in Britain.*

Marcus persuaded four of the network's most effective programme executives to leave their companies and join him in this leap into the unknown. Drama producer Vernon Lawrence left Yorkshire Television to become the Network Centre's Controller, Drama and Entertainment; Stuart Prebble left Granada, where he had been Head of Factual Programmes, to become Controller, Network Documentary and Factual Programmes; Dawn Airey, in charge of Planning and Presentation at Central Television, left to join the Centre as Controller, Children's ITV; and my old film-buyer colleague at Thames, Pat Mahoney, joined the Centre to become Controller, Film Purchase.

It was an expensive operation. Like Andrew and Marcus themselves, the Controllers had to be compensated for the salaries and share options they were leaving behind – some of them were moving their homes too – but this was a new and heady challenge, infused with the same spirit of enthusiasm and excitement which had fuelled the pioneers of ITV in the fifties and, caught up in it, the network was prepared to foot the bill. The entire management team worked hard and fast throughout the autumn to meet the 1 January deadline.

Until it hit a brick wall.

On 3 December, the Office of Fair Trading published its Director General's Report, and this time it was the turn of the companies and the ITC to be outraged. Sir Bryan Carsberg had found that the arrangements for compliance and commissioning from the Centre failed the competition test set out in the Broadcasting Act. He concluded that the contractual terms relating to the acquisition of programme rights from independent producers were likely to have anti-competitive effects on the independents' production and revenue. And he required changes in the Networking Principles, the Network Supply Contract and the Terms of Trade Agreements. All these procedures and documents would have to be modified and re-submitted to the OFT for agreement before they could operate. And the clock was ticking: the new licences were due to begin in 30 days' time.

The Monopolies and Mergers Commission – the MMC – was the relevant appeal body under the Broadcasting Act, but appeals had to be lodged within a month of the Report's publication so the ITC and the companies went into overdrive with their respective legal advisers to agree the terms of the parallel referrals. They only just made it: ITV's referral was taken by hand to the MMC a week before the deadline, the ITC's was delivered on the deadline day itself, 48 hours before the new licences were to begin. It was worth the effort. The fact that an appeal to the MMC was in process meant that Channel 3 could follow through its transitional plans for the new licence period without the threat of prosecution by the Office of Fair Trading.

Meanwhile, what about Granada?

As Andrew Quinn's successor, Gerry Robinson had appointed Charles Allen, an executive with whom he had worked closely at Compass Catering. The Chief Executive of ITV's proudest programme-maker was now a manager who knew nothing at all about programme-making. Like his boss, however, Charles Allen knew all there was to know about the bottom line, and the two of them were dedicated to maximising the bottom line of the Granada Group. Did the faintest of faint warning bells not sound somewhere in the depths of Kent House?

Sunrise......

S o it was that with Sunrise – sorry: Good Morning TV – on Friday, 1 January 1993, ITV companies new and old sailed into the open waters of Channel 3 as proud and purposeful as a raft of mallards, with their feet, like the mallards', paddling furiously beneath the surface. The paddling paid off. ITV's submission to the MMC beat its 5 February deadline, although it had to wait until 6 April and the publication of the Commission's Report before it knew that its hard work had not been wasted. The *Financial Times* called the Report 'an elegant solution to an intractable dispute': an elegant way of saying that there was a little something in it for everyone.

The Report agreed with the OFT that, in dismissing the Centre's direct commissioning and contracting of independent programmes, ITV's net-working arrangements were anti-competitive, but it recognised that under the Broadcasting Act compliance could only be exercised through a licensed broadcaster. It ruled therefore that, for the purpose of compliance, a licensee had to be included in each case in a tripartite contract with the independent producer and the Network Centre, the work to be carried out by the licen-see's broadcasting staff and not its production personnel. At Kent House we promptly split the broadcasting function away from LWT Programmes and handed it to Robin Paxton to run as Managing Director of LWT Broadcast, with Warren Breach as Deputy Managing Director. Warren's downstairs loo still displays the plaque from his office door bearing his new and well-deserved designation. Nick's company became LWT Productions Ltd.

ITV's contractual procedures had proposed a licence period of ten years for the rights to independent productions, with an option for a further five. The OFT had reduced this to a licence of five years with an option for a further two. The MMC now set aside the OFT ruling and required all licence periods to be agreed in negotiation. Happily, it included the option to acquire Further Programmes, embracing Format Rights where appropriate, an option essential to the channel's own competitiveness since, without it, a successful independent series on ITV could have been offered by its producer to a rival UK broadcaster. The MMC also required several other variations and additions to ITV's contractual procedures, including a Code of Practice to demonstrate its even-handedness between independent and in-house productions, none of them contested by either ITV or the independents.

ITV's modified contractual processes and procedures and their associated documents now had to be re-submitted by the end of June to the OFT for its agreement. More furious paddling for Andrew and his crew, but Andrew had never stopped. He had already begun to consult PACT and the lawyers about a redraft of the networking documents and was also in the middle of arranging the Network Centre's move from Knighton House to ITN's new building in Gray's Inn Road. Both tasks were completed by the end of June and the OFT's agreement was obtained in good time for Marcus Plantin's plans for the autumn schedule to be realised. Sighs of relief all round.

The year 1992 had been one of furious activity at Kent House too. The restructuring of the company was complete, giving greater autonomy to its constituent parts, each of them a separately accountable profit centre including the 23-storey building itself, now renamed The London Television Centre.

The franchise awards had fallen well for us. When the Carlton-led consortium lost its bid for breakfast television, Michael Green picked up the unallocated 20 percent of Good Morning TV and was already installed – and paying rent – as a Television Centre tenant.

London's new weekday licence holder was a publisher-contractor and not an owner of production or transmission facilities, but why build or buy its own? Why not use the production and transmission facilities at the London Television Centre, where it was already a tenant? And since Carlton and LWT were each required by their licences to provide a local news service during their respective periods on air, why not combine with LWT to provide a London news service which could operate across the entire week, based at the Television Centre from where it could so conveniently be transmitted? Why not indeed?

The London weekday company became not just LWT's friendly rival, as Thames had been, but its friendly colleague. LWT and Carlton set up a jointly-owned London News Network company to produce not only news and news magazines for London across the week but also sports programmes as required for each of its joint owners as well as GMTV and, as would later transpire, for Meridian TV too. Working 24 hours a day every day, the transmission centre would be responsible for transmitting all LWT, Carlton and GMTV services to the network, producing considerable cost savings for each company and considerable rental income for the London Television Centre. Under the previous franchise regime there had been three separate transmission centres in London, for Thames, TV-am and LWT. Now there would be only one.

A small army of workmen and engineers spent most of 1992 adding to the work they were carrying out on GMTV's studio and facilities, transforming the old Kent House canteen and its spacious outdoor terrrace into a news-room and news studio for the London News Network and building a new transmission suite for the use of all four of its broadcasters with its facilities, like those of all the Centre's studios, highly automated, its equipment at the cutting edge of existing technology.

Half way through 1992, when Andrew Quinn was still Granada's Chief Executive, he and Greg had agreed that a merger of the international sales divisions of LWT and Granada would not only produce significant admin-istrative cost-savings for both companies but also create a programme catalogue whose volume and variety would be able to take maximum advan-tage of the increasingly international marketplace. With Andrew as Chairman and Sydney Perry as its Chief Executive, Granada LWT International began trading on 1 January 1993, out of The London Television Centre.

The Centre was filling up. Carlton brought in its Presentation and Pro-motion Department to be near its transmission facility. ITV's Engineering Laboratories were transferred to the Centre. And Emma Mandley, the Cen-tre's Controller, was busily marketing its unique location and facilities to non-broadcasters too: P&O Bulk Shipping was now tucked away at the top of the Centre's tower.

Half way through 1993 Emma also had to make room for the rebirth of Laser Sales. In May LWT acquired 14 percent of Yorkshire Tyne Tees Tele-vision and Ron Miller went up to Leeds to find out why its advertising sales department appeared to be failing in the market place. He discovered that a flawed sales policy had oversold the station, given too much discount to its advertisers and dragged revenue forward from one month to another on a regular basis, creating a serious airtime sales debt in spite of YTT's area being larger in terms of set count and consumer spending than its network neighbour Granada.

Clive Leach, YTT's Chairman and Chief Executive, resigned and Ward Thomas, the Chairman and Chief Executive of the original Yorkshire-Tyne Tees merger as Trident Television, was invited back to take charge of the company. Greg went on to the YTT Board as a non-executive director, Ron's sales department was asked to take over the YTT sales operation, and Laser Sales was reborn. The ITC ruled that it had to have separate sales teams for each region to deal with agencies and media independents so, with something like six times the amount of airtime now to sell, Ron had to increase his sales department numbers by approximately 60 percent. And Emma had to house them all.

This little two-and-a-half day company was on a dizzy, exhilarating roll. It had already overtaken seven-day Granada in 1986 as ITV's third largest company by share of Net Advertising Revenue, Granada declining to fifth place. Now, once YTT's sales debts were resolved, YTT's additional airtime would bring Laser's share of Net Advertising Revenue to an estimated 21.4 percent, giving it significant clout in the advertising market-place.

LWT's programme sales to the network had grown by 39 percent since 1991. Now, the new system of commissioning and scheduling by the Network Centre meant that the major ITV companies were no longer limited in the amount of programming they could offer the network, and by the autumn of 1993 LWT had already negotiated commissions for 154 hours of programmes for the autumn schedule of 1994. The staff and production facilities of The London Studios were increasingly in demand from independent producers and other broadcasters, including the BBC: 57 percent of its business in 1993 came from other programme makers. And in spite of Laser's increased numbers LWT was still lean as well as lithe: between 1987 and 1993 we had reduced our permanent staff from 1,468 to 613.

The Management Incentive Scheme handcuffing its 54 participants to the company was due to mature in June 1993. As originally conceived, the market price of the company's shares at that point had to have reached 268p – "Let's face it," Robin Paxton had said, "the company's listed shares will never get as high as 268p". By the time the scheme had been signed and sealed the trigger figure had moved up a little to 278p and the 54 managers had purchased their Management Shares at 83p. Now, in June 1993, the market price of LWT shares had reached 385p and the ratchet it triggered made the fortunate 54 richer than any of us could ever have hoped.

The news was greeted with a tidal wave of press criticism. The rewards, the newspapers proclaimed, were out of all proportion to the risks LWT managers had run. The *Financial Times* claimed that the initials LWT stood for Lottery Winning Ticket. No one had thought so back in 1989. No one remembered how precarious the new franchise era of blind bids and quality thresholds had seemed for the incumbent companies, how necessary it had been to lock their best people away from competitors. No one had believed that the handcuffs four years later might turn out to be made of gold.

LWT staff at the Centre were unhappy about the size of the rewards too. They still shared 5 percent of the previous year's profits under the Profit Related Pay Scheme which had succeeded our Employee Share Scheme when the Group's capital was reorganised but they now put together a petition calling for a share of the newly triggered proceeds. Greg organised a scheme for managers to contribute a minimum of one per cent of their pay-out to it, rising to three per cent for those who had received more than a million, to be distributed as bonuses. It created a pot of £2.4 million, with Greg, Ron and me contributing £200,000 each and Christopher £250,000 – making it clear to journalists as he did so that "the motive was generosity, not guilt."

Charles Allen, Granada Television's Chief Executive, was now well acquainted with all that was going on at the London Television Centre, visiting it regularly in his capacity as Chairman of Granada LWT International in which he had succeeded Andrew Quinn. He would have reported his observations on the company's remarkable progress to Gerry Robinson at Granada Group, and that Group was decidedly not on a roll. Its mainstay was still Granada TV Rental, the orginal core of the business, which rented television sets to less well-off customers who couldn't afford to buy them. This produced more than half the Group's operating profit in 1993, but according to Granada's 1992 Accounts the rental business was facing a "continuing slow erosion of the contract base". Granada needed a growth strategy for the Group. In March Gerry Robinson bought a contract catering company for £360 million, so it looked as if his growth strategy was going to be based on acquisition. Did we not at LWT, even then, begin to hear a warning bell?

As Deputy Chairman of the Holdings Board I was party to all these developments, and although I was no longer the television company's Managing Director I didn't exactly have time on my hands. I was still a Governor of both the British Film Institute and the National Film and Television School, a Director of the Services Sound and Vision Corporation and ITV's representative on Harold Wilson's British Screen Advisory Council. Until the reorganisation of LWT (Holdings) was complete I was still Chairman of the television company, and I continued to chair LWT's Programme Advisory Board and take the chair or sit as a non-executive director on the Board of most of the company's divisions. But I was itching for more executive action, and most unexpectedly it was supplied by the Lord Chancellor, Lord McKay.

Christopher walked into my office at the beginning of November 1990 to say that the Lord Chancellor's Department had asked if he would agree to my being considered for appointment to the Lord Chancellor's Advisory Committee on Justices of the Peace. How would I like him to respond? Positively, I suggested. Later that month the Committee's Honorary Secretary wrote to ask if I was content for my name to go forward to the Lord Chancellor. I was; it went forward; and in January 1991 the Committee's Chairman Dame Margaret Booth, herself a Justice of the Peace, invited me to a drink at her home in Hampstead to put me in the picture in advance of the Committee's business meeting in February.

The picture was beguiling, and the work easily compatible with whatever demands for my time there might be at the Centre. This was the Lord Chancellor's Committee for Inner London, a body of some fifteen individuals, seven or eight of them serving magistrates in their own right. Based at Southwark Crown Court, its function was to interview prospective candidates for the Magistracy and make suitable recommendations for appointment to the Lord Chancellor. This fitted most agreeably with the remaining years of my contract at LWT, due to end with my 65th birthday in February 1994. I greatly enjoyed my time interviewing and recommending prospective Justices of the Peace – I was *casting* again, albeit Magistrates benches not TV programmes – and in December 1993 I was delighted as well as honoured to be invited by the Lord Chancellor to succeed Dame Margaret as Chairman of the Committee. I just hoped my colleagues on the Committee would be happy to be chaired by a show-business ham rather than a bona fide magistrate.

By now, though, the warning bells had begun to ring at last at Kent House. On 29 June 1993, Granada bought a near-15 percent shareholding in LWT, at 500p a share: 30 percent higher than the previous day's closing price. The shares came from Mercury Asset Management, an institutional investor with large stakes in both LWT and Granada. Two weeks later Granada bought another 5 percent elsewhere, bringing its stake up to 20 percent, the maximum allowed by the present rules. But those rules were about to change. The responsibility for broadcasting had been transferred from the Home Office to the Department of National Heritage, which announced that the moratorium on takeovers of one ITV major by another would be lifted on 1 January 1994. Companies would be allowed to own two franchises, and Granada was clearly preparing to go after LWT's.

After his first share purchase in June Gerry Robinson had expected a seat on the Holdings Board. It had not been given. With his second, Christopher and Greg met Robinson at his Holland Park home to see how much he would be prepared to pay for a friendly takeover. They said they would consider offers above 900p per share. Robinson offered less than 700p, and Christopher and Greg received the Board's backing to reject it. Now, in December, Robinson announced a hostile bid at 528p per share and the Board felt that the cash figure was so low in the light of our increasingly strong share performance that we could easily see him off. Besides, we had a secret weapon. Christopher and Greg were involved in preliminary discussions with Anglia TV about a three-way merger with Yorkshire Tyne Tees TV. Anglia would take over Tyne Tees and LWT would own Yorkshire Television, leaving each of us with two franchises, the maximum allowed under the forthcoming new rules, which would block any attempt by Granada to take us over.

On 19 December we issued a glossy brochure to all holders of LWT shares explaining why they should reject Granada's offer. Advised by Samuel Montagu, the brochure showed that LWT was one of the best performing shares in the UK. Since its capital reorganisation in 1989 LWT's share value had increased by 622 percent. Over the same period Granada's share price had risen by 70 percent. LWT ranked fifth among the 811 companies listed in the *Financial Times* All Share Index, the shares of only four other companies having more greatly increased in value. Granada's position in the list was 247th. The sum of £100 invested in each company's shares in December 1989 would have returned £756 for LWT's, £177 for Granada's.

The brochure pointed out that Granada was a conglomerate earning half its profits in the low growth sector of the rental business, whereas LWT was a television company with its investments exclusively in the high growth business of television. LWT was a major and profitable supplier of programmes to the ITV network, a leader in the studio and post-production facilities market, a founder-shareholder of ITV's breakfast television licence-holder, a founder and co-owner of the London News Network, and a co-founder with Carlton of the consortium which had acquired control of ITN that year. We had a strong case, and the brochure made it effectively. It listed the company's BAFTAs of the past ten years, its Emmys, its Prix Italias, its Montreux Rose Prizes, its Royal Television Society Awards. It indicated the company's large and highly regarded programme library, for which LWT's international sales division had already earned a Queen's Award before it amalgamated with Granada's to form Granada LWT International. Granada may have needed LWT to make sense of its television business, the brochure emphasised, but LWT didn't need Granada.

The brochure's closing message to the company's shareholders was "Your Board believes that you should not exchange your investment in such a valuable television company for shares in a conglomerate nor accept a poor cash offer." In the coming weeks, Christopher and Greg would do the City rounds persuading shareholders of the strength of the Board's case, just as the three of us had done four years earlier with Christopher's Scheme of Arrangement. This time, however, City Man and Action Man would be doing it without me. Front Man was nearing the end of his Long Goodbye.

...Sunset

" The Long Goodbye" was the heading of the memo I sent to Christopher Bland in 1990, when I handed the Managing Directorship over to Greg.

I was proposing a slow fade to black, gradually reducing my remaining executive and non-executive duties until my service contract ended in 1994. I'd borrowed the heading from one of Raymond Chandler's Philip Marlowe novels. John Freeman, who shared our affection for Chandler, would have been amused: Christopher's reply was headed by another Marlowe title: "Farewell My Lovely".

I was trying to avoid a farewell speech. I didn't make farewell speeches in those days: I made speeches for people who were saying farewell. But Christopher snookered me half way through the slow fade. On the day I retired from my remaining executive duties, he turned the Board lunch of March 1992 into a celebratory one and invited the indispensable Andrea Turner, who had been my secretary for 13 years, to join us. The venue certainly helped to make it celebratory. Christopher had booked Le Pont de la Tour, Terence Conran's delightful riverside restaurant at London Bridge, and the river was sparkling in the early spring sunshine.

I hadn't intended to make a speech, let alone a retirement speech. After all, I wasn't going anywhere: as Deputy Chairman I would be sitting round the Board table with the rest of the directors for another two years. But we were all still relishing our barely four month-old franchise success, and in that atmosphere post-prandial speeches were inevitable. In his, Christopher said some very complimentary things about what I had done for LWT over the past 18 years. In thanking him I said I liked to think I had been the right man at the right time for the company, just as John Freeman had been before me and Greg after me; but I thought the single most valuable thing I had done for LWT was to hold out for Greg as my successor. No outside manager would have had the combination of skill, energy and authority that was necessary to boot LWT into the new era of competitive broadcasting.

And Christopher? I said that for all of us who had combined to win the new licence – the staff, the management, the executive and non-executive members of the Board, the members of the bid team – it had been a great achievement. For Christopher, with that brilliant concept of capital recon-struction, his business vision and the drive with which he had galvanised us all, it had been a personal triumph. I raised my glass to him and to the finest of winning teams.

In the end it turned out to be Andrea's retirement lunch. Without my executive duties there wasn't enough secretarial work to occupy her and Personnel declared her redundant. She was scooped up by Carlton Televi-sion, where she was appointed Compliance Officer, ensuring that all the company's feature films and imported programmes were suitable for their scheduled slots. Andrea had acted as John Freeman's secretary as well as mine in that inter-communicating office suite in Kent House and when she retired from Carlton eleven years later John and I surprised her with an unexpected visit to her farewell party. It might not have made her day but the look on her face certainly made ours.

Now, in 1994, it was time for my own retirement. This time I really was going. My departure would be in the middle of Granada's attempt to take over the company so Christopher and I agreed to delay the farewell Board dinner until the dust of battle for LWT's ownership had settled. The Royal Television Society had been generous enough to propose a celebratory even-ing for me in May. Why not hold the Board dinner in May too? To complete a flattering trio of celebrations, the company's managers were also planning a farewell drinks reception for me, and that was arranged around the RTS function as well: Management would be on the 9th of May, RTS on the 12th, Board on the 19th. *Three* farewell speeches to make. Oh well... In the mean time, Audrey and I said our goodbyes privately and quietly and flew off into the sunset to stay with friends in Florida.

It was meant to be *my* sunset. It had never occurred to me, nor to anybody else at the London Television Centre, that it might also be LWT's. In the flurry of takeover bids that followed derestriction in January, Anglia had succumbed to Clive Hollick's Meridian Television so our secret weapon was never activated, but we believed that LWT's case was cast-iron nevertheless. Granada had grudgingly increased its cash bid but it was still under 700p per share. We were invulnerable, weren't we? Peter Coppock's Press Department kept me in touch with the battle by faxing its press digest to Florida each day, and sure enough each day Granada's bid failed to make any serious ground.

Until Friday, 25 February 1994.

Ironically, what happened that day had been foreshadowed by ourselves in the brochure we issued to shareholders in December 1993, the beginning of the battle. "Granada needs LWT more than LWT needs Granada," we said, and on 25 February Mercury Asset Management, Granada's biggest shareholder, agreed. It owned 17.5 percent of Granada and 14 percent of LWT. Across the previous four years LWT had delivered a compound rate of return to its shareholders of 66 percent and it was the fifth most valuable company in the All Share Index. Granada's performance had improved in 1993 but its Index position was still 247th. It very much needed the boost it would obtain with the acquisition of a buoyant LWT – and so did MAM's Granada shareholding.

On the morning of 25 February the Director of Mercury Asset Management, Carol Galley, rang Christopher Bland to say that she was going to accept Granada's offer. Christopher remembers hatching up a wild plan with Greg that morning to block Granada by borrowing £50 million and snapping up the LWT shares still in the hands of arbitrageurs and hedge fund operators, and Samuel Montagu were ready to lend them the money. But it was too late. Early that afternoon Granada's Chairman, Alex Bernstein, rang Christopher to tell him that the Group now had 57 percent acceptance of its offer and as a consequence controlled LWT. More than two decades later, Christopher still says that 25 February 1994 remains the worst day of his business life.

The daily press digest was full of the takeover but it told us very little of the reaction at Kent House. I learned afterwards that LWT's managers had been hit particularly hard. John Howard, Controller of Programme Finance and Business Affairs, remembers his reaction as being one of stunned disbelief. Warren Breach says he was devastated, shell-shocked. In his autobiography Greg finds it difficult to explain how devastated he himself felt then. His world disappeared, he says. He and Christopher had organised a drinks party to be held whatever the result of Granada's bid; the bar was opened early that evening and there were wryly funny speeches and attempts to find a bright side to look on, but there wasn't one. What had been anticipated as a victory celebration became a wake.

The staff mood was a little more mixed. With the decentralisation of LWT most of them now worked for The London Studios and the London Television Centre, which had become thriving businesses in their own right. The majority of the programmes being made at the London Studios were now for producers other than LWT; the Studios were contracted to supply Good Morning TV daily to the network, they transmitted Carlton's television service from Monday to Friday, and they operated the jointly owned London News Network every day.

Mike Southgate was Managing Director of The London Studios, Chairman of the London Television Centre and Chairman of the London News Network. He had to reassure his studio, production and transmission staff that the Studios and News Network were strong businesses and would survive in spite of Granada's takeover. He had to ensure that all transmissions that Friday proceeded hitch-free – Granada were concerned that they might be disrupted by LWT personnel spilling over from the drinks party. And, together with Penny Lent and Emma Mandley, he needed to set the minds of the Centre's clients and tenants at rest about the change of ownership. He eventually got to the party long after anyone else and for the rest of the evening had to remain relatively composed since he was also the Television Centre's bar licensee, on duty in case proceedings got out of hand. He remembers being too busy that day to be anything other than sad about Granada's victory.

Gerry Robinson attended the weekly Management Breakfast Meeting the following Wednesday and Warren Breach recalls that he set out to defuse with charm the hostility that greeted him. Ron Miller agrees. Robinson was an astute politician, he says: there was no triumphalism; he had nothing but praise for LWT's managers: they were what he had paid a great deal of money for and he wanted them to stay. Warren remembers Greg's reaction, that he would stay if he was Chief Executive Officer, and Robinson's response, that it wasn't possible because Charles Allen would be filling that role. In that case, said Greg, he wouldn't be staying. A week later, on 9 March, Granada issued a press release announcing changes in Board responsibilities at London Weekend Television, "now part of Granada Group".

Sir Christopher Bland was resigning as Chairman of LWT and would be replaced by Gerry Robinson. Greg Dyke was resigning as Chief Executive of LWT but would remain until the end of the month to ensure a smooth handover. Charles Allen, Granada Group's Executive Director responsible for television, would become Chief Executive Officer of LWT with immediate effect. He would retain his role as Chief Executive of Granada Television. Quoted in the release, Alex Bernstein, Granada Group Chairman, said "We would like to thank both Christopher and Greg for their support and advice and for the amicable way in which we have established relationships since the acquisition. We wish them well for the future." The amicability was reciprocated. I understand that Charles Allen gave his blessing for my planned Management drinks reception and Gerry Robinson gave his for the farewell Board dinner.

In the meantime it was business as usual at Kent House. There were productions to complete, advertising breaks to be filled, businesses to run. Granada wasn't able to move in completely until it had declared its offer unconditional and mopped up the entire ordinary share capital of the Holdings company. That happened on 20 May. It devoted the intervening period of limbo to studying the complexities of a split-week franchise and the workings of LWT's various operating divisions. As the process of integration took shape there were meetings and interviews, presentations and working parties, at Granada's offices in Manchester and Golden Square in London as well as at Kent House. No sackings, no compulsory redundancies. Not yet at any rate. Certainly the managers' mood had lifted by the time I returned to the Centre for the reception on 9 May. Perhaps the takeover battle's effect on their LWT shares had delivered some consolation: Granada's final offer was 686p per share in cash or 748p per share in Granada stock.

The reception was a happy and convivial occasion, a bookend to match the one with which my time in LWT had begun 20 years earlier in that same Westminster Room. I was presented with a massive, leatherbound tome 17 inches wide, 12 inches deep, 3 inches thick, a stone in weight. It was inscribed in gold lettering – forgive me for quoting this – "The friends and colleagues of Brian Tesler have put together this book of tributes and photographs in recognition of his distinguished career in British broadcasting and as a testimony of the affection and regard in which he is held". Its 70 pages of thick dark-green card contain contributions from 221 of those friends and colleagues, dating back from LWT to my days at Thames, ABC, ATV and the BBC.

I thanked the gathering for what is still today one of my most treasured possessions and said how good it was to see those familiar faces again. I carried with me marvellous memories of so many of them: my monthly encounters with the shop stewards at Consultative Committee meetings, my weekly meetings with my Directors of Programmes, my technical discussions with members of the Engineering Department, all of whom had the gift of being able to explain the most complicated piece of equipment in clear, simple layman's language so that after five minutes you still didn't understand a word but you were confident that they did. I said that LWT was still the best company in ITV, the most successful, the one with the greatest spirit. It had been through some tough times but it had always come through, and it would continue to do so now it was owned by Granada. I wished them all continued success, prosperity and good health.

It wasn't until I started researching this memoir that I discovered the book had been devised and masterminded by Joy Owen, Barry Cox's secretary. Barry had inherited John Freeman's old office in our intercommunicating suite and Joy, in its centre, had acted as required as my secretary too after Andrea's departure. To compile a list of contributors she had spread the word of what she intended doing, asked Audrey for suggestions and, she says, "found that once I asked one contact they recommended ten others and so the ball kept rolling". It rolled as far as the Chairmen and Directors General of the regulatory Authority in its successive incarnations, and took in on the way artistes and producers, writers and executives, department heads and managers, Chairmen, Managing Directors and Directors of Programmes across the industry with whom I had worked in the previous 42 years. She had written letters to each of them enclosing notepaper cut to a uniform size for written contributions, together with a hard-backed pre-addressed envelope to protect any photographs they might have chosen to send. And then she had worked with the Art Department to position the messages and photographs she had received in a most attractive layout in the book. An inventive, well-organised and hard-working young woman was Joy – and still is today, running several little one-woman businesses far removed from television.

One of the signed photographs was not included in the book and Joy took pleasure in presenting it personally. She had found a Press photograph of me receiving on behalf of LWT a reward from Princess Diana to recognise the company's support for theatrical charities. Joy had sent the photograph to Clarence House explaining what it would be used for and asking if the Princess would be kind enough to sign it. The presentations at the award ceremony had been made on the stage of the National Theatre and the photograph has Diana and me laughing heartily as we shake hands – the sort of photograph the Tatler would have captioned "Princess Diana sharing a joke". The joke was me. Running up the steps to the stage to receive the award I tripped and nearly fell. As the Princess shook my hand she was saying "We very nearly lost you there!"

There were plenty of jokes at the Royal Television Society's celebration three days later. These amiable RTS functions often take the form of 'roasts' in which the individual being celebrated is sent up sky high by some of his or her oldest friends and colleagues. On this occasion I sat there drowning while my professional life flashed before my eyes. The speakers were Bob Monkhouse, who had known me ever since the debacle of *Why?* in 1953; Bill Cotton, who had known me since I started to produce his father's show in 1954; and Paul Fox, who was already at the BBC when I joined in 1952. As I explained to the audience, "I was training to be a producer and Paul was training to be God, and as you know we both succeeded."

The fourth speaker was Lloyd Shirley, one of the great unsung creative heads of independent television, who had been at ABC Television when I joined and went on to Thames with me as Controller of Drama and Head of Euston Films. No send-up from Lloyd: he was straightforward and touchingly sincere about my time as Director of Programmes at both companies.

I told the RTS audience that I had had the best of times in the 42 years of my professional life. I had worked with remarkable men as my bosses; I had been a producer when cash-flow was not a problem, budgets were practically unheard of and no programme ambition seemed unattainable; as a Director of Programmes I had had the best Programme Heads in the business working for me; as a Managing Director I had been able to appoint young tyros as my successors who had gone on to become some of the most powerful figures in our industry. And throughout the ITV years I had been fortunate in having an excellent relationship with our regulators at the ITA, the IBA and the ITC – different officials, same folk.

I told the audience that my relationship with Lady Plowden when she was Chairman of the IBA was particularly special, but confessed "now that we're talking intimately within these four walls" that I had never been fortunate enough to bring it to the climax I hoped for it. Bridget Plowden, Audrey and

I shared the same hairdresser: Simon and Peter St John in Launceston Place. What I dearly wanted was for Bridget and me to be sitting side by side in our respective hairdresser's chairs one day, wearing our respective hairdresser's gowns, chatting merrily away. "You know, Brian, I think you were taking an unnecessary risk with that dialogue so close to the watershed – just a snip there, Peter please." "Yes Bridget, but don't you feel that in these days that sort of four-letter word is not only acceptable but expected – not too much off the top, please Simon"... and so on. Alas, it was never to be.

I thanked the audience for turning up, thanked the best PA in the business, who was sitting there in the front row, for being with me for 37 of those 42 years, and thanked the Royal Television Society for their generosity in celebrating them with me.

Two down, one more to go.

The Board's farewell dinner was as lighthearted and convivial as the other celebrations. I was particularly glad to see Greg again. I reminded our fellow ex-directors that two years earlier, at what had been my non-retirement retirement lunch, I had praised Greg for having exactly the right combination of skills to boot the company into the new competitive era of broadcasting. It was the most bizarre irony that he had been so successful in doing so that he had also booted himself and the entire Board out of a job. Greg would rise again, I said, and achieve still greater things in broadcasting. The rest of us would have to do the best we could.

Christopher had invited John Birt, Michael Grade and Marcus Plantin, my other ex-Directors of Programmes, to join us and it was a delight to see them all. I treasured my memories of our Friday morning routine meetings: Marcus in his Hell's Angels leather jacket; Michael wreathed in cigar smoke throughout; John, balancing files and folders and schedules and ratings on his lap; Greg, firing off ideas like a machine-gun in all directions, not finishing half of them because he'd suddenly thought of something else. I said I used to spend half an hour after each meeting with Greg on my hands and knees on the floor, picking up the ends of his sentences. And now Marcus, as the Network's Director of Programmes, had made that job in every ITV company redundant.

Because they were all together in the same room, I said I felt I could at last reveal that their remarkable progress in the industry after being Director of Programmes at LWT was no accident. I had deliberately infiltrated them into the most powerful positions in British television, programming them to spring into action when triggered by a simple but special phrase, to carry out a mind-blowing media coup. Finally, I said, at the end of the previous year I had got them all into position: John as Director-General of the BBC, Michael as Chief Executive of Channel 4, Marcus as ITV's Network Director, Greg as Chief Executive of the LWT Group, Chairman of the ITV Council, Chairman of GMTV – all the spoons in all the glasses as Cyril Bennett used to say, all poised for that mind-blowing media coup. Unfortunately, by that time I'd forgotten what it was. What was worse, I'd forgotten what the trigger phrase was. I used to look in the newspapers every day in trepidation in case I'd used it unknowingly and some ill-timed creative cataclysm had taken place somewhere in British television...

Well, it was a lighthearted and convivial occasion: I could be forgiven for trying to tell a funny story – and actually it went down rather well. As I looked round the table at the smiling faces of my fellow ex-members of the LWT Board and their partners it occurred to me, for the very first time, that I was the oldest person in the room. It was an odd experience for someone who for most of his professional life had always been the youngest: the youngest producer, the youngest Director of Programmes, the youngest Managing Director, the youngest Chairman... and now I was the oldest, in some cases by a generation.

It was time for me to go.

Postscript

I never returned to television.

I liquidated my private company but retained its name as the title of the charitable trust that Audrey and I set up when I retired. The Multithon Trust celebrated its 21st anniversary in 2015.

When my tenure as Chairman of the Lord Chancellor's Advisory Committee for Inner London ended in 1996 I was asked to serve as a lay interviewer for the Judicial Appointments Division, and for the next four years happily interviewed prospective Assistant Recorders, Acting Stipendiary Magistrates, Presidents of Industrial Tribunals and Circuit and District Judges. I was also invited by the Office of the Commissioner for Public Appointments to serve as an Independent Assessor and found myself working both for the Home Office, in the search for a head of the Parliamentary Boundary Commission of England, and for the National Health Service, in appointing Non-Executive Directors for the new primary care trusts.

These absorbing and enjoyable preoccupations somehow managed to extend beyond their statutory end, which should have been my 70th birthday in February 1999. Almost three years later I was still interviewing prospective Non-Executive Directors for the Wandsworth Primary Care Trust in the august company of the Chair Designate of the Wandsworth PCT and the Chair of the Queen Elizabeth Hospital NHS Trust. My P45 didn't finally arrive until 2010.

Meanwhile, my fellow LWT alumni continued their extraordinary progress through the upper echelons of television. After five years as Deputy Director General of the BBC, John Birt became its Director General in 1992. Greg

Dyke succeeded him as Director General in 2000. Sir Christopher Bland was appointed Chairman of the BBC Board of Governors in 1996 so both John and Greg had the pleasure of renewing their working relationship with him, just like old times. And Michael Grade achieved a unique double by being appointed Chairman successively of both the BBC (2004-06) and ITV (2007-09).

If mine had been the best of times in British television the two succeeding decades were among the most tumultuous. The flurry of ITV takeovers at the beginning of 1994 became a flood. When I retired from LWT there were 15 companies holding ITV licences. By 2005, ITV's 50th Anniversary, there were four. Today there are three: ITV plc, the STV Group (formerly Scottish Television) and UTV Media plc (formerly Ulster Television). As I write, ITV has acquired UTV Media, so there are now only two.

With satellite and digital channels as well as Channels 4 and 5 competing for the same pot of advertising gold, the takeovers were intended to increase efficiency, increase growth and reduce costs. It took a while for Granada and Carlton, the principal predators, to realise that the best way to achieve these ends was for the two of them to merge, which they did in 2004 as ITV plc.

As it consolidated, ITV found itself with more studios and broadcasting facilities than it needed, so some of the regional studios were sold off to independents and others were closed down and demolished. Even Granada's hallowed Manchester studios were abandoned, and the northern arm of what was now known as ITV Studios Ltd was moved lock, stock and *Coronation Street*-set to MediaCityUK, on the banks of the Manchester Ship Canal at Salford. To compete with its now numerous competitors, ITV plc finally introduced three new advertising-supported channels, ITV 2, ITV 3 and ITV 4, but it made no attempt to start up a subscription channel: its two owners had found their fingers too badly burned in 2002 by the collapse of ITV Digital, their joint venture into pay-tv.

The huge MediaCityUK development became the northern outpost of both the major terrestrial broadcasters. The BBC had already begun to move some of its activities there as part of a strategy not to consolidate but to decentralise. Its aim was for the BBC to become less metropolitan, to be spending half its programme budget in the regions and producing half its programming outside the capital by 2016, when its Charter would be coming up for review. It also pledged to reduce its costs by 20 percent, not an easy task in the light of the expenditure incurred by the move to MediaCityUK, but it had little choice: the Chancellor of the Exchequer had frozen the licence fee in 2010 until 2016 and directed the Corporation to take over not only the funding of the BBC World Service from the Foreign Office but also the cost of the supply of free television licences to pensioners over the age of 75.

As a result, the BBC put its landmark Television Centre at White City up for sale and began to build New Broadcasting House for its television activities next to what would now be Old Broadcasting House, which remained its radio headquarters. It also sold some of its operational divisions to private owners, including BBC Outside Broadcasts and BBC Costumes and Wigs, and began to make cuts in its staff, in its management and management salaries and in the fees it paid top talent.

It has been beset by problems, in the course of which the television careers of two of its Directors General have ended in resignation: the scandal of a *Blue Peter* phone-in competition in support of Unicef being won by a rigged phone-call made in the studio; the harsh criticism of BBC management procedures and journalistic standards by the Hutton Report of the enquiry into the death of Dr David Kelly; the attacks on the size of its pay-offs to departing managers; the mishandling of the *Newsnight* programme on Jimmy Savile; the green paper of July 2015 on the BBC's future, asking searching questions on its scope and how it should be financed...

ITV has had problems of its own: dissension within its board; a steadily declining share of audience; an over-reliance on advertising just as competition for it was proliferating; a belated recognition of the online market's potential; a mountain of debt; an increasing shortfall in its pension scheme... And at the beginning of 2016 it announced the departure of both its Chairman and its Director of Television.

Tumultuous times indeed. The official history of *Independent Television in Britain* doesn't cover them: its final volume, published in 2001, takes the history only to 1992. Nor are they covered in the official history of the BBC, the latest volume of which was published in 2015, covering the years from 1974 to 1987. Perhaps someone, somewhere, is writing his or her own personal history of British Television, bringing it up to date with the review of the BBC Charter in 2016. I look forward to reading it. But mine...

...ends here.

Brian Tesler, January 2016

Bibliography

Barfe, Louis: *Turned Out Nice Again: The Story of British Light Entertainment.*
Great Britain: Atlantic Books, 2008.

Birt, John: *The Harder Path: The autobiography.* Great Britain: Time Warner
Books, 2002.

Black, Peter: *The Mirror in the Corner: People's Television.*
Great Britain: Hutchinson & Co, 1972.

Bonner, Paul with Lesley Aston: *Independent Television in Britain Volume 5:
ITV and the IBA 1981-92.* Great Britain: Macmillan Press Ltd, 1998.

Bonner, Paul with Lesley Aston: *Independent Television in Britain Volume 6:
New Developments in Independent Television 1981-92.*
Great Britain: Palgrave Macmillan, 2003.

Bose, Mihir: *Michael Grade: Screening the Image.* Great Britain: Virgin
Books, 1992.

Brown, Maggie: *A Licence to be Different: The Story of Channel 4.*
Great Britain: British Film Institute, 2007.

Catterall, Peter, Editor: *The Making of Channel 4.* Great Britain: Frank Cass
Publishers, 1999.

Cotton, Bill: *Double Bill: 80 Years of Entertainment.* Great Britain: Fourth
Estate Limited, 2000.

Darlow, Michael: *Independents Struggle:The Programme Makers who took on
the TV Establishment.* Great Britain: Quartet Books, 2004.

Davidson, Andrew *Under the Hammer: Greed and Glory Inside the Television
Business.* Great Britain: William Heinemann Limited, 1992.

Davies, Hunter: *The Grades: The First Family of British Entertainment.*
Great Britain: Weidenfeld and Nicolson, 1981.

Docherty, David: *Running the Show:21 Years of London Weekend Television.*
Great Britain: Boxtree Ltd, 1990.

Donaldson, Marie: editor *Both Sides of the Camera.*
Great Britain: Weidenfeld and Nicolson, 1960.

Dyke, Greg: *Inside Story.* Great Britain: HarperCollins*Publishers,* 2004.

Fitzwalter, Raymond: *The Dream That Died: The Rise and Fall of ITV.*
UK: Matador, 2008.

Grade, Michael: *It Seemed Like a Good Idea at the Time.*
Great Britain: Macmillan, 1999.

Greene, Sir Hugh : *The Third Door Front: A View of Broadcasting in the Sixties.* Great Britain: Bodley Head, 1969.

Hill, Lord: *Behind the Screen: The Broadcasting Memoirs of Lord Hill of Luton.*
Great Britain: Sidgwick & Jackson, 1974.

Hobson, Dorothy: *Channel 4: The Early Years and the Jeremy Isaacs Legacy.*
London: I.B.Taurus, 2008.

Horrie, Chris & Steve Clarke: *Citizen Greg: The Extraordinary Story of Greg Dyke and How He Captured the BBC.* Great Britain: Simon & Schuster UK Limited, 2000.

Isaacs, Jeremy: *Look Me in the Eye: A Life in Television.* Great Britain: Little, Brown, 2006.

Isaacs, Jeremy: *Storm Over 4: A Personal Account.* Great Britain: Weidenfeld and Nicolson Limited, 1989

King, Cecil Harmsworth: *The Cecil King Diary 1965-70.* Great Britain: Cape, 1972.

King, Cecil Harmsworth: *The Cecil King Diary 1970-74.* Great Britain: Cape, 1975.

Lawson, Nigel: *The View from No. 11.* Great Britain, Bantam Books, 1992.

Lewisohn, Mark: *Radio Times Guide to TV Comedy.* Great Britain: BBC Worldwide Ltd, 1998.

Milne, Alasdair: *DG: The Memoirs of a British Broadcaster.*
Great Britain: Hodder and Stoughton Ltd, 1998.

Newman, Sydney: *Square Eyeballs in a Round World.* Unpublished and incomplete autobiography dictated to Marion McDougall 1987-89. Held in the Archive of The Royal Television Society, Great Britain.

Potter, Jeremy: *Independent Television in Britain Volume 3: Politics and Control 1968-80.* Great Britain: Macmillan Press Ltd, 1989.

Potter, Jeremy: *Independent Television in Britain Volume 4: Companies and Programmes 1968–80*. Great Britain: Macmillan Academic and Professional Ltd, 1990.

Sendall, Bernard: *Independent Television in Britain Volume 1: Origin and Foundation 1946–62*. Great Britain: The Macmillan Press Ltd, 1982.

Sendall, Bernard: *Independent Television in Britain Volume 2: Expansion and Change 1958–68*. Great Britain: The Macmillan Press Ltd, 1983.

Tesler, Brian: *Before I Forget: A Family Memoir*. Great Britain: Mind Advertising Ltd, 2006.

Thomas, Howard: *With an Independent Air: Encounters During a Lifetime of Broadcasting*. Great Britain: Weidenfeld and Nicolson, 1977.

White, Leonard: *Armchair Theatre: The Lost Years*. Great Britain: Kelly Publications, 2003.

Wilson, Angus: *TEMPO*. Great Britain: Studio Vista Ltd, 1964.

Whitney, John CBE: *To Serve the People: My Years at the IBA*. Great Britain: John Libbey Publishing Ltd, 2013.

Index